FRANCIS SCOTT KEY

LIFE AND TIMES

FRANCIS SCOTT KEY

From the portrait by Charles Willson Peale

Francis Scott Key

LIFE AND TIMES

Edward S. Delaplaine

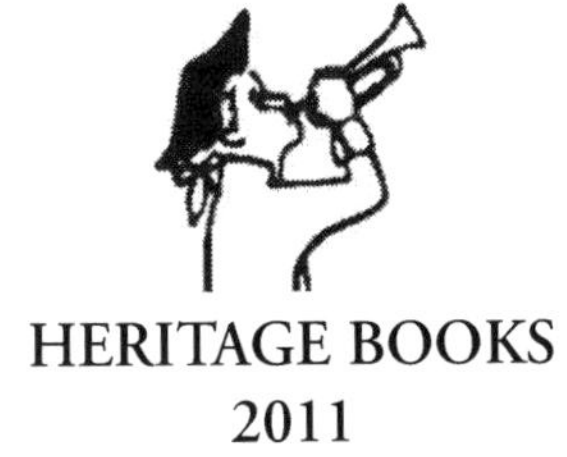

HERITAGE BOOKS
2011

HERITAGE BOOKS
AN IMPRINT OF HERITAGE BOOKS, INC.

Books, CDs, and more—Worldwide

For our listing of thousands of titles see our website
at
www.HeritageBooks.com

A Facsimile Reprint
Published 2011 by
HERITAGE BOOKS, INC.
Publishing Division
100 Railroad Ave. #104
Westminster, Maryland 21157

Reprinted for the heirs of the author by
Willow Bend Books, 2001

— Publisher's Notice —
In reprints such as this, it is often not possible to remove blemishes from the original. We feel the contents of this book warrant its reissue despite these blemishes and hope you will agree and read it with pleasure.

International Standard Book Numbers
Paperbound: 978-1-58549-685-3
Clothbound: 978-0-7884-8907-5

PREFACE

MORE THAN TWO centuries ago Andrew Fletcher remarked in a letter to the Marquis of Montrose: "I knew a very wise man that believed that if a man were permitted to make all the ballads, he need not care who should make the laws of a nation."

Certain it is that the fame of Francis Scott Key flowed almost entirely from the fact that he wrote *The Star-Spangled Banner*. Yet his life is significant for many other reasons. For many years, from the time when he first appeared before Chief Justice Marshall to plead for the release of Aaron Burr's messengers, Key was one of the leaders of the American Bar. He defended Sam Houston in his dramatic trial in the House of Representatives; he figured in Peggy Eaton's quarrel; he opposed Nullification and the United States Bank; and he was Andrew Jackson's conciliator in Alabama in one of the most stirring episodes in the history of the State.

I believe the story of Key's attitude on the burning issues of his day will shed some light upon the times in which he lived. In this volume I have brought together, for the first time, all the important utterances of his known public speeches. Some of these, like his Fourth of July Oration in the rotunda of the Capitol, proclaim his convictions on the fundamental principles of the American Government. His Washington's Birthday Address in Alexandria radiates his sturdy Americanism. In his discourse to the alumni of St. John's College in Annapolis, he gave his views on public education. His eloquent pleas for colonization of the Negro explained America's duty in reference to the throbbing issue of slavery.

All of this vivid panorama, however, is but the background for the portrait of an unusual character — a lawyer, orator, churchman, statesman, and poet, who was deeply patriotic and deeply religious.

The American people have always held Francis Scott Key in high veneration. After the World War, with monuments already erected to his memory in Baltimore, in San Francisco, at his birthplace, and at his grave, the Congress of the United States made an appropriation for a memorial at Fort McHenry. I attended the dedication of the towering monument on June 14, 1922, and heard the exquisite address delivered there by President Warren G. Harding.

I completed my manuscript of *The Life of Thomas Johnson* in 1927; and I think it was within a year after the publication of that biography that I began collecting fragmentary data on the life of Francis Scott Key. It seemed strange to me that, with all the admiration of the American people from coast to coast for *The Star-Spangled Banner*, no definitive biography of its author had ever been written. Most of his poems had been collected and published several years before the outbreak of the Civil War; but very little had been preserved concerning his career at the Bar, his rôle in National politics, or his achievements as a public speaker.

The story of Key's life is fascinating, and it was unusually so to me since the collection of data was contemporaneous with the restoration of the Roger Brooke Taney Home in Frederick, Maryland — for a Key museum was to be established in the Home, inasmuch as Mrs. Taney was Key's sister. The articles of incorporation, which I drafted to prepare for the acquisition of the historic property, were signed in the Govenor's office in the Maryland State House in Annapolis on September 9, 1929, Governor Albert C. Ritchie serving as one of the incorporators. The old dwelling and its slave quarters were purchased, restored, and equipped during the seven months that followed; and on April 15, 1930 the patriotic shrine was opened to the public.

Many valuable relics from the Taney and Key families were presented to the Home for exhibition. A number of Key's letters and documents were given by Colonel Francis S. Key-Smith, a great-grandson of Key. A reproduction of the painting of Key's Georgetown Home, autographed by John Ross Key, the artist, was given by the artist's widow. A law book from Key's library, and bearing his bookplate, was received from State Senator Alpheus H. Favour of Arizona. Mr. Henry Walters, the famous collector, then far advanced in years, sent a photograph of the original manuscript of *The Star-Spangled Banner*, a facsimile of which is included in this volume. Mr. Walters died shortly afterwards; and on January 5, 1934, the manuscript was offered for sale at an auction in New York, and it was bought by an agent for the Walters Art Gallery of Baltimore for $24,000.

At the time of the opening of the Taney Home, patriotic citizens from the Atlantic to the Pacific were signing petitions urging Congress to adopt *The Star-Spangled Banner* as our National Anthem. I learned that John Philip Sousa, the composer of *The Stars and Stripes Forever* and many other famous marches, was opposed to the scheme of offering prizes to select another song to supplant *The Star-Spangled Banner.* I asked Sousa if he would sign a statement containing his ideas on the subject. He cheerfully agreed to do so; and the autographed opinion of the great composer has been preserved in the Key room of the Taney Home. The statement concludes with these words: "It would be as easy to make a stream run uphill as to secure a new National Anthem as the result of a prize contest. The only possible chance that we might have a new National Anthem would be when the eyes of all Americans are directed toward some particular cause and another genius captures the spirit of the moment in a thrilling song of patriotism. Until that time I do not believe the veneration for Francis Scott Key's anthem will ever be displaced."

Finally, after many years of effort, the advocates of *The Star-Spangled Banner,* led by Congressman J. Charles Linthicum of Maryland, succeeded in securing the passage of an Act declaring "the composition consisting of the words and music known as *The Star-Spangled Banner* is designated the national anthem of the United States of America." The Act was signed by President Herbert Hoover on March 3, 1931.

Public interest in Francis Scott Key has never diminished, but has grown, with the passing of the years. Patriotic groups continue to unveil tablets of bronze and other memorials in his honor. From time to time I received invitations to speak at public ceremonies on various aspects of Key's life and character. My last address on this theme was delivered on August 7, 1934, before the Maryland State Camp, Patriotic Order Sons of America, on the lawn of Key's birthplace, Terra Rubra. On that occasion I took as my subject, "If Key Were Here." I had culled the gems from Key's public speeches, and I told how I believed Key would stand on the problems of the present age, if he were alive today.

The publication by Victor Weybright of his *Spangled Banner* in 1935 brought new interest in the life of Key. This book not only narrated in detail the story of the writing of the National Anthem, but presented much new material regarding the patriot poet.

I would be unable to name all of the many friends who assisted me in the collection of data for this biography. But I shall always have pleasant recollections of the active interest and encouragement of Mr. Sewall Key, of the Department of Justice; the late Dr. Ezra Z. Derr, Captain, United States Navy, retired, and Dr. and Mrs. John S. Derr, of

Frederick County; and the late Dr. Arthur B. Bibbins, of Baltimore, for some years President of the Star-Spangled Banner Flag House Association.

I extend my thanks to Mr. V. Valta Parma, Curator of the Rare Book Collection, Mr. J. Franklin Jameson, Chief of the Manuscripts Division, and Mr. Hugh A. Morrison and Mr. George H. Milne, of the Representatives' Reading Room of the Library of Congress, who have courteously aided me with the resources of that library. I also appreciate the help afforded by the Maryland Historical Society, and I particularly thank Miss Florence J. Kennedy, one of the librarians of the Society, for her gracious coöperation.

In affording me all the sources at their command, I express my appreciation to Mr. Charles Elmore Cropley, Clerk, and Mr. Frank Key Green, Marshal of the Supreme Court of the United States; the officers and their assistants in the Public Library of Washington; the United States National Museum; the office of the Register of Wills of the District of Columbia; the office of the Adjutant General, United States Army; the office of Naval Records and Library of the Navy Department; the Enoch Pratt Free Library of Baltimore; the Peabody Institute of Baltimore; the Maryland Diocesan Library; the St. John's College of Annapolis; the Boston Public Library; and the Department of Archives and History of the State of Alabama.

I am indebted to Mrs. Emily Wilkins Stryker, of Pasadena, California, for the miniature of Roger Brooke Taney, which is reproduced in this volume, and for Anne Key

Taney's poetry album. The miniature and the album are among the exhibits in the Stryker Collection at the Taney Home. I am also grateful to Mr. Charles McHenry Howard, of Baltimore, great-grandson of Francis Scott Key, for the picture of Key, the reproduction of which appears as the frontispiece of this volume; and to Mrs. Arthur T. Brice, of Washington, granddaughter of Key, for permission to reproduce the miniature of her grandmother, Mary Tayloe Lloyd Key.

Among the others who aided me were Dr. Carl B. Swisher, until recently a member of the faculty of Columbia University, and now of the Johns Hopkins University; Mrs. Robert L. Annan, and Mr. Preston B. Englar, of Taneytown, Maryland; Chief Judge Carroll T. Bond, of the Court of Appeals of Maryland; Mrs. Thomas J. Fickling, of Columbia, South Carolina; Mr. Claude G. Bowers, now Ambassador to Spain; Mr. W. B. T. Belt, of Omaha, Nebraska; Rev. Edward D. Johnson, rector of St. Anne's Church, of Annapolis; Rev. F. Bland Tucker, rector of St. John's Church, of Georgetown; Mr. Peter Baumgardner, owner of the Terra Rubra farm, near Keysville, Maryland; Miss Eleanor Murdoch Johnson and Mrs. Francis H. Markell, of Frederick; Miss Maud Burr Morris, Colonel Francis S. Key-Smith, Mr. C. B. Riddle, Mr. Monroe Johnson, Mr. William H. Ramsey, Miss Anne B. Cushman, Dr. Daniel W. Fetterolf, and Mrs. R. Woodland Gates, of Washington; and Mr. Walter W. Beers, Dr. Jesse W. Downey, Jr., and Mr. Francis B. Culver, of Baltimore.

I wish to acknowledge with sincere gratitude the generous aid of Alexander H. Carasso, Ph.D., of Brooklyn, New York, in editing the manuscript of this book and arranging for its publication.

EDWARD S. DELAPLAINE

Frederick, Maryland
July 3, 1937

Contents

Illustrations

FRANCIS SCOTT KEY

Life and Times

CHAPTER I

The Boy at Pipe Creek

I think of thee — of those bright hours,
Rich in life's first and fairest flow'rs,
When childhood's gay delights were ours, —
My sister!

The mountain top — the wood, the plain,
The winding creek — the shaded lane
Shall shine in both our eyes again,
My sister!

THUS DID Francis Scott Key, after fifty years, look back upon the golden hours of childhood. He and his sister Anne had been born under favoring circumstances. Their birthplace was a spacious mansion owned by their father, John Ross Key, in the fertile, well watered Monocacy Valley of Western Maryland not far below the Pennsylvania line. The Key estate was situated west of the stage road that led from Frederick Town to York and Philadelphia. About five miles up this road lay Taneytown with its tavern for accommodation of travelers. A short distance to the south ran Big Pipe Creek and Little Pipe Creek. A few miles to the west the Monocacy flowed in its meandering course toward the Potomac. And still further beyond lay the hills of Catoctin, a range of the Blue Ridge.

The broad acres that stretched about the mansion had belonged to the Key family for several generations. A tract of 1,865 acres had been patented under the name of Terra Rubra (Red Land) to Philip Key,[1] progenitor of the Key family in America. This gentleman, who received a splendid education in London, came of proud lineage. Members of his family had held important civil and military positions for a hundred years in England. Their crest — a griffin's head, holding in its beak a key — tells the history of their name. He began the practice of law; sat in the Provincial Assembly; served for a time as High Sheriff; was later the Presiding Justice of the County; and, during his last years, occupied a seat in the Council of Governor Sharpe. He was an active member of Christ Episcopal Church at Chaptico. When he died in 1764, one of the newspapers described him as "a truly pious and devout Christian, an affectionate and tender husband, an indulgent and fond parent, a humane master, a warm friend, a friendly neighbor, and a most agreeable and chearful companion."[2]

Philip Key had six sons and a daughter, all of whom inherited splendid intellects. One of the sons, Edmund, after studying law in London, became Attorney General of Maryland. Following the passage of the Stamp Act, Edmund Key served on a committee in the Assembly at Annapolis — Thomas Johnson, who later became the first Governor of the State,

1.—Philip Key, son of Richard and Mary Key, was born in the parish of St. Paul, Covent Garden, London, in 1696, and came to America in his early twenties. He settled in St. Mary's County, Maryland, where he built a mansion, called Bushwood Lodge, overlooking the Potomac.

2.—*Maryland Gazette*, August 30, 1764. Original will in the Maryland Historical Society, Baltimore, Md.

was also on this committee — to draft a paper setting forth "the constitutional rights and privileges of the freemen of the province."

Another son, Francis, married Ann Arnold Ross, daughter of John Ross, Register of the Land Office of Maryland. Mr. Ross lived in a fine mansion on the Severn, named Belvoir, about seven miles from Annapolis. When Francis Key and Miss Ross were married, one of the papers referred to the bride as "a well accomplished and deserving young lady, with a pretty fortune." Francis Key was appointed Clerk of the Cecil County Court in 1765. He added largely to the real estate holdings of the family, for, in 1767, a tract of 3,677 acres of land in Frederick County was patented under the name of Runnymeade to him and Dr. Upton Scott, a physician at Annapolis.

Francis Key had three children. The eldest was John Ross Key, born on September 19, 1754. The next child was Philip Barton, born on April 12, 1757. The youngest was Elizabeth, born in 1759. When the father died in 1770 without a will, Terra Rubra at Pipe Creek became the property of John Ross Key under the British law of primogeniture.

John Ross Key was only sixteen when his father died. Already the people of the Province were rising against the oppressive measures of the Government. When Governor Eden fixed the fees of proprietary officials without the approval of the Assembly, the scion of the Key family had his first appearance in public affairs when he attended a meeting at Taneytown to protest against the Governor's Proclamation. In 1775, when not yet twenty-one the stalwart young man from Pipe Creek was one of the freemen who met at the Court House in Frederick Town to discuss the resolutions of the Continental Congress. John Hanson — later first President of the United States in Congress Assembled — presided. Key was appointed on the Frederick County Committee of Observation to carry out the resolutions of Congress and to provide for the defense of the Colony. A few months later came stirring news from the North. Congress asked Pennsylvania, Maryland, and Virginia to send recruits to Boston. On June 21, 1775, Mr. Hanson read the appeal to the Committee of Observation; and the Committee decided to raise two companies of riflemen without delay.

In one of the companies John Ross Key was named second lieutenant. Within three weeks the volunteers were ready to march to Boston. The length of Key's military service is not exactly known. Certain it is that a few months later he was back in Frederick Town on an entirely different mission — this time to procure a marriage license. On one of his visits in the county seat the young patriot from Pipe Creek had met a very attractive 19-year-old girl with a very long name — Anne Phoebe Penn Dagworthy Charlton.[1] The Charltons, like the Keys, were of English descent and had been living in America for several generations. Edward Charlton of Prince George's County had a son, Thomas, whose widow kept a tavern in Frederick Town. Arthur Charlton, a son of Mr. and Mrs. Thomas Charlton, married Eleanor Harrison, and their daughter was the girl with the very long name. John Ross Key's proposal met with favor. For not only was he at-

1.—Born February 6, 1756.

tractive in appearance and manner, but he owned a spacious mansion, thousands of acres of productive land, and a number of loyal Negro slaves. The wedding ceremony was solemnized on October 19, 1775.

The mansion to which Key brought his bride was the largest within a radius of many miles. Across its entire front, measuring nearly a hundred feet, was a two-story portico with columns two feet in diameter. Extending from the main building were wings, in one of which lived the tenant and his family, and in the other the Negro slaves. The main dwelling was a plastered frame structure, while the wings were brick. The wings were connected with a double porch and a brick-paved court.[1]

On December 28, 1776, John Ross Key was commissioned a captain in Col. Normand Bruce's battalion of militia. But the demands of the plantation prevented his military service from being of long duration. The wheat he grew, ground into flour at nearby grist mills, was a necessity in the years when Governor Johnson was doing all in his power to send supplies to the troops of General Washington. In 1778, and again in 1779, and 1780, he was appointed justice of the peace. In 1781, before the surrender of Cornwallis at Yorktown, he was commissioned lieutenant in Captain Philip Thomas's troop of horse.

The first child of John and Anne Key was a daughter, Anne Charlton, born on July 19, 1777. The little girl died soon after birth. The next child was a son, born August 1,

1.—In 1858 a part of the house was blown away by a storm. In 1859 it was torn down to make way for a new structure.

1779. The parents decided to call him Francis Scott Key. The first name was given for his grandfather; the middle name was a tribute to Dr. Upton Scott, the husband of the infant's great aunt. The Annapolis physician was a man of prominence in Maryland. So great was his influence that after a lapse of eighty years, when Congressman Daniel E. Sickles of New York was tried for the murder of Francis Scott Key's son, Philip, Dr. Scott was recalled as a "wily Scotchman" and was charged with having obtained a commission for Philip Barton Key in the British Army at the time of the Revolution, when his brother, John Ross Key, took a commission in the American Army.

After the outbreak of the Revolution, the Established Church of England met with disfavor in the Colonies. No permanent rector resided at Frederick Town during these exciting days. So the Keys from Pipe Creek called upon Rev. Frederick L. Henop, pastor of the Reformed Church, to baptize the infant and christen him Francis Scott Key.

The boy at Pipe Creek was only four years old when General Washington surrendered his sword at Annapolis, but the lad heard from his father's lips some of the thrilling stories of the Revolution. Thus by his own fireside were instilled in him the first lessons in American patriotism. From his mother the youngster inherited a sublime faith. His soul was keyed to spiritual influences. He was taught to have absolute reliance in God. The saintly mother used to call the slaves on the plantation at sundown and conduct them in prayer. And here the growing farm boy learned to treat the black man with kindness. From her he also inherited a love for the Muse, for there was poetic talent in the family. Instilled in him, too, were courtesy and hospitality.

Key's ancestors were hardy pioneers who had developed those sterling qualities which nerved them to make their living on the frontier and to assert their rights against King, Parliament, and Colonial Governor. Such ancestry laid the foundation upon which could be built a character of strength.

Another child was born to the Keys on December 15, 1781. It was a girl, and they named her Catherine Charlton, but she died on August 10, 1782.

Mrs. Key gave birth to another daughter on June 13, 1783, and she was christened Anne Phoebe Charlton Key. This little girl grew up and became a devoted playmate to her brother. She, too, was bright and talented. Together they often heard the old melodies at their mother's knee. Little Anne was so talented in music that, when she was only twelve, her father ordered for her a handsome pianoforte from England at a cost of more than twenty-two pounds.

Francis and his little sister were fond of Nature. In Summer the shady lawn and the "terraced garden adorned with shrubbery and flowers" was a fine playground for the slender boy with dreamy blue eyes and for winsome little Anne. From the piazza and the front lawn, on a sunny day, they could gaze out across the fields and see the foothills that formed the horizon in the West — blue and green tints of the Blue Ridge which at sunset were "curtained in clouds of crimson and gold."

At the foot of the hill, scarcely more than a stone's throw away, was a spring. To this spot the children of the neighborhood often came on hot Summer days to rest under the oaks and to get cooling drinks of the sparkling water.

In the distance were Big and Little Pipe Creeks, murmuring through woods and meadows on their way to the Monocacy. These streams received their names, says an old legend, from the "pipe clay" in the vicinity, for in this country were beds of red clay from which the Indians used to make their pipes. Often the barefoot boy was lured to the "winding creek," which lingered in his memory through a span of fifty years. The great outdoors was his playground, and the fields and the swimming hole gave him tough sinews and bounding blood.

A few miles to the east of the Key mansion stood Col. Normand Bruce's flour mill, where the stage road crossed Pipe Creek. Here Frank spent many of his boyhood hours. Col. Bruce was a Scotchman who claimed descent from royalty. Espousing the patriot cause against the tyranny of George III, he had accompanied the Flying Camp, which had been led by Thomas Johnson to the Headquarters of General Washington in New Jersey. The quaint old aristocrat had many stories of daring and romance to tell, as the pensive boy listened to him with rapt attention.

Key never seemed to mind rough roads, the inclement weather, and the inconveniences of the country. A half century later he remembered only "life's first and fairest flow'rs" — the flaming dawn, the daisy-dotted meadows, the shaded lane, the rippling creeks, the melody of the pines, the blue mountains, the flaming sunset, and the starlit night.

FRANCIS SCOTT KEY

At the age of 14

CHAPTER II

Seven Years at St. John's

THE FIRST teacher Francis and Anne had was their mother. There were no schools in the vicinity of the Key home before the Eighteenth Century.

In 1789, when Francis was ten years old, his parents decided to send him to St. John's College, then preparing to open its doors in Annapolis. Charles Carroll of Carrollton, Samuel Chase, Thomas Stone, and William Pace, Maryland's four signers of the Declaration of Independence, were among the founders of the college.

Annapolis, at this time, was a town of three hundred houses, with upwards of two thousand inhabitants. It ranked as an aristocratic place, and was therefore a favorable college location. The institution was to be maintained by annual appropriations from the State, private contributions and tuition fees. A contemporary newspaper announcement supplies the details: "It is expected that the rooms will be ready in a few weeks for the different professors, by whom youth will be instructed in all the sciences usually taught in colleges. The tuition is fixed at five pounds per annum, and good board, lodging and washing may be had, as the public is already informed, in respectable families, at the rate of £30 current money, per annum."

The student from Frederick County, however, did not need to search for "good board, lodging and washing" in Annapolis; for he had been invited to make his home with his great-aunt, Elizabeth Ross Scott, and her husband, Dr. Upton Scott. They lived less than a mile from the college and they were eager to have Francis stay with them.

Accordingly, on the opening day, November 11, 1789, the boy from Pipe Creek enrolled in the grammar school. His matriculation was recorded on the college register: "Name of student — Francis S. Key. Age at admission — 10. Father — John Key, Planter, Frederick County." On this day the students, the professors, the members of the Board of Visitors and Governors, members of the Legislature, Judges of the General Court, members of the Bar, and other officials gathered at the State House, formed in line, and marched in procession to the College, where dedicatory exercises were held. Dr. William Smith, who had been asked to serve as principal *pro tem,* delivered a sermon; and Rev. Ralph Higginbotham, rector of St. Anne's Church of Annapolis, spoke on "The Advantages of a Classical Education." Rev. Higginbotham, the former head master of King William's School, had agreed to teach Latin and Greek in the College. In order to give a thorough knowledge of grammar to the younger children, daily exercises were given "with critical exactness." Strict attention was to be directed towards Latin and Greek, for an acquaintance with "the learned languages" was thought to be the surest foundation for other branches of literature.

Efforts to obtain a principal from England having failed,

Prof. John McDowell, a Pennsylvanian, nineteen years old, who had been teaching mathematics at St. John's, was elected in May, 1790, as the first principal of the College. He had graduated at eighteen from the University of Pennsylvania.

The institution progressed; and at the end of the first year the Visitors and Governors advertised for a vice principal to assist the principal in teaching Latin and Greek classics, mathematics, and natural and moral philosophy. A master of the French language and an usher for the grammar school were also sought.

At the Scott home, Francis found life very pleasant. Dr. Scott, now advanced in years and retired from the active practice of medicine, used to tell about his school days in Ireland, his experiences with General Wolfe in Scotland, and his early years as physician for Governor Sharpe in the days of British rule. Long before the Revolution Dr. Scott had built the mansion where he still lived.[1] As a former officer in the British Army and physician and friend of Governor Sharpe, Dr. Scott took the side of the Mother Country at the outbreak of the Revolution; hence he returned to Ireland and remained there until peace was restored. Much of his time now he used in looking after the lovely flower garden which stretched back of his home down to the water front. Aunt Elizabeth gave the little guest her love and spiritual guidance. Each night she led the young student in prayer for the protection of the "providential arm"; and many a guest at the house, it is said, used to catch a glimpse of the small white-

1.—The house is located on Shipwright Street. It is one of the scenes in Winston Churchill's novel, *Richard Carvel.*

robed figure at the head of the Colonial stairway as he was getting ready for bed.

Before noon on Saturdays, after delivering their weekly declamations, the boys were released from the class room. Sometimes they went on long walks along the Severn. All through life Key used to look back with fond recollections on the rambles he used to take around Anne Arundel County with some of his college chums. One of the places he frequently visited was the home of his grandmother, Mrs. Ann Arnold Key, on the Severn. His grandmother was totally blind. Many years before, in trying to rescue the servants who had rushed into her father's burning home on the Eastern Shore, she had been trapped by the flames and the contact with fire and smoke had brought on her affliction. She now lived at Belvoir with her daughter, Elizabeth, the wife of Col. Henry Maynadier. The soul of the young student was strengthened by contact with the kindly old grandmother.

All around Annapolis colorful scenes associated with Colonial and Revolutionary history made indelible impressions upon the adolescent boy. On the college green was a giant tulip poplar, hundreds of years old, under which the settlers had signed a treaty with the Indians. Here Continental soldiers had encamped during the Revolution; here Governor Johnson drew up a regiment of recruits, on the verge of mutiny, and ordered them to march to the Headquarters of General Washington. A few hundred yards away, in plain view, was the State House, where the sessions of the Legislature were held, and where Washington resigned his commission to

Congress a few years before. These scenes instilled in the growing boy a spirit of patriotism.

One of the most notable occasions in Annapolis, at the time Key was attending the grammar school, was the visit of George Washington. About 10 o'clock on the morning of March 25, 1791, the President, accompanied by Governor Plater of Maryland, made his appearance at the college. It was inspiring to come into the presence of the Father of his Country. The President enjoyed his trip of inspection; and when Prof. McDowell, the principal, wrote him a letter of appreciation, he replied that he had derived satisfaction from his visit to the "infant seminary" and that "the very promising appearance of its infancy must flatter all its friends (with whom I entreat you to class me) with the hope of an early and at the same time mature manhood." In closing his letter, Washington said: "I sincerely hope the excellence of your seminary will be manifested in the morals and science of the youth who are favored with your care." Francis Scott Key, now in his twelfth year, was one of the students destined to fulfill George Washington's hope that they would reflect credit upon the promising institution. A few months later Washington passed through Frederick County on his way to Philadelphia. He stayed over night in Frederick Town, and on July 1, crossed Little Pipe Creek and Big Pipe Creek on his way north. He found that the land in this locality was "remarkably fine." While he is said to have visited Terra Rubra, he made no mention of such a visit in his diary.

Francis was promoted to the French School, or intermediate department, on January 7, 1793. The requirements for admission to college were not so comprehensive in those days; and on May 5, 1794, when only fourteen, he was allowed to matriculate as a member of the novitiate class of the college.

In 1794 there were eight members of the faculty, including Prof. McDowell, the principal, and Rev. Higginbotham, the vice principal. Key studied under McDowell and Higginbotham during all three of his collegiate years.

During his novitiate year he was instructed by Prof. McDowell in algebra, logarithmal arithmetic, Euclid's elements, and plain and spherical trigonometry. Under Rev. Higginbotham he had the higher classics — Livy, Xenophon, Plato, and Demosthenes, and logic and metaphysics.

In the junior year the studies under McDowell were geometric principles, surveying, navigation, mensuration, fortification, conic sections, fluxions and gunnery. Under Rev. Higginbotham came geography, Well's *Dionysius*, Horace's *Art of Poetry*, Longinus, Aristotle *Poetics*, and Quintilian.

In the senior year, McDowell taught astronomy, use of the celestial globe, projections of the sphere, natural philosophy, and chronology and a sketch of natural history. Under Rev. Higginbotham in the final year were Epictetus, Tully's *Offices*, Xenophon's *Memorabilia*, moral philosophy, and introduction to civil history.

The other members of the faculty in 1794, in addition to Prof. McDowell and Rev. Higginbotham, were Patrick McGrath, professor of languages; Dominick Blake, assistant master of languages; Hugh H. McKearne, professor of English and grammar; John J. Tschudy, assistant in English and grammar; Richard Owen, master of writing and arithmetic; and Nyel de L'Allie, master of French.

The student body was small; hence the boys came to know each other intimately, sometimes forming life-long friendships. Three boys received the Bachelor of Arts degree at the first Commencement in 1793. There were only nine novitiates in 1794. President Washington mentioned in his diary that there were about eighty pupils "of every description" at St. John's College, but this number included the grammar school. In the College itself there was an average of about twenty-five in all.

One of the most intimate friends that Key had at St. John's was Daniel Murray of Annapolis. Key and Murray became intimate when they entered the grammar school. Key was then ten and Murray nine. They were brought up together, as Key expressed it, "almost in the same family." They were both spiritual souls. "From my earliest recollections of him," said Key in a glowing tribute to Murray, "his character and conduct were so remarkable, that he seemed to me without a fault. No temptations ever seemed to surprise him. No allurement or persuasion led him from his course. I remember well how strong his influence was over me, and how it was always used for my good. But I ascribed to natural causes altogether the peculiarity and excellence of his character, and did not see how religion could change him, who seemed already as perfect as a human being could be. This was not only my thought; all who knew him well thus estimated him." [1]

1.—*Daniel Murray,* from a letter of Francis Scott Key, Maryland Historical Magazine, XX, 200, 201.

Another classmate was John Shaw, who was about a year older than Key. Shaw was quite different from Key in appearance and nature. Key was slight of build, active, and agile, "throwing himself headlong into any plan for amusement that had aught of adventure, risk, or difficulty of any description."[1] Shaw was a large, heavy-set boy, usually quiet and reserved. He did not care much for the out-door games, such as shinney-stick; but was often alone, his favorite amusements being skating in Winter and swimming in Summer. The boy from Pipe Creek bubbled over with humor and enthusiasm. So happy and gay was he that sometimes he fell into mischief. Years later one of his college mates said: "Key was engaged in devising tricks against unpopular ushers, ever and anon getting into scrapes by writing pasquinades on odd characters in the town, his impudences sometimes rising to the height of sending his shafts among the prim and starch ladies of Annapolis of a certain age. But — shall I tell it? — his highest point of glee was to take a gallop round the college green mounted on an unfortunate cow."

While Key and Shaw were quite unlike, they became intimate friends. One bond between them was their love of the Muse. The "glow of poetry" began to thrill Shaw, according to one of his classmates, when he was about ten or twelve; and it must have taken hold of Key about the same time. One of Shaw's favorite poems was Gray's *Bard*, and often he recited it to the other boys "in his pensive moods, with a tone of melancholy wildness that was irresistibly touching." Hearing some of the terrifying stories of the French Revolution,

1. — Philip I. Thomas, one of Key's college mates, in a letter written on July 25, 1856.

Shaw wrote an ode, patterned after Gray's *Bard,* which he called *The Voice of Freedom.* The ode began with these lines:

Whither tyrants do ye haste?
Whither press your murd'rous bands?
Why, with hostile fury, waste
Peaceful unoffending lands?

But the young poet looked hopefully into the future:

Rhine! thou again shalt hear the roar
Of battle bursting on thy shore,
Again shall blood thy crystal stain,
And corpses strew thy shores again.
France shall the vollied thunder deal,
Oppressors shall her lightnings feel.

Shaw then penned a terrible denunciation of the man who was trying to enslave the Nations of the world:

Ruin on that miscreant fall
Who would Nations dare enslave!
Freedom Nature gave to all;
All an equal share should have.
Sons of Freedom, snatch the sword!
Quick! revenge your country's woes!
Soon shall heav'n your toils reward:
Soon the bloody scene shall close.

Out of the Reign of Terror came one of the classics of the literature of the world. For nearly a year Thomas Paine languished in prison, hourly expecting to be led to the guillotine. With an unconquerable spirit he employed his time in prison writing a book advocating "the religion of humanity" — turning the light of reason on the Devil, the demons, the witches, and all manner of superstitions and bigotry that had crept into Christianity. Thomas Paine believed in God. He was not an atheist. But, believing in a God of mercy, not a God of vengeance, he took issue with the threats of hell fire, which the clergy had been using to intimidate their congregations. "To do good," he declared, "is my religion." He judged a man, not by his creed, but by the way he treated his fellow men. James Monroe, the American Ambassador to France, succeeded in securing Paine's release from prison; and the final pages of *The Age of Reason* were written in Monroe's home in Paris. In 1794 and 1795 one of the epoch-making books of the world came from the press in Paris and London. Because of it Thomas Paine was branded as an atheist. Many church members shrank from it in horror, and many of the preachers tried to suppress it. But *The Age of Reason* soon found its way to America; and before long a copy of it reached the campus of St. John's.

Key did not read *The Age of Reason,* for he had heard the terrible criticism that it was atheistic. The boys handled it as if it were dynamite. Some years later Key graphically described the way in which the book was received by the students:

"While we were yet boys, a pupil of the William and Mary College in Virginia came to St. John's. He possessed talents and sprightliness, and a great fondness and facility for disputation. His mind unhappily had been poisoned by the doctrines of Godwin and other infidel writers, and he had no little zeal and a considerable dexterity in making converts. After his examination, he was placed in Shaw's class, and he immediately began to teach his accomplishments, particularly those of chewing tobacco and vending Paine's *Age of Reason* to his new companions. They were certainly in some danger and would have been utterly unable to answer the objections of a much less formidable opponent; as they knew little of Christianity but what they had imbibed in the nursery: its peculiar doctrines and the evidences of its truth formed no part of our system of education. My *alma mater* will excuse this reproach.

"In the disputes which arose, Shaw always took a distinguished part and stood forward as the advocate of sound principles. He had, manifestly, on every occasion, the best of the engagement, and induced, perhaps, a little by our prejudices, we unanimously sided with him and voted down Godwin and Tom Paine. We did not, to be sure, give either side a fair hearing; not feeling a sufficient interest in the question. We were repeatedly challenged to read these books but we had something more engaging for our leisure hours, and felt also, probably, some apprehensions as to the impressions which they might make.

"Shaw, however, offered to read Paine, and there was something like a general consent that he should do so, and decide upon it. I remember very well feeling an anxiety to know how he would determine, and I do believe that he would have made infidels of most of us, if he had determined in favour of the book. But he pronounced against it and avowed his conviction in the truth of the Bible to be unshaken.

"In a conversation afterwards with him on the subject,

he told me that some of the objections had given him some trouble to investigate and refute, that the work was plausibly written, and he thought I might as well not read it."[1]

Thus Francis Scott Key looked upon Tom Paine as a man of "inquity and cunning" and his works as "subtle snares and artful sophisms". It was not long before a rebuttal of Paine's religious views appeared. This was Bishop Watson's *Apology for the Bible.* The boy from Pipe Creek was thrilled with Bishop Watson's stirring defense of orthodox doctrines. "Never shall I forget," said one of his college mates many years afterwards, "the animated manner in which, while lying on his back under the shade of the old poplar on the college green he would read what he considered its eloquent passages. Even now, in my mind's eye, I can see the flush on the youthful cheek, and the bright beaming of his clear blue eyes, as he read from it the following brush of the good Bishop's honest indignation against the reviler of the Holy Book: 'You say (addressing himself to Paine) you have gone through the Bible like a man with an axe through a wood, cutting down the trees; and the priests, if they can, may replant them. Vain and preposterous boaster! You have, indeed, gone through the Bible with the best intention to destroy its fair trees of life; but the lofty cedars of Lebanon have derided your vain attempts, and laughed, unhurt, at the feebleness of your stroke. The Bible, sir, has withstood the learning of Porphery, the wit of Voltaire, and the satire of Bolingbroke, and it will not fall by your hands!' "

In the class room John Shaw was the outstanding student. In Latin he was a wizard. The teacher, Rev. Higgin-

1.—John Hall, *Poems by Shaw,* published 1810, introduction, 9.

botham, a native of Ireland and a graduate of Trinity College, Dublin, used to call the class, in which Shaw and Key were members, the Tenth Legion, to remind the boys of Caesar's Tenth Legion, those famous Roman battalions that were always receiving fresh recruits, and whose valiant soldiers kept advancing over the dead bodies of their comrades. Whenever guests arrived at the college, Rev. Higginbotham was glad to "order out the Tenth Legion for parade." At the head of the Tenth Legion stood John Shaw.

Among the Latin poets with whom Key became familiar was Marcus Valerius Martialis, known commonly as Martial. From 66 A.D. to 100 A.D. Martial flourished in Rome as a master of epigram. From his writings the young Latin scholars at St. John's received some valuable advice. One of Key's translations dealt with Martial's warning against procrastination:

Translation from Martial

To-morrow he will live, Lorenzo swears,
Quite a new life; and hath so sworn for years.
"Tell me, Lorenzo, when will come this day
Thou call'st to-morrow? Is it still distant? Say,
Where is it, and how is't to be got?
What is the price at which it may be bought?
Will it by Parry at the pole be found?
Or brought to light by Semnes from under ground?
To-morrow, dids't thou say, Lorenzo? Why,
Is that a day that hath not yet gone by?
'Twas known before the flood; its years outweigh
E'en those of Nestor, or Methuselah.
To-morrow thou wilt live! To-day is quite
Too late; he who lived yesterday, did right."

In the month of July, 1796, Prof. McDowell, in the presence of several members of the Board of Visitors and Governors, examined the applicants for the degree of Bachelor of Arts. Key was one of the six successful applicants for the degree. The other five were John Shaw, Daniel Murray, and William Cooke, of Annapolis; Robert H. Goldsborough, of the Eastern Shore; and Carlysle F. Whiting, of Virginia.

Key left the College on August 11, 1796, and arrangements were made to confer the degrees in October. Shaw was chosen to deliver the salutatory oration in Latin. Key was selected as the valedictory orator of the class. He took "Eloquence" as his subject.

Thus Key was graduated with honors at seventeen. In seven years he had been transformed from a rustic farmer boy with virtually no education into a baccalaureate.

It is true, he had written to his sister:

> Sad was the parting — sad the days,
> And dull the school — and dull the plays,

but seven years of discipline were also years of character unfoldment, and in these years of hard study he found many hours of happiness. During all the rest of his life the boy from Pipe Creek remained one of the most appreciative and loyal alumni of St. John's.

CHAPTER III

Law Student. Delia

KEY DECIDED to study law, as soon as he received his degree from St. John's College. It was a natural course: he had come of a family of lawyers. His father who, since the adoption of the Federal Constitution, had risen from the ranks of justice of the peace to a seat on the bench as Associate Justice of his Judicial District,[1] encouraged the idea. Besides, young Key was fond of books and had a quick mind and a good memory. His uncle, Philip Barton Key, a leading member of the Maryland Bar, and now located in Annapolis, invited the young man to begin the study of law in his office. Uncle Philip had an exciting career. Captain of the Maryland Loyalist Regiment, and prisoner in Florida, then Spanish territory, his Maryland property had been confiscated because of his allegiance to King George III. He practiced law for several years in St. Mary's County, and in 1790, at the age of thirty-three, married Ann Plater, sixteen-year-old daughter of George Plater, who was Governor of Maryland from 1791 until his death in 1792. Philip Barton Key settled in Annapolis soon after his marriage. His ability and pleasing personality helped to allay the ill feeling which many had for him because he took the side of the King during the Revolution.

1.—John Ross Key was appointed in 1791 as Associate Justice of the Fifth Judicial District, comprising Allegany, Washington and Frederick Counties.

Because the leading lawyers of Maryland congregated in Annapolis to argue their cases before the General Court, Annapolis was the best place in the State for a young man to study law. Francis was quite glad to remain a few more years in Annapolis. There was a very happy social life here; and with the restrictions of college discipline removed, he was able to enjoy some of the gayety of the State Capital.

At the time Key was studying under his uncle's guidance, there were in Annapolis between twenty and thirty other law students from different parts of the State. Among them was a very slender youth, about six feet tall, from Calvert County, who had graduated from Dickinson College in Carlisle, Pennsylvania. He had keen blue eyes, thick black hair, and a solemn demeanor. This young man was Roger Brooke Taney, and he was studying in the office of Jeremiah Townley Chase, Judge of the General Court. Here, in the Maryland Capital, began the life-long friendship of the graduate of St. John's and the graduate of Dickinson. Of the two young men, Taney, who was several years older than the other, was the more studious. He kept aloof from everything except his law books. He determined not to go into society until he had completed his legal studies and he adhered to that determination. Practically no one did he associate with, except law students, and for weeks together read law twelve hours in the twenty-four. In the midst of the highly polished and educated society of Annapolis he never visited any family but, instead, declined the kind and hospitable invitations that he received. Many years later he said it would have been better for him if he had occasionally "mixed in the society of ladies and gentlemen older than the students."

Quite different in temperament from Taney was young Key. Although a farmer's son like Taney, he sprang from an aristocratic family, a cavalier family that enjoyed the amenities of life. While a good student, and a boy of high ideals, he was gayer by nature than the dignified young man from the Patuxent. A good mixer, and rather fond of the drawing-room, Francis did not plunge into the Common Law as eagerly as Roger. He found relaxation and pleasure in Annapolis society.

Often his thoughts went back to Pipe Creek, not only for mother and father and sister, but also for a girl named Delia with whom he had fallen in love. One biographer of Key says: "Who she was we do not know, a near neighbor, perhaps a guest of his sister. She was certainly his first sweetheart."[1] Key's first poems were those written to Delia. The few quoted stanzas tell how he imparted his vow of love to Delia on the trunk of a beech tree:

For Fortune's fickle smiles let others pine;
Delia, thy smile, thy witching smile, be mine.
Content, though poor, each easy idle day,
Cheered by that smile, steals unperceived away.
With thy fond arm in mine, when Spring's soft power
First bursts the bud of every blushing flower,
Then let me guide thy light steps o'er the green,
And show thee all the beauties of the scene;
Or when the sultry suns of Summer pour
A warmer ray, then many a rapturous hour
Awaits us, where the beech-tree's arching shade
Has formed a secret bower for lovers made:

1.—Victor Weybright, *Spangled Banner,* 32

That beech, whose tender rind didst first impart
To Delia the soft secret of my heart —
Carved on whose trunk the faithful vows appear
Which Delia heard not with disdainful ear.[1]

In another poem the young student makes a pun on the word "key" — hoping he would be the "happy Key" to guard the treasures of his Delia's heart:

To A Golden Key

Long had a golden key concealed
   The treasures of my Delia's breast;
Treasures one half so sweet and rich
   Sure never key before possessed.

* * * * * *

But ah! that little golden key,
   Could I but dare unlock its store,
And with the trembling hand of Love
   Those treasures, long concealed, explore.

In this poem Key refers to Delia as a slowly-budding rose:

To A Rosebud

Ah! why so tardy, timid Rose,
   Thy opening beauties to display?
Ah! why within their mossy cell
   So long thy shrinking petals stay?
Full many a morn, and many an eve,
   Thy gently swelling bud I've seen,
And fondly strove, with many a kiss,
   To wake thee from thy bed of green.

1 — Key's Poems, 83.

But, as Victor Weybright says of Key's Delia, "She, unfortunately, must have been a redlands girl who did not winter along fashionable tidewater. Love at Terra Rubra, on a care-free summer holiday, was very different from the practical, well-directed love that prevailed in Annapolis."

The home that attracted Key the most in Annapolis was the mansion of Mrs. Edward Lloyd, 4th. Mrs. Lloyd was the widow of one of the Lloyds of Wye House, and Wye House was one of the show-places of Maryland. The masters of this estate, in Talbot County, had lived in each successive generation in utmost luxury, with hundreds of Negro slaves to do their bidding. Edward Lloyd, 3rd, had served as Governor of Maryland. His son Edward, 4th, was educated in England. He traveled down to Tidewater, Virginia; spent many hours at Mount Airy, the fashionable home of John Tayloe, on the Rappahannock, and brought home with him in 1767 Tayloe's daughter, Elizabeth, as his bride. From London he ordered blue liveries for his servants, and the "best colored and most approved prints" for his walls. Having a stylish pleasure-boat of 60-ton burden, he ordered from London six brass guns to rest on swivels, and fitted to fire with locks, and engraved with his initials; and he also ordered 200 balls, 200 cartridges filled with powder, and a supply of powder-horns and powder; also a flag with his "arms painted theron, the field azure, the lion gold." He also ordered a phaeton to be built by the best maker in London, a fashionable four-horse carriage, not too high, he "being a Gouty man." It was this Eastern Shoreman who, when he entered the Assembly in 1771, bought the uncompleted dwelling which

Samuel Chase had started to erect in Annapolis on the corner of Maryland Avenue and King George street. Lloyd completed it; and when it was finished it was the only three-story house and one of the most imposing mansions in the town. It was a great square Georgian structure, with severe exterior, and lofty chimneys. Broad steps in front led to a pretty fan-lighted doorway. This was the "town house" of Col. Edward Lloyd, 4th, who helped to draft the State Constitution, sat in the Council of Governor Johnson, occupied a chair in Congress at the time Washington resigned his commission, and served as a member of the Convention which ratified the Federal Constitution.

At the time Key was working for his degree at St. John's, Lloyd was a member of the State Senate. A short time before Key's graduation, Senator Lloyd died. The lavish entertainment for the ladies and gentlemen of official circles in the Capital gave way to mourning; but Mrs. Lloyd continued to live in the "town house," and her daughters continued to attract the young men of Annapolis. The youngest was the chief attraction for young Key. Her name was Mary Tayloe Lloyd. Mary was beautiful and charming and had a number of admirers. One of her suitors was Daniel Murray, Key's intimate friend, who later entered the Naval Academy. John Shaw, the head of Rev. Higginbotham's Tenth Legion, also cast his eyes longingly at the lovely girl.

Even when he was a student at St. John's, young Key had often talked to Mary; but at the time of his graduation, when he was seventeen, she was only in her thirteenth year. He was captivated by her winsome loveliness. Indeed, it was she who gave an impetus to his talent as a lyric poet. According to the accepted story, he wrote in verse the feelings of his heart but the rhymes did not meet with the response that he expected. Instead of being appreciated, his love ballads made her burst into laughter. She thought the missives were a huge joke. This was not unusual for the youngest daughter of the aristocratic house of Lloyd, reared in the lap of luxury, and surfeited with attentions. The story has been handed down through the years that the unresponsive Miss Lloyd, to taunt the romantic young Key, took mischievous delight in making the rhyming messages into curl papers. Tradition says that when the faithful swain was seen from her window, she would wave to him and point to her curls, and Frank would understand, much to his chagrin, that she had made good her threats and used his sonnets for curl papers.

Miss Lloyd's harsh reaction to Key's love songs brought deep remorse to the lovesick law student, for he was a romantic youth. And in her jesting she robbed posterity of the very first outbursts from the heart of the future poet lawyer. If it be true, however, that she did destroy all of the love ballads which she received, there survives a poem which Key dedicated "to Mary," which reveals the faithful and dauntless soul. Should he be downcast, he said, merely because his offers of love were not appreciated at the start? No. While "colder lovers" might shrink from the "gloom of clouds and storms," and "calmly wait for peaceful skies," he swore that he would keep striving to win his way to the idol of his heart:

To Mary

Frown on, ye dark and angry clouds;
  And, Winter, blow that blast again,
That calls thy wrathful host to pour
  Their fury on the wasted plain.
'Tis thus I choose my way to win
  To her whose love my bosom warms;
And brighter seems the prize I seek
  Seen through the gloom of clouds and storms.
Let colder lovers shrink from these,
  And calmly wait for peaceful skies;
Be mine, through toil and pain to win
  The beam of Mary's gladdened eyes.
Perhaps she'll value more my love,
  Perhaps give more of hers to me,
Perhaps may greet me with a smile
  More sweet, if smile more sweet can be.
O! Mary, could'st thou know this heart,
  Could words or deeds its truth declare,
'T would higher raise love's flame in thine,
  Or light it, if it be not there.

Francis Scott Key completed his law studies in Annapolis as the Eighteenth Century was drawing to a close. Since there were few American law books, the study of pleading at that time was confined almost entirely to the English digests. "Chitty," as it was pointed out by Taney many years later, "had not made his appearance, and you were obliged to look for the rule in Comyn's *Digest*, or Bacon's *Abridgment*, or Viner's *Abridgment*, and the cases to which they referred." Some of them were ponderous tomes; one of the volumes of Viner's *Abridgment*, weighing five pounds, and bearing Key's bookplate, is one of the exhibits in the Francis Scott Key room in the Taney home in Frederick.

There was no moot court for the law students in Annapolis in Key's day. Some of the students organized a debating society, but even in this group the questions that were discussed were rarely legal questions.

Nevertheless, before he was twenty-one, Key had acquired a sound foundation in the law. Not only had he received valuable training in Uncle Philip's office, but he had also acquired considerable experience by attending the sessions of the General Court. Here Key and Taney saw the three judges, in their scarlet cloaks, presiding on an elevated platform. The rough, often intoxicated, but powerful Luther Martin was "the acknowledged and undisputed head of the profession in Maryland" and nobody disputed this rank with him until William Pinkney returned from Europe. In addition to Mr. Martin, among the leading lawyers who appeared before the General Court were Key's Uncle Philip and his Cousin Arthur Shaaff. Enthused by hearing the array of legal talent, Key and Taney looked forward to the day when they, too, might occupy a commanding position at the bar.

It was about the dawn of the Nineteenth Century when the scion of the Key family was ready to commence the practice of law. He left Annapolis with a heavy heart, for he left behind him the sixteen-year-old girl who had won his heart.

MARY TAYLOE LLOYD KEY

From the miniature by Robert Field

CHAPTER IV

Professional and Married Life

KEY DECIDED to begin his professional life in Frederick Town. His father, still an Associate Judge, was now living there. This enabled the young lawyer to settle under the parental roof. It seemed to be the wise thing to do. Judge Key had grown in popular esteem with the passing of the years, his prestige arising largely from his readiness to respond at all times to appeals for help both in military and civil life. When President Washington called for troops at the time of the Whiskey Rebellion in 1794, Judge Key offered his service as lieutenant colonel in the Frederick County Militia; and in 1798, when a movement was on foot to remedy effects in the Militia Law of the State, he was chosen as one of the officers of his brigade to attend a state-wide conference in Annapolis. So popular had he become, that when Dr. John D. Carey in 1798 started a little periodical, he called it *The Key*, in honor of the Judge.

It was in *The Key* that the first history of Frederick Town appeared. It was a brief history, telling that the first house in Frederick was built by John Thomas Schley, the leader of a band of immigrants from Germany. At the time of the publication of *The Key*, Frederick numbered 449 dwellings, "built principally of brick and stone, and mostly on one broad street." The population had grown to more than 2,600. One reason for its growth, in addition to the fertility of Monocacy Valley, was the town's location. It was built on the intersection of the roads running from Baltimore and Georgetown to the West and the North. The days were enlivened by the stagecoaches and Conestoga wagons that lumbered up and down the rough highways.

It was in 1800 that Judge Key's son, now twenty-one, was admitted to the Frederick County Bar. The Court House was small but attractive; nearby was the Academy built in 1796. The people also boasted of a "spacious and handsome Poor House," and " a stone jail with a large yard surrounded by a stone wall." On Market Street, which rivalled Patrick Street as the main street of the town, was the Market House, erected in 1769. In the upper part of it was the official town office, and atop the building was a belfry.

All things considered, Frederick Town presented an attractive opening for the young lawyer. To be sure, it was no rival of Baltimore with its 26,000 inhabitants; but, with this single exception, it was the largest town in the State. Not only was it a fine flourishing inland town, but it was the seat of a rich smiling county. The fertile valley yielded abundant crops. It was estimated in *The Key* that upwards of eighty grist mills along the streams of the county were engaged in grinding wheat into flour. Then, too, there were two iron furnaces, two forges, two paper mills, and two glass works. There was another industry which flourished in Maryland — the distilling of rye whiskey. A single distillery sometimes produced more than 10,000 gallons a year. And Frederick County boasted of between 300 and 400 stills! The population of the county at the beginning of the Nineteenth Century was between 31,000 and 32,000, but about 4,500 of these were Negro slaves.

In Frederick Town the guttural German was spoken by a large part of the population; but young Key had an opportunity to form the acquaintance of a number of people of English blood. One of these was Thomas Johnson, Revolutionary War Governor and former Associate Justice of the United States Supreme Court, who was now enjoying the sunset years. It was he who delivered the panegyric on George Washington at the great mock funeral on February 22, 1800, when the patriotic Keys bowed their heads in tribute to the memory of the Father of his Country.

Life at Frederick Town promised to be pleasant for young Key; but his thoughts kept reverting to the scenes of his college days in Annapolis. Occasionally he heard from his friend, Daniel Murray, who became a midshipman. John Shaw, the Latin wizard, studied medicine and accepted a position as surgeon with a squadron that set sail from Philadelphia for the Mediterranean. When the fleet reached Tunis, Dr. Shaw's duties took a sudden turn. The Bey of Tunis threatened to declare war against the United States unless certain provisions arrived within a limited time; and Shaw was sent by the American Consul to our representative at the Court of St. James to take the instructions from the American Minister at Lisbon. The Marylander set sail from Tunis in September, 1799; but his little vessel, driven by wind and wave from one port to another, did not reach Gibraltar until March, 1800. It was while at Gibraltar that Dr. Shaw received a letter from his classmate at Frederick. Key said that he regretted he was not along with Shaw on his ramble to foreign lands. He would have especially enjoyed, he said, "a moonlight walk among the ruins of Gibraltar." In his reply, Shaw said he wanted to leave the ruins of Carthage behind him, and return to Annapolis to take "an evening's walk around the college green." He had his wish gratified; for he found his way back to the campus some months later.

Key, too, was always anxious to return to Annapolis—for he could never forget Mary. He made frequent trips to the college town; and, whenever he went back, he called at the Lloyd home. It was soon after he began the practice of law that his alma mater conferred upon him the degree of Master of Arts. The award was made at the Commencement held on November 12, 1800. Shaw and Murray and the other members of the Class of 1796 were also among the alumni honored with the Master's degree at the final exercises in St. John's Hall.

In the month of March, 1801, the young lawyer gave an enthusiastic welcome to one of his chums who had decided to locate in Frederick Town for the practice of law. It was Taney. This earnest young man from Calvert County had already won the distinction of serving in the House of Delegates, but he had been defeated for reëlection in 1800. Soon afterwards he made up his mind to settle in Frederick, for this appeared to be the most profitable point of practice in the State, with the exception of Baltimore and Annapolis. Another reason for his selection was the fact that he had formed friendships in Annapolis with some young men near his own age who now lived in Frederick Town, and he felt he would not be "as lonely and without friends" on his arrival here as he would be in Baltimore.

Taney frequently visited the Key home in Frederick Town as well as the plantation at Pipe Creek, and he was much interested in Key's sister Anne. One of Key's contemporaries recalled that Anne had the most cheerful face and the most pleasant smile that he had ever seen. About three miles south of town was Arcadia, the handsome estate of Arthur Shaaff, Key's bachelor cousin. Mr. Shaaff gladly lent a helping hand to the young lawyers: indeed, it was he who gave to Taney his first opportunity of appearing before the Frederick County Court. Before long the two young men were journeying together in legal business to adjoining counties. Together they were admitted to the Montgomery County Bar at Rockville on November 5, 1801.

In the meantime Attorney Key's principal suit had been to win the heart of Mary Tayloe Lloyd. He had been persistent in his courtship; and, at last, the promise of marriage was given. The announcement of the engagement was received with favor by both the Key and the Lloyd families, for the members of these two families had long been on terms of intimate friendship.

Mary wanted to have the wedding in her own home — the very house in which she had once made Frank's love sonnets into curl papers. It was decided to call on the rector of St. Anne's Episcopal Church to perform the ceremony. This was none other than Rev. Ralph Higginbotham, the jovial vice principal of St. John's College, under whom Frank had studied the ancient classics. The wedding was planned for the evening of January 19, 1802.

The town was aflutter as the hour of the marriage approached. William Faris, the Annapolis diarist, penned in his diary: "To night Miss Polly Lloyd to be married to Mr. Fk. Key."

When the wedding guests had assembled, the bride and groom marched into the great drawing room which gleamed with crystal and silver. Here the bride, not yet eighteen, tall and lovely, and the groom, twenty-two, slight of build, with heavy brown hair and blue dreamy eyes, exchanged their wedding vows.

It was on a bleak winter day that Frank and Polly arrived in Frederick Town. The groom had been living with his father and mother and Anne, and he had no home of his own; but the newlyweds "went to housekeeping" in a little house on Market Street.

Polly found life here in sharp contrast to that of Annapolis. The church, which was to be their house of worship, was a sample of the contrast. It was a plain brick building that had been put up about fifty years before for the frontier parish of the Colony — All Saints. Standing on a hill in the southern part of town, and surrounded by low marshy land, it was particularly uninviting in bad weather. The parish had neither vestry nor rector; but it managed to survive, with services conducted every other Sunday by Rev. George Bower, a gay and light-hearted preacher from Hager's Town. The hill church in the dead of winter was a barren place for a dainty bride accustomed to fashionable St. Anne's and the society of Annapolis and the Wye House. "There was no fire," says the church history. "People carried their foot warmers — wooden boxes lined with tin, some with an iron drawer which held about a tin cup of hot coals; these to keep the feet warm." It was a cheerless place even to those who came warmly bundled up.

In the Fall of 1801, the pillar of the church, William M. Beall, started an enrollment of members, looking to a reorganization of the parish and an election of a vestry. One of the men who was approached on the subject of church membership was Francis Scott Key, then twenty-two years old. There were six other churches in Frederick Town — German Reformed, German Lutheran, Presbyterian, Catholic, Baptist, and Methodist. Perhaps the strongest congregation was the German Reformed, one of whose pastors had baptized Key during the Revolution. Their church had one of the handsomest steeples this side of the Atlantic, and in the steeple were two bells that had been brought from London and installed at a cost of more than six hundred dollars. But Key was an Episcopalian; his relatives were Episcopalians; he was fond of the church's ritual; and he included his name as one of the active members of the struggling parish.

Key was a Federalist at this time. But the only record of his Federalism came in 1804, when he volunteered to assist in the defense of a man, whose prosecution was being engineered, so it was believed, by Roger Nelson, one of the anti-Federalist leaders. Others who offered to aid the defense were Shaaff and Taney and John Hanson Thomas, all Federalists.

While Key, strangely enough, was not ambitious for a political career, he was quite interested in public affairs. He was deeply patriotic. His patriotism was stirred when he heard of the preparations for the war against the Barbary powers — Tripoli, Algiers, Tunis, and Morocco. These countries had been demanding large sums of money from the United States and other nations before they would allow the merchant vessels of those nations to enter the Mediterranean; and, whenever the tributes were not paid, the corsairs resorted to plunder and cruelty. Key had heard John Shaw tell about some of the outrages along the African coast. The American Government had been compelled to pay twenty thousand dollars a year to enable our merchant vessels to sail the Mediterranean. But even this did not satisfy the pirates, who captured our sailors, held them in slavery, and treated them like beasts of burden under the lash. In 1801 the Pascha of Tripoli declared war on the United States; the insolent ruler cut down the Stars and Stripes, demanded that the American tributes be increased, and started on a campaign of rapine and cruelty. President Jefferson determined that no further tributes should be paid to the Barbary powers.

Key was thrilled in 1804 when he heard the news of the daring exploit of Stephen Decatur in the harbor of Tripoli. The young lawyer rejoiced not only because his country was victorious but more especially because Christians had triumphed over Mohammedans.

Later, when Decatur and his gallant comrades returned from the Mediterranean, they were greeted with wild ovations. Key sent up his paean of praise for the bravery of the sailors and exulted because the "Star Spangled flag" had eclipsed the Crescent.

The following poem bears the germs of the immortal anthem which he later composed:

The Warrior's Return

When the warrior returns, from the battle afar,
  To the home and the country he nobly defended,
O! warm be the welcome to gladden his ear,
  And loud be the joy that his perils are ended;
In the full tide of song let his fame roll along,
To the feast-flowing board let us gratefully throng,
Where, mixed with the olive, the laurel shall wave,
And form a bright wreath for the brows of the brave.

Columbians! a band of your brothers behold,
  Who claim the reward of your hearts' warm emotion,
When your cause, when your honour, urged onward
    the bold,
  In vain frowned the desert, in vain raged the ocean:
To a far distant shore, to the battle's wild roar,
They rushed, your fair fame and your rights to secure:
Then, mixed with the olive, the laurel shall wave,
And form a bright wreath for the brows of the brave.

In the conflict resistless, each toil they endured,
  'Till their foes fled dismayed from the war's deso-
    lation;
And pale beamed the Crescent, its splendor obscured
  By the light of the Star-Spangled flag of our nation.
Where each radiant star gleamed a meteor of war,
And the turbaned heads bowed to its terrible glare,
Now, mixed with the olive, the laurel shall wave,
And form a bright wreath for the brows of the brave.

Our Fathers, who stand on the summit of fame,
  Shall exultingly hear of their sons the proud story:
How their young bosoms glowed with the patriot
    flame,

How they fought, how they fell, in the blaze of their
glory,
How triumphant they rode o'er the wondering flood,
And stained the blue waters with infidel blood;
How, mixed with the olive, the laurel did wave,
And formed a bright wreath for the brows of the brave.

Then welcome the warrior returned from afar
To the home and the country he nobly defended;
Let the thanks due to valor now gladden his ear,
And loud be the joy that his perils are ended.
In the full tide of song let his fame roll along,
To the feast-flowing board let us gratefully throng,
Where, mixed with the olive, the laurel shall wave,
And form a bright wreath for the brows of the brave.

THE GEORGETOWN HOME OF FRANCIS SCOTT KEY

From the painting by John Ross Key

CHAPTER V

First Year in Georgetown

WHILE Francis Scott Key had his office in Frederick, his Uncle Philip practised law at Georgetown. In 1801 Philip was named by President John Adams as Chief Judge of the United States Circuit Court of Maryland, but this Court was abolished when Congress established a new judicial system. During the next few years he enjoyed a lucrative practice in the District of Columbia. Perhaps the most dramatic trial in which he was ever engaged was the defense of Justice Samuel Chase. Justice Chase's lawyers before the Senate—regarded as "five of the most eminent Federalist lawyers" of the day—were Philip Barton Key, Luther Martin, Robert Goodloe Harper, Charles Lee, and Joseph Hopkinson. Francis Scott Key watched the development with keen interest. On one side was his uncle; on the other Joseph Hopper Nicholson, who had married a sister of Polly. On March 1, 1805, after a month of testimony and argument, Vice President Aaron Burr announced the verdict. The acquittal of Justice Chase was received by the Federalists with great rejoicing. Senator William Plumer called it "the greatest and most important trial ever held in this nation." The Republicans were incensed; Henry St. George Tucker regarded the acquittal of Chase as "a foul disgrace upon our country."

It was soon after the close of this trial that Philip Barton

Key decided to withdraw from active practice. He was quite well-to-do. It occurred to him that he might turn over much of his practice to his nephew if he would come to Georgetown. Frank talked the matter over with Polly, and she felt happy at the prospect of moving away from Frederick Town. She had missed the social gayeties of Annapolis for nearly five years. She was now the mother of two children — Elizabeth Phoebe, born in 1803, and Maria Lloyd, born in 1805. It did not take them long to accept Uncle Philip's offer. So it was that at the close of 1805, when Key was twenty-six, he gave up his Frederick office, bade farewell to his parents, Taney and Anne, and bundling up the two small children, set out for their new home in the District of Columbia.

Georgetown, when Key and his family arrived there, was a flourishing community of nearly four thousand people. Standing at the head of tidewater on the hills that rolled back from the Potomac at the mouth of Rock Creek, it was one of the chief shipping ports in the New World; and also the central depot for stages that started off with passengers for Baltimore, Annapolis and Frederick. Among the places of interest in Georgetown was Georgetown College, founded in 1795 by Bishop John Carroll, and now accommodating about two hundred students. The town also boasted of an institution which Frederick lacked — a bank; it was the Bank of Columbia and had a capital of a million dollars.

As soon as the Keys had established themselves in their new home, Uncle Philip announced in the press that he was withdrawing from active practice, but that Mr. Francis S. Key would attend to any professional business confided to him. A splendid opportunity awaited his twenty-six year old nephew. His uncle's recommendation was in itself a fine introduction.

Then, too, Georgetown was in its heyday: it was crowded with lawmakers and foreign diplomats who sought the quiet charm of the Georgetown heights in order to escape the mud or the dust of the Federal City. This new seat of government had grown to be a place of more than four thousand people. The Capitol and the President's House, surrounded by woods and underbrush, were separated by a swamp: through this was a road with deep mud holes, stagnant, malarial pools, breeding places for myriads of mosquitoes in rainy seasons.

"No one, from the North or from the high country of the South," said Rufus King, "can pass the months of August and September there without intermittent or bilious fever."

And a French diplomat, speaking of the city of Washington, exclaimed: "Mon Dieu! What have I done to reside in such a city?"

One fine home in Washington was Octagon House, the mansion of Colonel John Tayloe of Mount Airy, Virginia. This home was famous for its entertainments for President Jefferson and other distinguished men in the early part of the Nineteenth Century.

Many of the Senators and Representatives crowded into boarding houses and inns near the Capitol; but others preferred to sojoin amid more attractive surroundings on the other side of Rock Creek, about four miles to the west. And so the young lawyer from Frederick County came into contact with some of the foremost political leaders of the day. Union

Tavern was a favorite rendezvous for the Nation's legislators – among them Aaron Burr and John Randolph of Roanoke – and Philip Barton Key and his nephew often came to the tavern to chat with the distinguished visitors.

Nearby was St. John's Episcopal Church. Services for Episcopalians had been held in Georgetown as early as 1794; and in 1796 the young rector, Rev. Walter D. Addison, started a movement to erect a church building; but lack of funds prevented it from rising any higher than the first range of windows until 1803, when contributions were solicited again, and President Jefferson was one of the contributors. The edifice was completed in 1804; and Rev. Johannes J. Sayrs, of Port Tobacco, Maryland, was chosen rector of the parish. Rev. Sayrs was one of the first persons whom Frank and Polly met in Georgetown. They promptly decided to join St. John's Church.

The houses along Bridge Street (later known as M Street) commanded a fine view of the Potomac. One of the houses on the south side of this street was purchased by Francis Scott Key. This home, in which he lived for many years, was built by Thomas Clarke about the year 1802, just east of the old aqueduct bridge (west of the present Francis Scott Key Memorial Bridge). It was built of brick; and, besides its two main stories, had a basement and a floor under a gable roof. The front door opened into a wide hallway. To the right of this were two large parlors. In the basement were the dining room, kitchen, and cold-storage pantry. In the rear was a sun porch, looking out upon the terraced flower garden sloping all the way down to the river bank. At the rear end were the coach house and a smoke house.

Before leaving Frederick, Key understood that his sister had promised to marry his friend Taney. The wedding of Anne Phoebe Charlton Key and Taney was set for the evening of January 7, 1806. They were married in the mansion at Pipe Creek. Taney, it was recalled years after, was "a tall, gaunt fellow, as lean as a Potomac herring, and as shrewd as the shrewdest." His marriage to bright little Anne was likened to "the union of a hawk with a sky-lark."

Even after his removal to Georgetown, Key kept in close touch with Taney, professionally and socially. Their friendship remained steadfast. And Key came to Annapolis from Georgetown and Taney from Frederick to appear together in the Court of Appeals of Maryland.

One of these cases – *Keefer vs. Young* – was an action of dower brought by Mrs. Barton Keefer, a widow, to recover her interest in fifty acres of land that had belonged to her husband. Arthur Shaaff, counsel for Mrs. Keefer, undertook to prove by parol evidence that her husband had owned the land at the time of his death. Key and Taney, representing the defendant, resisted the widow's claim by objecting to the introduction of the evidence. When the Court instructed the jury that the evidence was insufficient to entitle the widow to recover, Mr. Shaaff took an appeal. The Court of Appeals reversed the decision of the Frederick County Court and held that parol evidence was admissible to show that land owned by the husband was the same land in which the dower was demanded.

Another case that came before the Court of Appeals—*Sheely vs. Biggs*—was an action of slander brought by Biggs to secure satisfaction for an accusation that he had sworn to a lie. Schaaff, attorney for Biggs, explained in an *innuendo* that this meant "the plaintiff had committed perjury before a magistrate." Key and Taney were the attorneys for the defendant. When a verdict for twenty-two pounds was given to Biggs, Key and Taney moved for an arrest of judgment on the ground that the utterance was not actionable *per se* and that no *colloquium* had been inserted in the declaration to connect the utterance with a judicial proceeding. Their motion overruled, they took an appeal. The case was now argued in Annapolis before Chief Judge Jeremiah Townley Chase, Taney's old preceptor, and Judges Joseph Hopper Nicholson, John Buchanan and John Mackall Gantt. The result was a triumph for Key and Taney, as the decision of the Frederick County Court was reversed. Chief Judge Chase held that the word *foresworn* did not necessarily imply perjury; and, to make it constitute slander, it had to be prefaced by a *colloquium* setting forth the judicial proceeding in which it was uttered, the *innuendo* being insufficient to make the utterance actionable.

It was in 1806, during Key's first year in Georgetown, that his Uncle Philip ran for Congress. He announced his candidacy for Representative from the Third Maryland District, which included Montgomery and a part of Frederick County. Uncle Philip, while he spent much of his time at his mansion in the District of Columbia, also owned a farm in Montgomery County. Representative Patrick Magruder, Jeffersonian Republican, was running for reëlection. The campaign was exceedingly bitter. The Jeffersonians charged that Key was a Tory and a refugee during the Revolution. They accused him of having joined the British Army while his brother served as a patriot, at the instigation of their father so that , regardless of the outcome, his property would be safe from confiscation. It was also claimed that Mr. Key was a resident of the District of Columbia and therefore was ineligible to serve as Representative from Maryland. In order to stir up prejudice against Mr. Key, the Jeffersonians published a charge that the British Ambassador had visited in Frederick, insinuating that he had been helping to "build the fences" of Mr. Key for Congress. Which side would Mr. Key take, they inquired in derision, in the event of war between the United States and Great Britain?

A campaign of this kind at a time when feeling ran high against England, would have defeated a candidate of mediocre ability; but Philip Barton Key was a man of sterling character and winning personality. Then, too, he had the help of his brother and many of Frank's friends in Frederick County; and so, in spite of all the accusations of the Jeffersonians, he was elected.

Accordingly, within a short time after Francis Scott Key located in Georgetown, his talented uncle took his seat as a Federalist member of the House of Representatives. His seat was contested by the friends of President Jefferson; but in a speech denying the charge that he was a British sympathizer, Congressman Key said: "I returned to my country like a prodigal to his father. I have felt as an American should feel. And I have been received and forgiven, of which the most convincing proof is — my election."

CHAPTER VI

Aaron Burr's Messengers

KEY HAD BEEN living in Georgetown little more than a year when the opportunity came to him to appear before the Supreme Court of the United States. The case in which he appeared was the habeas corpus hearing for two prisoners charged with treason as accomplices of Aaron Burr. When, in the Spring of 1806, Burr received a message from General James Wilkinson, Governor of Upper Louisiana and one of his associates in the Mexican conspiracy, he decided to send a reply before setting out himself on his expedition. He selected Dr. Justus Erich Bollman of Philadelphia and Samuel Swartwout of New York as his couriers.

Bollman was a Göttingen graduate, now about thirty-five years old. It was he who, with the aid of Francis K. Huger of Charleston, South Carolina, helped General Lafayette to escape after months of planning from the dungeon at Olmutz. Lafayette was soon caught, however, and brought back to solitary confinement; and Bollman was captured too and thrown into prison. On condition that he would leave Austria, Bollman was released, and he sailed for America. With young Huger he called on President Washington and described the horrors of Olmutz; and Washington wrote to his Ministers at London and Paris and to the Emperor of Germany to enlist their aid in behalf of Lafayette.

Samuel Swartwout, the other messenger of Burr, was about twenty-two. He was a brother of Colonel John Swartwout, who had been removed by President Jefferson from the office of United States Marshall for the District of New York largely on acount of the Colonel's friendly relations with Burr.

While preparations were being made along the Ohio and the Cumberland for the flatboat flotilla that was to carry Burr and his men down the Mississippi, Bollman was carrying one copy of Burr's message by sea, while Swartwout carried another copy by land. General Wilkinson, when he received the message in New Orleans, meditated over the best method by which he could save himself and brighten his own reputation. He decided to denounce his associates in the Mexican plot as traitors and assume the disguise of loyalty to the United States Government. Bollman and Swartwout were arrested, denied counsel and access to the courts, and ordered to be taken under military guard to Washington.

When Jefferson received the letter of warning, he called the members of his Cabinet together in alarm and issued a Proclamation ordering the seizure of the conspirators and their supplies. Then he informed Congress of the conspiracy. Burr, declared the Chief Executive, was plotting an insurrection against the National Government. The awful charge of treason was preferred. From that time on the masses demanded the life of Aaron Burr.

Bollman and Swartwout were taken on a warship to Baltimore. From Baltimore they were rushed under heavy guard to Washington. Arriving in the Capital on January 22, 1807

— the day the message from President Jefferson denouncing Burr was read in the Senate — the dazed messengers were thrown into the military prison at the Marine Barracks. Here they were guarded day and night as desperate criminals.

On the day after the arrival of the prisoners, Senator Giles, Jefferson's Senate spokesman, moved that a committee be appointed to draft a bill to empower the President to suspend the right of habeas corpus. This extreme step was intended to throttle the counsel for Bollman and Swartwout. The bill to suspend the writ for three months in cases of treason was passed by the Senate, but was rejected in the House of Representatives by an overwhelming vote. Thus was defeated the attempt of the Jeffersonians to prevent the Judiciary from deciding whether Bollman and Swartwout were entitled to the benefit of "the most sacred writ known to the law."

The young prisoners were brought into the United States Circuit Court for the District of Columbia. The prosecutors were Caesar A. Rodney, Jefferson's Attorney General, and Walter Jones, Jefferson's appointee as United States Attorney for the District. On the bench sat two Jefferson Republicans and a Federalist. The Jeffersonians, Nicholas Fitzhugh and Allen B. Duckett, committed the accused to prison to await trial for treason; while the Federalist, William Cranch, dissented. For the first time in American History a National Court found itself divided on political grounds.

Harper and Lee now decided to apply for the writ of habeas corpus to Chief Justice Marshall. Luther Martin, the crimson-faced leader of the Bar, offered to enter the case.

Congressman-elect Philip Barton Key was in sympathy

with the luckless young prisoners but he refused to enter the case. His nephew from Western Maryland, however, was invited to participate in the proceeding before the Nation's highest tribunal. So it was that on February 10, 1807 — the very day that the application for habeas corpus was brought before John Marshall — Francis Scott Key was admitted to the bar of the United States Supreme Court. Seated with Marshall on the Bench were Bushrod Washington of Virginia, William Johnson of South Carolina, and Brockholst Livingston of New York.

After listening to the arguments of the lawyers, Chief Justice Marshall decided on February 13th that the Supreme Court had jurisdiction to issue the writ of habeas corpus under the provisions of the Judiciary Act in order to revise the proceedings of the Court below. The application was, in effect, an appeal from the Circuit Court.

The next step was a motion by Mr. Lee on February 16th that the Court order the prisoners discharged. Mr. Lee pointed out that, under the Fourth Amendment to the Constitution, warrants should not be issued except upon "probable cause supported by oath or affirmation." He then launched his attack on the commitment of Bollman and Swartwout on the ground that probable cause had not been shown in the Circuit Court. Nothing had been shown except an intent to start an expedition against Mexico in the event of war between the United States and Spain. He accused General Wilkinson of seizing Bollman and Swartwout in New Orleans without due process of law and sending them two thousand miles to Washington to be disposed of by the President. The prisoners had never been committed for trial by the court of any District. What was the necessity of proceeding in such an unprecedented manner?

Francis Scott Key now made his début before the Supreme Court. He advanced the view that, under the Federal Constitution, there was no such thing as *constructive treason.* He admitted that the English law recognized it, but he explained why he believed a strict construction should be given to the word *treason* in the United States.

"The Constitution," he said, "declares that treason against the United States shall consist *only* in levying war against them, or in adhering to their enemies, giving them aid and comfort. An adherence to rebels is not an adherence to an enemy, within the meaning of the Constitution. Hence, if the prisoners are guilty, it must be of levying war against the United States."

"By using the word *only,*" he maintained, "the Constitution meant to take away all pretense of *constructive treason.* Every man is to answer for his own acts only." If, for example, one hundred men conspired to overthrow the Government, and only fifty of them actually levied war against the Government, only those fifty were guilty as principals of the crime of treason.

"But why," he asked, "should not the same distinction between principal and accessory obtain in the case of treason as in any other crime?" He answered the question himself: "In a republican government, whose basis is the affection of the people, it is unnecessary to guard against offences of this kind with the same vigilance as in a monarchy or a despotism whose foundation is fear."

Key then passed on to the next step in his argument. Even if this construction of the Constitution were not correct, and even if the English authorities were considered to be in full force in the United States, still two things had to be shown: (1) that war had been levied; and (2) that the accused were confederates in that war.

Key, after objecting to the affidavits of General Wilkinson because they were not in proper form, said that even if they were accepted by the Court, they did not show any act of treason. "They prove no assemblage of men nor military array. There is not a tittle of evidence that any two men have been seen together with treasonable intent, whether armed or not. The supposed letter from Col. Burr speaks indeed of choice spirits, but he does not tell us they are invisible spirits."

"The Territory of Orleans, if it was to be revolutionized," the young lawyer continued, "might be revolutionized without levying war against the United States. There is no evidence that the prisoners knew that Col. Burr had any treasonable projects in view. Even if he had such views, he might have held out to them, as he did to others, only the Spanish expedition."

In conclusion, Key maintained that the bench warrant issued for the arrest of Bollman and Swartwout was illegal. He contended that no court has authority to issue a bench warrant except upon a presentment by a grand jury or for an offense committed in the presence of the court. "And it is a power," he said, "inconsistent with a fair trial, because the court would have thereby prejudged the case, and decided upon the guilt of the prisoner. No such practice is known in Maryland, under whose laws the court below was acting."

Thus did Key, at the age of twenty-seven, expound the Constitution before John Marshall. His maiden speech before the Supreme Court was formidable. So much concern did it give to the prosecution that on the following morning, February 17th, the Attorney General devoted most of his time in attempting to refute the points the young attorney had made.

Mr. Rodney, the Attorney General, was followed by Walter Jones, United States Attorney for the District of Columbia, who continued the Government's reply. Mr. Jones was a native of Virginia, and but a few years older than Key. His fluency of speech and simple analytical style had served to advance him rapidly in his profession. After a discussion of technicalities Jones came to the main question: What is treason? Key had construed Article III, Section 3, of the Constitution — containing the word *only* — to mean that the framers intended to exclude constructive treason. Jones took the view that the framers, by writing the definition in the Constitution, wished merely to prevent Congress from inventing definitions of treason. What constitutes treason? Jones declared that no special warlike array is necessary; no specific amount of force; no specific number of men. If soldiers are recruited, he maintained, and if there is intent to levy war, there is treason, he maintained, even though none of the men are actually armed. Therefore, he said, the only question that remained was whether Bollman and Swartwout had knowledge of Burr's treasonable intent.

The next speaker for the prisoners was Robert Goodloe Harper. Mr. Harper claimed that the affidavits did not prove that Bollman and Swartwout had participated in any crime. He expressed the hope that the Supreme Court would not sanction treatment of prisoners such as that given to the two messengers. If a military officer were allowed to seize a man and send him as a prisoner two thousand miles with only an *ex parte* affidavit as the basis of his commitment, then, declared Mr. Harper, the security provided by the law for the protection of liberty is broken down!

On the third day, February 18th, the Supreme Court listened to Luther Martin, the last speaker for the prisoners. It was a wanton exercise of arbitrary power, he exclaimed, to send Bollman and Swartwout from New Orleans to Washington. A District Court had been established by act of Congress for the territory of Orleans, he thundered, and this court was competent to try the offense of treason committed within its jurisdiction.

On the fourth day, Chief Justice Marshall announced that the Court was puzzled over two questions: (1) Is General Wilkinson's affidavit admissible in evidence in the habeas corpus proceeding? and (2) If it is admissible, should the Court consider the contents of a letter when the original is in his possession?

If, said Marshall, the counsel could find, over night, any authorities on these points, the Court would like to hear them.

When the jurists had taken their seats on the bench on

February 20th, the Chief Justice asked whether the lawyers had found any authorities on the points he had mentioned. The Attorney General replied that he had not been able to find anything on the questions. Francis Scott Key then arose. He said he could present an English case that would assist the Court in reaching a decision. He cited the case of *The King vs. The Inhabitants of Eriswell,* in the Court of Kings Bench, wherein the question was whether an *ex parte* examination of a pauper before two justices could be accepted as evidence by two other justices five years later, upon an application for removal after the pauper had become insane. One of the judges upheld the principle of Common Law that no person charged with a crime can be bound by an examination taken in his absence. And the Chief Judge, Lord Kenyon, held that the *ex parte* examination of the pauper before the first two justices had not been made for the purpose of securing an order of removal, and it was consequently extrajudicial. Marshall and the Associate Justices gave close attention to the young lawyer from Western Maryland as he expounded Lord Kenyon's opinion and strove to show the analogy between the English case and the case at the bar.

"So in this case," said young Key, "we say that as General Wilkinson did not apply to Justices Carrick and Pollock for a warrant to arrest Dr. Bollman and Mr. Swartwout and as he did not make the affidavit for the purpose of obtaining from them such warrants, the whole proceedings before those justices were extrajudicial. . . . In the language of Lord Kenyon, 'they deserve no more credit than if they had been made before the parish clerk.' If the affidavit be a judicial proceeding, it ought to be authenticated according to the act of Congress. If it be not a judicial proceeding, it is not evidence."

Perhaps Key had received some assistance from his Uncle Philip; but in any event he made a favorable impression.

At noon on February 21, 1807, the Court was ready to render its decision. Was the evidence sufficient to hold Bollman and Swartwout, the despatch-bearers of Aaron Burr, for treason against the Government of the United States? Or should they be discharged? On the bench with the gentle-mannered John Marshall sat Bushrod Washington, Samuel Chase, and William Johnson. The decision which these judges were now about to make was to be one of the landmarks in American jurisprudence. The Court proceeded to analyze the message that Aaron Burr had written. Burr's scheme, it appeared, was to move down the Mississippi River to Natchez, there to confer with General Wilkinson to determine whether it was expedient to seize Baton Rouge or to pass on. It was plain, said Marshall, that there was not a single word in the message to indicate that any part of the United States was the objective of a military expedition. Rather, he said, the language seemed to point to an expedition against Mexico. Nor, said the Court, had a single word been uttered by Bollman and Swartwout to support an accusation that they were engaged in a treasonable enterprise. Therefore, said Marshall, the Court held that there was not sufficient evidence of a levying of war by Bollman and Swartwout against the United States to justify their commitment on the charge of treason. So the long-suffering despatch-bearers were discharged. The Chief Justice explained, however, that the discharge of the prisoners did not acquit them of treason, for, he said, fresh proceedings could be instituted against them. But since the alleged crime had not been committed in the District of Columbia, the Court believed the accused could not be tried in this District.

The case of Bollman and Swartwout caused Jefferson's anger to blaze against John Marshall. But the decision was heralded by the Federalists as a noble example of the judicial safeguard of individual liberty. Judge Cranch, gratified by the confirmation of his decision, exclaimed: "I congratulate my country upon this triumph of reason and law over popular passion and injustice—upon the final triumph of civil over the military authority." And General Lafayette, worried because Bollman, who had rescued him from the dungeon of Olmutz, had been charged with the crime of treason, was greatly relieved when he heard that the Supreme Court had ordered his release.

The experience of the couriers had been a dear lesson to them; but no war with Spain developed and the West soon turned away from the adventure. President Jefferson's suspicions were now to cause him to use all the influence of the Administration to urge the punishment of Aaron Burr. Burr was brought before the Circuit Court in Richmond, but Chief Justice Marshall held him merely on the charge of violating the neutrality laws. Jefferson was inclined to believe that the Federalists were trying to shield Burr from punishment; it was unfortunate, he said, that Federalism was "still predominant in our Judiciary Department" and thwarting the Executive and Congress. Indeed, Jefferson suggested that Luther Martin be arrested as *particeps criminis* with Aaron Burr. He declared that this "unprincipled and impudent federal bull-dog" and the other "clamorous defenders" of Burr were his accomplices.

At the time the grand jury was in session, Swartwout and General Wilkinson happened to meet in Richmond. Swartwout, then about twenty-four flew into a rage and shoved the bulky officer into the street. General Wilkinson ignored the attack. Swartwout then challenged him to a duel; but Wilkinson declined. Whereupon Swartwout branded the commander of the United States Army as guilty of treachery, perjury, forgery, and cowardice!

Swartwout was possessed of a frank and engaging manner, which brought him many friends. His courage in facing General Wilkinson endeared him to Andrew Jackson, who had been summoned to Richmond to appear as a witness against Burr but was not called to the stand because he was found to be on Burr's side. This man whom Key represented in the Supreme Court was basely dishonest; thirty years later he embezzled more than a million dollars of public funds while Collector of the Port of New York.

On the grand jury in Richmond were some of Aaron Burr's most bitter political adversaries. And so when he was indicted, no one was surprised. Jefferson had been convinced by General Wilkinson that Burr was guilty of treason. And Jefferson was now at the height of his popularity.

When the great trial of Aaron Burr was held in Richmond, the habeas corpus case of Justus Erich Bollman and Samuel Swartwout was discussed, and Francis Scott Key's views regarding constructive treason were given consideration by the Court. The penetrating mind of John Marshall saw that the prosecution had failed to prove any overt act of levying war. And Marshall held that, irrespective of the English doctrine of accessories, no person could be found guilty of treason under the Constitution of the United States except for the performance of an overt act of levying war. The case went to the jury, but in less than thirty minutes the jury brought in the "Scotch verdict"—that Burr was not proved guilty by any evidence submitted to them.

Along with other Federalists of his day, Francis Scott Key approved Marshall's ruling and the verdict of the jury. He looked upon Burr's acquittal as an example of the justice of the law, which does not relax the safeguards of human liberty even in times of political rancor. But he was nauseated by the burst of fury from the followers of Jefferson; accusations that Marshall had connived at the escape of a traitor; the cries of politicians for Marshall's impeachment; and the reports that the expounder of the Constitution and Aaron Burr had been hung in effigy.

More than a century later a Missouri lawyer addressed the Bar Association of his State on the conspiracy of Aaron Burr. "It is now known," he said of Burr, "that he was never actuated with a traitorous intent, but wanted to conquer Mexico in order to attach it to American soil. His fight was for Texas, but he fought too early. What he tried to do was called treason, but less than fifty years afterwards when Texas was taken from Mexico, the act was applauded. . . . That Burr never intended to assault a city of his country cannot now be questioned; that he never intended to invade Mexico unless and in the event war was declared is now fully understood; that the entire southwest was with him is admitted. The only trouble was that he was forty years ahead of his time, but he lived to see his friend and associate, General Jackson, elected President of the United States. . . . Jefferson was honest, but imposed upon by the greatest traitor of all times, General Wilkinson. . . . How tragic that Jefferson did not know the truth!"

CHAPTER VII

Fruits of Character

FRANCIS SCOTT KEY inherited a deeply spiritual soul. When he came under the influence of Rev. Johannes J. Sayrs, a man of uncommon piety, his spirit burst forth into a fervent religious conviction. There was no communicant in St. John's parish more devoted and enthusiastic than Key. For hours at a time he poured over the Scriptures; and he regretted that he had not been more zealous in church work at Frederick.

In November, 1808, the young man opened his soul in a letter to his cousin, George William Murdoch of Frederick. The letter was inspired by the news of the death of Murdoch's brother-in-law, Judge Richard Potts. Murdoch and Judge Pott's second wife, Eleanor, were children of George and Eleanor Charlton Murdoch; and Eleanor Charlton Murdoch was a sister of Key's mother. Key reminded his Cousin George that they both had been blessed with mothers of unusual piety. He also disclosed a feeling which clung to him all the rest of his life — that he was polluted with sin but that he was battling courageously with his temptations. This is his letter:

Key to George William Murdoch

G Town —

Nov[r] 29, — 06

My D[r] George

I have rec[d] your letter confirming the accounts I had before received. Indeed I sincerely share in the feelings which this loss must have excited in you all. If I did not know the piety of your dear good mother & sister, I might well suppose them inconsolable; but I am sure their trust in Heaven is proof against all affliction; & that they have borne this trial (as they have many others) with all the fortitude and submission of Christians, & will receive their reward in another world where there is no sorrow or weeping. —

This event, my Dear George, calls upon you for the most vigorous & persevering exertions — In Mr. Potts your mother & indeed all your family have lost the most invaluable friend; whose kindness, advice & assistance were ever at their command — It is therefore more than ever your duty to become useful, respected & beloved, to be the stay of your mother & the comfort & joy of your sisters.

Higher duties than these cannot be conceived — And while your heart is warmed by considering them, resolve, with an humble hope in God's assistance, piously & faithfully to perform them. You are young & surrounded with the most dangerous temptations — Restraint, self-denial & an inflexible adherence to duty are not so easy as you may imagine. Nothing but Christianity will give you the victory — Fix the firmest conviction of its truth in your understanding, study it's evidences, establish it's principles in your heart & keep it's most glorious rewards forever in your view. Never suppose that it is enough for you to equal the bulk of professed Christians in your devotion to it — It is inconsistency more stupid even than infidelity to imagine that merely believing, or rather professing to believe, will excuse us before the Searcher of all hearts for the defectiveness of our practice & the sinfulness of our lives.—

As I am a few years before you in life, I would wish you to have the benefit of my experience—Take then my word for it. Until a man becomes seriously & strongly impressed with religious sentiments, until he believes *in his heart* that Jesus Christ is his Lord & Master, & joins in the earnest & eloquent application of the converted Paul, "Lord! what would'st Thou have me to do?" his course through life will neither be safe nor pleasant.—The thousands around you who are careless & indifferent upon this subject may seem happy, but they are not so—I had once no more religious concern than they & full as much right to be happy without it as most of them.—My only regret now is that I was so long blinded by my pleasures, my vices & pursuits & the examples of others from seeing, admiring & adoring the "marvellous light of the Gospel."

I hope you, my Dr George, will be able to commence a religious life at an earlier period, with a resolution less weakened & a heart less polluted.—We have both been blessed with mothers of rare & fervent piety; a signal advantage in these degenerate times. Never should we be unmindful of it—That alone entitles them to the gratitude & devotion of our hearts.

I wish, George, you would now & then write to me, let me know what you are about. I will not undertake to be a very punctual correspondent as I am generally a good deal engaged. But I shall always read your letters with pleasure—

Present me most affectionately to my Dear Aunt, Cousin Nelly & the Girls.—& believe me

Sincerely yrs

F. S. KEY

In 1809 Key heard the sad news of the death of another friend, Rev. Sayrs, the rector of St. John's Church. Key wrote an epitaph in which he referred to the beloved rector as one who had turned aside from worldly pleasures to the career of "an humble minister" and whose exemplary life was an inspiration for "a life of peace," "a death of hope," and "endless bliss" in the world to come. The epitaph is inscribed on a tablet in the church and it reads:

JOH. J. SAYRS
hu. ecl.
Rector primus
Hic,
(quo, christi servus
Fideliter ministravit,)
Sep. jac:
Ob: 6 jan: A: D: MDCCCIX.
AEt: XXXV.

Here once stood forth a Man, who from the world
Though bright it's aspect to his youthful eye,
Turn'd with affection ardent to his God,
And liv'd & died an humble minister
Of his benignant purposes to Man.
Here lies he now—yet grieve not thou for him,
READER! he trusted in that love where none
Have ever vainly trusted—Rather let
His marble speak to thee, and should'st thou feel
The rising of a new & solemn thought,
Wak'd by this sacred place & sad memorial,
O listen to it's impulse!—'tis divine—
And it shall guide thee to a life of joy,
A death of hope & endless bliss hereafter.

The influence exerted by the pious Rev. Sayrs in

strengthening Key's character was deep and lasting. Many years afterwards one of the chroniclers of Georgetown recalled how Rev. Sayrs had impressed Key with "a deep respect for his memory."

Key was thirty years old when he made his first appearance in a slavery case before John Marshall. A Negro named Ben was seeking his freedom from bondage. Maryland had a law intended to stop the influx of slaves: it provided that the importation of any slave into the State operated to give that slave his freedom, except a slave living in this country not less than three years, whose owner intended to settle in the State. In the Circuit Court of the District of Columbia it was shown that the slave owner on coming into Maryland had failed to prove Negro Ben's residence of at least three years in the United States to the satisfaction of "the naval officer, or collector of the tax," as the law prescribed. An effort was made at the trial to introduce evidence to show that Ben had nevertheless been living in this country at least three years before he was brought into Maryland. But the Circuit Court refused to admit this testimony; and the jury awarded the Negro his freedom. The master, Sabrett Scott, took an appeal. His lawyers contended that it was necessary for them only to prove the residence of three years to the satisfaction of the jury. What should prevail — property rights or human rights? A similar question was destined to come before the Court many years later when Key's brother-in-law as an aged jurist was called on to write the opinion that was to precipitate the Civil War. But the time had not yet come for the fires of secession. The rights of human beings under the Federal Constitution were not raised before Marshall. Key, as counsel for the slave, based his argument merely on the construction of the statute. There was a difference of opinion among the members of the Bench, but Chief Justice Marshall, handing down the majority opinion on February 7, 1810, held that since the purpose of the law was to break up the traffic in slaves – not to prevent slave owners from bringing their own slaves with them – Mr. Scott should have been allowed to show that his slave had in point of fact lived in this country at least three years, even though the technical requirements of the statute had not been complied with.

At the same term of the Supreme Court, Key appeared in one case as a colleague of his Uncle Philip. In three other cases he assisted Charles Lee, with whom he had been associated in the defense of Bollman and Swartwout. One was an appeal from Georgia over an audit of a sheriff's sale; another was a suit to rescind a contract for the sale of land on the ground that one of the parties was not an American citizen. The third was an appeal from an inquisition taken to ascertain the value of a parcel of land needed by the Georgetown and Alexandria Turnpike Company. Before the finding of the jury was recorded, the turnpike company succeeded in having the inquisition quashed by the Circuit Court of the District of Columbia at Alexandria. Curtiss, the land owner, was satisfied with the valuation that had been placed on his land and took an appeal. Before the Supreme Court, Key, as counsel for the turnpike company, made the argument that a court must, of necessity, possess control over its own records. Such jurisdiction was exercised in England and, he contended, a similar power resided in the courts of America. But Marshall disagreed. He held that, under the act of Congress providing for the turnpike, the inquisition was returnable to the clerk, not to the Court; the recording was merely a ministerial act; and hence the Circuit Court should not have prevented the clerk from recording the inquisition.

As an accompaniment of Key's love of country, there appeared as early as thirty a genuine public spirit. An illustration of this was his interest in public education. He regarded education as an important factor in promoting the happiness and the general welfare of the people. And he was one of a group of men who organized a Lancaster Society in Georgetown to give free education to all children whose parents could not afford to pay tuition fees. The Mayor of Georgetown was president *ex officio* of the Society. This plan, said to have been originated by Dr. Andrew Bell, a Scotch priest, was named after Joseph Lancaster, a Quaker of unusual executive ability, who had established throughout England and Ireland upwards of one hundred schools that accommodated about thirty thousand children. The members of the Georgetown Lancaster Society agreed to contribute annually toward the expenses of the school. Key, who was now the recorder, or legal adviser, of the municipality of Georgetown, was one of the first citizens to join the Society, and was placed on a committee to supervise the building of the school house.[1] The young lawyer and his colleagues conferred regarding the plans and specifications; the directions sent from England by Mr. Lancaster suggested a school building with one room

1.—Elected recorder January 4, 1808. Re-elected 1809, 1810, 1813, 1815, and 1816.

large enough to accommodate three hundred and fifty scholars. Early in June, 1811, the building committee was ready receive proposals for the construction of the school house. In their advertisements for bids, the committee announced that they would gladly accept any "donation of materials" or any other assistance "which benevolent persons may be inclined to render." Very soon the corner stone was laid by the Mayor in the presence of the trustees and members of the Society, members of a lodge of Masons, the Marshal and deputies of the District of Columbia, and clergymen of Georgetown and Washington. In November, 1811, the Lancaster School of Georgetown opened its doors – the first free school in the District of Columbia. Before long a bill was passed by Congress incorporating the Lancaster School Society, with Key as one of the incorporators.

CHAPTER VIII

Clamor for War

WHEN CONGRESS convened in November, 1811, there sat in the House of Representatives a number of aggressive young members from the West and the South in whose breasts dwelt the spirit of American Nationalism. Among these fiery young Congressmen were Henry Clay of Kentucky, aged thirty-four, who was chosen Speaker of the House; Felix Grundy of Tennessee, thirty-four; and John C. Calhoun of South Carolina, twenty-nine.

The Congress had been in session but a short time before the young frontiersmen began their clamor for war with Great Britain. War was necessary, they said, to make the British stop taking seamen from American ships and forcing them into the British service. Strangely enough, while the firebrands from the frontier were eager to defend maritime rights, the Eastern States — the location of maritime interests — had no desire for war. The reason for this paradox was the fact that the people of New England had been prospering from their commerce and they did not want it blockaded by the British Navy.

As a matter of fact, the War Hawks, as the jingoes were called, were being urged by the fur traders of the frontier to declare war against the Nation whose trappers were making inroads into their fur trade. The Northwest was anxious to wrest Canada from the British in order to monopolize the Indian trade and otherwise exploit the vast area of the frontier. The South meanwhile dreamed of a conquest of Florida from Spain.

Francis Scott Key, always an apostle of peace, was depressed when he heard the shouts for war. He was wholly out of sympathy with the movement. Looking back on the great drama of history, he saw what a scourge wars had been to mankind. He was not a conscientious objector: it was necessary sometimes, he knew, to fight for self-preservation, as his father had done during the years of the Revolution. But the saturnalia of crime that passed under the name of war—legalized murder—human life sacrificed to please the whims of rulers—brought a shudder to his sensitive soul. Dipping into Ovid he had been impressed by the warning of Ajax to Ulysses: he translated into English the speech of the "master of the sevenfold shield" to the "warrior of the tongue." His imagination was stirred when he read of the siege of Troy; and his translation includes these lines:

Lo! Troy pours forth again the storm of war,
And sword and spear and torch commingled glare
From her thick ranks—the angry gods are there,
Guiding the fiery tempest to the fleet.

A description quite similar Key was destined soon to write in his immortal anthem of American patriotism—the only difference being the substitution of the "rockets' red glare" and the "bombs bursting in air" for the sword and the spear and the torch.

All through the Winter of 1811-12 the shouts of the War

Hawks rang in the halls of Congress. Key kept in touch with the combat through his Uncle Philip, who had been reëlected to the House in 1808 and again in 1810. The partisan feeling that prevailed in Washington and Georgetown was at white heat. Washington Irving, for instance, while on a visit to the Capital dined with a group of Federalists and heard them "damning all their opponents as a set of consummate scoundrels, panderers to Bonaparte," but when he dined with the Republicans he heard them condemn the Federalists as "the greatest knaves in the Nation, men absolutely suborned by the British Government."

While the question of war was pending in Congress, Key came to the Capital to engage in the argument of cases before the United States Supreme Court. It was the day of prolix pleaders; and Key was one of the most prolix of them all. In one of his cases at the 1812 term of the Supreme Court so tedious were he and his associate, Charles Lee, that the bored and weary Justices were hopelessly lost in the "cloud of pleading." Key had instituted the suit for James and John Dunlop against Postmaster Thomas Munroe of Washington. The plaintiffs alleged that a letter containing two thousand dollars had been mailed at Philadelphia to them at Petersburg, Virginia. They claimed that the letter reached Washington and then vanished. They lost their case; and when their appeal was brought before the Supreme Court their counsel, Key and Lee, wandered for hours through a labyrinth of technicalities. It is no wonder that the solemn men on the Bench were confused, if not exasperated. "It is necessary," said Justice William Johnson in his opinion, "to dissipate the cloud of pleading in which this case is enveloped, in order to form a distinct idea of the questions intended to be brought to the view of the court below." The object of the suit, said the Associate Justice, was to hold the postmaster liable for the loss of two thousand dollars as a result of his negligence or the negligence of his assistants. "But," he declared, "unfortunately, as not unfrequently happens in this complex and injudicious mode of conducting a suit, with all the clerical skill displayed by counsel in multiplying their counts and pointing their bills of exceptions, the principal questions are really, at last, not brought to the view of the court." But after finding their way out of the smoke-screen of confusion, the Justice clarified the atmosphere by laying down the law that in order to hold a postmaster liable for a loss in the mails it must be shown that the loss was the result of negligence. And in spite of the maze of arguments presented by Key and Lee, the Court saw no evidence of negligence on the part of Postmaster Munroe. Accordingly Key and Lee lost their case.

In another case at the 1812 term, Key represented Hezekiah Wood, a slave owner, in opposing the freedom of the children of a free mulatto woman. The Circuit Court for the District instructed the jury that the evidence was conclusive in favor of the freedom of the children. Key appealed; and in this case he was opposed by Mr. Lee. Key, relying on technicalities, advanced the argument that there had been no evidence to show that the mulatto woman had been born free, but only that she was free at the time of a judgment prior to the case at the bar. Therefore, he pointed out, it had not been shown that she was free at the time of the birth of her children. "She might have been manumitted after the birth of her children," Key explained, "and so entitled to her freedom at the time of the judgment, and yet the petitioners might remain slaves." Chief Justice Marshall accepted Key's contention and reversed the decision of the Circuit Court.

In the midst of his professional duties, Key continued to ponder over the jingoism of man. He shared the opinion of the Federalist leaders that war was unnecessary, unwise, and unrighteous. He followed with particular interest the stand taken against war by the Virginia aristocrat, John Randolph of Roanoke. Opposed to Federalism because he loved the Commonwealth of Virginia more than a strong Central Government, he became one of the followers of Thomas Jefferson. Then, falling into a quarrel with Jefferson, he found himself deserted by the Republicans: but he could never be a Federalist. Later he developed a hatred for Mr. Madison and fought him whenever he could. Now in his thirty-ninth year he looked upon himself as a crusader battling to save the Nation from destruction.

In spite of his eccentricities, Randolph's extraordinary eloquence fashioned the attention of the Nation upon him. Six feet tall, with small head, elevated shoulders, and long legs that resembled canes, he made a ludicrous appearance. His lips were thin, compressed; his dark hair lay close to his head; his eyes had a piercing brightness. He wore a swallow-tailed coat with a great array of buttons on his breast and down his back. He usually wore a large white cravat, in which he sometimes buried his chin as he moved his head in conversation. His waist was so slender that he could almost span it with his long, bony fingers. His thin legs were encased in tight breeches and white stockings fastened at the knees by gold buckles. When he walked he planked his big buckled shoes straight ahead like an Indian. The House of Representatives looked upon this strange character with alternate astonishment, disgust, and delight. His high-pitched voice often ended in a shriek; but he was able to modulate the tones so as to charm his audience. He was the most amazing speaker in American politics.

When Randolph shouted a shrill call to the Speaker for recognition and leveled his bony finger at one of the members of the House, it was the signal for an attack of scathing denunciation. The scourge he used has been described as a lash made of "thongs that cut deeply and left corroding gangrene in the wounds they made" leaving his victim to bleed under his merciless attack. Francis Scott Key saw and appreciated the finer elements in this venemous soul and understood that they were thwarted by a defect of temper that soured ambition into petty vanity and arrogance. He overlooked Randolph's eccentricities; and admired him for his wonderful intellect, the courage of his convictions, and his freedom from party spirit. "The temper in his case," says one of Randolph's biographers, "was not so much an inflamable anger, which burst out in self-forgetful fury, as a constant, irritable sensitiveness, which stung right and left, like wasps or scorpions, yet was always under the guidance of a fierce clear vision, planting the dart in the most vulnerable spot. It had something of the instinct of vindictive torment which had come to him through Pocahontas from the Indian ancestors in whom he took such pride."[1] Randolph's quick temper and stinging sarcasm brought him many enemies. He made the homes of Congressman Key and Francis Scott Key places of refuge from the turmoil and bitterness of the Capital.

Randolph helped the Federalists to oppose the clamor for war. When the War Hawks contended that it would be easy to accomplish the conquest of Canada as one of the principal aims of the war, Randolph offered a resolution in the House declaring that under all the circumstances it was inexpedient to resort to war against Great Britain. Key admired the strange man, venomous though he was, for his attitude against war. Like Randolph, he kept hoping until the end that America could remain in peace. He recoiled from the thought of human butchery; it was a disgusting method of settling a dispute.

But the noisy War Hawks insisted that the United States was called on to fight. The mild Mr. Madison, who was a man of peace like Jefferson, was reluctant to lead the country into war, and delayed committing himself as long as he could. But he was ambitious to be renominated by the Republicans; and he was afraid to ignore the young jingoes of his party. Finally a delegation from Congress headed by Mr. Clay visited the President. Whether or not the President yielded under pressure and made a secret bargain with the War Hawks, the fact remains that on the 1st of June, 1812, he sent a communication to the Senate and House recommending that the

1.—Gamaliel Bradford, *Damaged Souls,* 127.

question of war be given prompt deliberation. He referred to the "crying enormity" of the insults heaped upon the United States by Great Britain and declared that "exhausted remonstrances and expostulations" from the United States had been futile. Whether the United States should continue passive under "these progressive usurpations and these accumulating wrongs," or should commit the cause into the hands of God by "opposing force to force in defense of their national rights," was a question, Madison said, which was confided by the Constitution to the legislative department of the Government. Mr. Madison, still timidly fearing to ask directly for a declaration of war, made the statement that he felt sure the decision of Congress would be "worthy the enlightened and patriotic councils of a virtuous, a free, and a powerful nation."

So anxious were the War Hawks for the call to arms that, when the Message to Congress came from the White House, they were thrilled with delight. Six of the exuberant Congressmen who sat together at their meals and were popularly known as the "war mess" — Clay and Calhoun, Grundy and Langdon Cheves, William Lowndes and Bibb — joined hands and danced around the room ring-around-the-rosy.

The question was referred to a committee composed of six Republicans — Calhoun, Grundy, Smilie, Harper, Desha, and Seaver — and two Federalists — Philip Barton Key and Peter B. Porter — and John Randolph of Roanoke, an independent. Mr. Porter was kept home on account of sickness. The committee presented its report on the 3rd of June; and on the following day the House was prepared to vote for war.

All of the Federalists except three cast their votes against the bill; but it was passed 79 to 49, the House being overwhelmingly Republican.

The bill now went to the Senate. Six Republican Senators voted against it, but it was approved by the vote of 19 to 13.

Thus was America, with but seven vessels in her Navy and about five thousand men in her Army, brought by jingoism into armed conflict with the greatest Naval power in the world — a conflict which was not wanted by the President and not wanted by the majority of the American people. The cause of the War Hawks had now become the cause of a political party. On June 19, 1812, James Madison signed a Proclamation formally proclaiming war against Great Britain.

In Francis Scott Key's sensitive soul there surged grave foreboding. He realized that Mr. Madison and the people of the country were entirely unprepared for war. And somehow he was obsessed by a strange feeling of dread, a presentiment that grave disaster would befall the Nation.

Then, too, could a follower of the Prince of Peace justify the most hideous crime against Civilization?

FRANCIS SCOTT KEY

At the age of 38

CHAPTER IX

If This Be Treason

AS SOON AS Congress voted for war, the minority members—including Key's Uncle Philip—issued a warning to the country that the conquest of Canada was problematical, in view of the smallness of American military and naval forces; that Great Britain was in a position to devastate the Atlantic seaboard; and that she would do so, if American troops invaded Canada.

On June 20, 1812—just two days after war was declared—the *Federal Republican,* a newspaper published in Baltimore by Alexander C. Hanson and Jacob Wagner, printed an editorial denouncing the National Administration. It was like a spark set to dynamite. Two days after the publication of the editorial, a mob wrecked the printing office. This, however, did not daunt the publishers: they soon made arrangements to have their newspaper printed in Georgetown. Before the close of July, Hanson mustered courage enough to return to Baltimore and to distribute his papers from a house on Charles Street. A short while after, Key heard that another mob had gathered, broken into the house, pillaged it, seized Hanson and a group of his friends and locked them in jail. Key further learned that the jail was stormed at night, and the prisoners brutally attacked. General James M. Lingan, an intimate friend of Key, who was mixed up in the affair, died as a result of that brutality. The murder of the General came as a severe shock to Key. It lodged in his heart a deep abhorrence for party spirit. Along with Taney and Arthur Shaaff, he served as trustee, under the General's will, for the settlement of his estate.

It was not long before opposition to the war began to blaze in open defiance in New England. Pamphlets, condemning the Administration, were widely circulated. One of these, entitled *Mr. Madison's War*, was written pseudonymously by John Lowell of Boston, who took the position that Great Britain deserved to be excused for any objectionable measures on the sea, since she was in the throes of combat with Napoleon. Even the Pulpit indulged in vitriolic harangues—some even proposing Secession!

Moreover, Great Britain was not eager for war with the United States. Preoccupied with her colossal struggle with Napoleon, then at the zenith of his power, the British regarded the American declaration of war like the feeble cry of an infant; nevertheless, the British Government announced that all rights of American seamen would be protected if the United States would take measures to prevent British seamen from enlisting on American ships. But the American officials felt that they were obliged to wage war in order to uphold the position of the Republican party in favor of war. Congress authorized President Madison to issue a call to enlarge the Army and to hold the Militia in readiness to defend the seacoast and the frontier.

As the months went by, the Federalist resistance to the war grew more determined. The bolder Federalist leaders insisted that the Republicans had led the country into war without just cause; that the American people had never favored it; and that they had a right to refuse to engage in hostilities that were unjustifiable.

In Key's native State of Maryland, as in most of the Eastern States, there was widespread sentiment against the war. Many of the political leaders recommended that military operations should be limited to defensive measures. Benjamin Stoddert, a veteran of the Revolution, and the first Secretary of the Navy, and a friend of Key, started a boom for Chief Justice Marshall, as a candidate to oppose Madison for President, as the Chief Justice was known to have opposed the declaration of war.

In Frederick County the Federalist party split into two hostile camps: one accused Madison of going to war to keep the Republican party in power and swore vengeance upon him; the other, while regretting the declaration of war as a stupid blunder, decided to subordinate party to country and stand by the President. The Federalist supporters of the war were nicknamed Coodies; and Taney, because he was one of their leaders, was called King Coody. The schism in the Federalist party at Frederick Town led to a rupture between Taney and John Hanson Thomas, which was not healed until Mr. Thomas lay on his death-bed in 1815.

Key was in a quandary. He was not absolutely a conscientious objector to war; he was willing to don the uniform and shoulder a musket, if necessary, to help defend the country from invasion. But he was essentially a man of peace. To him war was abhorrent: it was brutal, un-Christian, and absurd. He was sorry that political leaders were so eager to rush into hostilities, instead of settling their disputes by means of arbitration.

By this time Key had won the admiration as well as the friendship of Congressman John Randolph. This strange man often visited at the Key home, and he became very fond of Mrs. Key and the children. Randolph used to chat by the hour on politics, literature, and religion. He possessed a rich vocabulary and a ready wit, could quote with ease from the Latin, and had a keen grasp of affairs. So thoroughly had the War Hawks exasperated him that he thought of declining to run again for Congress. Key, however, consoled him; flattered him for his unselfish public service; and urged him to run for reëlection. So Randolph did run again. But he met with defeat.

In sheer disgust the defeated Congressman retired to his log cabin in the woods, which he gave the name of Roanoke. On May 10, 1813, he sat down in his cabin and addressed a letter to his friend at Georgetown.

> Dear Frank: For so, without ceremony, permit me to call you. — he began. — Among the few causes that I find for regret at my dismissal from public life there is none in comparison with the reflection that it has separated me — perhaps forever — from some who have a strong hold on my esteem and on my affections . . . on every other account, I have cause of self-congratulation at being disenthralled from a servitude at once irksome and degrading. The grapes are *not* sour — you know the manner in which you always combated my wish to retire. Although I have not, like you, the spirit of a martyr, yet I could not but allow great force to your representations. To say the

> truth, a mere sense of duty alone might have been insufficient to restrain me from indulging the very strong inclination which I have felt for many years to return to private life. It is now gratified in a way that takes from me every shadow of blame. No man can reproach me with the desertion of my friends, or the abandonment of my post in a time of danger and of trial. . . . . I am again free, as it respects the public at least, and have but one more victory to achieve — to be so in the true sense of the word. Like yourself and Mr. Meade, I cannot be contented to do good for goodness' sake, or rather for the sake of the Author of all goodness. In spite of me, I cannot help feeling something very like contempt for my poor foolish fellow-mortals, and would often consign them to Bonaparte in this world, and the Devil, his master, in the next; but these are but temporary fits of misanthropy, which soon give way to better and juster feelings.

Mr. Randolph closed his letter by asking Key to look after his gun, flask, and shot-belt, and a trunk full of books and letters, which he had carelessly left at his hotel in Georgetown.

Key had already found Randolph's rifle and trunk of papers and had anticipated the request to care for them. In fact he had already written about them; but as he directed his letter to Farmville instead of Charlotte Court House, Randolph's postoffice address, the letter was not delivered into Randolph's hands until the 21st of May. At the same time Key tried to console his friend, tried to show him the philosophy of defeat; and moreover ventured the belief that the people of Virginia were growing fonder of the war as the preparations advanced.

Penning a reply on the following day, Randolph said:

"I have read your letter again and again, and cannot express to you how much pleasure the perusal has given me." He reiterated that he had been nauseated by the members of the House of Representatives. "To be under the dominion of such wretches as (with a few exceptions) composed the majority," he said, "was intolerably irksome to my feelings; and although my present situation is far from enviable, I feel the value of the exchange." He had fought the good fight; he acquiesced in the decision; but he would now stand aloof from the bedside of his delirious country. But did the people really want war? No! "You are mistaken," he assured Key, "in supposing that 'we Virginians like the war better the nearer it approaches us'; so far from it, there is a great change in the temper of this State, and even in this District, paradoxical as it may seem, against the war. More than half of those who voted against me, were persuaded that I was the *cause* of the war; that the Government wished for peace." Randolph explained in conclusion that his young relative, Theodore B. Dudley, who had just received his M.D. degree in Philadelphia, and had come down to visit him, served to cheer the solitude in which he was plunged. "He desires to be remembered to you," said the gloomy man. "Present my best love to Mrs. Key and the little folks."

From this time on a constant flow of letters passed between the Georgetown advocate and the lonely man at Roanoke. Francis Scott Key was tireless in his effort to cheer the discouraged Virginian: "I could not help smiling at the painting you have given me of Roanoke—*laudat diversa sequentes.* To me it seemed just such a shelter as I should wish to creep under,

> A boundless contiguity of shade,
> Where rumor of oppression and deceit
> Might never reach me more.

After all, was not Randolph in his rustic retreat better off than most people? Especially now, when the demons of hate were abroad in the land. Key had just been reading about the invasion of Canada by the United States troops. As the Americans were advancing on York (then a town of eight hundred people; now the city of Toronto) a magazine exploded killing more than two hundred American soldiers, including General Zebulon Montgomery Pike. But the invading army, undaunted by the disaster, continued their attack and finally captured and pillaged the town of York and burned the Parliament House there.

How often it happens in life that two men think they would like to trade places with each other! Randolph envying Key, and Key envying Randolph! "I do not wish you so ill as to see you banished to this Sinope; and yet," said Randolph, "to see you here would give me exceeding great pleasure. Every blessing attend you."

As the troops were waging their campaign along the Niagara frontier, Key was passing through the gloomiest and most discouraging period of his career. Many of his friends were entering the Army and the Navy. Activity in most lines of business was retarded. Litigation was greatly reduced. Key's income had fallen away. It was during the gloom of the Summer of 1813 that he gave serious consideration to the plan of foresaking the legal profession for the ministry. Or, if this course was impractical, he thought of seeking a position as teacher. Or, if there appeared no opening in a faculty, he might even resort to politics. Never in all his life had he sunk so far into the slough of discouragement.

It was a pity that Key's God was a God of Wrath — not a God of Love. He was steeped in superstition. And this explains why at times he was a man of faltering courage. He had no need to fear the wolf at the door; the Keys were people of means; and his wife came of a family of wealth and influence. Besides, just before the close of 1813 Key took possession of an estate of more than 700 acres of fertile Maryland soil. It was composed of portions of four tracts, one of them known as Terra Rubra — the name by which Key's farm became popularly known. He paid for it $8,500; and in order to conclude the transaction he borrowed $5,000 from his Uncle Philip. Yet when he saw the ominous clouds of war he threw up his hands in despair. Other men, with fewer opportunities, and with prospects just as gloomy, were courageously fighting their battles; but Key could see no silver lining to the cloud on the horizon. His faith failed him when he needed it most. Physically and morally courageous, he fell a victim to discouragement when it seemed that Fate was against him. He did not radiate optimism in days of darkness. He was too sanctimonious, too depressed, to be happy.

So the despondent Georgetown lawyer wrote to Randolph for his advice. But on July 15, 1813 — two days before Randolph received his letter—Key, still pondering over the comparative prospects of the pulpit, the school room, and the political arena, volunteered to join the District of Columbia militia. He still felt, like the majority of the Federalist leaders, that the War Hawks should not have plunged the Nation into war; but a British squadron commanded by Admiral Cockburn had been plundering a number of towns along the Chesapeake, and the marauders were already repulsed in their attacks on Norfolk and Portsmouth; he saw the expediency of doing what he could to defend Washington and Georgetown from the possibility of invasion. The Georgetown Field Artillery, which had been organized by his friend George Peter as a part of the District Militia, was now practising. In this company Key enlisted as matross.

John Randolph was reluctant to offer advice to his discouraged friend. He did think, however, that Frank was thoroughly qualified either for the school room or the pulpit. "I heartily wish," said the former Congressman, "that I were qualified in any shape to advise you on the subject of a new calling in life. Were I Premier, I should certainly translate you to the see of Canterbury; and if I were not too conscious of my utter incompetency, I should like to take a professorship in some college where you were principal; for, like you, my occupation (tobacco-making) is also gone. Some sort of employment is absolutely necessary to keep me from expiring with ennui... In fact, this business of living is, like Mr. Barlow's[1] reclamations on the French Government, *dull*

1.—Joel Barlow, a native of Connecticut, was appointed Minister to France in 1811. He was one of the few men of letters of his day to receive diplomatic posts. He died in Poland in 1812.

work; and I possess so little of pagan philosophy, or of Christian patience, as frequently to be driven to the brink of despair. 'The uses of this world have long seemed to me stale, flat, and unprofitable'; but I have worried along, like a worn-out horse in a mail coach, by dint of habit and whip-cord, and shall at last die in the traces, running the same dull stage day after day." Referring to the deplorable condition of the country, Randolph declared he was happy to reflect that never, during a period of eight years, had he faltered in his opposition to the National Administration. "I predicted," he said, "the result which has ensued. The length of time and vast efforts which were required to hunt me down, convince me that the cordial co-operation of a few friends would have saved the Republic. Sallust, I think, says, speaking of the exploits of Rome, '*Egregiam virtutem paucorum civium cuncta patravisse*'; and if those who ought to have put their shoulders to the work, had not made a vain parade of disinterestedness in returning to private life, all might have been saved. But the delicacy and timidity of some, and the versatility of others, insured the triumph of the court and the ruin of the country."

Key might have been qualified to teach or preach; but he was not fit for the life of a soldier. While he was but thirty-four, vigorous and active, he was unfamiliar with military tactics and unaccustomed to military discipline. He had scarcely joined the Georgetown Field Artillery before he was ready to withdraw. He retired from the company on the 26th of July. His military service in 1813 covered a period of twelve days!

Another month of anxiety passed. Key was in the depths of melancholy. He thought that if the war dragged on much longer he would have to seek some employment in a church or a school or probably join the Regular Army. But there was one thing of which he was sure: he would most certainly not run for public office. The trenchant, often scurrilous attacks of politicians were exceedingly distasteful to him; electioneering was anything but pleasant; and politics in general was permeated with corruption. Coincident with his decision to keep aloof from politics there burst into his soul a ray of hope: he would trust in the guidance of Providence; he would "take no thought of the morrow." In an hour of gloom he had found courage. This is how he unburdened his soul to the lonely man at Roanoke:

> I suppose Stanford told you that I was half inclined to turn politician. I did feel something like it — but the fit is over. I shall, I hope, stay quietly here, and mind my business as long as it lasts. I have troubled myself enough with thinking what I should do — so I shall try to prepare myself for whatever may appear plainly to be my duty. That I must make some change, if the war lasts much longer (as I think it will), is very probable; but whether it shall be for a station civil, military, or clerical, I will not yet determine. To be serious, I believe that a man who does not follow his own inclinations, and choose his own ways, but is willing to do whatever may be appointed for him, will have his path of life chosen for him and shown to him, and I trust this is not enthusiasm....

In September, 1813, came Commodore Oliver H. Perry's victory on Lake Erie, followed by his memorable despatch to General William Henry Harrison: "We have met the enemy and they are ours." Perry's victory brought great rejoicing in the United States; bonfires and illuminations lighted up the country as a tribute to the hero of the hour. But neither Francis Scott Key nor John Randolph of Roanoke was able to derive any consolation from the news of victory. Randolph insisted that nothing could change his conviction that the Nation was steadily heading toward destruction. He told Key that Commodore Perry's victory on Lake Erie would have no effect except to "add another year to the life of the war."

Replying to one of Randolph's letters Key announced the latest arrival in the rapidly growing family. Mrs. Key gave birth in September, 1813, to another child, a boy, named Edward Lloyd Key. He was the sixth. The eldest child, Elizabeth, was now nearly ten years old. On this occasion Key discussed the merits of Sir Walter Scott, and indirectly reverted to the "law of the Muses" — as if he were lifting the veil of the future and predicting the legacy of his own Muse to his country — that a poet never writes more than one great epic poem. His letter reveals his apprehensions for the future:

> As to Sir Walter Scott, I have always thought he was sinking in every successive work. He is sometimes himself again in *Marmion* and the *Lady of the Lake*; but when I read these, and thought of the *Lay of the Last Minstrel,* it always seemed to me that "hushed was the harp — the minstrel gone." I believe I am singular in this preference, and it may be that I was so "spell-bound" by the "witch notes" of the first, that I could never listen to the others. . . . *But does it not appear that to produce one transcendently fine epic poem is*

> *as much as has ever fallen to the life of one man? There seems to be a law of the Muses for it.* I was always provoked with him for writing more than his first. The top of Parnassus is a point, and there he was, and should have been content. There was no room to saunter about on it; if he moved, he must descend; and so it has turned out, and he is now (as the *Edinburgh Reviewers* say of poor Montgomery) "wandering about on the lower slopes of it."

But the Muses did not hold his attention completely. The war was now upon his mind. He writes:

> ..... The opposition making to the Administration may succeed (though I do not think it can); but if it did I should hope but little from it; and that, because party, it would be beaten again immediately; for of two it is the opposition of a party. If it is the honestest contending factions, the worst must be, generally, successful. This is just as plain to me as that of two gamesters; he who cheats most will commonly win the game. We should therefore, I think, burn the cards, or give up the game of party, and then, I believe, the knaves might be made the losers. "Keep up party and party spirit" should be (if they have any sense) the first and great commandment of the Administration to its followers. . . . Suppose some ruinous and abominable measure, such as a French Alliance, is proposed by the Government; will the scolding of the Federalists in Congress gain any of the well-meaning but mistaken and prejudiced friends of the Administration, and induce them to oppose it? Will not such persons, on the contrary, be driven to consider it a party question, and the clamor and opposition of these persons, as a matter of course? Will men listen to reasonings against it, judge of it impartially, and see its enormity, who are blinded by party spirit? But let such men as Cheves or Lowndes, men who are not party men, or who will leave their party when they think them

> wrong; let them try if conciliation, and a plain and temperate exposure of the measure, will not be effectual; and it is certainly reasonable to expect it would. I am, besides, inclined to think that the worst men of a party will be uppermost in it: and if so, there would, perhaps, be no great gain from a change. If every man would set himself to work to abate, as far as possible, this party spirit; if the people could be once brought to require from every candidate a solemn declaration, that he would act constitutionally according to his own judgment, upon every measure opposed, without considering what party advocated or opposed it (and I cannot think that such a ground would be unpopular), its effect woud be, at least, greatly diminished. This course might not, it is possible, succeed in ordinary times, and when this spirit is so universally diffused and inflamed; *but we are approaching to extraordinary times, when serious national affliction will appease this spirit, and give the people leisure and temper to reflect.* Something too might then be done towards promoting a reformation of habits and morals, without which nothing of any lasting advantage can be expected. Could such an Administration as this preserve its power, if party spirit was even considerably lessened? And is it too much to expect? If so, there is nothing, I think, to be done but to submit to the punishment that Providence will bring upon us, and to hope that that will cure us. I am, you will think, full of this subject.

It was obvious to Key that if righteousness exalts a Nation then its corollary must be true that divine punishment is speedily inflicted upon a sinful Nation. Key had read in the Old Testament that when the Israelites became disobedient they were visited with plagues. Accordingly he believed the depression, which set in after the War Proclamation of Mr.

Madison, was a chastisement sent by a God of Wrath upon the American people for their wickedness.

Mr. Randolph thoroughly agreed with Key that America was approaching a crisis; that the only hope of salvation was the suppression of partisanship and the reform of morals. "I have a great mind to publish your letter," Randolph declared. "If any thing could do good, that, I am certain, would open the eyes of many, as many, at least, as would read it. But I have no faith, and cannot be saved. . . . How can a foolish spendthrift young man be prevented from ruining himself? How can you appoint a guardian to a people bent on self-destruction? The state of society is radically vicious. It is there, if at all, that the remedy should be applied."

Randolph had read in the press that Charles Sterritt Ridgely had gone down to defeat, although he had made the highest run on his own ticket. Randolph regretted Ridgely's defeat from the standpoint of his need by his party in the Legislature; but for Ridgely's own sake he was gratified because he was better off out of the maelstrom of politics. "I am convinced," Randolph repeated to Key, "that it is best for him and his; and I am inclined to think no worse for the country."

And so the views of the gloomy lawyer at Georgetown and the still gloomier politician at Roanoke coincided regarding the vicious condition of society. But Key still held out hope that the people would reform, would thereby appease God, and ultimately save the country from annihilation. His next letter to Randolph contained his formula for the Nation's salvation:

Key to Randolph

Georgetown,

November 27, 1813.

My dear Friend —

I have heard indirectly that you are still sick. I hope this attack will not be such an one as you had at my uncle's. Pain and sickness are sad companions any where, but particularly in the country. It is hard to feel them and think them the trifles that (compared to other things) they certainly are. He alone who sends them can give us *strength and faith* to bear them as we ought. I wish you every relief — but above all, *this.*

Let me hear from you as often as you can. Your letters may be short, but I shall not find them "meagre". . . . . Maryland is in great agitation about the Allegany election. The returned members will take their seats, and when they have elected the Governor and Council, then their right to their seats will be tried. This piece of jockeyship will degrade and ruin the party for ever. Perhaps it is well it should be so; the more each party disgraces itself the better.

I agree exactly with you, that "the state of society is radically vicious," and that it is there that the remedy is to be applied. Put down party spirit; stop the corruption of party elections; legislate not for the next elections, but for the next century; build Lancaster schools in every hundred, and repair our ruined churches; let every country gentleman of worth become a justice of the peace, and show his neighbors what a blessing a benevolent, religious man is; and let the retired patriot, who can do nothing else, give his country his prayers, and often in his meditations "think on her who thinks not for herself" — *"egregia virtus paucorum,"* &c. I often think of your apt quotation.

I believe, nay, I am sure, that such a course, if honestly attempted, would succeed and save us. God bless you.

Your friend,

F. S. KEY

Before the end of the Summer of 1813 the American commanders had formulated plans for an expedition to Montreal. It was believed that if they could secure control of Lake Erie and Lake Ontario, they could wrest Canada from the British Empire. In October, General William Henry Harrison won undisputed control of Lake Erie; but the Americans never won supremacy on Lake Ontario. The population of the United States was more than 7,000,000, while that of Canada was scarcely 400,000; but the United States had gone to war with incompetent leaders and was largely dependent upon the Militia, always an undependable force in time of war. Then, too, the divergence of views of the political leaders confused the minds of the people. Thousands of American citizens opposed recruiting, refused to subscribe to the war loans, and indeed took steps that were little less than treason. There was confusion in the minds of the soldiers; and inefficiency in the military forces resulted. Francis Scott Key heard with disgust the news of the proposal to send troops across the Canadian border to capture Montreal. He regarded a punitive expedition as altogether unnecessary and villainous.

As Winter approached, the American troops abandoned the invasion. Key was overjoyed. He wrote Randolph that he would rather see the American flag, which he had always looked upon as an ensign of Liberty, lowered in disgrace than have it stand for persecution and dishonor. "The people of Montreal," exclaimed Key, "will enjoy their firesides for this, and I trust for many a winter. This I suppose is treason, but, as your Patrick Henry said, '*If it be treason, I glory in the name of traitor.*' I have never thought of those poor creatures without being reconciled to any disgrace or defeat of our arms."

In bold language did Francis Scott Key enter his protest against war of aggression. And it struck a responsive chord in the heart of John Randolph, who in November had left his retreat at Roanoke to spend the Winter in Richmond. So delighted was he with Key's attitude concerning the expedition into Canada that he wrote Congressman Josiah Quincy of Massachusetts, who had opposed the war, that he was glad to find "one righteous man" on their side. He referred to the pious lawyer at Georgetown. It is obvious, therefore, that Key was still disgusted with the war policies of the Madison Administration. He did not want to embarrass the Government; but he was reluctant to aid a cause that appeared to him vicious and absurd. John Randolph continued to insist, as he stated to Mr. Quincy, that the motives of the War Hawks in plunging the United States into war were more contemptible than the stand taken by North's Administration against the American Colonies at the time of the Revolution.

CHAPTER X

The Voice of Washington

AT THE beginning of the year 1813, as the war clouds grew blacker and more ominous, Francis Scott Key was writing an oration for Washington's Birthday. The invitation to speak on this anniversary came to him from the Washington Society of Alexandria. This Society had been organized on January 14, 1800, one month after Washington's death, by his neighbors and friends who wished to perpetuate the memory of the Nation's hero, whom they loved.

It was a distinction to deliver the anniversary oration before this Society, whose members were very prominent men, including Chief Justice Marshall. The list of orators in previous years included George Washington Parke Custis, Charles Fenton Mercer, Francis Lightfoot Lee, Robert Goodlow Harper, and others well known for their forensic ability.

When Key received the invitation to address the Washington Society, he realized that his audience would include many of the neighbors and friends who had intimately known the Father of his Country, and he felt his lack of ability to do justice to a eulogy of Washington. Nevertheless he decided to use the invitation as an opportunity to proclaim his convictions regarding the deplorable condition into which the American people had fallen as a result of their vice and stupidity.

And so it was natural that Key fell upon Washington's Farewell Address as the subject for his oration. This legacy of advice had been issued to the people of the United States just a few weeks after Key was graduated from St. John's College; and, in the years that followed, the young lawyer drew from it inspiration that guided him in the composition of his anthems and other utterances of American patriotism. It was too lengthy to analyze and interpret in its entirety. All he would undertake would be to discuss Washington's observations on Religion and Morality – "these great Pillars of human happiness, these firmest props of the duties of Men and Citizens."

As Key studied the great document of Americanism, which had been issued to the people after years of deliberation, he realized more than ever what sage truths it contained, and how it served as a beacon light in times of deepest gloom, such as the period through which the people were than passing. How true was Washington's unheeded warning against the fury of party spirit! No wiser words of advice have been given to the people of the new generation, even if Washington could have stepped from his tomb and uttered them in person. Was not his denunciation of party spirit borne out by the events of the past year? "It serves always to distract the Public Councils, and enfeebles the Public administration. – It agitates the community with ill founded jealousies and false alarms, kindles the animosity of one part against another, foments occasionally riot and insurrection."

Francis Scott Key agreed also with Washington that the true policy of the United States was "to steer clear of permanent alliances, with any portion of the foreign world." He saw the wisdom of avoiding anything that might "entangle our peace and prosperity in the toils of European ambition, rivalship, interest, humour, or caprice." But his time was so limited, that he determined not to amplify this part of the Farewell Address but simply to repeat the great chieftain's own words of warning against "the mischiefs of foreign intrigue." The young lawyer believed that this solemn warning was "inestimable," but he realized that to do justice to a discussion of it was a task too great for the limited time available for his speech. He did take the occasion, however, to express his belief that Washington's Farewell Address was prophetic in its vision of the perils of the future. He believed that the solemn warning against entangling alliances with foreign countries would be just as applicable a century in the future as when it was written. And so he hoped that the admonitions of the Farewell Address would continue to be "at all times and under all dangers" the guide and the refuge and the preservation of "the remotest of our descendants."

The gist of Key's oration was the belief held by Washington that the only salvation of the people lay in themselves: any form of government was but a means to an end; it could never be better than the ethos of the people.

The building where the oration was to be delivered on the 22nd day of February, 1814, was the Presbyterian Meeting House, whose thick brick walls and heavy hand-hewn roof timbers had been erected forty years before by the hardy Scotch-Irish pioneers of Alexandria. It was large enough to accommodate several hundred people.

The audience saw a youthful orator of slender and medium height. He had a mass of heavy dark brown curly hair. His large eyes were expressive of earnestness. His voice was pleasing, his gestures graceful.

The speaker began with a few introductory remarks about the appalling condition of the country; and he gave a hint of a presentiment – "the still more awful anticipation of approaching calamity" – declaring his conviction that the American people would need "patient courage, pious submission, and humble enquiry into the means of preservation." Key came by this notion naturally. It was the faith of his father and mother. His mother said in one of her letters: "When I reflect how much we deserve and require chastisement, I cannot but see impending judgments greater than has yet befallen us." He now expressed in public his belief that "the common guilt" had brought down "the common punishment" as a scourge from the God of Wrath.

He then proceeded to eulogize the immortal Virginian, whom he called "the Deliverer and the Father of his Country." But he soon turned to the Farewell Address and, in a few moments, to that special injunction which Key picked out as the most vital of all – the maintenance of Religion and Morality. Here he emphasized again his opinion in regard to the Nation's affliction. With serious countenance and a voice that gave evidence of deep emotion, he said that the arm of the Almighty had been raised in wrath against the people of the United States and that accordingly they were now suffering "under Divine correction." The imperative duty of the Republic, therefore, was to repent and to banish the iniquity that had brought down the chastisement from the throne in Heaven.

The oration closed with a discussion of the relationship between Religion and Patriotism. "Love of country," said Key, "springs from religion .... and is ever nourished by its influence." The true patriot like George Washington serves his country and his God; the politician all too often is a seeker for power and fame rather than the welfare of his native land.

But quotations hardly do justice to Key's classic oration. Here is the full text:

> The return of this day, in times like these, presents us with a new and affecting proof of the uncertainty of all human expectations, of the vanity stamped upon every work and purpose and device of man.
>
> A nation in the pride of its triumph, in the exultation of prosperity, sets apart the birth day of its deliverer as a day of national festivity, and decrees that its annual return shall be welcomed by acclamations of joy, and be the signal of universal gladness. But alas! a few short years pass away, and the pride of triumph and the exultation of prosperity are gone. The feelings that once prompted the song of deliverance and the voice of thanksgiving are dead.
>
> In the gloom of present distress, in the still more awful anticipation of approaching calamity, the usual exhibition of national rejoicing would be impossible. A period arrives in which patient courage, pious submission, and humble enquiry into the means of preservation, are the virtues demanded of us.
>
> That all the vicissitudes of human affairs are ordered and controlled by the Almighty Governor of the world, who means, in all his dispensations, mercy to man, is a truth we coldly acknowledge; but how faintly

do we feel it? How little do we manifest by our conduct the influence upon our hearts?

Hence, when affliction is sent among a people, we are all too ready to charge it exclusively upon those to whose fault or folly we choose to impute it, and each man deems himself an innocent sufferer for the offence of others. And hence those mutual revilings and reproaches which shew a spirit unsoftened by adversity, which present neither remedy nor alleviation, but serve to aggravate the common guilt and the common punishment.

If, then, in the dark and evil times that have come upon us, this day must lose its brightness; if the sad and dispirited heart seeks in vain to be revived by the recollections it excites, it will become us to observe it with a solemnity, suited to the circumstances in which it finds. If it may no longer give unmixed delight it may teach us wisdom, may prompt us to timely consideration, and prepare us for the trials we may be called on to endure.

I shall not endeavor to distress you by a display of the fall of our national prosperity, the causes which produced, or the consequences to be expected from it; nor shall I enter into a discussion of the many questions that occupy and disturb the public mind.

Was I to speak of these things, I should speak of them as they are, and it would be a task, I hope, as repugnant to the feelings of those, by whose request I have the honor to address you, as to my own, to excite in your minds those portentous forebodings, which at times fill and agitate my own bosom, which I feel to be adverse to my own peace, and the discharge of my own duties, and which I therefore strive to repress.

This day is here celebrated by a Society formed for no low or ordinary purpose, seeking no political distinction or emolument, seeking nothing for itself, but aiming with a substantial and devoted patriotism, to promote the good of all our country, by actual works of beneficence. A Society, which, if these were not its motives and its views, would be put to shame by the name which it has assumed.

I have thought that he who speaks to you at such a time, under such a sanction, should not be emulous of that distinction which is to be obtained by sounding the praises of one sect of politicians and denouncing another; that the speaker of a Society bearing the name of your Washington, a Society loving that name to enthusiasm, professing and cherishing his principles, imitating his example, should not be so unmindful of that name, of those principles, of that example, as to minister, at such a time, and in such a place, to the pride or passion of party-feeling, and avow allegiance to any thing less than his country? And I have the gratification of believing that such a discharge of the duty I have undertaken is neither expected nor desired by those who have condescended to call me here.

To give due honor to the illustrious object of our regard; to call up his image before you; to awaken your recollections of his worth, of his zeal and devotion to your service; to select, from the innumerable proofs of his affection, some signal and useful token of his love; and to make the memory of what he was, even now that he is no more, a continual defence and blessing to us; these are subjects well suited to the proper commemoration of this day; to these considerations I would lead you.

To do honor to the name of Washington; to awaken the glowing recollections of his countrymen; to warm, with those recollections, the hearts of those who were not only his countrymen, but his neighbors and associates — Is this the task I have undertaken? and can I hope to fulfill these expectations? Where is the human eloquence that shall be found equal to such a subject? Shall it be displayed in exhibiting to your view the bright course of a long and honorable life, the assemblage of all the varieties of virtue which have constituted him your hero, your patriot, the Deliverer and the Father of his Country!

Is his worth to be thus sought after, are his services to be thus enumerated? No, my friends! the excellence of your Washington is of no common character: It is that excellence that makes panegyric poor, that defies description, that overpowers eloquence.

This part of my duty is done — I call the feelings that are now glowing in your bosoms to witness that it is done, and "bid them speak for me." They have paid a ready tribute of affection and of reverence that I should be ashamed to attempt to express. The name of Washington has been sounded in your ears — at that sound where is the heart that is not kindled into rapture, where is the eye whose glance does not confess it? Can words, poor words, do justice to these feelings? Can I give language to that which the coldest bosom must feel to be too big for utterance? The memory of man can receive no higher homage, a mortal name cannot be more ennobled than when at the mere utterance of that name, as if a magic spell had been pronounced, the tide of transport rushes from every heart, and throbs through every vein of all who hear it. Let the advocate of false greatness, the asserter of a doubtful fame, the encomiast of successful ambition, let him exhaust the embellishments of rhetoric to blazen forth a worth which is neither seen nor felt, and to warm with some artificial heat the unaffected minds of his hearers; but let him who speaks to you of your departed chief remember that he cannot be exalted in your affections, let him name the name of Washington, and catching the contagious impulse it has excited, join you in the reverential homage of the heart.

In the midst of these contemplations, I trust, we shall all remember the high and solemn duty they so obviously suggest to us. That in a time of great national calamity a deliverer was appointed to us, that he was gifted with every quality required by every emergency, guarded for our sakes in the midst of danger, and preserved to establish us in peaceful security. That we have even yet left to us the benefit of his example, the deathless glory of his name and the inestimable excellency of his principles — these are blessings which a kind providence has bestowed upon us, and for which gratitude and praise cannot be withheld without impiety.

Let us then not be unmindful of this national duty, let us sanctify the commemoration of this day by this "reasonable and acceptable service."

It is not merely for some temporary purpose and only for the benefit of the age in which he lives, that Heaven in compassion to the necessities of a people, vouchsafes to raise up a great and favored man in their defence. The good as well as "the evil men do, lives after them," — and never was richer inheritance bequeathed by expiring Patriot to his country than we have received from ours. Lasting as his name will be the blessings achieved for us by his life if we are not wanting to ourselves — in that name alone he has left a defence and a perpetual excitement to the highest efforts of patriotism. If the native of England may justly boast that —

"Chatham's language was his mother tongue,
And Wolfe's great name compatriot with his own"

what should be his exultation who remembers that, in the name of American, he bears a title ennobled by the deeds of Washington? Deeds which asserted and established his country's pre-eminence over the proudest and greatest nation upon earth, in that conflict, when

— "All the budding honors on her crest,
Were cropt to make a garland for our own."

Nor has he left us only his name: I trust he never felt the chilling thought that that name would be forgotten or disregarded; but he well knew that even those who might feel the sincerest veneration for it would be frail and fallible, subject to the assaults of passion, the arts of prejudice, and all the various sources of error which might make their efforts, however well intended, worse than useless. He has provided for this, and I have chosen a subject for our reflections this day from that instance of anxiety for our welfare, which I consider the consummation of his character.

I allude to that last and most interesting act of his official life, when, on his retirement from the government, to the humbler duties of a private station, he made his parting address to his lamenting countrymen. That concern for your interest, which had animated all his labours, was still working at his heart, and would not suffer him to take his final leave of the nation he had saved, without adding to his prayers for his country, those maxims of political wisdom, which I trust will never be forgotten, and which at this time particularly becomes us to call to mind. In selecting any of the last words of our beloved chief, I need not fear that I have chosen an unwelcome topic. In our recollections of a departed friend, the mind naturally turns to the last acts of kindness, to the dying declarations of attachment—advice offered under such circumstances is received with peculiar regard, and though often neglected in the wantonness of prosperity, it recurs in the day of trouble with more than its original influence.

In this address we have every thing to excite our veneration and affection. It evinces a disinterested devotion to our good, which no folly can be preposterous enough to deny; and it will ever be our own miserable neglect if the wisdom and patriotism of the counsels it contains, do not continue to be at all times and under all dangers our guide, our refuge and preservation. He has here laid down for us a course, which in every situation in which we may be placed, will lead us safely and honorably, through all the difficulties that may oppose us. No evil can befall us against which he has not guarded us, no temptation can come upon us, where his monitory voice has not supplied us with a caution. The remotest of our descendants, to whom the political blessings we have received may be allowed to be transmitted, will find these parental counsels sanctified by experience, and the impartial historian will note the invariable connection between the happiness of the nation, and the observance of these hallowed precepts — and if the day shall ever come (which may Heaven be propitiated to avert!) that shall cast us down from our greatness, when civil discord, corruption or usurpation shall bend the necks of freemen to a miserable and hopeless bondage, then shall the sorrowing patriot who may survive the horrors of that day, point to the disregarded admonition of your Washington, and the tear, that he drops upon the ruins of his country, will be embittered by the recollection of her follies and her crimes.

The feelings which prompted him to endeavor to perpetuate our blessings are thus affectingly displayed in his own words in the conclusion of his address:

> "In offering to you, my Countrymen, these counsels of an old and affectionate friend, I dare not hope they will make the strong and lasting impression, I could wish — that they will controull the usual current of the passions, or prevent our Nation from running the course which has hitherto marked the destiny of Nations. — But if I may even flatter myself, that they may be productive of some partial benefit; some occasional good; that they may now and then recur to moderate the fury of party spirit, to warn against the mischiefs of foreign intrigue, to guard against the impostures of pretended patriotism, this hope will be a full recompense for the solicitude for your welfare, by which they have been dedicated."

To do full justice to this inestimable warning, to point out to your view the various excellencies that distinguish it, is a task far too great for the present occasion. I intend, therefore, only to offer to your consideration its most essential of solemn injunctions: one of which no individual of any nation should ever be unmindful, which, without exception or excuse, is the bounden duty of every citizen, the indispensable obligation upon the conscience of a patriot. It is that admonition of your Washington which recommends to your regard the religion to which he bore his honorable testimony. Hear then the important words which he addressed to you upon this all important subject.

> "Of all the dispositions and habits, which lead to political prosperity, Religion and morality are indispensable supports. — In vain would that man claim the tribute of Patriotism, who should labour to subvert these great Pillars of human happiness, these firmest props of the duties of Men and Citizens. — The mere Politician, equally with the pious man, ought to respect and to cherish them. — A volume could not trace all their connexions with private and public felicity."

I cannot avoid remarking that there is scarcely a memorable incident or official act of his life in which the strong and just impressions of his mind upon this subject were not manifested. In all our national deliverances we see him ascribing all the glory to their true and Almighty Cause, and calling upon his countrymen to acknowledge and praise the Power that defended them.

I hope I shall be pardoned for presuming to address you on such a subject. I have felt how little I was qualified for such an office, and I have undertaken it relying, for all claim to your attention, upon the influence of that name in which we are assembled; and believing that nothing could be presented to you more worthy of your thoughts, or more applicable to our present situation. When a people are suffering, under divine correction, when the arm of the Almighty is raised in wrath against them, surely it is not unreasonable to expect that they will "call their ways to remembrance," and endeavor to ascertain the iniquity that has provoked chastisement. If we do this faithfully, it will lead us to the only remedy for all the evils we either endure or anticipate, and affliction will have "done its errand." But if we are hardened against such suggestions, we need not look to the history of past ages, or the speculations of fancy, to learn the nature and extent of the visitation we may expect. The fall, in our own view, of many of the proudest nations of the earth, once peaceful and prosperous as our own, now groaning in unutterable wretchedness, gives awful warnings of the fate that may await us.

Let us then endeavor to ascertain what those duties are, which the religion we profess demands of us in relation to our country, and how they have been discharged.

It has been said that the exalted virtues of patriotism finds no place in this religion, and is incompatible with its tenets. So strangely erroneous is this opinion, that a just and disinterested love of country springs from religion as from its natural and proper source, and is ever nourished by its influence. Let the men of other principles tell us, whether that boasted divinity, the work of man's corrupt imagination, which they have set up, and which they worship, can supply the patriot with that armour of proof which religion furnishes; and if deluded by the error they have loved, they tell us that it can, let us look among the lives of those who live only for this world and in obedience to its rules, for instances to prove it. If we are dazzled by a few shining exceptions, how are they out-numbered by thousands of the fairest promise, whose lamentable fall shews us the weakness of the power that upholds their virtue?

A man may wear out his life in the toils of the cabinet, or hazard it by his daring in the field, yet if he is prompted to this from the love of power, the dream of ambition, the glory of a name, if these are his motives, who can doubt but that it is his own power, his own ambition, his own glory, that he seeks, that it is himself, and neither his country, nor his God, that he loves and serves.

A man may offer himself to death, may fall exulting in the trappings and decorations with which honor adorns its victim; but if unimpelled by that love to God and man, which is the only incense that can sanctify such an offering, it is a sacrifice unacceptable to Heaven, it is a sacrifice to self.

Look at the efficacy of these principles in the day of trial. Let temptation come upon him; let his evil passions solicit indulgence; let the pomp and glory of the world spread their allurements before him; let a secret path of crooked policy seem to lead to the eminence for which his heart pants; and what shall stop him in his way? Alas! feeble are the barriers which the wisdom of this world can present to the madness of ambition!

He who submits to be guided by the divine light of revelation has learned the nature and condition of man, the engagements to which he is called, and the dangers that oppose him. He has heard of his high original, of his wretched fall, of his glorious redemption, of the awful and everlasting destiny which awaits him. Grateful for his deliverance, thankful for all the blessings of life, and exulting in the hopes of eternity, he has acknowledged the Almighty as his Lord, and devoted himself to His service. Anxious to manifest the warmth of his gratitude by the fidelity of his obedience, he has humbly enquired into his will. Finding himself associated with numberless fellow-creatures, "framed with like miracle, the work of God," he has been solicitous to learn his relation to them. He is told they are his brethern, that he is to love them, and that it is to be his business to fill up the short measure of his life by doing good to them. Engaged in this work, he has perceived himself peculiarly connected with some, who are brought nearer to him, and therefore more within the reach of his beneficence. He has observed that he is a member of a particular social community, governed by

> the same laws, exercising the same privileges, and bound to the same duties. His obligations therefore to this community, are more obvious and distinct. His own country, to which he is immediately responsible, by whose institutions he has been cherished and protected, has therefore a peculiar claim upon him. That he may acknowledge this claim, that his zeal may want no excitement to rouse him, it is there that his blessings are fixed, that the charities of life have been exercised, and an impulse of filial affection is awakened within him, that binds him unalienably to the land of his birth.

When Key closed his address, a motion was made that the thanks of the Society be presented to the speaker "for the elegant and appropriate Oration" and that he be requested to furnish a copy of it for publication by the Society. The motion was unanimously adopted. Thus was Key's first oration preserved for posterity. And it is fortunate that it was. For not only does it show Key's admiration for Washington as the foremost of his heroes, but it also reveals the transcendent influence exerted by Washington upon the life of Key.

And, besides, it shows the well-springs of thought which were to be given expression by Key in his anthem of patriotism. It shows that although the anthem was to be dashed off in a moment of exultation its theme was the result of a deep-rooted conviction gathered from long hours of meditation and study.

Here in the old Presbyterian Meeting House in Alexandria the young orator recalled that in all our National deliverances Washington had ascribed all the glory to the "true and Almighty Cause" and had urged his fellow countrymen to "praise the Power that defended them." In a few months more Key would give the same thought in a poetic outburst destined to inspire patriotism through endless generations:

> Blest with victory and peace, may the heav'n-rescued land
> Praise the Power that hath made and preserved us a nation!

CHAPTER XI

At the Crossroads

WHILE KEY'S faith in his fellow men had been shaken, his faith in God remained steadfast. All of the troubles of America, indeed of the whole world, were the result, he believed, of man's misconduct. Herein he differed from John Randolph of Roanoke. Early in life Randolph had become a believer in Mohammedanism. "The Crescent," he said, "had a talismanic effect on my imagination, and I rejoiced in all its triumphs over the Cross (which I despised) as I mourned over its defeats: and Mohamet II himself did not more exult than I did, when the Crescent was planted on the dome of St. Sophia, and the Cathedral of the Constantines was converted into a Turkish mosque." This skepticism was the result of his perusal of Voltaire and other French philosophers.

But Key's faith had been strengthened, rather than weakened, by the books of infidel writers. "Our Church," he informed Randolph in 1814, "recommends their perusal to students of divinity, which shows she is not afraid of them." Key did not believe that any new objections could be found to the truth of Christianity, although it was to be admitted that old ones might be cleverly presented in a new dress. "Men may argue ingeniously against our faith — as indeed they may against any thing — but what can they say in defence of their own? I would carry the war into their own territories. I would ask them what they believed." He had no patience with agnostics. "If they said they believed nothing, you could not, to be sure, have any thing further to say to them. In that case they would be insane, or, at best, illy qualified to teach others what they ought to believe or disbelieve." He could not understand how anyone, who inquired into the subject earnestly, could become an atheist. One of the theological books he had read was *de Veritate* by Hugo Grotius, the celebrated Dutch writer. "I should like to see an infidel," said Key, "attempt an answer to that book."

John Randolph was impressed with Francis Scott Key's child-like faith in every line of the Scripture. He was beginning to see that his own soul had been warped, that many of his troubles emanated from within. Indeed, he wrote Key, he had been living in a "world without souls," until his heart was "as dry as a chip," and "as cold as a dog's nose." In the city of Richmond, as well as at his home in the wilderness, he found a certain amount of comfort in literature. One of the poems which he enjoyed was *The Giaour*, which Lord Byron had written in 1813. He read the posthumous works of Edmund Burke, whom he greatly admired. He also continued to find pleasure and instruction in many of the articles in the reviews. Occasionally he would come across something in the newspapers about himself. Once his eyes came upon a paragraph in a newspaper which accused him of being "an obvious imitator of Lord Chatham." Randolph burst into a rage. He knew that Lord Chatham occupied an exalted position; whereas his own face had become prematurely wrinkled and he had "lost his grinders"; but he objected to being classed with "the servile herd of imitators." He regarded the article as a foul attack. To Key he explained his resentment: "Any other man but yourself (or perhaps Meade) would take this long paragraph as proof that I am insincere, or self-deceived. To tell you the truth, I am sensible of the gross injustice that has been done me in the paragraph in question. I had as lief be accused of any crime, not forbidden by the Decalogue, as of *imitation*. If these articles choose to say that I have neglected, or thrown away, or buried my talent, I will acquiesce in the censure; but amongst the herd of imitators I will not be ranked, because I feel that I could not descend to imitate any human being."

Toward the close of February John Randolph was stricken at Richmond with severe illness — a "gouty affection of the alimentary canal." He grew more despondent than ever. But there were two rays of sunshine: one a cheerful letter from his friend, the poet lawyer; the other, a copy of Key's oration delivered on Washington's Birthday. Propping himself up in bed, the sick man read with delight every word of the oration. It was like a tonic to peruse his young friend's denunciation of the American people and his reaffirmation of the principles in Washington's Farewell Address. "Your letter found me in bed," Randolph replied to Key on March 2, 1814. "It was, I believe, the best medicine that could have been administered to me, but, aided by an Anniversary discourse, which Joe Lewis was considerate enough to send me, and which came also in the nick of time, the effect was wonderful. I am half disposed to be angry with you for passing over the said discourse, as if it never had existed, and especially for leaving me to the charity of Joe Lewis, but for whose contribution I might have been deprived of the pleasure of seeing it at all; for you need not flatter yourself that the newspapers generally will republish it." Randolph was overjoyed to read Key's rebuke of the political leaders; but Randolph had surrendered all hope that the politicians would ever put aside their selfish ambitions, their greed for power and gold, for true patriotism. "You are right, my friend," he said, "but who will follow you? Who will abandon the *expedient* to adopt the counsels of self-denial, of mortification, of duty? For my part, much as I abhor the factious motive and manner of the Opposition prints, and many of its leaders, if I could find as many men of my way of thinking as drubbed the French at Agincourt, I would throw off the yoke, or perish in the attempt." Nevertheless, the morbid Randolph was certain that Key's oration would produce "a most happy and beneficial effect on all ranks of the people"—if they would read it. "But," he said, "the people will not hear, cannot read, and if they could, cannot understand, until the paroxysm of drunkenness is over. Wanting your faith I cannot repress *my* forebodings. They weigh me down and immerse body and soul. I never stood more in need of your society. In this world without souls, everybody is taken up with 'the one thing needful'—what that is you must not consult St. Paul, but the Jewish doctors, to discover."

In the melancholy days of 1814, dark and uneventful though they appeared, Francis Scott Key was preparing himself for a dramatic event and an immortal fame. Finding little to do in his office, he occupied many hours with the Muse. Day after day he immersed himself in the rhymes of English and American men of letters. His favorite of all contemporary poets was Sir Walter Scott; his poems had a melody and a charm that appealed to Key's love of the beautiful; Mr. Randolph's favorite was Byron, whose romantic poems contained rugged strength and vigor, and who was threatening to surpass the Wizard of the North in literary supremacy. *The Bride of Abydos* was one of the productions that Byron hurled from his pen within a few days in 1813; but the poet lawyer at Georgetown was not particularly pleased with it. In a letter to Randolph, Key thus explained his preference for Sir Walter Scott over Byron: "I have not yet seen *The Giaour,* but have looked over *The Bride of Abydos.* It has some fine passages in it, but it is too full of those crooked-named out-of-the-way East Indian things. I have long ago, however, resolved that there shall be no such poet as Walter Scott as long as he lives, and I can admire nobody that pretends to rival him." Mr. Randolph could not agree with him; his poetic taste was different. "I cannot yield the precedence of Lord Byron to Walter Scott," he wrote to Key in reply. "I admit your objection to the 'crooked-named out-of-the-way Turkish things.' But this must be pardoned in a traveller, who has explored the woods that wave o'er Delphi's steep, and swam across the Hellespont. No poet in our language (the exception is unnecessary), Shakespeare and Milton apart, has the same power over my feelings as Byron. He is, like Scott, *careless,* and indulges himself in great license; but he does not, like your favorite, write by the piece. I am persuaded that his fragments are thrown out by the true spirit of inspiration, and that he never goads his pen to work. When you have read *The Giaour* — the first, I think, of his poems — I am persuaded that you will change your opinion of this singular author, and yet more singular man. His feelings are too strong to endure the privation of religious sentiment. His time is not yet come, but he cannot continue to exist in the chill and gloom of skepticism." Randolph's prediction that Lord Byron was eclipsing Scott as a poet was correct: Scott had already turned from poetry to prose; and the publication of *Waverly* in 1814 not only served to make Scott the king of romancers but also marked the beginning of the ascendancy of the novel as one of the most popular forms of literature.

But there was one writer upon whom Key devoted very little time. That man was Thomas Moore. John Randolph was delighted with Moore's polished satire and sometimes licentious verse. One of Moore's works that Randolph enjoyed was *The Twopenny Post-Bag*, which, in a letter to Key, he said was one of the "literary sweets" in which he had been revelling. But Key turned a deaf ear to any praise of Moore's verses. In the Key family there has long been a tradition that Francis Scott Key found the poems of "the sentimental Tom Moore" so distasteful that on one occasion he picked up a volume of these poems in the library of his home, handed it to Mrs. Key, and told her to burn it up.

But Key, in preparing himself — whether wittingly or unwittingly — for the writing of the National Anthem, did more than pore over the works of the poets; he actually made a study of song-writing. Here is an illustration of the truth that nothing is ever done without practice and preparation. One day, picking up a copy of *Bronson's Select Review,* he saw an article on American song-writing. Needless to say, he read it with keen interest. Was he aspiring even then to write a song that would breathe the spirit of true patriotism? An anthem that would praise the Divine Power that had guided the fathers in founding the Nation? Key did not know who wrote the review on American song-writing; but certain it is that it produced a profound effect upon him. He even went so far as to recommend that the author, whoever he was, should start a new magazine and become editor of it; for he felt that a new publication, preferably an American publication, was needed to take the place of the *Edinburgh Review,* which he thought had undergone a "great and shameful change of principle." "Is it not desirable," he asked Randolph, "that there should be a good American Literary Review? One inculcating the sound principles of the *Quarterly Reviewers,* and exposing our book-makers, would perhaps improve both our taste and habits. Have you seen an article in *Bronson's Select Review* on American song-writing? I do not know who the author is, but I think he could conduct such a work with much spirit. I have seldom, I think, seen a better piece of criticism." Randolph endorsed Key's suggestion for a new American periodical. "I *do* think a review on the plan you mention would be highly beneficial, and if I was fit for any thing, I should like to engage in a work of the sort. But fourteen years of Congressional life have rendered me good for nothing. It may be an excuse for idleness, for this devil attacks me in every shape.... I have not seen the article you mention in *Bronson's Select Review.* In its new form I think that a respectable and useful publication. To be sure, it is made of scissors; but it is so far beyond the *Port-Folio* as to be comparatively good. The last is the most contemptible thing ever imposed on the public in the shape of a magazine — and that is going very far."

It was early in April, 1814, while regretting that his law practice was far from lucrative, and musing over the songs of the Nation, that Key arrived at the crossroads of life. He had just received an invitation to become assistant rector of St. Paul's parish in Baltimore, the call coming in a letter from Rev. Dr. James Kemp, the rector of St. Paul's and Christ Churches. Dr. Kemp believed that the Georgetown lawyer was already thoroughly qualified to enter the ministry.

Key was in a quandary. The ministry was attractive to him in many respects; but in his path there were many obstacles. For one thing, he had become heavily involved in debt and other complications, which seemed to make it altogether impossible to abandon his profession for the pulpit, which paid just enough to provide shelter and food for his family, but little more. So he wrote back to Dr. Kemp that he would pray for Divine guidance as to the course to pursue — and, if he failed to receive it, he would consult two or three friends for advice. His letter indicates his perplexity and vacillation:

Key to Rev. Dr. James Kemp

Geo. Town —

April 4, 1814.

Rev[d] & D[r] Sir: —

Your letter should have been sooner answered, but it came while I was in Charles County whence I returned home the night before the last very much indisposed.

When I thought a few years ago of preparing myself for the ministry, it seemed to me, from all the consideration I could give it, that I was peculiarly situated, & had entered, almost necessarily, into engagements that made such a step impossible. — At the same time I hoped (as I still do) that if the path of duty would lead me to this change of life, I should be enabled to see it, & that my present course should be stopped if I could serve God more acceptably in the ministry. — I did not to be sure ever think of such a situation as you have suggested; but I have doubts how far, even in this way, an abandonment of my profession could be reconciled with the necessities of my present arrangements. — I have been obliged to contract (not on account of any concern of my own) a very considerable debt — and the relinquishment of my present pursuits would materially affect others (some even out of my own family) to whom I seem to have become bound. — Under these circumstances you will perceive I ought not lightly nor without mature consideration, to make so important a change in my situation; and I should be very glad of your thoughts upon the subject. — That I could support my family upon the terms you have mentioned I think probable: But I should find it difficult (if not impossible) to do more; and to do more I seem to be necessarily bound. Would it be practicable to make anything as an author of religious & Literary publications? And would I have any leisure for such engagements? —

The great advantage of entering the Church under an association with you I am fully sensible of, & this more than anything else inclines me to think it may perhaps be my duty.—At least it will induce me to give the subject a full deliberation & to endeavor to ascertain if the nature of the engagements I have intimated can justifiably allow of it.

I believe we differ upon the subject of Episcopacy—you consider it as the divinely established & only form of Church government & that there is no valid ordination elsewhere. I have never seen anything to satisfy me of this, but though I have been led to think it a *form,* I still think it the best form.—And this difference is, I believe, no more than has always existed among the members of our Church of whom many respectable names are on each side of the question.—As to our Church service, few persons can be more attached to it than I am.—I lament that any of our ministers should substantially depart from it, though I love and esteem some who occasionally do so. I regret also that others should insist upon a literal and universal compliance as absolutely essential to be enforced by strict Church discipline; and though I think such a design would introduce a spirit of controversy & persecution, and that it would perhaps make an irreconcilable schism in the Church, about things, that, if they were not disputed about, would create no differences, yet I have an equal affection & regard for some who I believe hold this opinion.—I have been remarkably influenced by the conviction of many most erroneous opinions of my own, to allow for those of others—& have been led to see great merit among the advocates of each side of a controversy. —I believe that God will sufficiently enlighten every man who hungers and thirsts after righteousness, & prays to be led into the truth, & that it may be consistent with His wisdom & goodness to leave us for a time under the influence of some errors.—

However we might differ in opinion I feel gratified

in believing that our hearts would be united in one great purpose, & our labours directed to the same end: & I am not so vain & self-confident as not to be fully persuaded of the importance of entering upon so solemn a calling with such a connection as you suggest. — I am obliged to leave home again for a week or a fortnight, & will not fail to think of this subject & write to you. —

Allow me to hope that I may have your candid advice and your prayers that I may be rightly directed.—

truly & resply
Yrs
F. S. KEY

P. S. — May I be allowed to mention this subject to two or three friends, whose counsel I should wish? — that is, if, on reflection, I find a difficulty in determining. — As far as I have been able to think at present, I do not see how I can extricate myself from my engagements. —

So for about four weeks the poet lawyer wrapped himself in solitude to ponder and pray. Finally, on April 28, 1814, the decision was reached. On this day he determined once and for all that he would continue in the path he had been following — the law. In the first place, the complications in which he had become involved apparently made it impossible for him to enter the ministry. These difficulties, which had occurred to him from the first, appeared, he told Dr. Kemp, insurmountable. In the second place, he was afraid that if he entered the ministry he would be accused of acting "under the influence of unworthy inducements" and thereby might injure "the cause of religion." It was not only an important decision for the man himself and the members of his household but also, so it turned out, a decision that was destined to have a part in preparing the way for the writing of the American Anthem, a song which was to have a profound influence on the soul of the Nation throughout all future generations.

When he had penned his answer to Dr. Kemp, Key felt relieved. Now he took on a new stature in courage. He had prayed for guidance; and he felt confident that his path had been charted. "I trust," he declared, "that if I have been incorrect in this determination, I shall be brought to see it, & that God will make plain to me his will and my duty & give me strength to perform it."

One of the battles of life had been fought and won!

THE FORT McHENRY BATTLE FLAG

The original flag which inspired Francis Scott Key to write "The Star-Spangled Banner"

CHAPTER XII

"The Star-Spangled Banner"

IN THE Spring of 1814 the fleet commanded by Sir George Cockburn reappeared along the Atlantic coast and in June the vessels were ascending the Patuxent. The design of the Enemy was obvious: they were preparing for a punitive expedition. The volunteers in the District of Columbia Militia assembled and made plans to hurry to the Patuxent.

The courts had adjourned because of the impending danger; and Attorney Key, with his practice at a standstill, volunteered his services to the Georgetown Light Artillery. Major Peter, the commander, was glad to have him join, and on the 19th of June he entered the Militia with the rank of lieutenant and quartermaster. There was no time to lose. Key dashed off a letter to his mother at Pipe Creek; gave good-bye to his wife and children; and off he went with the company in the direction of the Patuxent.

When the militiamen from Georgetown arrived at their destination, however, they found, much to their relief, that His Majesty's fleet had turned around and started down the river. The members of the Artillery bivouacked near Benedict, a settlement in Charles County, and decided to keep guard for any further appearance of the enemy. Lieutenant Key, in another letter to his mother, proudly announced that the British had been driven off and predicted that, as long as the Militia were stationed along the shore, the invaders would not likely return. The letter, like many others Key wrote, shows how intimately he kept in touch all through life with his mother:

Key to His Mother

Camp near Benedict—
June 23, 1814—

My Dear Mother—

I wrote you a few lines from Geo. Town just before we marched.—And I have now an opportunity to Town and only time to tell you that I am well.—

We came to this place on Monday night and after the Enemy had left it—a few of them, who had landed, being driven off that evening with some little loss of which I suppose you have seen the account.—They have now gone down the river—and nobody seems to think there is any chance of their coming back again, at least, while the troops are in the neighborhood—How long they will keep us here I cannot tell, but I trust not long—And as soon as we are discharged I shall try to be with you . . . . .

I will write you a line occasionally as I can—and hope to be able to be on the way to Pipe Creek.—With love to my Father, Anne and Taney, I am,

My Dr Mother
Y^r^ Most affec^t^
F. S. KEY

Key's hope for a speedy end of guard duty was realized: since there was no indication of an immediate return of the British, Major Peter ordered the Light Artillery back to

Georgetown. And on the 1st day of July Lieutenant Key was discharged from further attendance.

On returning to his law office within a fortnight, Key sent off a number of letters to relatives and friends. One letter went to John Randolph of Roanoke. He told of the expedition to Benedict, but admitted that the most thrilling adventure which he had on the trip was when he was knocked down by "a bone of bacon" and pitched over his horse's head into the river. The camp life had been irksome: the poet lawyer hoped that he had seen the last of warfare for the remainder of his life.

By this time efforts were being made to bring about a treaty of peace between England and the United States; and Randolph, in a letter to Francis Scott Key, July 14th, said: "I saw some account of your campaigns in the newspapers.... Your labors, my good friend, are drawing to a close. Rely upon it, we have peace forthwith." What Randolph was now afraid of was that the treaty of peace would be unfair to the United States. He looked with suspicion on the assertions of American officials, that the matters in dispute had been removed by the termination of hostilities in Europe. "Poor devils," he exclaimed to Key concerning the Republican leaders, "what a figure they do cut! Yet they will look as consequential as ever, and even carry the people with them."

Randolph was back at Roanoke again. St. George Randolph, his deaf mute nephew, was now with him and added to his despondency. This unfortunate young man of twenty-two, his proposals of marriage rejected, had developed into a frantic maniac; he had quieted down considerably so as to become manageable with little difficulty; and although he was quite irrational, his memory seemed to be unimpaired. The affairs of the plantation had been a great source of worry too. Fortunately he had not been having any trouble with his slaves. Not one of his two hundred Negroes had been sick since his return from Richmond. But there had been a number of heavy rains, and his crops, he said, had "drowned"; and then, when hot weather came in July, the crops "burned up."

Francis Scott Key felt sorry for the morbid man. He listened with infinite patience to the recital of all his vicissitudes. But their correspondence was now to be interrupted by events of transcendent importance.

The surrender of Napolean in 1814 enabled England to release a squadron of Lord Nelson's Marines and a division of Wellington's Invincibles for duty along the American coast. Several brigades were sent to Canada, one brigade was fitted out for service in the Chesapeake. The latter was placed under the command of Sir Robert Ross, of County Down, Ireland. This gallant officer, 48 years of age, had served in Egypt and in the Peninsular campaigns, had been wounded in the Battle of Orthes, and was made a Major-General after the Battle of Victoria.

On July 24th the squadron reached Bermuda, the British base for the Chesapeake operations, and joined the fleet commanded by Vice Admiral Alexander Cochrane. General Ross and his staff went on board the *Tonnant*, Admiral Cochrane's flagship. The reënforced fleet now sailed for the

Chesapeake, and on the 14th of August joined Rear Admiral Cockburn off the mouth of the Potomac.

The thousands of redcoats were welcomed ashore on the beach of Tangier Island by Joshua Thomas, "the Parson of the Isles," who preached to the veterans of the Peninsular campaign, warned them of their sins, and advised them not to try to capture Baltimore.

But the Parson's advice to them to return to England made no impression. The Royal vessels spread their sails again, sailed up the Chesapeake and entered the Patuxent. The British officers had decided to land their troops: their objective was Washington, the Capital of the United States. Nor did they make any effort to conceal their intention. Indeed they wanted it to be known that they were making ready to retaliate for the burning of the Parliament House at York by the American troops. Admiral Cochrane, in a letter to Secretary of State Monroe, wrote that he had been called upon by the Governor-General of Canada to retaliate upon the United States for the wanton destruction committed by the American soldiers in Upper Canada and announced that it was his duty to issue to his naval force "an order to destroy and lay waste such towns and districts as may be found assailable."

President Madison had chosen Brigadier General William H. Winder to command the Tenth Military District, comprising Maryland, the District of Columbia, and that part of Virginia lying between the Potomac and the Rappahannock, to afford military protection to the Capital. General John Armstrong, Secretary of War, preferred someone else to command this district; and when he was overruled by the President, he became indifferent and left further defense measures to President Madison, Mr. Monroe, and General Winder.

General Winder recommended that the President call out four thousand militia to guard the Capital; leading business men called at the President's Mansion and urged that the city be fortified. But although the British had long been ravaging the shores of the Chesapeake, Armstrong remained passive, arguing that fortifications would exhaust the Treasury and that bayonets would be "the most efficient barriers." But there were only about four hundred regular troops prepared to defend the capital from invasion. The people of the District of Columbia were alarmed. But the Secretary of War waived aside warnings and neglected to take adequate steps to fortify the Capital. He believed that Baltimore, and not Washington, was the Enemy's objective. It was not until August 20th that General Winder's recommendation was approved.

But imminent danger threatened the Capital. On August 19th upwards of five thousand British troops landed in Charles County about eight miles below Benedict, near the spot where Key and his comrades had camped in June, and started their march in the direction of Washington. Mr. Monroe advised that the Government records ought to be moved and suggested that explosives be in readiness for the destruction of the bridges. The frightened Secretary of War put General Winder at the head of the militia and urged him to do all he could to save the city. But General Winder could muster but four thousand militia and several hundred regulars. The Virginia militia had been called, but they had no flints for their firelocks.

General Ross said he "didn't care if it rained militia." He and Admiral Cockburn had the joint command of the troops. At daybreak on August 21st General Ross ordered the soldiers to march to Nottingham, a village on the Patuxent within forty miles of Washington. Here they bivouacked on the night of the 21st. Early on the morning of the 22nd they resumed their march by advancing along the shady road along the Patuxent toward Upper Marlborough. After the cramped confinement on the transports, the soldiers enjoyed the leisurely march through the country.

It was one o'clock on the 22nd when the houses of Upper Marlborough, sixteen miles from Washington, came into view. No one in the invading army appreciated the scenery more than did Rev. George R. Gleig, the literary chaplain who accompanied the expedition. He gave a glowing description of the countryside around Upper Marlborough: "The gentle green hills which on either hand enclosed the village, tufted here and there with magnificent trees, the village itself, straggling and wide, each cottage being far apart from its neighbors and each ornamented with flower beds and shrubberies; these with a lovely stream which wound through the valley, formed, as far as my memory may be trusted, one of the most exquisite panoramas, on which it has ever been my good fortune to gaze."

On arriving in Upper Marlborough, General Ross selected the mansion of Dr. William Beanes for his Headquarters. Dr. Beanes was a leading physician of Prince

George's county. His ancestors had lived in Scotland, but he himself was a native of Maryland. At the outbreak of the Revolution he had espoused the patriot cause, having served on the county committee to carry out the resolutions of the Continental Congress. At Philadelphia during the war he had helped to bandage the wounds of the Continentals wounded at Long Island and Brandywine. But now, at sixty-five, he assured the British officers that he was a Federalist, and that he had been opposed to the war with Great Britain. "And we believed him the more readily," said Rev. Gleig, "that he seemed really disposed to treat us as friends." On account of his hospitable attitude, his slaves, horses, and cattle were unmolested.

Upper Marlborough was about thirty miles from Baltimore; and about sixteen miles from Washington. General Ross was undecided about what to do next. On August 23rd, Ross held a council of war with Admiral Cockburn in the Beanes home. Here it was decided to move on toward Washington. That afternoon the British troops evacuated Upper Marlborough. At daybreak on the 24th they advanced toward Bladensburg, a village located about five miles from Washington on the Eastern Branch of the Potomac.

The approach of the British was the signal for alarm in Washington. General Winder had been mobilizing his troops around Bladensburg. One of the Washington newspapers tried to calm the people: "In a few hours thousands of brave men will be prepared to resist the host of mercenaries that now threaten us. Arrayed in defense of all that renders life a blessing, and for protecting from insult and desolation the metropolis of their country, hallowed by the venerable name of Washington, every arm will be nerved with valour irresistible!"

The agitated General Winder, bewildered by a myriad details, reported at the President's Mansion for a conference on Tuesday night. On Wednesday morning at ten o'clock he received the news that the British were advancing toward Bladensburg. Secretary of State Monroe had already started toward Bladensburg; General Winder now rushed to the scene; the President and members of the Cabinet followed.

Francis Scott Key, while he did not favor the war, was ready to give himself to the defense of the Capital. The firebrands were approaching. The Government buildings and his own home were in peril. He had volunteered to act as aide to General Walter Smith, whom General Winder had placed in command of a reserve force of Washington and Georgetown Militia.

The poet lawyer was given the duty of locating the regiments to their assigned positions as they arrived on the field. It was a stifling hot day—this 24th of August, 1814, when Key swung his horse up and down the dusty roads and across the fields in the vicinity of Bladensburg, helping to make final efforts to get the raw militia ready to stem the advance of the seasoned Invincibles.

Here too were President Madison and Secretary Monroe and Secretary Armstrong. It was a cruel fate which cast Madison, peace-loving and mild-mannered, into the vortex of war. And, like Mr. Madison, Key abhorred war and was unfit to cope with fire and sword.

Monroe and Key were posting General Stansbury's Militia with all possible haste. Stansbury commanded about two thousand Maryland Militia; General Winder commanded the Georgetown and Washington Militia under General Smith, a few Maryland Militia, and Barney's seamen, aggregating in all more than three thousand men.[1]

As General Winder arrived in the field about noon, a long column of British soldiers with scarlet tunics and shining bayonets were advancing, six abreast, about a mile away. They marched with the regularity and the easy swing of seasoned veterans.

As the Enemy came marching into Bladensburg, President Madison said to Mr. Monroe that it was about time for them to go and leave the rest to the soldiers. So the two men — the President frail in body but of powerful intellect; Monroe six feet tall, broad-shouldered and of powerful physique — hurried to the rear. After the battle was over the President was the target for ridicule. Characterized in a doggerel poem as "a citizen of courage and renown," Mr. Madison was quoted as saying to the Secretary of War and the Attorney General:

Armstrong and Rush, stay here in camp,
  I'm sure you're not afraid —
Ourself will now return; and you,
  Monroe, shall be our aid.
And, Winder, do not fire your guns,
  Nor let your trumpets play
'Till we are out of sight — forsooth,
  My horse will run away

1.—"Winder, pushing forward Smith's brigade, arrived in time to fight a battle on dispositions, not made by himself but by Stansbury and Smith, and their assistants, Colonel Monroe and F. S. Key. Of these dispositions, we need say nothing, as the gentlemen to whom they have been principally imputed were both ashamed of them." — *Inquiry Respecting the Capture of Washington by the British.* Rare Book Room, Library of Congress.

Shortly before 1 o'clock the invaders appeared – battle-scarred soldiers who had gone through the campaigns of the Duke of Wellington on the Peninsula, veterans who had served under Lord Nelson at Trafalgar and on the Nile.

A few of the Yankee companies were dressed in blue jackets. But all the rest looked like "country people who would have been much more appropriately employed in attending to their agricultural occupations than in standing with muskets in their hands on the brow of a bare, green hill." But there they stood! General Winder had not provided any obstruction to the road to Washington – not a single breast-work or ditch.

After a few volleys the front ranks of the British charged with the bayonet. The militia were panic-stricken. Most of the Yankee defenders had seen about as much experience as Francis Scott Key in military affairs; some had less. Formation after formation wavered, broke, turned, and fled. General Winder's artillery set up stiff resistance, shooting down quite a number of the British vanguard with grape-shot; but the hardened British campaigners, inured to hardships on the bloody fields of Spain, closed the gaps in their ranks and smashed through the American line. The redcoats also discharged a number of rockets: the glare from these caused a stampede among the battery mules.

Francis Scott Key was overcome with despair when he saw that the militiamen were fleeing with great rapidity in the scorching heat – exhausted, terrified, as if chased by some hideous beast. But there came a ray of hope with the arrival of Commodore Joshua Barney on the scene. Barney, a 55-year-old Maryland hero, had been striving to protect the Chesapeake and its tributaries with a flotilla of gunboats built and manned at Baltimore, and had kept back the British fleet as long as he could. He came ashore with about four hundred of his seamen when he heard that the British had landed, and he ordered his barges to be blown up along the wooded banks of the Patuxent, whence he had been chased, to keep them from being taken by the British. When the British troops were resting at Upper Marlborough, Commodore Barney and his bluejackets were at the Woodyard, the home of Mr. and Mrs. Richard W. West. Mrs. West, one of the Lloyds of Wye House and Annapolis, was an elder sister of Mrs. Key. It was here that Commodore Barney offered to come to the aid of General Winder and his Militia, then on the way to Bladensburg. As soon as it was learned that the British army was proceeding from Upper Marlborough in the direction of Washington, General Smith ordered his District Militia forward, while Commodore Barney took a position along the Eastern Branch of the Potomac. And when word came that the fight was about to take place at Bladensburg, Barney and his men hastened to the scene: on the way they found the militiamen running toward Washington.

The courageous defense made by Joshua Barney and his men was a dramatic and inspiring story that made Francis Scott Key believe that America was "the home of the brave" – in spite of the derision of the militia for running in what many people facetiously dubbed "the Bladensburg races." In addition to his bluejackets the Commodore had charge of 78 marines from the Barracks. His entire force of officers and men totalled 583. Less than six hundred men against approximately 4,500 hardened British soldiers! The sailors had a few cannon; they fought also with muskets, handspikes, and cutlasses. Barney's horse was killed under him. The gallant Commodore himself was shot in the thigh by a musket-ball; but he remained in active command. In the confusion of the retreat of the militia, the ammunition wagons were swept away. The supply of powder and balls for cannon and muskets was nearly exhausted. Barney did not want to retreat; but he saw the futility of prolonging the fight. To stand their ground any longer would be futile butchery. So the Commodore ordered his men to save themselves.

Thus came to an end, after a couple of hours, the Battle of Bladensburg. As the brave flotilla men, blackened with powder and dirt and drenched with sweat and blood, fell back before the British onslaught, the wounded Commodore, weakened by the loss of blood from his bullet wound, and in intense pain, lay down to rest. Three of his officers tried to carry him away. But he bid them to leave him where he lay. They did not want to leave him to the mercy of the Enemy. Barney commanded two of the comrades to go; one he permitted to remain. The Commodore was taken prisoner but he was treated witth "the most marked attention, respect and politeness" at the British hospital at Bladensburg.

The casualties on the battlefield of Bladensburg were comparatively slight. Only a few score men were killed on each side. But several thousand members of the militia were missing: they had scattered to their homes. Barney's artillery fell into the hands of the British, and General Ross ordered it to be destroyed.

It was now the middle of the afternoon, and the sun was sizzling hot. General Ross thought that it was now best for his troops to rest. After the long march and the battle in the intense heat, a chance for refreshment in the shade was welcomed by the men. When the shadows lengthened several hours later, General Ross ordered his men to resume their march upon Washington. The British army now had an unobstructed path to the American Capital. Mr. Monroe and General Winder had hurried back to the Capital and had decided to flee for their lives.

All during the day the excitement in the President's Mansion had been intense. A dust-covered messenger rushed into the mansion to bid Mrs. Madison seek a safer place. Then another. He too had panic in his eye. But Dolly refused to go. The President had been in the saddle since 8 o'clock in the morning. She would not leave until she knew he was safe.

"Since sunrise," Dolly wrote to her sister while anxiously waiting for her husband, "I have been turning my spyglass in every direction. . . . Three o'clock — Will you believe it, my sister, we have had a battle, or a skirmish near Bladensburg, and here I am still within sound of the cannon. Mr. Madison comes not! May God protect us!"

In those last moments the Chief Executive's wife lived a lifetime "in an agony of fear lest he might have been taken prisoner." He finally arrived about three o'clock. Dolly's prayers were answered. She gathered together the silver, the

Declaration of Independence, and everything else she could handle, pressing the Cabinet papers into trunks and loading them on a carriage. On one of the walls of the mansion was Gilbert Stuart's oil painting of George Washington. The portrait hung so high that a step-ladder was required to reach it. It was screwed fast to the wall. The process of unscrewing it was found to be too tedious in such a perilous moment. So Mrs. Madison ordered Jean Sioussat, the French porter, to break the frame and take out the canvas. Sioussat was the last person to leave the mansion. He handed the key to the Russian Minister, who was hurrying off to Philadelphia.

The President and Mrs. Madison fled into Virginia.

About sundown General Ross and Admiral Cockburn were approaching Washington. Into the Capital they rode at the head of their troops like conquering heroes. It was about eight o'clock when Ross and Cockburn and several other officers came galloping into Capital Square. A shot was fired by some one from a house on the northeast corner of the Square. The bullet killed General Ross's horse. General Ross ordered his men to burn the house from which the shot was fired.

Admiral Cockburn rode through the streets looking for the office of the *National Intelligencer*, the organ of the Madison Administration; his "friend Gales" had given him "some hard rubs" and he wanted to "pay his respects." Next to the newspaper office lived two women who nearly went into hysterics when the Admiral ordered the office set on fire. They begged the Admiral not to do it, screaming that their home would catch fire and be destroyed too.

"Be quiet, ladies!" Cockburn said. "You'll be just as safe under my administration as under Mr. Madison!"

The troops now swarmed into the halls of the Capitol, prepared to carry out the request of the Governor General of Canada to retaliate for the burning of the Canadian Government buildings. Admiral Cockburn ascended the rostrum in the House chamber and took the Speaker's chair. Calling the mob together in mock session, he put the motion:

"All in favor of setting fire to this harbor of Yankee democracy, say Aye!"

The vote was unanimous in favor of the affirmative, and the order was given amid the lusty cheers and jeers of the soldiers. Furniture and books were thrown in huge piles and set on fire. Soon smoke was arising from the Capitol, and before long the stately building was in flames.

General Ross and Admiral Cockburn now marched with several hundred men to the President's Mansion. Breaking into the mansion they found plenty of good things to eat and drink. The table in the dining room had been laid for supper; the hastily prepared meal had been left when Mr. Madison and Dolly hurriedly took their departure. The soldiers found "a fine dessert set out on the sideboards" and Mr. Madison's champagne "in coolers." So the British officers ordered everything appetizing that could be found; and General Ross, standing at the head of the table, drank to the health of His Majesty King George III with the President's wine.

After the marauders had finished their dinner and ransacked all the rooms, they made ready to set fire to the mansion. When a messenger from the French Minister arrived on the scene with a request that a guard be supplied so that his house might not be pillaged, he found "General Ross in the act of piling up the furniture in the White House drawing room preparatory to setting it on fire." This too was soon ablaze. M. Serrurier, who lived nearby in John Tayloe's Octagon House, reported in a letter to Talleyrand that he had never beheld a scene "at once more terrible and more magnificent."

The fires lighted up the sky for many miles round about. For Francis Scott Key it was a weird and tragic night, after a sweltering and hectic day, as he gazed with his wife and children toward the illuminated eastern horizon. It was another visitation, he thought, sent down by the God of Wrath upon a wicked people. There were many who threw the blame on President Madison; others blamed the Secretary of War; others General Winder. One writer says: "Of the American generals whose colossal incapacities had brought disaster in the War of 1812, William Hull, Alexander Smyth, Dearborn, Wilkinson, none had equaled the blunders and sloth of Winder." But Key looked upon General Ross and Admiral Cockburn as instrumentalities of the Deity carrying out the Divine plan of retribution. On that terrifying night of August 24, 1814, there were put to the torch "the Capitol, the arsenal, the dock-yard, Treasury, War Office, President's palace, rope-walk, and the great bridge across the Potowmack, in the dock-yard a frigate nearly ready to be launched, and a sloop of war." The Americans themselves had set fire to the Navy Yard and Arsenal, resulting in the destruction of immense quantities of stores. General Ross seized more than 200 cannon, 500 barrels of powder, 100,000 pounds of musket-ball cartridges, and other ammunition.

To cap the climax a terrific thunder storm early the next day finished the work of the flames. It was a "tremendous hurricane." Key heard the voice of God in the howling of the tempest. And yet, with it all, he did not bear up as bravely under the humiliation as a godly man such as he might have done. He looked on the spectacle as a prodigious disgrace. So unnerved was he that for several days afterwards he "had neither time or mind to do anything."

The Nation was at the nadir of its existence. The President and the members of his Cabinet had fled. The Capital had been captured and overrun by the Enemy. The only public building saved from the torch was that occupied by the Patent Office and the Postoffice Department.

The seizure and burning of Washington had caused deep anxiety to Key's father and mother at Pipe Creek and to Taney and Anne and other relatives at Frederick. But the people of Georgetown were safe, temporarily, at least, from the torch.

The remnant of General Winder's forlorn forces, after burning the bridges over Rock Creek, retreated to the heights of Georgetown and were reënforced by some militia from Virginia. Nor did General Ross and Admiral Cockburn intend to take the risk of having their troops trapped in Washington and cut off from the fleet. They destroyed the Government buildings "with the least possible delay, so that the army might retire without loss of time." Having accomplished their task they ordered their troops to start back to the ships in the Patuxent. They went back by way of Bladensburg, where General Ross left his wounded soldiers, and Upper Marlborough.

Meanwhile Frank and Polly had been urged by Taney and Anne to take refuge at Frederick; but the poet lawyer had declined the invitation, for, since he had enlisted in the District of Columbia militia, he felt it would not be honorable to leave home while the surrounding country was threatened by the British marauders. And Polly Key was like Dolly Madison: she refused to leave home as long as her husband was exposed to danger.

So the Taneys and the old folks from Pipe Creek had a family conference to determine what they ought to do. Taney agreed to journey to Georgetown and make a personal appeal to Polly. They all thought it would be prudent to bring Polly and the children to Frederick to take refuge there or at the parental home at Pipe Creek until the danger was over. "For," as Taney pointed out, "if the attack was made, Key would be with the troops engaged in the defense. As it was impossible to foresee what would be the issue of the conflict, his family, by remaining in George Town, might be placed in great and useless peril."

When Taney arrived on the scene, the Capitol and the President's home were in ashes, and he heard that a British squadron was anchored off Alexandria. This squadron had sailed up the Potomac at the time Ross and Cockburn were making their invasion. The people of Alexandria, having seen the reflection from the fires in Washington but a few days before, were terrified and in humble submission they asked for terms of capitulation. They gave a ransom of a hundred thousand dollars worth of flour and tobacco in addition to ships and their cargoes in the harbor. A few days later the squadron moved down the Potomac and joined the main fleet under Cochrane, which was preparing to make an attack on Baltimore.

On the evening after the departure of the British squadron, a visitor called at the Key home on an important errand. It was Polly's brother-in-law, Richard W. West. He had come to relate about the unfortunate experience of his family physician, Dr. William Beanes of Upper Marlborough. For Dr. Beanes had been taken prisoner by the British! Mr. West explained that on the afternoon following the burning of Washington the old doctor was entertaining Dr. William Hill and Philip Weems in his garden with some punch. They were jubilant because Upper Marlborough was finally free of the British, who had passed through the town on the way back to their ships. As Dr. Beanes and his guests were removing their inhibitions with potent beverage, three stragglers who had dropped out of the ranks and were lagging behind the British army wandered into the garden. They saw Dr. Beanes and his guests enjoying themselves at the spring, intruded upon the party, and demanded something to drink. The old doctor, his inhibitions removed by this time, ordered the intruders out of his garden. They became insolent and threatening, whereupon he had them arrested for disorderly conduct and lodged in jail. One of the soldiers escaped and hurried to the British camp and reported to the officers what had happened. Admiral Cockburn sent a detachment of marines back to Upper Marlborough with orders to release the prisoners from jail and seize Dr. Beanes. The marines arrived about midnight, broke into his home, dragged him from his bed, and allowed him but a few minutes to remove his nightclothes, and put on some other clothing. The 65-year-old doctor was put on a rough-gaited horse and hurried off on a midnight ride of thirty-five miles toward Benedict. Some of the old doctor's friends visited the British Headquarters to plead for his release; but the commanding officers maintained that he deserved no clemency. The officers considered Dr. Beanes not as a prisoner of war, but as a noncombatant who had feigned friendship for the British when the army first appeared and then broke faith. He was closely guarded, and his friends were not allowed to see him.

Francis Scott Key listened to the details of the story with intense interest. He knew Dr. Beanes intimately. The doctor was one of the most popular men in Prince George's County, as well as one of the most successful. In addition to his professional work, he had made a success with his farms and grist mill; he had also been one of the founders of the Episcopal Church at Upper Marlborough. As Key pictured the old physician in chains, surrounded by the Enemy soldiers on the ship, he decided to go immediately in search of the fleet in order to intercede for his release.

The poet lawyer decided to confer first with President Madison on the subject. The President had returned on the afternoon of the 27th from his hiding-place in Virginia and had established a temporary home in Washington. The prim little man was nearly prostrate from fright. The President upon whom Key called wore powder on his hair, which was dressed full over the ears, tied behind and brought to a point above the forehead to cover some of his baldness. He wore a black dress coat; his breeches were short, with black silk stockings and buckles at the knee. Key explained the object of his mission: he wanted the sanction of the Government. The gentle little man gave Key permission to proceed as an official emissary under a flag of truce. Armstrong had not yet returned to Washington; indeed at the insistence of Monroe he was to be driven from the Cabinet. Monroe was acting as Secretary of War *ad interim* as well as Secretary of State. The President requested John Mason, the Commissary General of Prisoners, to authorize Key to visit the Headquarters of General Ross in company with John S. Skinner, General Mason's agent and flag officer.

General Mason wrote the following letter to General Ross:

Office Comm. Gen. Pris.
Wash. Sept. 2, 1814.

Sir:

Having understood from sources not to be doubted that a detachment of the army under your command on its retreat from Washington — seized and carried off from their houses several of our most respectable citizens in the vicinity of Marlbro', unarmed and entirely of non-combattant character — and that one of them, Dr. William Beanes — sixty five years of age taken from his bed, in the midst of his family and hurried off almost without clothes is yet retained — I have been instructed to enquire into the causes of this Departure from the known usages of civilized warfare—and to request the release of Dr. Beanes.

To this end John S. Skinner agent and Flag officer for this office and Francis S. Key Esqr. a citizen of the highest respectability have been authorized to wait upon you and to express to you the views and expectations of the Government.

It is hoped that the seizure and detention of the person of the aged and respectable Dr. Beanes have been unauthorized by you — and I confidently trust Sir that when you shall have been more acquainted with the facts in the case you will order the immediate restoration to his family of that gentleman. He is far advanced in life, infirm, and unaccustomed to privations from which he must now suffer severely.

I beg leave to assure you that the utmost attention has been and will be paid to your wounded officers and men left in our possession. It was directed the Flag officer to take any letters they may wish to convey to the British army—and on his return to take charge of such articles of Supplies &c. as it may be desired to send them.

I have the honor
to be Sir
J. MASON

Major General Robert Ross,
Commander of the British Army.

In addition to this letter directed to General Ross, Key also received a letter from the Commissary General of Prisoners, addressed to Mr. Skinner and himself. This was a confidential letter of instructions. It mentioned the attitude taken by the British in justification of the arrest of Dr. Beanes— "that he was hostilely engaged against them in violation of propriety, inasmuch as he was one of the citizens who met them under a flag on their first approach and was under engagement tacitly at least to refrain from acts hostile to them." The letter went on to say that there was no just reason for Dr. Beanes's detention because the hostile act – merely that of picking up some stragglers of the British army – "was performed when he was absolved from any engagement he might have been before under expressed or understood, since at that time the British army had withdrawn and given up the country." Skinner and Key were authorized to endeavor "by all proper means" to get Dr. Beanes released as a noncombatant. But if the British officers refused to release him as a noncombatant, then Skinner and Key were instructed as a last resort to give a receipt for the doctor in behalf of the United States Government together with a statement of the facts of the case. This precaution was to be taken because of the fact that the bounty law had been accepted by the warring countries: no persons were to be captured or imprisoned by either country other than those designated as prisoners of war by the provisions of the Cartel; and the bounty was intended only for prisoners recognized according to the usage of war. Noncombatants captured at sea with real prisoners of war, for example, had always been struck off the bounty list before the bounties were paid. "It is impossible," General Mason's instructions concluded, "that the Government can yield a point of so much National importance involved in this case, as to admit that he [Dr. Beanes] is an exchangeable prisoner of War – since it would at once induce the Enemy to seize and carry off every unarmed citizen of whatever age they may have in their power."

General Mason also gave to Key a brief personal letter addressed to Mr. Skinner, which directed him to embark with Key at Baltimore and proceed down the Chesapeake Bay in search of the British Army. "Instructions," said General Mason, "are made out to you jointly which are in the hands of Mr. Key. They are shorter than they might have been, but you are as I have told Mr. Key so well possessed of all the general arrangements on our side and pleas on the side of the Enemy – it is unnecessary to be longer. I pray your utmost zeal and earnestness in endeavoring to withdraw the worthy Dr. Beanes."

Polly agreed to go to Frederick with Taney. They took the six children – Elizabeth, now nearly eleven; Maria, nine; Francis, eight; John Ross, five; Anna, three; and Edward, who was less than a year old.

That night the poet lawyer penned a farewell to his mother, telling her he was ready to start out on his mission to the British fleet. Once more he uttered his belief that the calamities of the Nation had been brought upon the people through their own folly and wickedness, and the American people wandered so far from the path of righteousness that their chastisement from the Divine Ruler, so he told his mother, was much lighter than they deserved. In his letter to his mother, dated September 2, 1814, he said:

Key to His Mother

My Dr Mother. —

You have made allowances, I hope, for our confusion & anxiety here, & have therefore excused my not writing sooner. Indeed for two or three days after our disgrace I had neither time or mind to do anything.— And since then I have been much engaged.—I had however a promise from Mr. Munro that he would write to Taney often & soon, so that you might know I was well.— You have since no doubt heard how mercifully we have all been spared here, the Enemy not even entering our Town, which I am sure they would have done, had they not gone off with such unnecessary precipitation — They have to-day left Alexandria, & I trust we shall see no more of them.—I hope we shall be grateful to God for this deliverance, & remember how much more light our chastisement has been than we expected or deserved.—

I am going in the morning to Balt^{e}. to proceed in a flag-vessel to Genl Ross. Old Dr Beanes of Marlbro' is taken prisoner by the Enemy, who threaten to carry him off—Some of his friends have urged me to apply for a flag & go & try to procure his release. I hope to return in about 8 or 10 days, though it is uncertain, as I do not know where to find the fleet.—As soon as I get back I hope I shall be able to set out for Fred^{k}.

The children will be delighted to see their mother.— Give my love to them & to Papa.—

God bless you my Dr Mother

Ever yr most affec^{e} Son

F. S. KEY

Early the next morning the poet lawyer rode out of Georgetown with the letter to General Ross and the confidential instructions from the Commissary General of Prisoners.

Arriving in Baltimore on the morning of September 4th, Key called on Skinner and handed him the instructions. Like Key, Skinner was a native of Maryland and a son of a Revolutionary veteran. Skinner was the younger of the two: Key was 35, Skinner only 26. Like Key, too, Skinner had taken up the study of law in Annapolis; but when war was declared he gave up his practice to become the Government's agent for the foreign mails and the exchange of prisoners. He was a daring young man, patriotic, energetic; but he did not possess the polished, gracious manner of the poet lawyer who was to accompany him in quest of the British fleet.

The vessel on which Key and Skinner embarked was a cartel ship used for communicating with the Enemy and flying the white flag of peace. Just as they were setting sail down the Patapsco River on September 5th, Skinner acknowledged the letter of instructions from the Commissary General by saying that he and Key were on their way. Skinner believed, however, that to obtain the release of Dr. Beanes by giving a receipt was, under the circumstances, as much as could be expected. "Making allowance for the opinion and feelings of an Enemy," said Skinner, "they will no doubt consider him as having waived all 'benefit of exception' from the general rule of combatant persons. The best however shall be done with the most ardent desire to accomplish your views and wishes."

For two days the little ship sailed down the Chesapeake as the two young lawyers scanned the horizon for the British fleet. Finally on September 7th the British sails came into view near the mouth of the Potomac. Key and Skinner were taken on board the *Tonnant*, Vice Admiral Cochrane's eighty-gun flagship. After a few exchanges of civilities, Francis Scott Key mentioned the purpose of their visit and presented the letter from the American Commissary General of Prisoners to General Ross. Rear Admiral Cockburn and Vice Admiral Cochrane also heard the plea. The situation did not look encouraging. Cockburn spoke of Dr. Beanes with harsh words, exclaimed that the old man deserved no consideration from the British, that they saw no reason for his release, and that they had decided to take him to Halifax for punishment. The hearts of Key and Skinner sank within them as they heard the denunciation. Skinner handed over a package of letters written by British officers who had been wounded during the battle at Bladensburg: the letters were directed to certain friends in the British fleet and spoke in complimentary terms of the medical attention and kind treatment given to the wounded Britons by Dr. Beanes. It was at this point that Key made his plea to the British commanders. He said that Dr. Beanes was a scholar and a gentleman of unimpeachable character and was esteemed most highly by the people of Maryland. He said he felt sure that when Dr. Beanes ordered the arrest of the soldiers after the main body of the British Army had passed through Upper Marlborough, he did not have the slightest idea that he was violating any obligation or faith. General Ross was impressed with the earnestness of the young attorneys. Seemingly less vindictive than the two Admirals, he said that while it was probably true that Dr. Beanes deserved punishment, yet the letters from the British soldiers wounded at Bladensburg showed that the doctor had been kind and generous to them; and as far as he was concerned he was willing to let him go. At length Cockburn and Cochrane gave their approval; and General Ross rendered the decision in reply to General Mason:

H. M. S. Tonnant

Sept. 7, 1814.

Sir:

Dr. Beanes having acted hostilely towards certain soldiers of the British army under my command, by making them prisoners when proceeding to join the army, & having attempted to justify his conduct when I spoke to him on the subject, I conceived myself authorized & called upon to cause his being detained as a prisoner. Mr. Skinner to whom I have imparted the circumstances will detail them more fully.

The friendly treatment, however, experienced by the wounded officers & men of the British army left at Bladensburg, enables me to meet your wishes regarding that gentleman; I shall accordingly give directions for his being released, not from an opinion of his not being justifiably detained, nor from any favorable sentiment of his merit, as far as the cause of his detention is to be considered, but purely in proof of the obligation which I feel for the attention with which the wounded have been treated.

I have the honor to be
Sir
Your Most Obedient
Humble servant

ROB. ROSS Major Genl.

Key and Skinner were given permission to see Dr. Beanes at once. They found him imprisoned in the prow of the ship, surrounded by a crowd of soldiers and sailors. Imagine the joy of the old man when he caught sight of the two Marylanders who had come to rescue him! He told them of his harrowing experiences and the rough way he had been handled by the soldiers; said he had been treated not as a prisoner of war — for he was not a combatant — but as a dangerous criminal; and that the commanding officers had ignored him completely. And, in addition, wild stories had been circulated on the ship that he had inflicted grievous injuries upon British soldiers. As a result he had a lurking dread that some of the men might grab him at any time and throw him overboard. And then unexpectedly the glorious news that he was to be released!

But the British officers were not ready to release him yet. They were just getting ready to attack Baltimore — the "hornets' nest" which had equipped and sent to sea on President Madison's request more privateers than any other city in America. They told Key and Skinner that they would not allow any one to leave the fleet until the attack was over. However, the two lawyers were treated with courtesy by the British officers: they were assured that they would be made as comfortable as possible during the time they were detained with the fleet. On the day they came on board the *Tonnant* they were given an invitation to dine at Vice Admiral Cochrane's table; but Cochrane said that he was unable to accommodate them any longer on his flagship because it was already crowded with officers. However, he told them that they would be taken care of by his son, Sir Thomas Cochrane, who commanded the frigate *Surprize*. So the Marylanders were transferred to the smaller vessel, on which they were entertained by young Sir Thomas until the Royal fleet arrived at the mouth of the Patapsco. The Vice Admiral decided now to shift his flag to the *Surprize*: the reason for this change was that he believed he could move further up the Patapsco in the smaller ship and thus be enabled to superintend personally the bombardment of Fort McHenry. Accordingly, on Saturday, September 10th, before starting up the Patapsco, Cochrane moved Key and Skinner again, this time from the *Surprize* to their own cartel ship, and allowed them to take Dr. Beanes with them. But to prevent them from returning to Baltimore until after the attack he placed them under a guard of marines.

In the meantime, with the disaster at Bladensburg and the burning of Washington fresh in everybody's mind, Brigadier General John Stricker and Commodore Barney had asked a widow, Mary Young Pickersgill, to make a flag for Fort McHenry, her mother having made flags during the Revolutionary War. She was related to both Stricker and Barney. Mrs. Pickersgill went to work with a will. She was given help by her little 14-year-old daughter Caroline. First they had to cut pieces of red and white and blue from four hundred yards of bunting. It was a mammoth flag which the officers asked the woman to make — 29 feet from top to bottom and 36 feet in width. "The flag being so very large," Caroline recalled when she was 75 years old, "my mother was obliged to obtain permission from the proprietor of 'Claggett's Brewery,' which was in our neighborhood, to spread it out in their malt-house, and I remember seeing my mother down on the floor placing the stars.... The flag I think contained four hundred yards of bunting, and my mother worked many nights until 12 o'clock to complete it in a given time." Night after night through the hot weather the widow and her daughter Caroline crawled over the big flag, and stitched the colored pieces together. Just a widow and her little daughter crawling at night on the floor of a brewery — but helping to write an anthem destined to be enshrined forever in the hearts of the American people! And when it was finished, this enormous ensign of freedom had fifteen stripes of alternate red and white; and a field of blue, with fifteen white stars. This was the National banner, intended to inspire the patriotism and the courage of the people. Each of the stars measured two feet from point to point: it was a flag that could be identified for many miles around. And when it was accepted it was hoisted on a tall staff that stood behind the guns of Fort McHenry.

On Sunday morning, the cannon on the Court House green in Baltimore announced that the British fleet was coming. Major-General Samuel Smith, 62-year-old veteran of the Revolution who was commander-in-chief of the forces around Baltimore, had more than 10,000 men under his command. That afternoon, about 3,000 infantry and several hundred cavalry and artillery marched out of Baltimore under Brigadier-General John Stricker to meet the invaders.

On Monday morning, September 12th, the British soldiers were aroused from their sleep before daybreak; the transports began to lower their boats; and about sunrise the veterans were landing on the low shores inside North Point on the east side of the Patapsco about ten miles from Fort McHenry and within fourteen miles of Baltimore. The commanding officers selected this place for landing because they were afraid of shallow water as well as obstructions that might have been thrown into the stream.

General Stricker sent out an advance guard when he heard that the British troops were landing. It was early in the morning when the opening skirmish came. Ross and Cockburn and several other officers had stopped at a farm house for some breakfast. The farmer asked whether they intended to come back in time for supper.

"No!" said General Ross, "I'll eat supper tonight in Baltimore — or in Hell!"

Hearing the sound of musketry the officers dashed to the door. General Ross mounted his white charger, and turning to Cockburn shouted he would bring up a column of men; but just as he wheeled his horse a shot rang out. General Ross fell with a bullet in his arm and chest. He was carried back toward the river. An officer galloped madly calling for a surgeon. But before Ross reached the shore he was dead. The loss of the gallant Sir Robert affected the morale of the British troops and "turned the tide of the war."

The battle began early in the afternoon. About 4,000 British troops were ordered to advance. Stricker was greatly handicapped. His force is supposed to have numbered 3,185; but the members of one of his regiments were held in reserve, much to their delight; and quite a few of the militiamen disappeared; so that the actual fighting force was reduced to about 1,600; most of these had never been under fire; some had run in the "Bladensburg races." Finally, the defenders wavered and began to fall back. In about an hour and a half the battle was over. As at Bladensburg the losses were small. On the British side 39 were killed and a few hundred wounded; of Stricker's forces only 24 were killed, 139 wounded, and 50 captured.

The little cartel ship, on which Key and Skinner were detained by the guard of marines, was anchored nearby. Admiral Cochrane felt confident that he would force the garrison at Fort McHenry to surrender within a few hours. He ordered the cartel ship to be placed near the bombing vessels so that Key and Skinner could witness the artillery duel.

But Fort McHenry was strongly built. Its walls, made of brick set in oyster-shell mortar, were fourteen feet high and thirty-five feet thick. It was garrisoned by about a thousand men. The commander of the fort was George Armistead, a native of Virginia, aged 34, now a Lieutenant-Colonel of the United States Artillery. Colonel Armistead's forces consisted of his own company of artillery, two companies of sea fencibles, two companies of volunteer artillery from Baltimore, an artillery company captained by Judge Joseph Hopper Nicholson of Baltimore, a detachment of Commodore Joshua Barney's flotilla men, a detachment of United States troops, and about 600 of General Winder's militiamen—about a thousand, in all.

Observing that their shells reached the fort, the Enemy kept up an incessant bombardment. Colonel Armistead opened fire from his largest cannon, 42-pounders, but the shells all fell short of the Enemy's vessels. Exposed to "a constant and tremendous shower of shells" without being able to do any injury to the attacking ships was, in Armistead's own words, "a most distressing circumstance." All that he could do was to reserve his fire, except an occasional shot to let the Enemy know that the garrison had not surrendered.

About two o'clock in the afternoon one of the Enemy's bombs dropped in the southwest bastion, occupied by the artillery company captained by Frank Key's brother-in-law, Judge Nicholson. The bomb exploded; dismounted one of the cannon; killed Lieutenant Levi Claggett of Captain Nicholson's company; and wounded several other men. The volunteers were frightened by the explosion; but they pulled themselves together; carried off the wounded men; and remounted the gun.

All day long Key and Skinner and the old Upper Marlborough doctor paced the deck of their cartel ship several miles away. With the aid of their field glasses, they could see the flag of Stars and Stripes that had been made by Mrs. Pickersgill. It was a manifestation that the Americans were still holding the fort. As it floated in the breeze a British shell pierced it and tore out one of the white stars from the field of blue. Toward evening a breeze unfurled the folds of the giant banner as though in a defiant salute to the departing day. The three Marylanders on the cartel ship were advised by their British guards to "look well at the flag" before night came on, because they would not see it waving over the fort in the morning. Indeed, all of the British officers and men were confident that it was only a matter of time before the fort would surrender and Baltimore would be taken. Francis Scott Key had heard Admiral Cockburn boast that the capture of Baltimore would be "only a matter of a few hours." And, as a matter of fact, His Majesty's forces were of such overwhelming superiority that the Admiral's boast seemed by no means extravagant. Sir George Prevost, Governor-General of Canada, was so confident of Baltimore's surrender that he proposed that a public jubilee planned at Montreal to celebrate the fall of Washington be deferred for a few days so that they could celebrate the fall of Baltimore at the same time. But as twilight fell Key saw through his field glasses that the flag was still waving defiantly over the fort.

Night came on. And through the long hours the steady bombardment continued. The missiles of terror — solid cannon balls and 200-pound bombs — went plunging through the sky. Would the garrison be able to endure this terrible bombardment? Key, with the picture of looted Washington still in his mind, dreaded to think of the fate of Baltimore. Occasionally the red glare of the rockets gave the poet lawyer a glimpse of the flag waving over Fort McHenry.

Shortly after midnight, when it was learned that the army had failed to reach Baltimore by land and had given up its expedition, Admiral Cochrane determined to close in on the front again. He ordered sixteen frigates and a group of bomb-ketches and barges to proceed toward the fort. A force of men, numbering about 1,250, were picked to climb the ramparts. They were equipped with scaling ladders. The crisis had now come. In the midst of a tremendous fire — sometimes several bombs would burst at once in the air — the British attempted a surprise attack. Believing that they could steal by the fort in the blackness of the night without being seen, they started up the main branch (the north channel) of the Patapsco in five barges and the rocket-ship. The vessels proceeded a short distance, when they were discovered by a patrol who heard the creaking of their oars. The patrol set fire to a haystack in order to give an alarm to the batteries on the north side of the main branch of the river. The illumination had the effect intended; it exposed the moving ships to the view of the seventy-five men entrenched at the Six-Gun Battery commanded by Lieutenant John A. Webster from the flotilla, and the sailors commanded by Lieutenant Newcomb of the Navy at Fort Covington. Had it not been for these small fortifications the midnight expedition of the British would probably have been successful and Francis Scott Key would not have written the National Anthem. Lieutenant Webster's battery was entirely exposed save for a dirt breastwork about four feet in height. His magazine for ammunition was nothing but a hole in the ground about twenty yards to the rear. He had his cannon loaded with 18-pound balls and grape shot ready for any emergency. And then a storm came up and the rain fell in torrents. For a while Webster lay in a blanket exhausted. "About 12 midnight," he recalled years afterwards, "I could distinctly hear a splashing in the water; the attention of all hands was aroused; we were sure it was the sound of barges and their oars. Very soon after we could discern a small glimmering light at different places. I was sure it must be the matches on board the barges, which at that time did not appear to be more than from two to three hundred yards off. Some of the lights were above me next to Fort Covington. As rapidly as possible, I mounted the cannon with my breast over the aprons of guns, and examined the priming, as it was then raining fast. All being right, I trained the guns to suit my own views before firing. When I opened on them, my fire caused the boats to cease rowing. A rapid firing followed from the barges as well as ourselves. I could distinctly hear the balls from our guns strike the boat. My men stated to me they could hear the shrieking of the men. Soon after I commenced, Fort Covington opened on them, although they had not got quite up to it. During the firing of the Enemy I could distinctly see the barges of the Enemy by the explosion of the cannon, which was a great guide to me to fire with more precision than I could otherwise have done. The Enemy had a large schooner with them, which they had propelled up by sweeps. This had an 18-pounder on board, and should have done much execution, but not a man was injured by the Enemy; they fired mostly too high and in the bank in front of my cannon." The cannonade from the shore crippled some of the Enemy's vessels, and the invaders turned and retreated to a safe distance.

By this time old Dr. Beanes was exhausted. He left the deck and retired below for some sleep. Skinner too went down to rest for a while. But Francis Scott Key continued his vigil throughout the night. Often he saw the blaze from the British guns and then a moment later heard the explosion of the bomb. The sky was filled with flame and smoke. He could not sleep until the mighty question of victory or defeat was answered by the Court of Eternal Destiny.

The British had stopped firing for fear that they might hit their own boats attempting to pass the fort. But before long the bombardment was renewed. Throughout the remaining hours of darkness Key watched "in painful suspense" on the deck of his little vessel, and waited for the first gray streaks of dawn. About three o'clock in the morning the British barges and rocket-ship retreated with rockets firing from them.

It was a long and spectacular battle. The firing continued until daylight. In the first gray beam of dawn Key turned his field glasses toward the fort. Over the harbor of Baltimore hung the morning mist and the smoke of battle. Was there any sign of the Stars and Stripes above the ramparts? Dr. Beanes, so the story goes, had been hauled off from his bedroom in Upper Marlborough with such precipitation that he encountered the British commanders without his spectacles and wig; and since his vision was none too good he kept asking Key what the field glasses revealed.

"Can you see –" he kept asking nervously, – "the flag?"

Suddenly there was a rift in the clouds. The soul of the poet surged with emotion as he saw that the flag was still there!

The fleeting glimpse told the story. The gallant defenders of Fort McHenry, of the Six-Gun Battery, and of Fort Covington had beaten off the invaders. Dr. Beanes and Skinner were jubilant; but an unusually radiant smile lighted the face of the poet lawyer. In the thrill of exultation at sunrise came the inspiration for a song. Had not his prayers been answered? Had not the new day brought a new day of freedom?

Turning his field glasses in the direction of North Point

as the mists began to clear away, Key was able to discern a hurried movement on the shore. Men were getting into boats; the boats were moving toward the transports. This was proof that the army and the navy of George III had been repulsed!

Key was now convinced that there had come a change of feeling on the part of Jehovah, the God of Battles. The Enemy were retreating. The siege was over. Baltimore was saved. God had been appeased. Might not the Nation, after all, be saved from destruction? In the joy of the moment he pulled a letter out of his pocket and on the back of it he jotted down a rhyme that poured from his soul in a song of thanksgiving.

Key and Skinner and the frightened old doctor were soon released from guard. Even while Key was meditating over his anthem, the marines were ordered off the cartel ship. By nine o'clock His Majesty's fleet with the Invincibles started down the Patapsco.

The cartel ship started back to Baltimore. On the way back Key finished the rough draft of his poem. That afternoon of the glorious 14th of September he went to a tavern and asked for a room: it was probably the Fountain Inn, a popular place for travelers, where George Washington lodged on his way to Congress in 1775, on the way to Yorktown in 1781, and before his inauguration as President in 1789.

That night at the inn Francis Scott Key was again alone with his God. During these quiet hours he penned the final text of his anthem of patriotism.

The poem begins with a question:

O say can you see by the dawn's early light
What so proudly we hail'd at the twilight's last gleaming,
Whose broad stripes & bright stars through the perilous fight
O'er the ramparts we watch'd, were so gallantly streaming?
And the rocket's red glare, the bombs bursting in air,
Gave proof through the night that our flag was still there,
O say does that star-spangled banner yet wave
O'er the land of the free & the home of the brave?

Then the mists begin to lift, and the poet lawyer exults as he catches a glimpse of the ensign of the Republic:

On the shore dimly seen through the mists of the deep,
Where the foe's haughty host in dread silence reposes,
What is that which the breeze, o'er the towering steep,
As it fitfully blows, half conceals, half discloses?
Now it catches the gleam of the morning's first beam,
In full glory reflected now shines in the stream,
'Tis the star-spangled banner — O long may it wave
O'er the land of the free & the home of the brave!

The third stanza asks where the invaders are who boasted they could take the country and lay it in ruins:

And where is that band who so vauntingly swore,
That the havoc of war & the battle's confusion
A home & a country should leave us no more?
Their blood has wash'd out their foul footsteps pollution.

No refuge could save the hireling & slave
From the terror of flight or the gloom of the grave,
And the star-spangled banner in triumph doth wave
O'er the land of the free & the home of the brave.

In the last stanza he gives all the credit for the repulse of the British invaders to the Supreme Being who makes, preserves, and punishes the Nations. He concludes by originating the motto of the American Government:

O thus be it ever when freemen shall stand
Between their lov'd home & the war's desolation!
Blest with vict'ry and peace may the heav'n-rescued land
Praise the power that hath made & preserved us a nation!
Then conquer we must, when our cause it is just,
And this be our motto—"In God is our trust,"
And the star-spangled banner in triumph shall wave
O'er the land of the free & the home of the brave.

After his night's sleep at the tavern, Key called on the following morning, September 15th, upon his brother-in-law, Judge Nicholson, who had just returned from his post at Fort McHenry, and showed him the four stanzas he had written about the repulse of the British. Judge Nicholson was pleased with the song and thought that it would help to inspire the people's patriotism. The tune to which it was to be played or sung was that of *The Anacreon in Heaven*. Certainly Key and Nicholson were both familiar with this tune, which had become a popular one in America. It had been composed by John Stafford Smith for the Anacreontic Society of London,

England; with words by Ralph Tomlinson, each stanza ending with a call to the Sons of Anacreon to "intwine the myrtle of Venus with Bacchus's vine." But it had also been sung in the United States to other words. It had been adopted by Robert T. Paine as the tune for his poem, *Adams and Liberty,* written for the Massachusetts Charitable Fire Society in 1798, and by Alexander H. Everett for an ode sung at a festival in Boston in 1813. It was a very sprightly tune.

Judge Nicholson was so delighted with the song that he wanted it published at once. He took it to the printing shop of Captain Benjamin Edes; but the shop was closed, as the captain had not yet returned from the front. Nicholson then went to the office of the *Baltimore American.* This newspaper had suspended publication for some days, as most of the printers had marched away with the volunteers to meet the Enemy. At the *American* office, however, the judge found an apprentice boy about fourteen years old named Samuel Sands, who was taking care of the plant in the absence of the publishers. The judge thought that the song ought to be printed without delay; so he asked the boy to start upon it. "When it was brought up to the printing office," Mr. Sands recalled years afterwards, "my impression is, and ever has been, that I was the only one of those belonging to the establishment who was on hand, and that it was put in type and what the printers call 'galley proofs' were struck off previous to the renewal of the publication of this paper, and it may be and probably was the case that from one of these proof slips handbills were printed and circulated through the city." Sands is thought to have been the person who first set the text of Key's poem in type, for it was only a few days after the bombardment of Fort McHenry that the song was published in broadsides. Key's name did not appear on them.

The first appearance of the National Anthem in a newspaper was in the *Baltimore Patriot* on September 20th, the first issue of the paper after its suspension during the days of feverish anxiety. This was still some time before the song was known as "The Star-Spangled Banner." It was titled "Defence of Fort McHenry." The editor praised it as a "beautiful and animating effusion" and prophesied that it was destined "long to outlast the occasion and outlive the impulse which produced it." But Key's name still did not appear on it. The editor explained, however, that the song had been written by a gentleman who had left Baltimore under a flag of truce to visit the British fleet to seek the release of a friend who had been captured at Upper Marlborough. On the following day the anthem was published in the *Baltimore American.* Thomas Carr, who kept a music establishment in Baltimore in 1814 and was the organist at St. Paul's Episcopal Church, set the anthem to music for the first time and published the song with the notation, "adop^{d}. and arr^{d}. by T. C." And before long it was sung from lusty throats in the taverns, on the streets, and in the camps.

When Key returned home he wrote to Randolph of his thrilling adventure on the mission to save Dr. Beanes. This letter is interesting because it shows that the poet lawyer had not altered his opinion that the War Hawks were unjustified in urging America into the war with Great Britain. True, he appreciated the bravery of the militia at North Point and of the garrison at Fort McHenry and at the Six-Gun Battery and at Fort Covington, and rejoiced over the retreat of the invaders; but the whole war was a "lump of wickedness" nevertheless. In his letter to Randolph he said:

> . . . . I have since then spent eleven days in the British Fleet. I went with a flag to endeavor to save poor old Dr. Beanes a voyage to Halifax, in which we fortunately succeeded. They detained us until after their attack on Baltimore, and you may imagine what a state of anxiety I endured. Sometimes when I remembered it was there the declaration of this abominable war was received with public rejoicings, I could not feel a hope that they would escape, and again when I thought of the many faithful whose piety lessens that lump of wickedness I could hardly feel a fear.
>
> To make my feelings still more acute, the Admiral had intimated his fears that the town must be burned, and I was sure that if taken it would have been given up to plunder. I have reason to believe that such a promise was given to their soldiers. It was filled with women and children. I hope I shall never cease to feel the warmest gratitude when I think of this most merciful deliverance. It seems to have given me a higher idea of the "forbearance, long suffering and tender mercy" of God, than I had ever before conceived.
>
> Never was a man more disappointed in his expectations than I have been as to the character of British officers. With some exceptions, they appeared to be illiberal, ignorant and vulgar, and seemed filled with a spirit of malignity against everything American. Perhaps, however, I saw them in unfavourable circumstances.

Key's trip down the Patapsco, even though it had been made under a flag of truce, had given deep concern to his wife, to his father and mother, and to the Taneys. So when he arrived in Frederick after his hazardous experience, there were many handclasps and kisses and shouts of joy.

The poet lawyer was pleased with the success of his trip. But he had a particularly strange feeling of pride in the song he had written. He carried a printed copy of it in his pocket, and he lost no time in showing it to Taney and Anne. They were pleased with it too.

"How did you manage to write it under such circumstances?" Taney asked.

Frank then explained the story of its composition.

And then the story was repeated to Polly and the children and to the old folks at Pipe Creek.

Many years afterwards, Chief Justice Taney declared that "The Star-Spangled Banner" revealed his brother-in-law's "genius and taste as a poet" and the "warm spirit of patriotism which breathes in the song."

CHAPTER XIII

Soldier of the Cross

HUMAN BEINGS may be divided into three classes, according to the method by which they study themselves and find their places in the Universe: religious, philosophic, and scientific. Francis Scott Key's heritage, his early home training, his education, his nurture in the strict orthodoxy of the day — all operated to make him a religious man. On one occasion, when he was at the Montgomery County Court House on March 4, 1807, he wrote to his mother:

> I trust in Heaven I may always feel it, as I now do, my strongest and most delightful inducement to walk in a path where you may see me with pride and pleasure. I would rather see you satisfied and hear you say with joy "this is my son" than receive the applause of the whole world. May I never be so wretched as to fail in making this return for your anxiety.

Moreover, to Key the invisible was quite as real as the visible. Others might try to explain the mysteries of the Universe; but certainly not he.

And it was the unseen that he feared. When any unfavorable events came to pass, he cringed in terror because of what he regarded as a manifestation of Divine disapproval. In Key's eyes God was not a benevolent Spirit, but an irascible

Sovereign, a mighty anthropomorphic Being, whose chief duty was to reward and chastise. God sent the rain. God brought the harvest. God gave the victory. God ordered the defeat. When war came to an end, the wrath of God had been appeased. Such was Key's feeling early in 1815, when he heard that a treaty of peace had been signed at Ghent on Christmas Eve between the United States and Great Britain. The people of these countries had grown weary of the war. Nothing had been gained by the British in America; indeed, many of the most sensible people of England shook their heads when they heard of the burning of Washington. Lord Grenville in a speech in Parliament deplored the fact that the British forces had destroyed buildings unconnected with military purposes; and in the House of Commons Mr. Whitehead condemned the warfare which Sir Alexander Cochrane was waging against noncombatants on the American coast, and called on the Ministers to explain whether England was fighting America on the question of new boundaries, impressment, or maritime rights. It is true that the Treaty of Ghent did not contain anything about the protection of commerce of neutral Nations; anything about the impressment of American sailors; or anything about the issue that plunged the two Nations into war. But after several years of calamity and disgrace, the tidings of peace, reaching Washington after General Jackson's victory at New Orleans, brought great rejoicing in America. Few people stopped to inquire whether the terms of the compact were good or bad. Federalists and Republicans alike were exultant because the war was over. Francis Scott Key saw in the dawn of peace a rainbow of promise — an evidence that the enraged Jehovah had finally been pacified and had bestowed the blessings of peace as a healing gift to the afflicted Nation.

During the war Key had fallen as a victim of worry and despair. He had been alarmed and depressed by John Randolph and other gloomy Cassandras who predicted the downfall of the Republic. But he was born anew. Never again would he question the dispensations of Providence. From now on his faith in God was to be invincible — a faith that all things are ordered according to a Divine plan. This applied to sickness as well as health, defeat as well as victory, sorrow as well as joy.

To Francis Scott Key the coming of peace was the dawn of a brighter day. Already his law practice was returning. He had found the road to success, as it often happens, just as he was on the verge of giving up. In the early part of 1815 — just about the time that the Treaty of Ghent was before the Senate for final ratification — Key was appearing before the Supreme Court as one of the counsel in a group of four cases that had been brought to test whether an equitable interest in real estate was subject to attachment under the law of Maryland. The cases were argued in the home of Elias B. Caldwell, clerk of the Supreme Court; for after the British had reduced the Capitol to bare walls and ashes, Mr. Caldwell offered his home to the Justices as a meeting place for the Court until the Capitol was rebuilt. Associated with Key in the attachment cases was William Pinkney, who had served as Madison's Attorney General. Mr. Pinkney, now fifty-one years old, was the leader of the Maryland Bar. The lawyers opposing them were Philip Barton Key and General Walter Jones. The younger Key and Mr. Pinkney won the cases: their view that an equitable interest in land could be attached was sustained.

This was the last time that Frank was to meet his Uncle Philip before the Supreme Court. For the master of Woodley was taken suddenly ill soon afterwards, and he died on July 28, 1815, at the age of fifty-eight. It was a great blow to the nephew, for Uncle Philip had been like a father to him both in Annapolis and in Georgetown; had helped him to get a start on the highway to success.

And yet, when Uncle Philip died, Frank urged his relatives not to grieve, but to take cheer from the thought that Heaven would be an unending life of bliss. He wrote the following lines to show his admiration for his uncle:

Philip Barton Key

If nature's richest gifts could ever,
If genius, wit, and eloquence, could charm,
If grief of sorrowing friends, or anguish wild
That wrings the widow's and the orphan's heart,
Could soothe stern death, and stay th' uplifted stroke,
Long had this vision of his wrath been spared.
Mourning survivors! let all care give place
To that great care that most demands your thoughts:
The care that brings the troubled soul to Christ;
Fix there your hopes. There is, beyond the grave,
A life of bliss where death shall never more
Part you from joys that know no bound or end.

Randolph asked Key if he was still thinking of editing a magazine. "What are you going to do—have you given up the editorial scheme? Do you really think that the mere restoration of peace has anticipated all your schemes to be of service to this poor country? Are the present men and measures riveted upon the Nation, at least for our lifetime?"

At this very time Randolph's friends were urging him to run again for Congress. But he was reluctant to go back into the dismal whirpool of politics—the vortex between "vexed Scylla and the hoarse Calabrian shore." If the voters of his District, whom he had served for fourteen years, didn't know him in 1813, why should they know him any better in 1815? Then too, as he had told Key, he felt like "a worn-out horse in a mail coach." But his friends prevailed upon him; and he announced his candidacy again for a seat in the National House; and after a brief campaign, he was triumphantly elected.

But even his victory at the polls failed to dispel the dark clouds of despair. In a letter dated April 25, 1815, the unhappy man told Key of his continued pessimism. "You will have heard," he said, "of my re-election; an event which has given me no pleasure, except so far as it has been gratifying to my friends.... I cannot force myself to think on the subject of my public affairs. I am engrossed by reflections of a very different, and far more important nature. I am 'a stricken deer,' and feel disposed of 'leave the hind.' The hand of calamity has pressed sorely upon me; I do not repine at it."

Key congratulated Randolph on his political victory. But at the same time the poet lawyer expressed the hope that in time of triumph the victor would exhibit humility, a most noble but difficult virtue. "Excuse me," said Key apologetically, "for thinking of reminding you of this. It springs from a heart, among whose warmest wishes it is, that you should exhibit every grace and dignity of which this poor frail nature of ours is capable."

The Congressman-elect was quick to reply that he most certainly did not exult in "unbecoming triumph" over his election. "I do assure you with the utmost sincerity that, so far as I am personally concerned, I cannot but regret the partiality of my friends, who insisted on holding me up on this occasion." Then it was that Mr. Randolph explained that he was engrossed with thoughts of a far different character: he was looking forward with "anticipations that forbid any idle expression of exultation." The truth of the matter was that his mind was filled with thoughts about salvation — "peace in this world, as well as in the world to come."

Key was delighted. Was it possible that the gloomy Virginian, so long a skeptic, would accept the teachings of the Gospels? The pious Georgetown lawyer knew Randolph's weaknesses, his high temper, his terrible vindictiveness, his scathing sarcasm; and yet there was something about the man that he admired as well as pitied. From now on he sought to bring peace to the distracted mind of the erratic man whose temper was more violent than Andrew Jackson's and who had dared the wrath of Jefferson and Madison and Clay and Calhoun and Webster.

"I cannot describe to you," said Key in a letter of felicitations on May 11, 1815, "the gratification your letter has given me. The sentiments show the Divinity that stirs within you."

Key then went on to present his credo. He believed in the fall of Adam and the corruption inherent in every descendant of Adam. He believed that every man was born in sin under a "sentence of Almighty condemnation." He believed that suffering, adversity, and sorrow are inflicted by God as blessings in disguise. He believed in a Resurrection from the dead and a day of judgment. He believed that Jesus Christ is the Son of God. He believed in an everlasting life of excruciating torture, unavoidable in every case, unless by salvation through the merits of the atonement of the Saviour, who alone gives "pardon, peace, and holiness."

On one occasion Key proclaimed his credo in rhyme; here are three of his stanzas:

Our Father Who Art in Heaven

Father in Heaven! does God who made
And rules this universal frame—
Say, does He own a father's love,
And answer to a father's name?

Saviour divine! cleanser of guilt,
Redeemer of a ruined race!
These are Thy cheering words, and this
The kind assurance of Thy grace.

My God! my Father! may I dare—
I, all debased, with sin defiled—
These awful, soothing, names to join;
Am I Thy creature and Thy child?

As devout as he was and as faithful in the discharge of his duties as a member of the Church, Francis Scott Key could never banish the notion that he was "all debased, with sin defiled." For many years Key served both as vestryman and lay reader; there were few laymen in his Diocese, if any, who rendered more valuable service to the Church; moreover, he conducted family prayers twice a day and insisted on the attendance of all the members of the family as well as the servants: and yet there was perhaps no Episcopalian of his day who groped more "in doubt and darkness" and cogitated more on his sin as a son of Adam than did this pious communicant of St. John's Church of Georgetown. This was a rather natural attitude because it was an orthodox doctrine of the day. The depravity of man, rather than his exalted place in the Universe, was taught in the Church.

"Few men," according to Rev. John T. Brooke, one of his rectors, "were more unfavorably circumstanced for a pious life; few had stronger inward impulses to control or a thicker array of outward temptations to encounter." He was a man of ardent convictions and strong impulses; these he had to grapple with continually. Having a very keen mind, he spoke and acted with unusual rapidity; and he was not exempt, his rector revealed, from "occasional slips of judgment or slighter deviations." Made of human clay, "a man, not an angel," Key was not faultless. "His character was, in many respects, unique; so much so, that strangers and mere passing acquaintances sometimes misapprehended both his excellencies and his failings." The rector explained that Key possessed quite "an ardent temperament" and was exposed to "the stormy strifes of public and professional life"; but "real faults" of Key were comparatively few and did not affect the "soundness of his heart." It is apparent that one of Key's chief faults was that he was sometimes overcome by the "disturbing forces" of his temperament; but his conscience was never affected in the slightest by these occasional deviations; on the contrary, his conscience was as true to his God as the needle is to the North Pole. "But whatever were his faults," said the rector, "they were not concealed. He had no concealments." The rector added that while Key "passed through some deep waters and fierce flames," he came off as a conqueror in the battle of life.

But Key made it plain, in sending his message of encouragement to Randolph, that no man needs to wait to become righteous first, before going to his Saviour. He emphasized that we can go to the Throne of Grace as sinners "to be pardoned for our sins, and cleansed from all our iniquities." Then, referring to the agreement in this respect of the doctrines of nearly all religious denominations, he said: "This is the true doctrine of our Church, and the plain meaning of the Gospel; and indeed it seems to me, notwithstanding some peculiarities (about which there has been much useless disputation), that in these essential points almost all sects agree."

The religious beliefs which Francis Scott Key held were the doctrines of the Gospel expounded in Wilberforce's *Practical View.* Like Wilberforce, he was neither a "latitudinarian" nor an "exclusionist." He was "eminently catholic in his spirit." "For," according to Rev. Brooke, "while he loved his own Church, he loved her as she is—just as she came from the hands of the reformers—sound in doctrine and moderate in her spirit and bearing towards her sister

Churches of the Reformation. With the later attempts of individuals, at different periods, to erect high and exclusive fences upon the original peculiarities of the Church, Mr. Key had no sympathy whatever. And although he loved the liturgy, and, by his loud and hearty responses in the sanctuary, always gave note that he was there; he could feed upon the truth administered by any faithful hand and enter into the spirit of prayer, no matter under what form or by whom offered. He loved the pious ministers and members of all Evangelical Churches; sympathized with them, and co-operated with them in promoting 'the common salvation.' For he was not only sound in doctrine and catholic in spirit, but zealous of good works. This was, indeed, his prominent — his distinguishing trait. He was a liberal contributor to all benevolent objects; and although we never heard him speak of what he gave, we were informed by one of his intimate friends, that a tenth of his income was sacredly devoted to benevolent uses. A hint of poverty or wretchedness in his neighborhood, was sufficient, and his example in giving was a fair illustration of the truth, that genuine charity, in the choice of her objects, is neither exclusively domestic nor exclusively foreign."

The only thing that Key regretted about the Episcopal Church was the fact that two factions within it were grappling at each other's throats. They were the Formalists or the High Churchmen, and the Evangelicals or the Low Churchmen. He thought it was extremely unfortunate that any man — rector or layman — should be "a violent party man." But since he had to choose between the two, he was inclined to favor the Evangelical party. After many years of service as a member of the Episcopal Church, he said candidly: "I am a Low Churchman. I never could believe (though I tried hard in the *jus divinum*), or draw any of the conclusions that are usually deduced from such a position by those who hold it. I know that the Church of England has not been unanimous upon the point, and that some of her highest and best men have at all times taken lower ground to place our Church on."

Key sat for the first time in the Diocesan Convention in 1813 as a lay delegate from St. John's parish. In the following year there arose an acrimonious contest in the Convention between the High Churchmen and the Low Churchmen over the election of a Suffragan Bishop. The High Church supported Rev. Dr. James Kemp; while Rev. G. J. Dashiell, rector of St. Peter's Church of Baltimore, and others were candidates from the Low Church. The delegates were unaware at the opening of the Convention that the election of the Suffragan Bishop would be rushed through by "steam-roller"; but the High Church delegates discovered unexpectedly that they had a majority of votes, and at the last moment they rushed through the election of Dr. Kemp. A protest against Dr. Kemp's consecration was sent to the House of Bishops. Francis Scott Key signed the protest on the ground that there had been insufficient notice, but he did not concur in the accusation that the election was engineered by "premeditated management." However, the House of Bishops decided that the election had been conducted properly, and Dr. Kemp was consecrated as Suffragan Bishop.

Rev. Dashiell, chagrined because of his defeat, attempted to make a schism by setting up a separate branch of the Church. He made such a great disturbance in the Diocese that Bishop Thomas John Claggett deposed him from the ministry. Bishop Claggett, the first bishop consecrated in America, had been serving as the head of the Diocese of Maryland since 1792. He was a distinguished looking man, six feet four inches in height; his long white hair fell in heavy ringlets on his shoulders and added to his venerable appearance. Key came to know him intimately, having met him at the sessions of the Diocesan Convention. His powerful voice was harsh and rasping and, it is said, he often terrified the congregations with his vivid descriptions of Hell and the Devil. In 1816, the prelate, then seventy-three years old, died at his home in Prince George's County, after having served as Bishop of Maryland for nearly a quarter of a century. The poet lawyer of Georgetown wrote the epitaph that was inscribed on the tombstone over the grave of the beloved Bishop at Upper Marlborough. The epitaph was written in Latin; and after giving the dates of Bishop Claggett's birth, ordination and consecration, and death, concluded:

FIDELITATE ET MANSUETUDINE
ECCLESIAM REXIT
MORIBUSQUE
ORNAVIT
UXORI, LIBERIS, SOCIISQUE
MEMORIAM CLARISSIMAM
ET PATRIAE ET ECCLESIAE
NOMEN HONORATUM
DEDIT.

About this time Key was chosen to represent the Diocese of Maryland as one of the lay delegates to the General Convention of the Protestant Episcopal Church. The General Convention was held in New York City from May 20th to 27th, 1817. It was a thrilling experience for the lawyer from Georgetown. At the sessions he met some of the leading churchmen in America.

While he was one of the younger delegates in the Convention, being not yet thirty-eight, he took the floor frequently and spoke with earnestness and effect. On Thursday, May 22nd, he offered a motion in the House of Deputies to place the Church on record against "the vain amusements of the world." The text of his motion was: "*Resolved*, that the Clergy of this Church be, and they are hereby, enjoined to recommend sobriety of life and conversation to the professing members of their respective congregations, and that they be authorized and required to state it, as the opinion of this Convention, that conforming to the vain amusements of the world, frequenting horse races, theatres, and public balls, playing cards, or being engaged in any other kind of gaming, are inconsistent with Christian sobriety, dangerous to the morals of the members of the Church, and peculiarly unbecoming the character of cummunicants."

Key's motion failed of adoption. It was too "Methodistical," too strict, in the eyes of the majority of the delegates. The House of Deputies declared it to be unnecessary for "the purposes of Christian discipline."

That very morning Key received a letter from his mother. It brought sad news: news of the death of his Cousin Arthur

Shaaff, his friend during his early years at the Bar. Key had accepted an invitation to take tea that evening with friends in New York, but he was so deeply shocked that he sent his regrets to his friends, and spent the time in quiet meditation.

In a reply to his mother at Pipe Creek, the poet lawyer referred to the grandeur of New York's churches, the charm of the chanting, and the inspiration in the speeches.

The Keys had been invited to spend the Christmas holidays with the Taneys at Frederick; but Key had but one day of rest—Christmas Day—and he plunged into work again. At this time Taney was a member of the Senate of Maryland, having taken his seat in that body in December, 1816; he was now attending his second session. Key, in a letter to his sister expressed the hope that Taney would stop for a visit in Georgetown on one of his trips to or from Annapolis. Key's letter to Anne attests to his godliness:

Key to His Sister

Geo. Town

Dec. 26, 1817—

My Dear Anne—

As I expected it has been quite out of my power to join you all in Fred[k] and spend these holydays with you. Our Court adjourned for but one day, & we are all at work again—and so I fear I must continue to be all the winter.—

I have been wanting to write to Taney but have been too busy, & have also had some hope he would call this way in some of his journeys to and from Annapolis.—If he is yet with you, tell him that he positively promised in his last letter to me, that he would come this way if they succeeded in turning out the Council, &

that I claim he will shew himself a true Coody by keeping his promise.—

As I do not come to Fred[k] I beg you will write to me—Let me know if Papa & Mama are with you & if not, write when they come. M— called to see me & gave us a particular account of your fright & fall (of which we had heard before). I hope you will take care of yourself, & put yourself under His protection to whose care and kindness we all owe so much—May you daily experience fresh proofs of His goodness!

Polly desires her love & begs you will remember her gloves.

God bless you my dear Anne.

Yr affec[e] Brother

F. S. KEY

CHAPTER XIV

Crusader for Colonization

FRANCIS SCOTT KEY was always a bitter foe of slavery. Although born and reared in a slave State — there were more than 107,000 slaves in Maryland when he was twenty-one — and although he himself was a slave owner, he declared, when he was approaching sixty, that there was no man who started out in life "with more enthusiasm against slavery" than he did. He envisioned the slave traffic as a dark blot on Civilization. Like many of the slave State statesmen — notably Jefferson, Madison, and Monroe — he labored diligently not only to prevent the extension of slavery but also to rid the country of it altogether.

Carrying his religion into the toil of everyday life, he sympathized with the man in bondage and championed his cause. Deeply was he impressed by the philippics against the slave trade on both sides of the Atlantic. One of the most powerful of these denunciations came from the pen of the English poet, William Cowper:

> Thus man devotes his brother, and destroys;
> And, worse than all, and most to be deplored,
> As human nature's broadest, foulest blot,
> Chains him, and tasks him, and exacts his sweat
> With stripes, that Mercy, with a bleeding heart,
> Weeps when she sees inflicted on a beast.

Then what is man? And what man, seeing this,
And having human feelings, does not blush,
And hang his head, to think himself a man?

Key read these lines and repeated them again and again. So profoundly stirred was he by the thoughts of Cowper that he dedicated a poem to him:

To Cowper

Cowper! who loves not thee deserves not love
From God or man, or aught that God hath formed.
Eloquent pleader for the works of God!
Pleading for all that breathes — from the poor worm
"That crawls at evening in the public path,"
To man, that treads the earth, and looks to heaven.
To the mute wonders of the Almighty hand,
As seen in mountain, valley, field, and flood,
Thou, too, hast given a voice of praise and love;
They speak to all unutterable things,
Till the full heart o'erflows, and pours "the tears
Of holy joy" into the glistening eye
Of Him to Whom they say — "We all are thine —
Works of a Father's hand, for thee, a child —
And given thee but as earnest of the gifts,
Richer than all thy thoughts, but now await
Thy joyful coming to a Father's home.

"O! worship then with us, while here below,
In this, the vestibule of heaven's high fane,
Whose outer lamps gild the blue vault above thee,
Whose inner courts shall call forth all thy praise."

Cowper declared that he would rather himself be the slave and wear the bonds of slavery than fasten them upon another. But slavery had been recognized as lawful in America for many years; it had become firmly imbedded in the body politic; and Francis Scott Key was one of those who saw the intricacies as well as the evils of the problem. Time and again he appeared in the courts to fight for the ownership of slaves as though they were mere articles of merchandise. One suit in which he participated was brought in Prince George's County by the administrator of Miss Jane Fishwick for the value of a Negress named Dinah and her descendants. Dr. William Beanes, some weeks before his arrest by the British invaders, had testified that he had heard it said that Dinah was the slave of Miss Fishwick. But although Miss Fishwick died about the time of the Revolution, her estate was not administered upon until 1812, a delay of about thirty-seven years. When the case came before the Court of Appeals in Annapolis at the December Term of 1815, Francis Scott Key and Luther Martin represented Miss Fishwick's estate. One of the opposing lawyers was William Pinkney. The case was sent back to Prince George's County and another trial was held. Then another appeal was taken and again the case was argued in Annapolis. This time Key and Martin were opposed by General Walter Jones. Key argued that Miss Fishwick had died in the home of her stepfather and while the slaves remained in his possession they never actually became his property. He admitted that no claim had been made for Dinah and her offspring for upwards of forty years, but he maintained that not until the appointment of an administrator was there any person authorized to sue for the property. Chief Judge Chase, accepting Key's contention, delivered the opinion that the Statute of Limitations could not operate to bar the claim until letters of administration had been granted, thereby vesting some one with authority to sue for the slaves.

But while there were occasional instances like the Fishwick case in which Key battled for the ownership of the slave, there were many other cases in which he represented the slave, often without any hope of remuneration. He was known as an ardent friend of the blacks. One of his contemporaries said: "He was their standing gratuitous advocate in courts of justice, pressing their rights to the extent of the law, and ready to brave odium or even personal danger in their behalf."

There was one case in particular that stirred the Georgetown lawyer. Near the close of 1815, a slave trader had bought a Negress and decided to separate her from her husband and children and drag her to the South. Preparatory to the journey the Negress was imprisoned in the attic of a tavern in Washington. She became hysterical, and jumped out of the attic window. She was so badly injured that she was no longer in "a marketable condition"; and so when the slave trader left for the South with his drove of male and female slaves, handcuffed in pairs and attached to a long chain, she was left behind. While it was unlawful at this time to bring slaves into Washington for domicile or for sale, there was no law prohibiting any one from bringing them through the city enroute to the South; and shortly afterwards Judge James S. Morsell, who was elevated to the bench in 1815, called the attention of the grand jury to the frequency with which the streets of Washington were crowded with Negroes in manacles – a sight that was revolting to the feelings of the humane. About this time a young man named Jesse Torrey Jr., happened to be visiting in Washington. Hearing the story of the Negress, he visited the tavern and found in the attic not only the injured woman but also a man and a woman and a child, who claimed that they were entitled to their freedom but that they had been kidnapped by slave traders in Delaware and were being driven to the South for the auction block. Young Torrey told the story to a number of leading citizens, and decided to make a trip to Delaware to look for evidence. When he returned he asked for the legal assistance of Francis Scott Key and others who were known to be sympathetic toward the man in chains. The lawyers worked on the case without receiving any fee. And in due course the captives won their freedom.

But the problem of the free Negro was quite as much a source of worry as that of the slave. What shall we do with the free Negroes? was a question solemnly pondered by the statesmen in the South and in the border States. How shall we dispose of them as they are emancipated from time to time? They had very little opportunity of obtaining employment, and often their influence on the slaves was bad. Many were sent to the free States; but a number of the free States passed laws forbidding the settlement of emancipated Negroes. As far back as the Revolution, Thomas Jefferson had devoted his attention to the problem: before Francis Scott Key was born, the sage of Monticello proposed a plan in the Virginia Legislature for the gradual emancipation of the slaves and their exportation to Africa. He never dreamed of the interfusion of the races, never dreamed of the possibility of incorporating the Negroes as free citizens of the Republic. About ten years later the plan of establishing a colony in Africa was suggested to the colored people of Massachusetts and Rhode Island, but the project failed for lack of funds. Finally in 1816 the Virginia Legislature revived the discussion by calling the attention of the National Government to the subject. Each year the problem seemed to be growing more alarming. A college president in Mississippi wrote in a book on slavery published in Washington during the lifetime of Key: "The venomous fangs thereof were spreading wider and wider, and all the while taking a deeper and firmer root." But it was the emancipated Negro more than the slave that Virginia feared. One of the Virginia orators who favored the plan of colonization said: "Upon our low lands it seems as if some malediction had been shed — the habitations of our fathers have sunk into ruins; the fields which they tilled have become a wilderness.... Those... thickets ... shelter and conceal a wretched banditti, consisting of this degraded, idle, and vicious population, who sally forth from their coverts, beneath the obscurity of the night, and plunder the rich proprietors of the valleys. They infest the suburbs of the towns and cities, where they become the depositories of stolen goods, and schooled by necessity, elude the vigilance of our defective police."

While the legislators of the Old Dominion were making a plea for an asylum in Africa for the free Negroes, a zealous advocate of colonization was on his way to Washington to urge the formation of a colonization society and to enlist the coöperation of the Federal Government. It was Rev.

Robert Finley, a graduate of Princeton, forty-four years old, now a Presbyterian preacher in New Jersey. He believed that it was possible to get rid of most of the Negroes by sending them back to Africa; and he published a pamphlet entitled, *Thoughts on the Colonization of the Free Blacks,* which had much to do with the awakening of public interest in the scheme. Rev. Finley conferred with several members of Congress and other prominent men in Washington, and made arrangements to hold a meeting on December 16, 1816, to discuss the plan. Justice Bushrod Washington, a nephew of General Washington, presided, and it was decided to arrange for a public meeting on December 21st. This meeting was held in Brown's Hotel on Pennsylvania Avenue. Henry Clay, Speaker of the House, who presided, endorsed the movement and promised to give it his unqualified support. "Can there be a nobler cause," he said, "than that which, while it purposes to rid our own country of a useless and pernicious, if not dangerous portion of its population, contemplates the spreading of the arts of civilized life, and the possible redemption from ignorance and barbarism of a benighted quarter of the globe?" Addresses favoring the movement were than made by Elias B. Caldwell, Congressman John Randolph, and Congressman Robert Wright, a former Governor of Maryland. A resolution offered by Mr. Caldwell named a committee on constitution and rules, and another committee to petition Congress to acquire a territory suitable for their purpose. The name of Francis S. Key appeared on both of these committees.

John Randolph was named on the committee to solicit

the aid of Congress. But this seems to have been the end of the cynical Virginian's interest in the plan of colonization. For he suddenly turned his back against the advocates of colonization and denounced them as religious fanatics and publicity seekers. He took the view that colonization might be liable to incite the slaves to insurrection, and furthermore would fail to get rid of one tenth of the increase of free Negroes — unless through some "miraculous interposition of the hand of God," such as occurred at the Exodus of the Jews. In 1826 Randolph, then United States Senator, refused to present a petition of the Colonization Society to the Senate, although entreated to do so by Francis Scott Key, his bosom friend.

On December 28, 1816, the colonizers assembled in the hall of the House of Representatives. The constitution drafted by Key and his colleagues was adopted: and thus was founded the American Colonization Society. The constitution declared the purpose of the society to be the promotion of "a plan for colonizing (with their consent) the Free People of Colour residing in our country, in Africa, or such other place as Congress shall deem most expedient."

The organization of the society was perfected on January 1, 1817, with the election of officers. Justice Washington was elected President. The following Vice Presidents were then selected: Secretary of the Treasury William H. Crawford of Georgia; Speaker Clay of Kentucky; William Phillips of Massachusetts; former Governor John Eager Howard, Samuel Smith and John C. Herbert of Maryland; Colonel Henry Rutgers of New York; John Tayloe of Caroline, Virginia; General Andrew Jackson of Tennessee; Attorney General Richard Rush and Robert Ralston of Pennsylvania; General John Mason of the District of Columbia; and Rev. Finley.

In addition to the recording secretary, the corresponding secretary, and the treasurer, twelve managers were named to promote the activities of the organization: and the first name on the board of managers was that of Francis S. Key.

The lawyers, clergymen, members of Congress, and other public men, who organized the American Colonization Society were idealists. Their aim was to eradicate slavery without causing political or economic violence. Statesmen from the North and South were able to stand together on the platform of the Society. According to some historians, the colonizers were "idealists with troubled consciences." And there is no doubt that this slur applied to a great many of the slave owners. Patrick Henry, for instance, reflected how strange it was that there were men who professed "a religion the most humane, mild, meek, gentle and generous" who were adopting nevertheless a principle that was repugnant to humanity and destructive to liberty. "Will anyone believe that I am master of slaves of my own purchase?" Patrick Henry cried, his conscience disturbed. "I am drawn along by the general inconvenience of living without them. I will not, I cannot, justify it. . . . Slavery is detested; we feel its fatal effects — we deplore it with all the pity of humanity. As we ought with gratitude to admire that decree of Heaven which has numbered us among the free, we ought to lament and deplore the necessity of holding our fellow-men in bondage. But is it practicable, by any human means, to liberate them without producing the most dreadful and ruinous consequences?" Francis Scott Key, a slave owner like Patrick Henry, must have been troubled occasionally, especially whenever he recalled that he had named the American flag the ensign of the "land of the free" and the "home of the brave."

And so there were many doubters in America who looked skeptically upon the scheme of the American Colonization Society. The more practical business men of the country sneered at the scheme. The cold and calculating John Quincy Adams criticized the idea as absolutely visionary. The critics doubted whether the free Negroes would be willing to leave the United States for tropical Africa; and, even if they did, whether they would be able to govern themselves after they arrived there. And so Francis Scott Key and his fellow colonizers were ridiculed as "Quixotic adventurers," as "amiable enthusiasts," and as "Utopians."

But the colonizers were not discouraged. They believed that as their purpose was humane it had the approval of Providence, and that if they persevered they would meet with success in the end. They also laid the flattering unction to their souls that the deported blacks would take with them what they had learned in America and would found in Africa a free and happy commonwealth.

Fortunately James Monroe, who succeeded Mr. Madison in the Presidential chair on March 4, 1817, gave his endorsement to the plan of colonization. And in a year or two representatives of the American Colonization Society were on their way to Africa with instructions to explore the west coast of the Dark Continent and to select a location for a colony for the free blacks of America.

Before long auxiliary colonization societies were formed in Baltimore, Philadelphia, New York, and other cities. Early in 1818 the people of Baltimore contributed several thousand dollars to the cause, and the Legislature of Maryland requested the Governor to urge President Monroe and the members of Congress to negotiate for a colony in Africa by cession or purchase. Similar resolutions were adopted by the Legislatures of Virginia, Tennessee, and other States.

As a result of the pleas of the friends of colonization, the Congress, on March 3, 1818, passed an act directing the United States Navy to capture all African slaves found in the possession of American slave-traders, and empowering the President to appoint agents on the coast of Africa to receive, shelter, feed, clothe, and protect the slaves so captured. The passage of this law brought cheer to Francis Scott Key and his associates. It meant the coöperation of the United States Government. The coast of Africa was lined with slavers; and without the aid of the Navy the little colony would be at their mercy.

It was now time for the American Colonization Society to raise money for expenses. At the beginning of the year 1819 thirteen collection agents were chosen by the Society to engage in what Key called "the begging business." Key was one of the thirteen men authorized to engage in this unpleasant work. From now on, for many years during the prime of life, the poet lawyer of Georgetown traveled up and down the land begging for money to further the plan of colonization.

One of the first cities to which he was invited was Annapolis, in January, 1819; but as he was busy in the courts he tried to secure one of the members of Congress to take his place as the speaker, or else have the meeting postponed until a more convenient date.

In the meantime President Monroe, while in favor of the plan of colonization, was not coöperating as wholeheartedly as the colonizers had expected. They were urgently appealing for Federal aid in the early part of 1819, for there was a large supply of slaves in Georgia which had been seized by the State because of their importation contrary to law; these captives had been advertised for sale; and the colonizers were anxious to buy them from the Governor of Georgia. About this time Key's friend, Rev. William Meade of Virginia, was presenting the plea of the Colonization Society in New England. On his way back he stopped in Philadelphia; and while in that city he received a letter from Key informing him that President Monroe had been procrastinating in carrying out the provisions of the colonization law. Then, too, his Attorney General, William Wirt, appeared to be cool toward the colonization scheme. Key had promised to present to Mr. Wirt a copy of Rev. Meade's sermon on *The Plea for Africa.* And so the poet lawyer urged Rev. Meade to hurry back to the Capital. The letter, which Key wrote at Georgetown in 1819 to Rev. Meade, gives an insight into a few of the countless problems that confronted the advocates of colonization. The letter also shows how thoroughly familiar Key was with the details of the movement:

My Dear Friend:

Mr. Crawford's[1] fears are realized. The President has forgotten his promises, and what simple courtiers were we, to suppose it would be otherwise.

We have it all to go over again. But never fear. We shall bring him back to the point we had gained. He is gone, and we must write to him, and get him to give his orders at once, in black and white.

Mr. Crawford had a talk with him and the Attorney General, and I have seen them both. All the difficulties that we had before removed about the vagueness of the law, and the difficulty of its execution, re-appeared. Mr. Crawford tried to remove them; *e contra* the Attorney General. The President thought that he could not purchase land, therefore could make no settlement, nor any provision for receiving the captured negroes in Africa. He desired the Attorney General to take the law and examine it, and give him his opinion. The Attorney General said, that without further examining it, he would at once advise him to do nothing, that Congress would soon meet and pass another law, in which they might say plainly what they wanted done. Mr. Crawford said the law was just what it ought to be, and presented neither doubt nor difficulty.

Thus they broke up. Nothing was done. Caldwell has seen Mr. Crawford and the Attorney General also, and we have not met to compare notes since. I went to see him, but he was gone to Alexandria.

I spent several hours with Mr. Wirt. He acknowledged that he was uninformed about the business; thought our plan impracticable, but concurred in all our wishes. I found him reading our report, and he says he will read everything about it and consider it. I think he will be a friend, at any rate, not an enemy. He seems to fear the danger of some ex-

1.—William H. Crawford was born in Virginia in 1772. In 1807 he entered the United States Senate; in 1813 he was named Minister to France; in 1816 Secretary of the Treasury.

citement among the slaves, in consequence of our proceedings, and made some observations on the subject that deserve to be considered. He said the President would certainly appoint Bacon the agent, and that we ought to write to him and remind him of what had passed between us; as to which, he had no doubt, he would do what he had promised, and intimated that he would not oppose us. He added that he would write to the President to-day upon the subject.

We must, therefore, immediately prepare to carry on a correspondence with the President, and I will prepare a letter for our Committee to sign and forward, as soon as Gen. Mason (who is one of us, and the only one who has any weight) returns, which I hear, will be to-morrow.

. . . . My idea is that the President will appoint an agent, two, if we can find another (which, by the by, we must do, and I wish you to look about for another), that he will send a ship of war to the coast, and probably a transport with the colored men from this country, as laborers, and some agricultural implements, and that he will authorize him to settle in our territory and make preparations for receiving the captured negroes, and I think this will do.

I wish you to bring on a dozen of the sermons you sent me, the "Plea for Africa." I have promised one to Mr. Wirt. The one I had, I lent, and cannot get again. I think it calculated to help us greatly.

If you have no meeting in Philadelphia, I think you had better bring on Bacon with you, and the sooner you are both here, the better, unless you are doing something material, of which you will be the best judge.

May God bless you.

Ever your friend,

F. S. KEY

So the task of the colonizers was a stupendous one. While there were quite a few idealists like Francis Scott Key and Rev. Meade and Henry Clay who looked for the solution of the slavery problem in colonization, there were innumerable others like William Wirt who believed that the colonizers were wasting their time and their money. For each year the menace of the slavery agitation was growing more acute. In March, 1820, the Missouri Compromise was approved by President Monroe. John Randolph, believing that Congress had no power to prohibit slavery in the Territories, called it "a dirty bargain" and called those who voted for it "doughfaces." The venerable Thomas Jefferson said: "This momentous question, like a fire bell in the night, awakened me and filled me with horror. I considered it at once as the knell of the Union."

But the colonizers thought that they had a solution of the difficulties. In the Summer of 1820 plans were set in motion for the formation of an auxiliary society at Frederick. A meeting was held in the Court House in August to consider the project, and a committee was appointed to make recommendations at another meeting in September. The committee, feeling that the people of Frederick County were not familiar with the colonization plan, invited representatives of the American Colonization Society to explain the movement at the meeting in September. Francis Scott Key and Charles Fenton Mercer, Congressman from Virginia, were selected to address the Frederick gathering.

In 1820 Sherbro Island was proposed as a colonization point, but it was found to be marshy and malarial. Accordingly in 1821 Cape Mesurado was selected as the home of the first group of free blacks from America. In 1822 Jehudi Ashmun, a 28-year-old New Englander who had come to the District of Columbia to edit a church publication, was sent to Africa by the United States Government to strengthen the infant settlement at Cape Mesurado. When he landed with his little band of Negroes on August 9, 1822, he found the colony in a state of wretched demoralization, practically on the verge of extinction. Of the 114 settlers sent over from the United States in 1820 and 1821, many had died of fever; of the survivors nearly all were sick. The white agents had deserted. The supplies were exhausted. The native chiefs were threatening to attack. Ashmun, who had taken his wife along with him, expecting to return within a short time on the same boat, heroically determined to remain: he assumed the leadership of the colony in caring for the sick and preparing for the attack of the savages. Only about thirty men were able to bear arms. The fatiguing labor brought on fever. Ashmun was prostrated. His wife sickened and died. Finally, on November 11th, just before dawn, eight hundred savages made an attack; but with his thirty men and boys he repelled them. On December 2nd an attack was made by a still greater force of barbarians; but again he repulsed them. Ashmun inspired the colonists with courage; he labored upon the reconstruction of the colony with diligence and ability.

Francis Scott Key was delighted to hear the encouraging news from Africa. "I suppose," he wrote to one of his coworkers in Philadelphia, "you have seen the late intelligence from Mesurado, and that therefore I need not state it to you.

Capt. Spence left our people all safe and well, and we think our prospects are flattering. The time now draws on for the appointment of a missionary, and for his making his preparations. Ashmun writes us that one is greatly needed, and will be eminently useful."

But alas! charges were brought against Ashmun that he had assumed the position of agent without due authority. In the Spring of 1823, a new agent, Dr. Eli Ayres, arrived on the African Coast. Ashmun was superseded, his sacrifices were unappreciated, and his motives were questioned.

In September, 1823, a vessel arrived from Africa appealing again for a missionary. In another letter to Philadelphia, Key said: "Ayres implores us to send out a missionary and it is now high time to make our arrangements. If Mr. Nash cannot go, can we get any other? Somebody we must send in the vessel which we expect to despatch in November. We have (as I told you) a Clergyman from New England offering, but I confess I shall regret it if Mr. Nash does not go. Do write to him and let me know his determination soon."

Key now took up his pen to aid the cause of colonization. Prevented from attending as many meetings as he wished on account of his work in the courts, he wrote his pleas to the people through the press. Several of his articles were published at Frederick. Copies of the newspapers were sent to Philadelphia, with the hope that they would be reprinted. "Would Mr. Walsh publish them?" the poet lawyer asked. "Perhaps he would, if the Bishop would ask him." Key assured that nothing would appear in the articles that would offend Mr. Walsh, the publisher, in any way. "His aid, or his neutrality even," Key explained, "would be important to us. His only objection is to the practicability of the Scheme, and of this he may, as he sees more, be convinced."

In the Spring of 1824 Dr. Ayres returned to America. In April Key announced he would try to come to Philadelphia if he could, but that General Robert Goodloe Harper could make arrangements for a meeting there. In May he wrote to Dr. Ayres, then in Baltimore, that he did not see how he could go to Philadelphia, on account of his engagements for some weeks to come. "Besides," said Key, "I have no doubt all is done in the way of speech-making that will be of any use. The begging part of the business ought now to begin. Indeed it ought to have been begun at once." Key also congratulated Dr. Ayres on his influence with Mr. Walsh, the publisher. "I think you have done wonders in Philadelphia, and have managed Mr. Walsh peculiarly well. We must let him get off smoothly: and I think will, after a little while, see him advocating our cause." In a postscript Key asked Dr. Ayres: "What do you think of this news from Africa? Can the Ashantees get to Mesurado?" Soon after this, at the suggestion of General Harper, the settlement at Mesurado became known as Monrovia in honor of President Monroe, while the entire colony became known as Liberia.

It was about this time that the *Antelope,* a Spanish ship engaged in smuggling slaves into the United States, was captured by a United States revenue cutter off the coast of Florida. The ship carried a cargo of about 280 Negro slaves. After it was brought into the port of Savannah for adjudication as prize, the *Antelope* and the slaves were claimed by subjects of Spain and Portugal. The United States Government resisted the claims on the ground that the slave trade was in violation of the laws of the United States; therefore, it was argued, the Negroes were entitled to their freedom.

It was brought out at the trial of the case in Georgia that a privateer manned at Baltimore, but flying the Artegan flag, had captured the *Antelope* and also several Portuguese ships and an American vessel along the coast of Africa, taking from each of the vessels a number of slaves. The privateer and the *Antelope* then sailed from there for South America, and the privateer was wrecked off the coast of Brazil, whereupon the master and a large part of the crew were taken prisoners, while the remainder of the crew were taken on board the *Antelope,* where the African slaves were imprisoned. It was then that the*Antelope* sailed north and was captured by the revenue cutter. The Circuit Court of Georgia dismissed the claim of the United States Government, except as to that part of the cargo captured by the privateer from the American vessel. All the other slaves were awarded to the Spanish and Portuguese claimants.

An appeal was taken by the Government to the Supreme Court of the United States. Attorney General Wirt asked Francis Scott Key to assist him in the argument of the case. Key had been a participant in a number of cases before the Supreme Court, had battled with many of the leaders of the American Bar on Constitutional questions, and had become recognized as one of the ablest practitioners in the District of Columbia. In 1819, for instance, he faced General Walter

Jones and Luther Martin in a case in which he discussed the right of trial by jury, guaranteed by the Seventh Amendment to the Constitution, and the meaning of the Law of the Land, guaranteed by the Maryland Declaration of Rights; and the opinion of Justice William Johnson, based on Key's argument is one of the landmarks of Constitutional interpretation. And in 1824 one of Key's rival gladiators in the legal arena was Daniel Webster, then forty-two years old. Key was counsel for the Bank of Columbia, which had brought suit against an endorser on a note. The endorser was represented by Webster and General Jones. Key was victorious in his contention that the bank was within its rights in offering evidence of the local custom regarding the number of days of grace allowed.

Then, too, Key was one of the leading advocates of the black man in America. He had a genuine sympathy for the wretched creatures that were captured by the man-hunters along the coast of Africa. Aside from the importance of the *Antelope* case — for the captured slaves had a monetary value of thousands of dollars — was it not, thought Key, his duty to lift his voice in America's highest tribunal against the slave traffic as a blot on Civilization?

When the *Antelope* case came before the Supreme Court early in March, 1825, the court room was crowded with members of Congress and other officials of the Government. The lawyers for the Spanish and Portuguese claimants were John McPherson Berrien of Georgia and Charles J. Ingersoll of the Philadelphia Bar. Mr. Berrien was two years younger than Key, but he had acquired considerable experience in the courts; had served on the bench in Georgia; had occupied a seat in the Georgia Senate; and in 1825 had entered the Senate of the United States. Mr. Ingersoll was three years younger than Key; had entered the House of Representatives in 1812; and had served for fourteen years as United States District Attorney for Pennsylvania.

As the eyes of John Marshall and the Associate Justices turned to Francis Scott Key, there came to him the opportunity of a lifetime to urge the Supreme Court to place its stamp of disapproval upon the slave trade as a violation of the Higher Law of Humanity. Now, at forty-five, he had reached the height of his powers as a debater and an orator. The poet lawyer was "slightly built; his head well formed; his features thin, and very expressive." His brown curly hair was thinning. His face, for many years of boyish "oval form," was beginning to show the marks of worry and responsibility, the indelible imprint of the struggle with life. His large dark blue eyes beamed with sympathetic expression under heavy arched brows. In his gayer moments his eyes sparkled, and his whole face broke into a radiance of kindliness.

Launching upon his argument, Key declared that the Government resisted the claim of Spain and Portugal on the ground that the Negro captives were to be considered as freemen, and not as slaves. He realized that unless he could show that the officers on the *Antelope* were outlaws, the Government would have difficulty in winning the case; for traffic in slaves was allowed at that time by Spain and Portugal, and the African cargo was claimed by subjects of Spain and Portugal. Furthermore, the *Antelope*, whatever its destination might have been, had been seized along the coast of Florida, at that time a province of Spain. So he denounced the officers of the *Antelope* as pirates. And the officers of the American revenue cutter, he said, were to be praised for rescuing the Negroes from the pirates' grasp.

Key then proceeded to state his contention that the Supreme Court was charged with the administration of the laws of the United States, not those of Spain and Portugal; and that the Negroes on the *Antelope* had been emancipated by virtue of the Slave Trade Acts, which stipulated that any slaves imported into the United States were to be entitled to their freedom. "These acts," said the Georgetown lawyer, "constitute a solemn pledge to all Nations interested in the suppression of this human traffic, and to Africa herself—a pledge that if the objects of it should seek our protection, where they may lawfully receive it, within our territorial jurisdiction, and at the feet of our tribunals of justice, they should be entitled to that protection."

It was now that the poet lawyer grew eloquent, as he proceeded to make his plea for the freedom of the captives under the Higher Law. The subjects of Spain and Portugal, he said, were claiming the ownership of the slaves by right of possession of merchandise; but the Justices of the Supreme Court were considering something more than merchandise: they were considering human beings made in the image of the Creator.

"These are men," he declared, "of whom it cannot be affirmed that they have universally and necessarily an owner. In some particular and excepted cases, depending on the local law and usage, they may be subjects of property and ownership; but by the Law of Nature all men are free!"

In conclusion Key pictured the horrors of the slave trade as a relic of barbarism. Pleading for the wretched creatures captured by cruel man-hunters on the coast of Africa and carried away in bondage, his speech as assistant to the Attorney General placed him in the front rank of American orators. An idea of the deep impression which he had made on this occasion is afforded by Henry Stuart Foote, a graduate of Washington College, Lexington, Virginia, who in after years served as United States Senator and as Governor of Mississippi:

> Mr. Key was tall, erect, and of admirable physical proportions. There dwelt usually upon his handsome and winning features a soft and touching pensiveness of expression almost bordering on sadness, but which in moments of special excitement, or when anything occurred to awaken the dormant heroism of his nature, or to call into action the higher power of vigorous and well cultivated intellect, gave place to a bright ethereality of aspect and a noble audacity of tone which pleased while it dazzled the beholder. His voice was capable of being in the highest degree touching and persuasive. His whole gesticulation was natural, graceful and impressive; and he was as completely free from anything like affectation or rhetorical grimace as any public speaker I have known. He had a singularly flowing, choice, and pointed phraseology, such as could not fail to be pleasing to persons of taste and discernment; and I am sure that no one ever heard him exhibit his extraordinary powers of discussion, to whom the ideas to which he essayed to give expression seemed at all cloudy or perplexed, or his elocution clogged and torpid, even for the shortest possible per-

> iod of time. On this occasion he greatly surpassed the expectations of his most admiring friends. The subject was peculiarly suited to his habits of thought, and was one which had long enlisted, in a special manner, the generous sensibilities of his soul. It seemed to me that he said all that the case demanded, and yet no more than was needful to be said; and he closed with a thrilling and even an electrifying picture of the horrors connected with the African Slave Trade, which would have done honor either to a Pitt, or a Wilberforce in their palmiest days.

Mr. Berrien and Mr. Ingersoll, in replying to Key's arguments, declared that an African slave was nothing more than merchandise under the law—this was the opinion reached many years afterwards by Chief Justice Taney in the Dred Scott case—and that the slave trade was sanctioned by the Law of Nations. On behalf of Spain and Portugal, the lawyers demanded the slaves on the *Antelope* as personal property acquired "in the regular course of legitimate commerce." The argument was closed by Attorney General Wirt, who replied that the captured Negroes were not merchandise, but human beings.

John Marshall, delivering the opinion of the Court, said that the case was one of "momentous importance." Clashing in conflict with each other were "the sacred rights of liberty and of property." These conflicting claims, he said, drew from the bar "a degree of talent and of eloquence worthy of the questions that have been discussed." But, said Marshall, he was a jurist, not a moralist. And the Supreme Court must obey the mandate of the law; it must not yield to "feelings which might seduce it from the path of duty." And whatever might be the answer of a moralist, the slave trade could not be pronounced at that time by a jurist as a violation of the Law of Nations. Any Nation had the right to engage in the slave trade; any Nation had the right to renounce that right; but the traffic remained lawful to those Governments that had not forbidden it. The Court therefore decided that a foreign vessel such as the *Antelope* engaged in the African slave trade, captured on the high seas in time of peace by an American cruiser and brought in for adjudication, should be restored to the claimants.

After Key had passed fifty, he was still devoting a large portion of his time to the crusade for colonization. On October 21, 1829, he delivered an address on the subject before the Pennsylvania State Colonization Society in the hall of Franklin Institute in Philadelphia. At this time he made the announcement that the American Colonization Society, for which he was speaking, had been prevented for some time from sending any free Negroes to Liberia on account of lack of funds. "There are now," he deplored, "more than six hundred slaves willing to go to Africa and offered by their owners to the Colonization Society on condition of their being sent to the Colony." He pointed out that "the laws of most, if not all the Southern States discourage the manumission of slaves, unless they are removed from the State." Besides this, the propriety of emancipation was often questionable, inasmuch as the condition of a slave suddenly thrown upon his own resources was very far from being improved. "By providing a refuge for these unhappy beings," said Key, "the Colonization Society removes a great obstacle to their manumission, and directly promotes the cause of Abolition . . . . That this is the cheapest and most direct method of promoting Abolition is evident, since the emancipation of thousands might be procured for the mere expense of transporting them to Africa; whereas, in the ordinary mode, it requires a large sum to liberate a single individual, whose liberty when attained is frequently anything but a blessing."

Key concluded his speech by appealing to the people of Philadelphia to give financial aid to the American Colonization Society. His remarks were warmly received, and a committee headed by Bishop White was appointed to solicit funds for the cause.

While the colonizers had been criticized in the North as a group formed for ulterior political purposes, and had been denounced in some quarters as a part of the Clay machine, Francis Scott Key was encouraged by the hospitable reception which he received in Philadelphia. Upon his return home, he wrote to Dr. William Bradley Tyler, one of the prominent residents of Frederick, explaining how the Pennsylvania Society had been "taking up the business in a way to do her credit" and expressing the hope that he would "make a zealous effort as soon as possible." He recommended that solicitors should appeal to each man and woman in Frederick County to contribute one dollar:

Geo. Town
28 Novr 29.

My Dear Sir —

I rec^{d}. your letter to day & am glad to find that you are determined to do something in Frederick for our Col^{n} cause.

I approve entirely of your suggestions, & believe that by making your efforts point to something local, you will do more than in any other way. Dividing your funds in the way you propose, giving us half for the general object, & applying the other half to pay for such as go from your County, will aid us as effectually as any other way, & will enable you to obtain more.—I am glad to tell you that I believe Philadelphia is taking up the business in a way to do her credit.—They have determined there to send out at their own cost entirely, 200, immediately.—They are to be Slaves manumitted for the purpose, & we are to select them from those that are offered to us.—They send none now free; and this is because they thought the abolitionists there would be more easily brought into the scheme, if it was confined to such as were now Slaves, & were to be free on the condition of going.—Would there be any of this description from Fred^{k}.? I think Judge Shriver told me of some of his father's that could be sent. I have two boys at Pipe Creek that I wish to go, & they have agreed to it. But they would be more willing if there were any others from the County. They can be called for at Balt^{e}.—It is important to send some from Maryland, as otherwise we shall lose the benefit of the annual appropriation of 1000$. Dr. Rideout has one to send from Annapolis, & I hope there may be some (but am not sure there will) from Balt^{e}.—I suppose the vessel will be ready in 3 or 4 weeks. 30 or 40 of Col^{o}. Early's from Georgia are to go, & some from Virg. & N. Carolina—so that the vessel will have to stop at Norfolk & Savannah or Charleston. Those from Balt^{e}. can be sent to Norfolk in the steam boat.—

I think it not very important either as to your success or as to the aid it would afford us, whether you act in the way you propose, as an independent Society under another name, or as an auxiliary to us.—adopt therefore either as may be more agreeable to yourselves — your course would be the same in either way, & receive our approbation & thanks.

I hope you will make a zealous effort as soon as possible — for the drafts on us from the Colony & the last shipment have emptied our treasury and put us in debt. — Would not an active & intelligent agent with a short address from your Society, by going thro' the County & distributing it & asking every man & woman for a dollar, bring in, in a few weeks, a handsome contribution? I think you could find such a man, or two or three of them to go into different parts of the County — They should make it their only business for the time they would be so engaged, & should be paid for their time and trouble. —

Yrs truly

F. S. KEY

And so for many years Key took an active part in the crusade for colonization. Liberia now embraced about one hundred and fifty miles of coast and extended inland about forty miles. It had a population of upwards of three thousand in addition to several thousand natives. By the year 1832 American newspapers were giving glowing accounts of the Colony and pointing out that with little attention the fertile soil would yield coffee and cotton, sugar cane, indigo, rice, and other products in abundance.

From original cut at Terra Rubra by Francis Scott Key

Anne Phoebe Penn Dagworthy Charlton
1756-1830
(Mrs. John Ross Key)

John Ross Key
1754-1821

CHAPTER XV

Sunshine and Shadow

A STRONG BOND of affection existed among the members of the Key family. Francis Scott Key himself was deeply affectionate. He poured out his love for mother and father, for his sister Anne, and for Polly and the children. The family was a happy one. When Key reached forty, Polly had already given birth to eight children. Their eldest child, Elizabeth, was nearly sixteen. Maria was over fourteen. Frank, named after his father, was approaching thirteen. John, named after his grandfather, was ten. Ann was eight. Edward, named for Polly's father, was nearly six. Daniel Murray, named for Key's old college mate, was three. The baby, Philip Barton, named for Uncle Philip, was a year and four months.

Traditions are redolent of the many happy hours in Georgetown. "The shady lawn and orchard sloping to the Potomac's edge," wrote one of Key's granddaughters many years after his death, "and the terraced garden with its lofty walnut trees and Lombardy poplars shading the walks, made a happy playground for the household band. Here, for each child, a tiny round garden had been made by the gardener, under their father's directions, and what ecstasies of delight abounded when the sprouting seed took the shape of names, and 'Maria,' 'Lizzie,' 'Anna,' etc., were clearly spelled out in the centre of the green seedlings!"[1]

The story has also been told that Key used to take the children out to hunt for eggs, as the hens often laid their eggs some distance from the chicken coops. He filled some of the nests with eggs dyed in bright colors. As a joke on the children he printed on some of the eggs this inscription:

> Look for the hen with yellow legs,
> For she's the hen that lays these eggs.

These stories are only traditions; but they give color to the scene of the happy home in Georgetown along the north bank of the Potomac and testify to the adoration that the poet lawyer had for his children.

Still another legend describes the care with which Key selected schools for his children. "If a school was to be selected for any of the children," said Key's granddaughter, "their father had his own way of choosing one. He called the children, put a Latin grammar under his arm, and started forth. The teacher would be called on for a Latin quotation. If his pronunciation was satisfactory, the children and the grammar were left there, otherwise not."

And then there were the merry days of Summer, when Frank and Polly returned with the children to the old homestead at Pipe Creek. Elizabeth gave a glimpse of the family when she wrote a letter to her grandmother in July, 1819, in anticipation of their vacation in the country. The young lady told how busy her father was—"so much engaged at Court that he has hardly time for anything"—but he hoped Court

1.—Anna Key Bartow, *Recollections of Francis Scott Key*, published in 1900.

would soon be over; she was sorry her Aunt Anne Taney's children had the measles, and hoped they would soon recover; she reported that little Barton, the baby, had been "very sick, indeed," but was well again; she and Maria were hoping they would soon go to school; Frank sent word that his tent should not be cut up; and John wanted his colt broken; and finally she asked about her cow.

At the bottom of Elizabeth's letter her father wrote the following message to his mother:

> My Dearest Mother
>
> As Elizabeth tells you we have a long & most fatiguing Court — I rarely get home till tea-time & then as soon as I can make my arrangements I hope to come up & see you. —
>
> Meade is here, attending to our Colonization affairs — I believe I shall have to go to Philadelphia & New York & perhaps farther this Summer in that business if I can spare the time. — I suppose Taney has got home, & I hope to hear soon how the children come on with the measles.
>
> Tell Papa I hope he has an abundant Harvest. —
> God bless you my dear Parents —
>
> Yr affec[e] Son
>
> F. S. KEY

In February, 1820, Judge John Ross Key, the master of Terra Rubra, was stricken critically ill. Frank rushed to his bedside at Frederick. "What must it have been," remarked John Randolph of Ronaoke, "to have his bedside attended by such a son! He [Francis Scott Key] is indeed as near perfection as our poor nature can go, although he would be shocked to hear it said. Severe to himself, considerate and indulgent to others, speaking ill of none."

Judge Key gradually recovered. But in the following year he was stricken again; this time fatally. In October, 1821, the happy family circle was broken by his death at the age of sixty-seven. Judge Key's death was a heavy blow to the family, especially to the saintly wife. The devoted son at Georgetown and his sister Anne at Frederick bowed their heads in sorrow. Here, as in every crisis, they fell on their knees and prayed for a revelation of the will of God. The poet lawyer envisioned the happenings of life with the godly meditation of a saint. And the death of his father deepened his godliness.

But in the following Summer there came to Key an even more poignant test of grief — the death of one of his children. The tragedy occurred on July 8, 1822. On that day his son Edward, a bright and attractive lad of nearly nine, was playing with his toys after lunch, when his mother called him to go to school. Edward immediately put up his playthings, bade his mother an affectionate good-bye, and ran off to school. About four o'clock, when school was over, the lad and one of his schoolmates went down to the river for a swim. It was a hot day and the cool water of the Potomac was inviting. Venturing out in the stream too far, Edward sank in the deep water and was unable to get back to shore. His little companion was terrified: he was afraid to tell what happened until after six o'clock that evening. Then he told the victim's brother John. John ran to the river bank, and seeing no trace of his younger brother, waded in and dove around in search of the dead body. A number of neighbors joined in the search. Finally the little boy was found, and about nine o'clock he was carried back to his mother. The father was not at home; he had left on a business trip to Annapolis a few days before.

In some mysterious way Key had been prepared for the ordeal. On Sunday — the day before the tragedy — a weird feeling of humility came over him. He detected a strange "murmuring" in his soul. This is his own description of the uncanny feeling that came over him, as he recorded it in his diary a few weeks later:

> On Sunday the Sacrament was administered and after renewing my Covenant with God, I spent a considerable part of the evening and several hours at night alone. I became much impressed with a sense of the ungrateful return I had made for all the goodness I had experienced. I think I was never before so sensible of some of my faults and failings and was particularly struck with a discontented murmuring and impatient spirit that seemed latterly (under the pressure of some little troubles) to have been growing upon me. I became much humbled, and felt doubts whether I had indeed ever given myself to the Lord.

Had he not been "estranged and engulfed" by the things of the world? Was not this a presentiment of some impending calamity? All day Monday — the day of the drowning — the same mysterious sensations gripped his mind. Of his sensations on the fatal day he wrote:

> The next morning I rose with the same thoughts and feelings. I walked out, and my mind was much exercised with the reflections of the day before. I never saw the folly and ingratitude of my conduct so plainly. I lamented it and protested against it for the

> future, and tried to bring my heart into a total renunciation of all its own desires and a complete submission to the will of God. Through the day these exercises continued and my mind was unusually engaged and impressed. I remember thinking at the close of the day, that I had spent a most spiritual day than I had done for some time.

And when twilight fell in Annapolis, Franics Scott Key went to his room, fell on his knees, and offered prayers for forgiveness and strength. Finally, when he went to bed late that night, he had a feeling of confidence that, whatever misfortune might befall him on the morrow, he would accept his fate with humility and resign himself into the hands of his Creator. This is how he felt on the night when his little boy lay dead, but before the news had reached him:

> At night, I was again alone in my chamber, and did not go to bed till a late hour. I here renewed my surrender to God, lamented my past failings and prayed for mercy and grace. I prayed against my impatience and discontent, and felt gratified at the peace and freedom with which I felt enabled to devote myself to His will and service, and I thought I had never given myself to God so faithfully and entirely before. I thought that before I had always kept back something, but that now I could put myself and all my concerns into His hands with a perfect resignation to His will, and a desire that "not my will" but His should be done.

When he awoke on Thursday morning, Key received the news of the drowning from a special messenger. Immediately he packed his belongings and hurried from Annapolis. So well had he been prepared by the unusual presentiment, that his mind was "more composed and subdued" than he "could have supposed possible." As he hurried back to his home in

Georgetown, his principal worry was for Polly: for he was afraid that he would find her in a "state of distraction." But when he walked across the threshold, and Polly threw her arms about him, he found to his surprise that she was just as composed as he was.

And then without delay the pious husband began to tell his wife about the mysterious thoughts that had been surging through his mind — a feeling so clear, so distinct, so irrepressible, that he felt sure it was a supernatural admonition. Polly was amazed; for she too, all day Sunday, had felt a strange sensation in her soul. Could this be but a mere coincidence? Or was it a psychic phenomenon? Certainly it was worth describing in great detail in his diary:

> She told me that she also recollected an unusual impression on her mind on the day (which was Sunday) before this occurrence. She was led to think of her neglect of religious duties and among other things, as to the instruction of her children, and she called Edward who was with her in her room and the rest of the children and heard them the Catechism. She had never done such a thing in her life but once before, and she said it was a great comfort to her to think that she had done so, and to remember how cheerfully and well Edward had said it.

In the gloom that followed the death of the little boy, the godly lawyer and his wife at Georgetown sought comfort in the Scriptures. Particularly the Psalms of David they found comforting in time of tribulation. One of the poet lawyer's favorite passages in the Scriptures was Psalm 50:15: "And call upon me in the day of trouble: I will deliver thee, and thou shalt glorify me." One day he wrote a poem based on this verse:

Help in Trouble

Thy trial day on earth must bring
  Trouble in mercy given,
To fit thee for thy conflicts here,
  And for thy crown in heaven.

But when they come, remember then
  A promised help is nigh;
A Father's kind and pitying ear
  Is open to thy cry.

Then may the light of these blest words
  On all thy pathway shine:
"I will, thou shalt"; the hearing ear
  Be His, the praise be thine.

Key still clung to the belief that death and illness as well as troubles of every kind are afflictions sent down as punishment by the omnipotent Judge. The angel of death had made the visitation to take away a child on the direct command of an angered God to chastise the parents. And evidently they had been so extremely negligent in their religious duties that the chastisement was deserved.

But here appeared a problem in his credo. Why should an obedient little boy be chosen as a mark of "judgment and condemnation"? Could a just God strike down an innocent child "in wrath and for punishment"? In the Psalms Key read David's assurance: "Like as a father pitieth his children, so the Lord pitieth them that fear him." Frankly he was puzzled. And so he bowed his head in humility, hoping to learn a lesson from the terrible chastisement. Of one thing he was convinced: "Afflictions come not out of the ground and such an awful shock as this is never ordered by a merciful God, but for some wise and good purpose." And so he tried to find out what the Divine Ruler was aiming to teach in the drowning of the boy in the Potomac. In the first place, he realized that he could be grateful because the judgment had been tempered with mercy. Had he not been brought by the grace of God into an extraordinary state of mind that "greatly softened" the shock of the chastisement? "Surely," he meditated, "I may believe that the Lord, who saw it necessary to chasten me, had compassion upon me, and prepared me for the correction of humbling and bringing me into a more childlike spirit, that I might see that it was in love and mercy that He thus visited me." Then too he was thankful that he was away from home at the time that the search was being made in the river for the body of the little boy. "I was spared," he said, "all that stormy tumult of feeling endured by my poor wife and children who were at the scene of suffering, all that agony . . . of hearing he was in the water, that they were searching for him, that he was found, that they were attempting to revive him, that it was in vain." Furthermore, he had a feeling of gratitude because of the fact that Polly had been given strength to bear the ordeal. He was glad that her soul had been purified in the crucible of grief. Ought he not praise the Lord for leading Polly, even though by punishment, "into the way of peace"? And finally, he was grateful because it appeared that after Edward's sudden death the other children all appeared to have "softer and better felings." There were still eight children left, the youngest a baby girl who arrived on the scene less than a year before. The eldest daughters, Elizabeth and Maria, were now thinking of romance. The father was disappointed because the girls failed to appear as pious as he thought they ought to be. Once in a while he thought he detected in them "some contritions and some care for the soul"; but alas! those outward and visible signs, so quickly they vanished, were like "the early dew and the morning cloud." But he did not blame his children: evidently it was his own fault. Ever since the close of the war, he had been exceedingly busy in office and in Court; and the children had suffered from his carelessness and their want of discipline. He did not hesitate to confess his "unfaithfulness as a parent." How could he expect "any fruits from labors and efforts" as defective as his had been? He particularly regretted that he had neglected to give adequate religious instruction to Edward, who had been so bright and easy to teach. "What an excitement should this be," the bereaved father soliloquized, "to make me more diligent and faithful in my prayers and efforts for my remaining children!"

So the death of the little son in the Summer of 1822 had the effect of making Francis Scott Key more humble and pious than ever. He condemned himself for being a "slave of the world" rather than a "servant of God." He felt ashamed of himself also because he had worried so often over his troubles. "I ought also to remember with shame," he said, "my past impatience and fretfulness under the little ordinary troubles of life." How little, he mused, can one appreciate "his hopes and his privileges" when he allows himself to become upset over the vicissitudes of life! Therefore he resolved again, as he had done during the war days, to banish the demon of worry. This is how he jotted down his resolution to seek a richer experience in "the comforts of religion":

> Let me endeavor carefully to guard against this un-Christian spirit for the future! How little in my late sorrow, did all these things seem to me, which I had suffered so as to trouble me! Let me consider them always as they seem now, in this affliction and as they really are! This trial is certainly for the improvement of my faith and patience. . . . May my faith increase till it overcomes the world! . . . May it make me heavenly-minded, opening to my view the things that are unseen and eternal and weaning me from the things of time and sense! . . . May I never suffer a murmuring word to pass my lips, however sharp may be my trials, nor a murmuring thought to rise in my heart!

It was in one of his buoyant moments that he penned a song of thanksgiving, acknowledging that his soul had been a "wretched wanderer, far astray," but praising the Lord for His "pardoning grace" and the peace that flows from it. This is his best known hymn:

Lord, with Glowing Heart

Lord, with glowing heart I'd praise thee
For the bliss thy love bestows,
For the pardoning grace that saves me,
And the peace that from it flows.
Help, O God! my weak endeavor,
This dull soul to rapture raise;
Thou must light the flame, or never
Can my love be warmed to praise.

Praise, my soul, the God that sought thee,
Wretched wanderer, far astray;
Found thee lost, and kindly brought thee
From the paths of death away.

Praise, with love's devoutest feeling,
  Him who saw thy guilt-born fear,
And, the light of hope revealing,
  Bade the blood-stained Cross appear.

Lord, this bosom's ardent feeling
  Vainly would my lips express;
Low before thy foot-stool kneeling,
  Deign thy suppliant's prayer to bless.
Let thy grace, my soul's chief treasure,
  Love's pure flame within me raise;
And, since words can never measure,
  Let my life show forth thy praise.

Devoted as he was to his wife and children the happiest moments in Key's life were those he spent at his own fireside. As a result of his authorship of *The Star-Spangled Banner*, he was invited to become an associate member of the Delphian Club of Baltimore, a social group organized in 1816 to stimulate interest in literary pursuits. The club was named after the oracle at Delphi; the president was supposed to be a representative of Apollo, and each member had one of the Muses as his consort; and in this way the club maintained a classical background which afforded great amusement. Meeting each Saturday night at the home of one of the members, the men exchanged epigrams, puns, and humorous stories, and then adjourned for oysters, or partridges, or canvasback duck. A few of the members wrote some splendid essays and poems; but they indulged more in pleasantries than in literature. Francis Scott Key was not fond of conviviality; but as the author of a popular song he was invited to membership in the club, as were also Samuel Woodworth, author of *The Sweet Home.*

Old Oaken Bucket, and John Howard Payne, author of *Home,*

One of Key's poems, entitled *On a Young Lady's Going into a Shower Bath,* is said to have been written for the Delphian Club:

"O that this too too solid flesh would melt
Thaw and resolve itself" to water clear,
And pure as that which flows through flowery vales
Of Arcady, and stays its gentle wave
To kiss the budding blossoms on its brink,
Or to encircle in its fond embrace
Some trembling, blushing maid, who doubting stands,
And hopes and fears to trust the smiling stream!
Then, as the amorous rise of Gods and men
From Heav'n descended in a golden show'r
To Danae's open'd arms, another heav'n,
So from the bath, that o'er the shrinking charms
Of Sweet Nerea hung, would I more blest
Than rapturous love, upon a form more fair
Than Danae's a silver show'r descends.
O then those charms of which the lighted touch
Would fire the frozen blood of apathy,
Each drop of me should touch, should eager run
Down her fair forehead, down her blushing cheek
To taste the more inviting sweets beneath,
Should trickle down her neck, should slowly wind,
In silver circles round those hills of snow,
Or lingering steal through the sweet vale between
And when at length perplex'd with the rich store
Of nature's varied, most luxuriant charms,
Amid the circling tendrils which entwine
An altar form'd for love's soft sacrifice,
Insinuating creep, there as a bee
In a fresh rosebud hid, a refuge find
From the rude napkin's meriligious touch.

The Delphian Club went out of existence in 1825. While Key had become acquainted with many of its members, his contact with the organization was quite limited.

"One would think," he once said, "that when a man had just got a good wife, he would be willing to sit down quietly at home, get to work and provide for his family." This was the advice that he gave to his Cousin Thomas U. P. Charlton (son of his Uncle Thomas Charlton) in 1824, when the young Savannah lawyer was aspiring to be Minister to Mexico. President Monroe had appointed Ninian Edwards of Illinois to this position; but Edwards was accused of being the author of a scurrilous attack on Secretary of the Treasury Crawford; was brought back to Washington to be quizzed; and soon was forced to resign. While Key had no influence with President Monroe, or with John Quincy Adams, Secretary of State, nevertheless he agreed to urge the appointment if Cousin Tom insisted on it. Key referred to John Quincy Adams as "a cross grained piece of stuff" with "stiff sinews" and "hard face" — a description somewhat like that given by a contemporary who said that Adams was "hard as a piece of granite and cold as a lump of ice." Key's letter of advice to his ambitious cousin gives an illustration of the poet lawyer's humor:

Key to Thomas U. P. Charlton

My dear Tom.

On going home for a day or two last week I found your letter, but had not time to answer it, as I was obliged to return here in a hurry — I heartily wish you joy of your marriage. Judge Johnson had informed me in the winter of your good fortune. And now what a strange, discontented fellow you are — One would think that when a man had just got a good wife, he would be willing to sit down quietly at home, get to work & provide for his family. And yet this is just the time when you are full of going abroad, & think of relinquishing a profession by which you can gratify every reasonable desire to take up a vagabond sort of life subject to the calls & re-calls of whoever may happen to have the command of you — You may tell me (& I suppose it is so, of course; & I would take the privilege of a relation to tell Mrs. Charlton to insist upon it that it should be so, though I dare say she will require no such hint) that your wife is to accompany you: but this does not remove all objections. You will spend your outfit, your Salary, & probably more; & when you come back again in two or three years you will, I fear, be too lazy for the drudgery of the law, & you will I know, be too proud to come to the city & beg & bow & lie to get another place. — I hope therefore you will think of this matter more seriously — I know you despise money & prudence & all such matters, & shall therefore only use the *argumentum ad hominem* — Take therefore your idol — fame — & consider whether you cannot in a fair professional career, gather as bright laurels, as those that have been stinking on the foul head of a poor dirty wretch like Edwards — However I forget that you did not ask me for advice, but for intelligence as to the prospect of success, & aid, if there was any way in which I could render it — As to aid, you know I have no political influence, & therefore nothing to give for anything I might ask. To get anything with out having something to give for it is, I presume, out of the question at Courts: unless perhaps to some very particular Court-favorites; & they too, poor Devils, have to give something, that is, themselves (if that is anything,) for all they get — As to intelligence, if you wish to know what Mr. Monroe would say in case I called upon him, & asked how you stood, and what prospect there was of your appointment, I can give you his answer now, just as well as if I had waited upon him & taken it down in black & white. And if you chuse it, I will call upon him & let you know exactly what he says — But as I can do it just as well before hand, I do not see why I need make you wait for it — Here it is then —

(*presidens loquitor*) "Mr. Charlton of Georgia — O yes — I recollect him Sir very well — We have received his letters & his recommendation very strong — very high & from the very first men, nobody can come before us with greater claims to consideration. And he is a man we know independently of recommendations. — We know personally his great worth & fitness for such a place — indeed Sir, for any place — He was much distinguished in Congress I believe" —

"He was not in Congress Sir — He attended the Supreme Court when you saw him here. — And was Mayor of Savannah during the great mortality there."

"O yes Sir I recollect — the Supreme Court — it was the Supreme Court — And at Savannah Sir, he acquired the greatest credit by his heroical conduct — I doubt not Sir, but that such services & a such character will be thought to present very strong claims to any office. But Sir there are so many things to be considered on these occasions — there are so many applications & so many & such very warm recommendations — & sometimes so many that are all equally meritorious & equally recommended, that really Sir, you can hardly conceive our embarrassments" —

"Suppose Sir (excuse me for suggesting anything) suppose in such cases you were to put them all in a bag, shake them well together, & see who would come out first" —

"Why really I thank you Sir — That might do often — I think we might have tried it sometimes to advantage — I really wish we had thought of it — I wish we had put Edwards in a bag — But Sir as to Mr. Charlton you may assure him that there can be no such thing as overlooking the pretensions of such a man. And, to be candid Sir, I will express to you my sincere hope that when the matter comes up before us Mr. Charlton's services & standing may be duly estimated, & that it may be in our power to gratify our wishes in regard to him"—

So much for the President—Now if you can find out from this what your chance is, you are far more quick sighted than our Court followers here, who have been studying such answers for years without being able to make anything out of them yet.

And now do you want to know what Mr. Adams will say of your prospects?—That would depend entirely upon the person that called upon him. If he was a man that could turn a state or perhaps even a county on the presidential question, the Secretary would try to bend his stiff sinews & soften his hard face, & would be as polite & promising as possible, & would look more smooth than it could be thought such a cross grained piece of stuff ever could— But if *I* was to call upon him, as soon as he saw him, he would feel pleased to *think* that there was a fellow to whom he could be as short and crusty as he liked, & you would have but a poor view of the matter from the monosyllables that I could force out of him.—

As to Lloyd, he could serve you no better than I—rather worse—for I am but a Cypher, where as he is a figure of some size against the palace. Being an open and violent friend of Crawford they would rather spite him than please him—Besides do you think you are fit to succeed Edwards?—Are you fit for anything that fitted him? You may say so, but I would not say it for you—I have hardly paper enough to tell you that whatever you may think of my notions on this subject, I hope you know that I am

Sincerely your friend & Kinsman

FRANCIS SCOTT KEY

"Take therefore your idol — fame." Francis Scott Key was giving his sincere conviction when he wrote these words. He did not covet any office in the government. When his friend William Hemsly, a quiet, modest man, died in 1826, he wrote an epitaph for his grave that bespoke his preference for a tranquil life over a career of pomp and power. This is Key's tribute to his friend:

William Hemsly, Esq.

Here lies a man whose life proved and adorned
The faith by which he walked. By all esteemed,
By many loved, hated or feared by none,
He moved, secluded from the world's vain gaze,
Within a narrow, but a glorious sphere
Of Christian duty, shedding love and peace
Around his path, where many an eye that once
Beheld and blessed him, now is dim with tears.
Reader! if thou dost know the grace of God,
Thank Him for this His gift; and pray that thou
May'st live, like Hemsly, to thy Maker's praise,
And, like him, die with steadfast hope in Christ,
The victor, not the victim of the grave!

Many years before Key had become known as an expert writer of epitaphs. When a relative or friend died, the poet lawyer would pen a dozen or so lines of verse to express his sympathy and his admiration for the departed. Among those who called forth his Muse were two beautiful young sisters, Isabella and Sarah Steele.

The following lines were written in memoriam to Isabella who died in 1825:

Isabella M. Steele

Why must the grave hide one whose light would
shine
To bless the world? Why friends and kindred mourn?
And this cold stone — why must it vainly strive

To tell a mother's love, a mother's grief?
The grave must hide the young, the fair, the good,
To prove the grave to be the gate of life
Through which they pass to joys that bloom not here.
Kindred and friends must mourn, that they may long
To meet again, where they shall part no more.
A mother's heart must bleed that He who wounds
Only to heal, may call its hopes from earth
To fix them with a sainted child in heaven.
When graves give up their dead, O! then may all
Who weep o'er this, reap blessings from their tears.

Another epitaph was written for the grave of Mrs. Mary Ann Morsell, who died in 1831 in her thirty-second year:

Mary Ann Morsell

A little while, this narrow house, prepared
By grief and love, shall hold the blessed dead;
A little while, and she who sleeps below
Shall hear the call to rise and live forever;
A little while, and ye who pour your tears
On this cold grave, shall waken in your own,
And ye shall see her, in her robes of light,
And hear her song of triumph. Would ye then
Partake with her the bliss of that new life?
Tread now the path she brightly marked before ye!
Choose now her Lord! live now her life! and yours
Shall be her hope and victory in death.

There were many poems, too, which Key composed for living friends in token of sympathy or affection. One of these was written in 1828 for a deaf and speechless boy. William Darlington, who was on a visit to Washington. It was a thrilling experience for the lad when he shook hands with the author of *The Star-Spangled Banner.* A feeling of deep sympathy surged through Key's soul as he dashed off the stanzas:

Lines Given to William Darlington

The deaf shall hear, and the dumb shall speak,
In the brighter days to come,
When they've pass'd through the troubled scenes of life,
To a higher and happier home.

They shall hear the trumpet's fearful blast,
As it breaks the sleep of the tomb;
They shall hear the righteous Judge declare
To the faithful their blessed doom.

And the conqueror's shout, and the ransomed's song,
On their raptur'd ears shall fall,
And the tongue of the dumb, in the chorus of praise,
Shall be higher and louder than all.

Oh Thou, whose still voice can need no ear,
To the heart its message to bear,
Who canst hear the unutter'd reply of the heart,
As it glows in the fervor of prayer—

Speak in thy pity and power to these
Who only Thee can hear,
And bend to the call of their speaking hearts,
Thine ever-listening ear!

As Key placed his hand on the deaf boy's shoulder and handed him the poem, he wondered if poetry could be appreciated fully by the deaf. The grateful lad picked up his slate and wrote: "I think the minds of those who cannot hear may perceive the beauties of poetry." Then he wrote on his slate:

"Your lines, though I have only read them over hastily, I observe are intended to describe the happiness of the deaf and dumb in the future state, when after this life they shall be received into Heaven with great joyfulness and open ears."

The longer Key lived, and the more opportunity he had to observe unfortunate people — the sick and insane, the blind, and the deaf — the more he appreciated his own lot in life. But to him life gave no greater joy than the thought that after the brief existence on this earth his body would be resurrected for a life eternal.

The poet lawyer sang with David: "I will bless the Lord, who hath given me counsel. . . . Therefore my heart is glad, and my glory rejoiceth. . . . For thou wilt not leave my soul in hell. . . . Thou wilt shew me the path of life: in thy presence is fullness of joy: at thy right hand there are pleasures for evermore." He was so happy over his prospects for the life beyond that he wrote a poem of ecstasy in which he expressed his assurance that he would avoid the dread gloom of Hell:

Psalm XVI

O! bright and happy is my lot,
And sweet the path of life to me;
All praise to thee, eternal King!
Whose favor fixed the fair decree.

He guides me through the busy day,
And through the long and lonely night;
Fills me with hope and holy joy,
And guards me with his matchless might.

My mind, in all I act or plan,
Looks to my God, and His commands;
And, to uphold my feeble steps,
Protector, by my side, He stands.

My heart shall beat with grateful joy,
  My ready tongue thy praise proclaim;
For thy benignant grace shall still
  Preserve and bless this mortal frame.

And thou this warm, aspiring soul,
  That breathes its humble vows to thee,
From hell's dread gloom wilt kindly save,
  And from the grave's corruption free.

Thou the bright way to heaven wilt show,
  Thy blissful courts the just receive,
Thine hand bestow celestial joys
  No tongue can tell, no heart conceive.

Key was beginning to dispel the thought of Divine anger and chastisement; he was now acquiring a brighter conception of life. Like his forefathers, he found in the Bible a strength that gave him self-reliance and steadfastness in faith. From the Bible he took, like Milton and Bunyan, inspiration for his poetry. As he studied the life of the Teacher of Galilee, he was impressed to find how promptly sinners were forgiven. In St. Luke, for instance, was the story of the woman of sin, who, when Jesus sat at meat in the house of Simon, the Pharisee, brought "an alabaster box of ointment," and began to wash the feet of Jesus with her tears, and "did wipe them with the hairs of her head, and kissed his feet, and anointed them with the ointment."

Key was stirred as he read the declaration of the Prince of Peace to the Pharisee: "Her sins, which are many, are forgiven; for she loved much." And then the assurance given to the erring woman: "Thy sins are forgiven. . . . Thy faith saved thee; go in peace."

According to many commentators of the Bible, there is no

foundation for the belief that the woman who anointed the feet of Jesus in Simon's house was Mary Magdalene; but this assumption found its way into a number of books, and when Key wrote a poem about the repentant woman he called it *Mary Magdalene*:

To the hall of that feast came the sinful and fair,
She heard in the city Jesus was there;
Unheeding the splendor that blaz'd on the board,
She silently knelt at the feet of her Lord.

The hair on her forehead so sad and so meek,
Hung dark o'er the blushes that burn'd on her cheek;
And so sad and so lowly she knelt in her shame
It seemed that her spirit had fled from her frame.

The frown and the murmur went round thro' them all,
That one so unhallow'd should tread in that hall,
And some said, the poor would be objects more meet,
For the wealth of the perfume she shower'd on his feet.

She heard but her Saviour, she spoke but in sighs,
She dar'd not look up to the Heav'n of his eyes;
And the hot tears gush'd forth at each heave of her breast,
As her lips to His sandals were throbbingly press'd.

In the sky after tempest as shineth the bow,
In the glance of the sunbeam as melteth the snow,
He looked on that lost one — her sins were forgiv'n,
And Mary went forth in the beauty of Heav'n.

More and more too was Key appreciating the beauties and the bounties of Nature, and discovering in them the hand of a God who was sympathetic and kind, rather than stern and vindictive. His theory of the Creation was the one advanced by Moses: God ordered the sun to light the earth by day; the moon by night; then placed the stars in the "firmament of the heaven" — all within the period of six days. He was deeply impressed by Voltaire's lines:

> "Toutes ces vastes pays d'azure et de lumière
> Tirés du sein de voide, formés sans matière,
> Arrondis sans compass, et tournants sans pivot,
> Ont à piene contés la depense d'un mot."

Key translated the thought of Voltaire into verses of his own, constituting one of his most superb poems:

The Creation

From the dark depth of Nature's void arise
Unnumber'd worlds, and glitter in the skies.
No bright materials the vast orbs demand,
Nor rule, nor compass, nor a forming hand;
Self-pois'd the axis, self-sustain'd the poles,
Each in his order'd path, obedient rolls.
They were not, and were call'd — were call'd and heard,
And cost, and scarcely cost, the effort of a word.

Key's sister Anne, who had left Frederick with Taney in 1823 and was now living in Baltimore was delighted with this brief but excellent poem. She copied it into her poetry album, for she too shared the poet's love of the beautiful; she too gazed often into the starlit night; she too was unable to understand how any one could doubt the existence of a God.

Key's conception of the Universe was similar to that of the ancient Jews — a great machine operated day and night by an anthropomorphic God. Like Darwin, some years later, he believed that the Universe was so "grand and wondrous" and so far beyond the scope of man's intellect, that it was impossible to conceive that it arose through chance — this constituted an argument for the existence of God. He recalled the words of the English poet, Edward Young, "By night the atheist half believes a God."

Another bit of verse which struck Mrs. Taney's fancy was a poem dated at Georgetown on February 14, 1828, describing the landscape by moonlight:

'Tis Midnight

'Tis midnight — on the mountain brown
The cold round moon shines deeply down;
Blue roll the waters, blue the sky
Spreads like an ocean hung on high,
Bespangled with those isles of light,
So wildly, spiritually bright!
Who ever gazed upon them shining,
And turned to earth without repining;
Nor wished for wings to flee away,
And mix with their eternal ray?

As the years rolled by, Key found in each joy and each sorrow a deeper meaning in life. The decade from forty to fifty was a period of kaleidoscopic change. In 1823 a new experience came to him — the marriage of one of his children. It was Maria, the eldest of all except Elizabeth. Maria, at the time they settled in Georgetown, was an infant in swaddling clothes; now she was eighteen. On June 3, 1823, she became the bride of Henry Maynadier Steele.

In November, 1823, Polly gave birth to her tenth child, now her ninth living child. It was a girl; and they christened her Mary Alicia Lloyd Nevins Key. She was called Alice.

In 1825 Elizabeth, then a young lady of twenty-two, was married to Charles Howard of Baltimore. The groom was a son of General John Eager Howard, who had won distinction in the Revolution and later served as Governor and United States Senator.

In 1826 Francis Scott Key, Jr., joined the ranks of the benedicts, taking as his bride Miss Elizabeth Lloyd Harwood of Annapolis.

The author of the National Anthem became a grandfather at forty-five; Polly a grandmother at forty. So large was the family that after they were grandparents they became parents again: for in the Summer of 1827, when Polly was over forty-three, the eleventh child was born. It was a boy, named Charles Henry.

Although responsibilities were piling upon him mountain-high, Key never lost his vibrant enthusiasm for the Church. Frequently, as a lay reader, he held services in churches with vacant pulpits; frequently visited the poor, the sick, and the prisoners in jail; gave money to the destitute and prayed with them, as one of his daughters recalled, with "great fervor and earnestness." While he frowned on some of the sects like Socinianism, he was always glad to lend a helping hand to any of the sister denominations which taught the Apostle's Creed. When he heard that plans were on foot to consolidate the English Presbyterians and the German Reformers of Taneytown and to raise funds to erect a union church for the two congregations, he gladly gave his coöperation to the movement. To help his friends, Clotworthy Birnie and Nicholas Schnider of Taneytown, he wrote a letter of recommendation, as they started on a trip to Philadelphia to solicit contributions. "The union of these Societies," he said in his recommendation, "is a gratifying event, and the example, if followed (as may be hoped) in other places, will produce many good consequences."

Even in the Summer time, on his vacation at Pipe Creek, Key never neglected his religious duties. He journeyed up and down the countryside with John Snook, one of his country neighbors, it is said, and held prayer meetings. Snook, who was ten years younger than Key, had become interested in revival work largely through the inspiration of the "unsectarian ministers" who established the United Brethern Church near Frederick in 1800. The need for a church and a school in the Pipe Creek region was apparent, and an appeal was made for contributions. The poet lawyer from Georgetown offered to donate a half acre of ground from his Terra Rubra estate for the purpose. The offer was accepted; and in September, 1828, he and Polly deeded the land to John Snook, Frederick Dutterer, Jacob Maring of F, and Jacob Maring of G, as trustees, for the erection of "a school and meeting house for preaching." By and by the little log buildings, about a mile west of Terra Rubra along the road leading from Bruceville to Emmitsburg were completed. Key had already erected a dwelling nearby; soon several other houses were built; and in the course of time the village became known as Keysville. It is still known by that name in memory of the author of the National Anthem.

Key also continued in his later years to attend many of the Conventions of the Episcopal Church. In 1820, when he was one of the lay deputies to the General Convention in Philadelphia, he and Rev. Dr. William E. Wyatt were chosen to represent Maryland on the board of trustees of the General

Theological Seminary at Alexandria, a position which he held during the rest of his life. At the same Convention he was appointed a member of a committee to consider the formation of a missionary society: and thus did he become one of the organizers of the Domestic and Foreign Missionary Society of the Protestant Episcopal Church.

An example of Key's influence in the councils of the Church was manifested at the General Convention of 1826. At this Convention, held in Philadelphia, a canon was introduced in the House of Bishops to modify the liturgy. Some of the lay deputies raised objections, but Key gave his enthusiastic coöperation. One of the prelates, Bishop J. H. Hobart, appreciating the support of the lawyer from Georgetown, wrote to him: "I do assure you, that my object was to settle the discrepancies which prevail in the use of the liturgy, in a manner suiting all parties; and I was highly gratified by the frank and cordial support which this attempt received from yourself, Mr. Meade, Mr. Henshaw, and others."

On July 8, 1830 – after Key had passed fifty – death took away the saintly mother who had formed the godly character of the Nation's patriot poet. At her knee the son had learned humility and charity. He had loved her throughout all the years from the time he was a barefoot boy at Pipe Creek. Her death was a poignant grief to his sensitive soul. It is no wonder that, as blow fell upon blow, a tenderness of expression "almost bordering on sadness" was chiselled upon his face.

Key recalled David's song in the Psalms: "In the day when I cried thou answeredst me, and strengthenedst me with strength in my soul." With this in mind he wrote a poem to explain the value of prayer in time of trouble:

Efficacy of Prayer

When troubles, wave on wave, assailed,
And fear my soul appalled,
I knew the Lord would rescue me,
And for deliverance called.

Still onward, onward came the flood;
Again I sought the Lord,
And prayed that he the waves would still
By his resistless word.

But still they rushing came; again
Arose my earnest prayer,
And when I prayed for faith and strength
Whate'er he willed, to bear.

Then his felt presence was my strength,
His outstretched arm was nigh;
My head he raised, my heart he cheered;
"Fear not," he said, "'tis I."

Strong in that strength, I rose above
The tempest's fierce alarms;
It drove me to a sort of peace,
Within a Saviour's arms.

All about him Key saw conditions of misfortune and suffering. One of the most pathetic figures in Georgetown was Rev. Walter Dulany Addison, who was Key's rector at St. John's until the founding of Christ Church. In 1824 Rev. Addison's eyes were gradually failing; finally they were operated upon in Philadelphia, but without success; and then in 1827, with blindness and poverty upon him, he was forced to abandon his flock. In 1830 his son, Francis Key Addison, who had entered the Military Academy at West Point through Francis Scott Key's influence, died. A few years later came the death of the rector's daughter. But even as late as 1831, Rev. Addison, when totally blind, occasionally officiated at church services; and the radiance on his face impressed all who saw him. As old age came on, he accepted the will of God with humble submission.

During all these years of shadow and sunshine, the love between Key and his sister remained steadfast. In Mrs. Taney's poetry album under date of January 1, 1832, is the poem written for her by her brother:

To My Sister

I think of thee — I feel the glow
Of that warm thought, yet well I know
No verse a brother's love may show,
My sister!

But ill should I deserve the name,
Of "warmth divine" that poets claim,
If I for thee no lay could frame,
My sister!

I think of thee — of those bright hours,
Rich in life's first and fairest flow'rs,
When childhood's gay delights were ours,
My sister!

Those sunny paths were all our own,
And thou and I were there alone,
Each to the other only known,
My sister!

In every joy and every care,
We two, and we alone, were there
The brightness and the gloom to share,
My sister!

As changing seasons o'er us flew,
No changes in our love we knew,
And there our hearts together grew,
My sister!

And then there came that dreaded day
When I with thee no more must stay,
But to the far school haste away,
My sister!

Sad was the parting — sad the days,
And dull the school and dull the plays,
Ere I again on thee may gaze,
My sister!

But longest days will yet be past,
And cares of school away be cast,
And home and thee be seen at last,
My sister!

The mountain top, the wood, the plain,
The winding creek, the shaded lane,
Shall shine in both our eyes again,
My sister!

Who then shall first my greeting seek?
Whose warm tears fall upon my cheek
And tell the joy she cannot speak?
My sister!

My sister! those bright days are gone
And we thro' life have journey'd on
With hearts which still, as then, are one,
My sister!

A parting hour at last must come —
To meet again beyond the tomb —
O let us then make heav'n our home,
My sister!

In 1833 Key received the news of the death at Frederick of a little granddaughter of his Cousin Eleanor Potts. The little girl was the daughter of Richard H. and Harriet Potts Marshall. Mr. Marshall, a native of Southern Maryland, had come to Frederick to study law under Taney. He was now thirty-three and was engaged in the practice of law at Frederick.

Key wrote a letter of sympathy to Mrs. Potts, expressing one of the cardinal tenets of his philosophy of life — that the visitations of God are always for the best:

Key to Mrs. Eleanor Potts

Geo Town

26th. Mar — 33

My Dear Cousin Nelly

The enclosed little book I will thank you to give to Harriet with my love. Tell her I hope she is able to say from her heart — "it is well," — It is only saying what is infallibly true and certain; as she will one day know — Now we "see through a glass darkly" — but when all the hidden ways of God's providence are revealed to us, we shall see & own that "He hath done all things well."

It is only the weakness of our faith that keeps us now from being, "in whatsoever state we are, therewith content" — If we believed & trusted as we have a right to do, we should always be enabled to say of everything that happens to us — "it is the Lord —let Him do what seemeth to Him good."

God gives us many helps in this our weakness of faith — We see around us in the world many & severe sufferings. The child for whose life we would pray we cannot guard from them. We must commit it to God: and if He sees best to remove it from "the evil to come," & take it from scenes of trouble and danger, to mansions of rest & happiness in his own presence, how can we repine?—When it is thus taken what shall we pray for?—that we may see it again—that this dear object of our affections may be again in our arms? This is a natural & reasonable desire—and it shall be granted.—And that is the best possible way for us & it. —"I shall go to him," said David of his child, "but he shall not return to me."

Now if God, in such circumstances, was to give us our choice of either of having our child returned to us here, or of taking us to it in heaven, could we have a doubt as to which was best?

I trust that Harriet & Mr. Marshall will encourage each other in looking forward to a meeting with their dear child, where there will be no more sorrow or separation, sickness or death, and that they will see & own in this dispensation, the hand of a father & say—"it is well."

With love to them & Eleanor & all our friends

I am my dear Cousin

Affec^{ly}. yrs

F. S. KEY

Through many ordeals passed the poet lawyer, with Polly by his side, to the sunset years of life.

FRANCIS SCOTT KEY

From the original
supposed to have been cut by him

CHAPTER XVI

A Plea for St. John's

ABOUT TEN years after Key's graduation, the Maryland Legislature discontinued its appropriation to St. John's College. It was a hard blow to the institution — that "infant seminary" which George Washington hoped would develop into "an early and at the same time mature manhood." President McDowell resigned as President of the College to take a position elsewhere. The College had no graduates at all for several years. It sank into decay because of the false economy of the members of the Legislature. This is how Francis Scott Key explained the cause of the misfortune:

> At the unfortunate period to which I refer, when the brightest ornament of the State [St. John's College] was cast away from her protection, it was not the voice of the people, but the strife of party, by which it fell. It is not censorious to say of the opposing politicians who then divided and distracted the State, that in their struggles for pre-eminence, each class considered its own ascendancy as the greatest concern of the State. In their eager search for pretexts to catch the popular ear, the College was thought of. As the people at large seldom saw it or heard of it, and a great proportion of them, from their situation, felt no immediate interest in its continuance, it was thought the saving of the funds could be called economy, and that the many, who were to be flattered, would be pleased with the destruction of what appeared to be only for the

> benefit of the few. Had a fair appeal been made by either side to the intelligence and patriotism of the people, and their own great interest in the institution been set before them, there is no reason to doubt but the sound policy which had originally appropriated these funds to such a purpose, and of which no complaint had been made, would have been sustained. But no such appeal was made. Each party caught at the advantage to be gained by the apparent popularity of the measure, and the real interests and honour of the State were sacrificed by each.

While St. John's was in this predicament the lawyer from Georgetown visited Annapolis and strolled over the College green. He was distressed at the lamentable transformation. Although he had never before been ambitious for public office, now, for once, he wished he were a member of the Legislature, for, his pride for his Alma Mater wounded, he wanted to lift his voice against what he termed "the madness" of the legislators to erase a foul blot from the State. As he paused on the steps of McDowell Hall under the branches of old Liberty Tree, he saw the ghosts of yesteryear:

> Thirty years ago I stood within that hall, with the associates of my early joys and labours, and bade farewell to them, to our revered instructors, to the scenes of our youthful happiness, and received the parting benediction of that beloved and venerated man [John McDowell] who ruled the institution he had reared, and adorned, not more by the force of authority than of affection.
>
> In a few short years I returned; and the companions and the guides of my youth were gone—and the glory of the Temple of Science, which the wisdom and piety of our fathers had founded, was departed. I saw in its place a dreary ruin. I wandered over its beautiful and

> silent green, no longer sacred to the meditations of the enraptured student, nor vocal with the joyous shout of youthful merriment. I sat upon the mouldering steps of that lonely portico; and beneath the shadow of that ancient tree, that seemed like me to lament its lost companions—and the dreams of other days came over me—and I mourned over the madness that had worked this desolation.
>
> If I have ever felt the impulse to mingle in the councils of my country, it was in these scenes and at these moments, when filial affection to my Alma Mater, and love to my native State, united to impel me to redress the wrongs of the one, and efface the foulest blot upon the name of the other.

In 1811 an appropriation of one thousand dollars was restored by the Legislature; this was far less than the amount needed from the State; but it was better than nothing. Then in 1824 the College conducted a lottery: from this a fund of twenty thousand dollars was raised; but when it was invested in bank stock it brought an income of only about one thousand dollars a year.

St. John's languished so long that many of her patrons were apprehensive that she would be unable to survive. It was in this extremity that the alumni stepped forward to offer their aid. An appeal was issued to the alumni to attend the Commencement exercises on February 22, 1827. Francis Scott Key was one of the loyal sons of St. John's who visited the College on that day. After the exercises were over, the Faculty, Board of Visitors and Governors and the alumni adjourned to St. Anne's Church to hold a meeting there in the interest of the College and to form an Alumni Association.

John C. Herbert, an alumnus from Prince George's

County, acted as chairman of the meeting. A. C. Magruder, James Murray and Francis Scott Key were selected to prepare a constitution for the Alumni Association.

Key had been invited to deliver the address at the meeting. He had already conferred with a number of the members of the Legislature, urging them to save the struggling institution of learning. He felt confident that the people of the State would eventually force the Legislature to give adequate aid to St. John's. On the subject of the expectation of State aid he said:

> I may have spoken in vain to the legislators and the citizens of Maryland. Public opinion may be slower in its discernments and operations than one as inexperienced as I am on such subjects may have supposed. But I have the consolation of knowing that Experience if a slow, is a sure teacher; and that it cannot be long before Maryland will be made to feel her need of men of high attainments in political and natural science, gifted with the powers necessary to successful service, and to see that the only way to secure them is to rear them herself.

Key declared that he felt a sense of gratitude for "the richest of all earthly blessings, in the culture and discipline of my earliest and happiest years." Accordingly he had "an ardent desire to see this venerable seat of learning restored to her former splendour, and dispensing these blessings to the rising generation of Maryland, the future ornaments and pillars of the State." To the loyal teachers, who had been sticking to their tasks at St. John's in spite of their difficulties, he expressed his sincere appreciation. Brighter prospects loomed ahead. "We owe our thanks for this," he said, "to those whose zeal and ardor have excited them to renewed efforts in her behalf, who with limited means, and against many difficulties, have exhibited before us on this occasion the interesting and gratifying fruits of their labours."

Key then called upon his fellow alumni to pledge themselves to come to the rescue of their Alma Mater. The alumni, he declared, ought not to need a speaker to awaken emotions in their breasts. They were in the midst of scenes that recalled the days of yore – the days "when the morning of life, and the light of intellectual improvement, and the warm associations of early friendship, gave all their brightness to the joys and the visions of youth." They were assembled "as brethern, bound by the same ties of love and veneration to their common mother." In her behalf he called upon them to make an appeal "to the patriotism and justice of their fellow-citizens – to make it till it is heard throughout the bounds of the State – to make it till it is successful."

Key's address was a cogent argument for State aid to Education. This was his syllogism: The State is founded to promote happiness; Education confers happiness; therefore the State should foster Education. To use his words:

> A government administered for the benefit of all should provide all practicable means of happiness for all. It must also provide useful citizens competent to the discharge of the various services the public interests may require. Education confers happiness and usefulness, and therefore demands attention. No maxim is more readily admitted than that a wise and free government should provide for the education of its

> citizens; but the maxim seems not to be admitted to its just extent.

He then divided the people into two classes—the rich, or the "men of leisure"; and the poor, or the "labouring class." Himself a scion of an aristocratic family, he branded the socialistic idea as Utopian and dangerous. "There are, and ever will be," he declared, "the poor and the rich, the men of labour and the men of leisure, and the State which neglects either, neglects a duty, and neglects it at its peril, for whichever it neglects will be not only useless but mischievous. They have equal claims to the means of happiness. They are capable of making equal returns of service to the public."

From the very nature of things, Key declared, it would be neither possible nor desirable that all men should be alike in any political society—limited by the same necessities, or destined to the same employments. "If they could be reduced to the same level," he maintained, "they could not be kept to it. Idleness and vice would sink below it; honourable effort would rise above it."

And so he emphasized the vital importance to the State of training her "men of leisure" in order to qualify them for broad spheres of usefulness. To neglect the rich man's son—allowing him "to rust in sloth, or to riot in dissipation"—he thought would be worse than to neglect the poor boy, for the wealthy person "has more in his power either for good or evil; will be more apt, from his greater temptations, to be depraved himself and the corrupter of others."

Francis Scott Key, as afraid as any Puritan of the "vain

amusements of the world," believed that failure to provide the discipline of College life would irreparably damage a country like the United States. Said he:

> This neglect would be peculiarly unwise in a government like ours. Luxury is the vice most fatal to Republics; and idleness, and want of education in the rich, promote it in its disgusting forms.

Indeed, he believed that the evil of luxury was already beginning to undermine the foundations of the Republic. "Nor let it be thought," he exclaimed, "that we have no cause to guard against this evil. It is perhaps the most imminent of our perils." Pictured in his mind were the wealthy ambassadors who came to Washington from the luxurious Courts of Europe. He caught occasional glimpses of the extravagant trappings and riotous living at the Embassies. He was apprehensive that these emissaries might import "foreign vices" into this country. "Whoever notes the change of manners thus introduced," Key warned, "will see that we have departed far from the Republican simplicity of better days."

Another argument in behalf of the College was the part it played in the advancement of Science. To Science, he said, "a people's greatness and happiness" are largely due. And, instead of conflicting with Religion, he believed that it prepared man for the life beyond.

> What gives to Agriculture her plains of smiling plenty? To Commerce, her wide domain upon the mighty waters? To the Arts, the very materials of their labour, as well as the skill to mould them? And what gives the power to defend, and the wisdom to govern the country they enrich?

And has Science accomplished all her conquests for man? Has she no further rewards for her votaries? Is she not now, in our own days, analyzing the earth for Agriculture, and revealing the very elements of fertility? Has she not just given to the Arts that safe and cheering light [Sir Humphrey Davey's lamp for miners] which descends into its deepest caverns, and makes its hidden treasures the prize, no longer of the fearful daring, but of the commanding wisdom of man? And is not her richest boon to Commerce, the mightiest power with which she rules her dominions, the gift but of yesterday?

She has, and will have, as long as man is doomed to labour, rewards for his labour, blessings to fit him for the enjoyment and diffusion of happiness here, and to prepare for the brighter glory of a higher state to which she teaches him to aspire.

Key then undertook to rebut the argument that it is not the duty of the State to provide for higher institutions of learning, but that they should be privately maintained. As a matter of fact, he declared, philanthropy is seldom, if ever, sufficient for such a purpose without State aid. "I do not mean," he explained, "that such persons [the wealthy] should have their children educated at the public expense, as should be the case with those whose necessities require it, but that they should be enabled to find within the State an establishment founded by its bounty and governed by its care."

The orator now proceeded to analyze the school system of Maryland. "She has established her primary schools, and in this she has done wisely. . . . She affords support, in most of the counties, to Academies for teaching the rudiments of some of the learned languages, and some of the sciences. In this also she has done wisely." But, he added, with these schools only a part of her duty had been fulfilled, and without a higher institution much of the efforts of the teachers would be fruitless:

> A boy of ten or twelve years of age at one of the primary schools, or elsewhere, has acquired a plain English education. His parents are affluent, and have the means of enabling him to devote his youth to education, and are desirous he should do so. When he has passed through his English school, he must either go home, and spend his youth in idleness, or be removed to some higher institution, where he can improve what he has acquired, and engage in other studies. The County Academy furnishes generally the means of accomplishing this. But in three or four years he has passed through this also; and though the ability and inclination of the parent may still continue, the State has afforded no means of doing more.

Since the collapse of St. John's College, the State of Maryland had not a single institution where the higher branches of Literature and Science could be taught. "Hundreds of her youth," he charged, "are either excluded from the degree of improvement required by their condition in life, or obtain it by being sent to other States." This, he felt, was extremely unfortunate. A youth of fifteen, he believed, ought to be placed under the wholesome restraint of College discipline, and not turned loose upon the world to pass "the most perilous period of his life." Key was not unmindful of the lures of "a deceitful world": he termed it "the deepest cruelty" to permit a lad to follow the reckless course to which "his own passions or the vices of others may allure him." Discipline, gentle but persevering, and some employment to consume the restless energies of an awakening mind — these are essential for the safety of youth.

In addition to discipline, the Colleges open the avenue to the highest satisfactions of life:

> Nor is it only as a refuge from the dangers of youth that such an institution is to be regarded. It is to give strength and preparation for the whole life. It is then that habits, principles and tastes, that fix the colour of succeeding years, are to be formed. Then are the victories to be achieved over the temper and disposition, over the temptations from within, and from without, that make the man master of himself through life. Patience in investigation, accuracy of research, perseverance in labour, resolution to conquer difficulty, zeal in the cause of learning and virtue, are then to be acquired. Then is Science to display her charms, and Literature her delights, and a refined and exalted taste to lure him, by higher gratifications, from the vain pleasures of the world. Then is he to be made familiar with the sages and heroes of antiquity, to catch the inspiration of their genius and their virtues, and the great and the good of every age and of every land are to be made his associates, his instructors, his examples.

Key now advanced his next argument — that the Colleges, in addition to promoting the happiness of the students, also serve to promote the welfare of the Nation, The educated man, enriched by the wisdom of the ages, holds not "these sacred trusts" only for himself; his greatest joy should be to wield them for the benefit of his country. And therefore the Colleges cultivate patriotic devotion:

> Will not a grateful sense of these benefits heighten the ardour of his patriotism, and will he not serve a

> country that cherished and adorned his youth with more devotion, as well as with far more ability? It may be that love of country springs from some undefinable and hidden instinct of our nature, wisely given to the heart of man to fit him for the filial duties which he owes to the land of his birth. But this impulse, however pure and high its origin, must submit to the common destiny of all human affections. It may glow with increasing ardour, elevate itself above all our desires, and reign the ruling passion of the soul. And it may grow cold, languish and expire. A country, like a parent, should meet this instinctive feeling of her children with a corresponding affection; should call it forth to early and continual exercise, by early and continual blessings, by setting before them illustrious examples, and all the high rewards of virtue, and preparing them for all the enjoyments and duties of life. Such a country will not want patriots. But the land that does nothing to cherish or reward the natural affection of her sons. . . . must look for them in vain . . . And the name and the thoughts of their country awakens no emotions but those of shame and reproach.

And so he enunciated this principle as indisputable: "A Nation is loved in proportion as it mérits the love of its people." Said he:

> The history of the world tells us from what altars the highest and purest flames of patriotism have ascended. The slave of the despot, who leaves an ill-fated country, and wherever he may wander, finds a fairer heritage and a better home, knows nothing of the *maladie du pays*. It is the free and hardy Swiss, who hears in distant lands the notes that charmed his ear upon his native mountains, and sickens, pines and dies, with love of country.

Therefore, he contended, it was the duty of the State to

establish institutions for her youth, institutions that would knit their hearts by the strongest ties to the land of their birth, institutions that would animate them to the highest zeal, and fit them for her greatest exigencies. "To what can a Nation look for her strength, security and glory," he asked, "but to a succession of patriots thus trained for her service?"

But the Colleges did more than benefit the Nation; they benefitted all mankind. Herein lay the challenge to America! Key agreed with Longinus, the Athenian philosopher, and David Hume, that "free governments are best adapted to the successful cultivation of literature and the arts." If that be true, then it was all the more the duty of America, the land of the free, to encourage such pursuits:

> Nations and individuals are alike under obligations to uphold the general cause of humanity, to contribute to the common stock of human happiness. The beneficent Creator, who has placed us in this scene of probation, has made this both our duty and our interest.
>
> Our Country has already been made the instrument of signal blessings to many portions of the earth. In the science of government particularly, much of the improvement made and now making in the condition of the world is to be attributed to the free and enlightened discussion of its principles among us, and to the influence of our example. America has held forth the light of Liberty to the world. To exalt still higher the lustre of her fame, to give perpetuity to our own institutions, and to dispense more widely the same blessings to others, let her now hold forth the torch of Science.

Finally and more important than all else, Key turned to the highest of all motives — gratitude to the Giver of all mercies. The lot of the American people, he declared, had been cast in a "land of light and liberty"; and God required some evidence of appreciation for the blessings bestowed. This obligation must be fulfilled; it is evaded at our peril:

> We profess to be a Christian people. We have received a revelation, to which everything within us and around us bears testimony of the high destiny of man, to which he is to be exalted when the ever changing scenes of this probationary state shall have passed away, and for which he is to be fitted by the due cultivation and employment of the faculties conferred upon him here. Whatever improves these faculties, enlarges the understanding, and exalts the affections, tends to prepare man to receive this faith and qualifies him to adorn it — makes him a shining light in a world of darkness, enables him to endure the conflicts of a life of trial, to "rejoice in the hope set before him," and fits him to communicate the blessedness of that hope to others.

Having completed his general argument in favor of Higher Education, Key now advanced to the need of Higher Education in Maryland. While it was true that the Legislature had withdrawn its support from St. John's College, he denied that the sentiment of the people of Maryland had been expressed on the subject. He was confident that the people of the State would favor an adequate appropriation to St. John's. He said:

> To suppose that the people of Maryland would now, upon a full and impartial consideration of this great subject, with all the light which experience has thrown upon it, . . . refuse to afford support to such an institution, would be to impute to them a degree of ignor-

> ance and prejudice, of which I trust and believe they are undeserving. If there were once doubts upon this subject, there can be none now.

Key hastily surveyed the political situation in the Nation. Since the election of John Quincy Adams in 1824, party spirit had been blazing with intensity. President Adams named Henry Clay for Secretary of State; and immediately there arose the cry of a corrupt bargain between Adams and Clay. Key's Virginia friend, John Randolph of Roanoke, added fuel to the flame. In the Senate this sepulchral figure denounced the friendship of the Puritan President and "Harry of the West" as a dangerous conspiracy. "I was defeated," shrieked Senator Randolph, "horse, foot, and dragoon – cut up and clean broke down by the coalition of Blifil and Black George – by the combination, unheard of till then, of the Puritan with the blackleg." This accusation led to a duel between Randolph and Clay, in which Clay put a bullet through Randolph's coat. All during the year 1826 the opposing political parties were strengthening their organizations. The followers of Adams and Clay united under the banner of the National Republicans. They stood for a protective tariff and for internal improvements by the National Government. It was at this time that many of the Federalists in Maryland joined the anti-Administration forces. Before long Roger Brooke Taney, who had been a Federalist for a quarter of a century, was to become an ardent follower of Andrew Jackson and one of the leading Democrats in Maryland. The sensitive soul of Francis Scott Key was disturbed. He could hear the call to arms; he could hear the tramp of the armies of the North and the South; he could hear the reverberations of the guns that were to shake the foundations of the Nation. He spoke now as a prophet:

> We have lived to witness the operation of the political institutions founded by our fathers. Events of the greatest interest have occurred, questions of the utmost moment have arisen, and principles vitally affecting us have been discussed and settled, and others are continually recurring. In all these events and questions and discussions, to see and feel the force of talent, the power of mind, and sometimes also to see and feel the want of them. Talent and mental power, if not always conferred, yet are always increased by education. . . . Therefore in almost all the States, particularly in such of them as have been most interested in these occurrences, public attention has been drawn to this subject, and wisely determining to call forth all the strength of their people, the public patronage has been given to the institutions of education. Maryland is a member of the American confederacy, united with the other independent States in one General Government. It is her concern that her own political course should be directed by wisdom, and for this she must necessarily look to her own citizens. It is also and equally her concern that the General Government should be wisely administered, and with a just regard to her own peculiar interests. She must furnish her quota of talent there. Her duty to the Union requires this; her own preservation demands it. It is not enough for her that there should be found there, wisdom and talent and patriotism; but she must see to it that Maryland wisdom and talent and patriotism are found there.
>
> There is a great common interest among these States—a bond of Union, strong enough, we all hope, to endure the occasional conflicts of subordinate local interests. But there are and ever will be these interests, and they will necessarily produce collision

and competition. Hence will continually arise questions of great National concern, and more or less, according to their respective interests, of vital importance to the States. These are all to be considered, discussed and settled. That they may be settled with justice to herself, Maryland must meet this competition with all her strength. It is not in the number of her delegation that she is to trust. She may send one man who may be in himself a host. It is essential to her that her interest should be seen and felt, and that those who see and feel it, should maintain it with all the power that talent and patriotism can wield. It is essential to her, and to every member of the Union, that the agitations excited by these collisions should be kept from endangering the foundations upon which the fabric of our free institutions has been reared — that men of the highest powers and the purest principles should rule the deliberations of our National councils on these occasions of difficulty and danger, and preserve, through every storm that may assail it, the Union — the ark of our safety.

It is no reproach to the wisdom of those who framed our Constitution that they have left it exposed to danger from the separate interests and powers of the Sates. It is not to be avoided but by incurring far greater dangers. Nor is our situation in that respect without its advantages. These local interests are powerful excitements to the States to prepare and enrich their public men with the highest possible endowments. . . .

If Providence shall preserve us from these dangers, and give perpetuity to our institutions, Maryland will continue to see an increasing necessity . . . for calling forth and cultivating all her resources. And if this hope fails us, if the Union is dissolved, in the distractions and dangers that will follow, she will, if possible, still more require the highest aid that the wisdom of her sons can afford, to guide her through that night of darkness.

As an illustration of the rivalry between the States, Key alluded to the foremost issue — the question of internal improvements. The Erie Canal had been completed in 1825 at the expense of the State of New York; and President John Quincy Adams, in lauding the people of New York, urged the Congress to follow their example by undertaking public works "important to the whole country." Plans were now on foot in Maryland to construct a railroad from Baltimore to the Ohio River as a means of hauling freight in cars drawn by horses and mules; and Governor Kent appealed to the people to give their support to the Baltimore and Ohio Railroad as well as to the Chesapeake and Ohio Canal. Whether internal improvements should be made by the States alone, or whether they were within the province of the National Government, had not yet been determined. But in either event, said Key, it was the bounden duty of Maryland to qualify and call forth all the talent that the subject required.

The speaker refrained from giving his own opinion on the political aspects of internal improvements. He evaded the issue by saying that the most needed improvement was the improvement of the intellect. To Francis Scott Key the mind was more important than matter. This was his tribute to the mind of man:

> I mean not rivers, roads, canals, nor all the facilities of commerce — but that which is above them all — which commands them all — at whose bidding the mountain opens to its base, and the waters of the cataract are still. I mean the mass of mind, the native talent of her population.
>
> And what is this without improvement? Inert and

dead as the rocks and mountains upon which it would labour; wild and wasteful as the torrents it would control — a chaos of confusion, till called into life and form and vigour by the light of Science; and then able to reduce into subjection all the elements of Nature.

This is the power which has placed a sister State [New York] foremost among the competitors for internal improvement; that has achieved for her the work [the Erie Canal] to which she justly looks for the continuance of her pre-eminence. It is not to the instruments of labour, with which the work has been accomplished, nor to the hands that wielded them, that the people of that State are to ascribe the success of their efforts. These instruments might have been wielded forever in vain, even by their whole population. A far higher power must be called to these labours. The man of Science must go before, and shew blind strength where he is to strike. And by the side of this Man of Science, or before him, must go the Man of another, and a higher Science. The Patriot and Statesman, who makes all the powers of Nature and the resources of Art tributary to his Country's greatness — who works upon the noblest of all materials — the mind of man — and achieves higher conquests than he who overcomes the obstacles of Nature. For he has mountains of prejudice to remove, floods of passion to controul, mightier than those of Nature. He is not only to form his own designs, but he is to be ever prepared, to convince, to refute, to persuade, and to turn the judgments and affections of others into the channel of his own conceptions. This is the power which has given to New York the work to which she owes her ascendancy.

The gist of Key's argument, therefore, was that, so that mind could conquer matter, it was wise to cultivate the mind. "Shall Maryland apply her resources to roads and rivers, and make no effort to obtain the Science that is to form them into the veins and sinews of her strength? Shall we give millions for canals, and nothing for the makers of canals?"

Arriving at the close of his argument, Key paid a tribute to the men of attainments who mold the thought and shape the destiny of mankind. "Let it also be remembered," he said, "that every well-taught citizen, whatever may be his condition, to whatever station in life he may belong, is generally speaking, an advantage to the public."

Key then recalled an oration delivered by Cato in the Roman Senate at a time of imminent peril. Cato's oration was so eloquent that the Roman historian was led to look back upon the past dangers and deliverances of his country and remark of the "*praeclara facinora,* that adorned her history, that their success and glory are to be attributed to the exalted excellence of a few citizens *paucorum civium eximia virtus.*" What a deep influence one man can exert for the welfare of a Nation!

Turning to "the short but eventful history" of the United States, Key recalled the galaxy of intellects who "led the way in the career of glory, and will ever be remembered as the Fathers of the Republic." Then he asked: "Who can say they would have attained — who can say they would have attempted success, if destitute of that intellectual and moral power which impelled and fitted them to the crisis?"

The poet lawyer alluded to Thomas Jefferson, author of the Declaration of Independence, who "left a memorable proof of the value at which he estimated literary institutions." Speaking of the sage of Monticello, Key said: "His last and most zealous labours were devoted to the accomplishment of this object for his native State; and he regarded it as the greatest work he had been permitted to effect, expressing his desire, in preference to every other memorial of a life of public service, to be remembered as the founder of the University of Virginia."

Key then referred to George Washington, the Commander-in-Chief and the first President. In his Farewell Address Washington had said: "Promote, then, as an object of primary importance, institutions for the general diffusion of knowledge. In proportion as the structure of a government gives force to public opinion, it is essential that public opinion should be enlightened." Referring to Washington's advocacy of Education, Key remarked:

> Take also the opinion of another, who stood pre-eminent above them all — who will ever hold the first place in the hearts of his country men, and in the admiration of the world. Read it in his Farewell Address and in the generous appropriation of his private funds, to secure this safeguard to the liberties of his rescued country.

The speaker also asked his fellow alumni to remember their own forbears, the Marylanders who had directed their efforts to the founding of educational institutions with the aid of the State as "the surest basis of the stability and glory of a free Republic." He repeated his belief that the comparatively few who received the advantages of College education would make "full returns to the State." "Every eminent and gifted man who may be thus prepared for usefulness," he avowed, "becomes the property of the State, will be of more value, and will be more valued, than all the wealth that a parsimonious policy could heap together in her treasure." He wanted the members of the Legislature to know that one of their most important duties was to secure "successive generations of enlightened patriots" for the service of the State. "May I not call upon them," he said, "to make perfect and effectual the system of instruction they have commenced; to apply in this age of improvement the spirit of improvement to its greatest and noblest objects; and to lay the deep and broad foundations of their country's greatness in the religious, moral and intellectual culture of her people?"

In conclusion, Key pointed out that the State was not the sole founder of St. John's College; on the contrary, private citizens had made liberal donations to its funds upon the plighted faith of the State. This, he contended, was another reason why it was the duty of the Legislature to make appropriations for the College. He also asserted that Annapolis was the logical location for Maryland's College. "Where else," he inquired, "can interest, inspection and patronage of the State be adequately called forth, and advantageously exercised, but at the seat of government?"

His final exhortation to his fellow alumni was eloquent and inspiring:

> Let not this filial duty be delayed. Death has already thinned your ranks. Your eldest brethren [Alexander, Carr, and Lomax] have run their brief but honourable course, and are no more. He too, [John Hanson Thomas, who had represented Frederick County in the Legislature] who had caught within that hall the bold

spirit of the ancient eloquence from its mightiest master [Demosthenes]; who, if he had been spared to stand before you this day, would have roused you from your seats and called you to join your hearts and hands in a sacred covenant to restore its honours to St. John's, and to swear to its fulfillment by the memory of the dead, the hopes of the living, and the glory of unborn generations.—He alas! is a light shining no more upon the earth.

He, also, [Dr. John Shaw] who excelled in all the attainments of mind, and charmed with all the attractions of virtue; who could descend at will from the highest soaring in the regions of fancy and be found foremost in the steepest ascents of the paths of Science; he who had here caught

> ". . . . . the glow,
> The warmth divine that poets know";

and whose lyre, upon a theme that touched these scenes of inspiration, would have poured forth its most impassioned strains, and compelled the hearts that eloquence could not subdue to bow to the magic of its song. He, too, the ornament of St. John's and the leader of her Tenth Legion has had our tears, and sleeps, not in an honoured grave, but beneath the wave of the ocean.

Nor can he be forgotten, [Henry M. Murray of Annapolis] the last but not least lamented of our departed brethren, who would have been among the foremost to offer the feelings of a warm heart and the powers of a gifted mind to the labours to which I have invited you. . . . The awful Providence which removed him, in the midst of life and usefulness, from the profession he adorned, the society he blessed, and the friends he delighted, has called upon our College to mourn the double loss of an honoured son and a devoted patron. But it becomes us not to murmur under this mysterious dispensation—rather to be thankful that it has left, to console and animate us, a cherished memory and a high example.

You have lost the assistance of associates like these. And we who survive are soon to follow them. But let the thought of your diminished strength and the remembrance of what you have lost urge you — not to despair, but to effort. Remember the truth declared and attested by history, that the accomplishment of great events depends often, if not always, on the ardour and energy of a few.

And when Maryland shall receive from the institution, your labours shall have revived, her able and well-trained advocates, the promoters of her future greatness; when, by the aid thus afforded, she shall attain her just rank in the American Union, and the full measure of her prosperity, then shall it be said of *praeclara facinora*, as those of Rome, *paucorum civium eximiam virtutem cuncta patravisse.*

CHAPTER XVII

Peggy Eaton's Quarrel

FRANCIS SCOTT KEY shunned politics until his fiftieth year. Often he cried out — as George Washington had done — against party spirit. Often he denounced public officials for being hypocritical. The result of this attitude was that he never became one of the "Court-favorites" — as he told his Cousin Tom Charlton when James Monroe was President. Nor did he have any influence at the White House during the years when John Quincy Adams was President: President Adams to Key seemed just as stern and hard-faced, just as "short and crusty," as he did when he was Secretary of State.

But in 1828, when the Nation was ringing with lusty cheers for General Andrew Jackson, the poet lawyer was one of the many thousands in whose breasts Jackson's leadership kindled enthusiasm for Democracy. Key is said to have met Old Hickory about a year after the Battle of New Orleans. According to the story, a copy of the anthem written by Key after the repulse of the British in the Chesapeake was sent to New Orleans at the time General Jackson was stationed there; it was read by the General and Edward Livingston, his aide-de-camp, and they were so pleased with it that they ordered copies of it to be printed and distributed to the soldiers. After the close of the war, the old warrior from Tennessee met the poet lawyer in Washington, complimented him on the inspiring anthem, and avowed that it had helped to bring victory to the American troops at New Orleans.

The fact that Key had been a Federalist, and that he was the son of a Federalist Judge and the nephew of a Federalist member of Congress, could not prevent him from becoming a follower of General Jackson. Political parties were in a nebulous state; the Federalist party had disappeared from American politics; the friends of Adams and Clay clung to the ideals of Federalism. But thousands of voters who had been Federalists for many years – among them Mr. Taney – had decided to espouse the cause of Democracy: and Francis Scott Key was one of those who followed the Jackson banner. It was a turning-point in his life, for he was soon to be transformed into a politician.

If it was strange that Key was a friend of the eccentric John Randolph, it was equally strange that he was an admirer of the uneducated Andrew Jackson. Key, in his address to the alumni of St. John's College, had publicly stated that college-trained men serve their country "with more devotion as well as with far more ability" than the uneducated. Yet Old Hickory's attainments in scholarship were negligible. Key must have been aware that Jackson lacked mental training, if not moral discipline, so essential to sober statesmanship in the highest office in the gift of the people. But apparently the poet lawyer was willing to judge men by their virtues: not by their defects. He understood that Jackson's shortcomings sprang largely from his lack of advantages; and, although he was hot-tempered and obstinate, nevertheless he was loyal to his friends, and deeply patriotic. Whether in battle, on the duelling-field, or in the wilderness, he always displayed amazing courage; and side by side with the vials of wrath in his nature there were to be found the wellsprings of tenderness and kindness. It was because of Andrew Jackson's outspoken frankness, and the courage with which he asserted his beliefs, and the seeming unselfishness of his motives that he captured the confidence of the American people. And it was these same qualities that made Francis Scott Key admire the brave old warrior.

The campaign between General Jackson and President Adams was a very bitter one. Never had Key heard such scathing denunciations. Jackson had once killed a man in a duel: hence he was accused as a murderer. He had been endowed with a quick temper: hence he was called a drunken brawler. He had married backwoods Rachel Robards before her decree of divorce had been signed: hence he was an adulterer. He had come from a plebian family: hence he was a vulgar barbarian who went for a week without shaving and chewed tobacco; while Rachel was a dowdy woman who smoked a corn-cob pipe. But the people had risen. President Adams, a dignified and cultured aristocrat from New England, was overwhelmed. And Francis Scott Key was jubilant when the Jacksonians bore their old hero from the frontier to the White House.

When Key drove into Washington to witness the inauguration of the old warrior, the city was seething with excitement. Thousands of people had been crowding into the city to see their old hero take the oath of office. March 4, 1829, was a sunny day with a suggestion of Spring. By ten o'clock

Pennsylvania Avenue was filled with marching men, many of them carrying hickory canes, on the way to the Capitol. No plans had been made for a special inaugural parade; but a group of Revolutionary war veterans formed an escort for the President-elect and marched beside his open carriage. Key, wending his way to the scene of the inaugural ceremony, found a crowd of about fiften thousand people on the Capitol steps and in the yard east of the Capitol. "I never saw such a crowd before," said Daniel Webster. "Persons have come five hundred miles to see General Jackson, and they really seem to think that the country is rescued from dreadful danger." On the portico was a table covered with a red cloth; behind it the closed door to the rotunda. The door opened; and out walked the Judges of the Supreme Court, headed by John Marshall. Behind them appeared the tall form of General Jackson. The white-haired hero bowed gravely, as the throng responded with a great shout.

The poet lawyer from Georgetown was thrilled by the colorful scene. As he stood gazing upon the spectacle from the gate of the yard, Key exclaimed: "It is beautiful! It is sublime!"

Before Chief Justice Marshall administered the oath, General Jackson read his inaugural address in a low voice — so low that thousands in the crowd were unable to catch his words. His address was brief and cautious. In reference to internal improvements, he said nothing further than that they were highly important "so far as they can be promoted by the constitutional acts of the Federal Government." In reference to states' rights, his only hope was to be "animated by a proper respect for those sovereign members of our Union, taking care not to confound the powers they have reserved to themselves with those they have granted to the Confederacy." Near the conclusion of his speech he promised to appoint to public office men of integrity, diligence, zeal and talents. Little did Francis Scott Key imagine that he himself would be called upon to serve in public office as an appointee of President Jackson. And little did he imagine that before long he would be called to the White House and delegated to urge Taney to enter the Cabinet.

The appointment of Mr. Taney was made following the disruption of the Cabinet as a result of the quarrel over Peggy Eaton, wife of the Secretary of War John H. Eaton. For more than two years the quarrel raged in the National Capital. And Georgetown's poet lawyer was thoroughly familiar with all phases of the dispute. He could recall when Secretary Eaton's wife was a barmaid for her father, William O'Neale, a rollicking Irishman, at his tavern on Pennsylvania Avenue. O'Neale's was a popular tavern; here were kept a "post coach and four horses" to convey members of Congress to and from the Capitol; here could be had a night's lodging at twenty-five cents, fire and candle extra; and here could be had toddy at twenty-five cents, and bitters and brandy for twelve and a half cents. And here grew up one of the chief attractions, Margaret O'Neale, the innkeeper's daughter. She was an exquisitely beautiful girl with dark brown curly hair, and pert red lips, and merry blue eyes. Little "Peggy" won her first triumph at a school exhibition at the Union Hotel, just a short distance from Key's home in Georgetown. In this contest she was selected as the prettiest girl and was crowned Queen of Beauty by Dolly Madison, the First Lady of the Land. When school was interrupted by the war, she went behind the tavern bar and served drinks to Senators, Representatives, and other high officials. She confessed she was "the wildest girl that ever wore out a mother's patience . . . as gay as a lark, full of fun and nonsense . . . sometimes, maybe, a little original and lawless." A born coquette, she flirted furiously with the Nation's lawmakers, who liked her marvelous beauty and her sprightly Irish wit. But at sixteen she married a handsome but dissipated purser named Timberlake, after an acquaintance of but a few weeks. Timberlake was absent from home for long periods. Peggy had a baby, but it died. So she went back to the tavern, to entertain the distinguished boarders again. One of the gentlemen who was attentive to her was Senator Eaton, a cultured young man, who had been admitted to the Nashville Bar and was now one of the Senators from Tennessee. Occasionally she sat and chatted at the table with Senator Eaton and General Jackson, also a boarder there when he was a member of the Senate. In 1828 came the news of Timberlake's sudden death — possibly a suicide — after a drunken debauch in a Spanish port. Senator Eaton was now seen with Peggy oftener than ever. Soon the gossips began to whisper about them in social circles. Finally the Senator asked Jackson for his advice on the advisability of marrying the widow Timberlake: the old warrior instantly replied that if he loved her he ought to marry her. The Senator was thirty-eight, Mrs. Timberlake was thirty-two. They decided to marry, and the wedding was performed on January 1, 1829.

Washington was aghast when it heard that the dashing widow had become the wife of the Senator from Tennessee, certain to be a power in the Jackson Administration. Old Hickory entered the White House with a grudge against any one who took advantage of a woman's reputation for political purposes; for he considered that the scurrilous slander of the Presidential campaign had helped to put his beloved Rachel in her grave. Accordingly, when accusations were brought against Mrs. Eaton, the grim old warrior, eager for revenge, gladly championed her cause.

It was but a few weeks after the inauguration when Key heard that complaints had been made against the vivacious bride of the Secretry of War. The first stones were cast at her reputation by ministers of the Gospel. And it was a client of the poet lawyer — Rev. J. M. Campbell, pastor of the Presbyterian Church where General Jackson worshipped in Washington — who was the first to advocate the filing of a remonstrance with the President against Mrs. Eaton. Rev. Campbell was afraid to make the protest himself, but he discussed the matter with an older clergyman, Rev. Ezra E. Ely, of Philadelphia, who had come down to Washington to attend the inauguration. Rev. Ely solemnly agreed that the dubious reputation of Mrs. Eaton made an alarming situation, and he promised to sound a warning after he returned to Philadelphia. So, on his return home, Rev. Ely drafted the charges against Mrs. Eaton — accusations of the blackest kind, based on whispered tales — and sent them to the President. "For your own sake," wrote the pious man, "for your dead wife's sake, for your Administration, for the credit of the Government and the Country, you should not countenance a woman like this."

President Jackson, instead of being disturbed, was indignant. He retorted that he believed Mrs. Eaton was an innocent and maligned woman – nothing short of absolute proof would convince him to the contrary – and moreover it was his duty to select a Cabinet for the Nation; he had not come to Washington to "make a Cabinet for the ladies of this place."

Shortly afterwards Francis Scott Key heard that Peggy had made a trip to Philadelphia to seek the source of Rev. Ely's charges. With reluctance Rev. Ely disclosed that the information came from President Jackson's pastor. When Peggy returned to Washington, a lively scene was enacted in the parsonage of Rev. Campbell. In the excitement, Peggy fell and sustained an ugly bruise on her head. The old warrior from the White House made a personal call at the home of Major Eaton, and found Peggy in bed as a result of her mishap at the parsonage.

It was at this juncture that Key became involved – as an attorney – in the petticoat entanglement. Rumor had it that Peggy was going to give the two clergymen trouble. Rev. Ely, in a letter from Philadelphia, expressed the hope that Mrs. Eaton would make the Secretary of War a good wife and that she would make no trouble. But the preachers had told a contemptible story, and the friends of the Eatons were incensed. The possibility of a suit for slander worried Rev. Campbell. President Jackson said this was what his pastor deserved. Rev. Campbell prayed that some way could be found to pour oil upon the troubled waters. In his anxiety he called upon the poet lawyer for his legal advice, to be prepared for any damage suit that might be instituted against him. Key was consulted not only because he was a leading member of the District Bar, and a leading churchman as well, but also because he was a friend of President Jackson: thus he occupied a position of influence that might facilitate conciliation. General Duff Green, editor of the *Telegraph*, while admitting that the whole trouble had been started by "petty jealousy and idle tittle-tattle," apprehended that Rev. Campbell would be unable to evade responsibility for uttering the slanderous charges unless he denied the accusations or else substantiated them by giving the source of his information. Key realized, after hearing all the details of the episode, that the best thing he could do as Rev. Campbell's attorney was to announce that his client had possession of "sufficient proof" to protect himself in the event Mrs. Eaton filed suit against him. But Rev. Campbell's chief hope was that he might be able to keep the unfortunate affair out of Court. So he retained the Georgetown lawyer for the purpose of fending off litigation, if possible. Striving for delay, Key proposed that Mrs. Eaton refrain from instituting Court proceedings until the matter could be investigated — at least until after Rev. Ely had a chance to tell his side of the story. He thought that the tempest would blow over.

In the meantime the old warrior in the White House was gathering evidence on the subject. During the Summer of 1829, he collected about a hundred pages of data. This showed that, while Mrs. Eaton was a little more animated and imprudent than convention decreed at that time, there was not a shred of evidence to substantiate the accusations that had been made against her. In September the President called his Cabinet together to hear the evidence; and at the same time he called in Rev. Ely and Rev. Campbell to testify in their own behalf. Major Eaton did not attend; but Major William B. Lewis, his brother-in-law, — Lewis lived at the White House as Jackson's confidante and was known as "his man Friday"— was present at the meeting. The President first called on Rev. Ely. In the course of his testimony Rev. Ely admitted that he had no evidence of any improper conduct against Major Eaton.

"No!" exclaimed the old warrior. "Or against Mrs. Eaton either!"

"On that point," said Rev. Ely blandly, "I would rather not give an opinion."

Whereupon Jackson shouted in a rage: "She is as chaste as a virgin!"

What Jackson wanted was an apology; but Rev. Ely refused to apologize. With his blood boiling the President now called on Rev. Campbell, the client of Francis Scott Key. Rev. Campbell remarked that he had no intention of finding fault with the President or his Administration: on the contrary, his purpose had been to "save the Administration from reproach, and the morals of the country from contamination." In a few moments he was trying to discredit the evidence which the President had produced.

"Remember!" thundered the old warrior with anger

blazing in his eyes. "You are here to give evidence, not to pass on it!"

Jackson managed to restrain himself from incandescent profanity, but he gave the clergymen a verbal lashing that made the witnesses gasp.

The President left Rev. Campbell's church. And, before long, Key's client left Washington.

But Mrs. Eaton's position was no better than before. Mrs. John C. Calhoun, wife of the Vice President, refused to accord her social recognition. So did Mrs. Samuel D. Ingham, wife of the Secretary of the Treasury. So did Mrs. John M. Berrien, wife of the Attorney General. So did Mrs. John Branch, wife of the Secretary of the Navy. The more the President championed Peggy, the more did the ladies of society shrug their shoulders and insult her. She was but a barmaid and a social upstart, and they refused to invite her to their social affairs. It was apparent that the ladies were jealous, for Peggy was exquisitely beautiful and charming and outshone those from the upper ranks of society.

But in the Cabinet there was one active champion of Mrs. Eaton. It was Martin Van Buren, the Secretary of State. Suave, ingratiating, and cunning, the Red Fox of Kinderhook saw his opportunity to win favor with the President. Mr. Van Buren was a widower: so, if he showed any attentions to Peggy, he had no explanations to make. He called upon her; gave dinners in her honor; danced with her — knowing all the while it was politic to please General Jackson, while others were arousing his ire. Indeed the prediction was made by Daniel Webster that the "desperate turmoil in the social and fashionable world" might result in determining who would succeed Jackson when he retired to private life. And so it eventuated. For the Red Fox, endearing himself to the old warrior, was paving his own way to the Presidency.

Meanwhile the conviction was gripping Jackson's mind that Vice President Calhoun was fomenting a conspiracy to stigmatize Mrs. Eaton. Was it not all a malicious persecution aimed at his "little friend Peg" to drive Major Eaton from the Cabinet – a sinister scheme of the Vice President to become President? Jackson wrote a trenchant letter to Calhoun on the subject, but Calhoun retorted that it was a ladies' quarrel in which he would not interfere, and that the laws of the ladies were "like the laws of Medes and Persians, and admitted neither of argument nor of amendment."

Francis Scott Key and many other friends of the Chief Executive were still hoping that the storm would blow over. But before long the poet lawyer heard that Mrs. Andrew J. Donelson, Jackson's niece, who was acting as the mistress of the White House, was siding with the Calhouns and snubbing Peggy. The grim old warrior told her that unless she yielded to his wishes by recognizing Peggy, she would have to leave the White House. Her husband was private secretary to the President. But Emily Donelson chose to leave, rather than comply with her uncle's wishes. It was now whispered that Peggy Eaton was the unofficial First Lady of the Land. Jackson's enemies chuckled. They were anxious to see the quarrel injected into politics. Would it not be strategy, they thought, to incite the General's wrath to his own destruction? For the old warrior was more convinced than ever that many of his unwary friends were falling into the trap set by "the great intriguer Mr. Calhoun."

The tempest raged for two years. Finally Jackson, grimly determined to compel social recognition for Mrs. Eaton, called for the Red Fox and showed him a paper that he was planning to read to his Cabinet. He summoned Mr. Ingham, Mr. Berrien, and Mr. Branch to a conference. To them he avowed that their attitude toward the Secretary of War and Mrs. Eaton was insulting to them, as well as offensive to the President. Any member of the Cabinet, he said, who could not harmonize with the other members had "better withdraw." So he sent away the Attorney General, the Secretary of the Navy and the Secretary of the Treasury with the warning that they must "arrange their parties in the future" so that the world would not get the impression that they were snubbing Mrs. Eaton.

But the warning was in vain. In order to help the President out of his dilemma, Mr. Van Buren offered to resign as Secretary of State; whereupon Jackson could ask the others to resign too. But Jackson was reluctant to lose his shrewd adviser; but he consented to the scheme with the understanding that he would send the Red Fox as Minister to London. Arrangements were now made for a conference between President Jackson, Secretary of State Van Buren, Secretary of War Eaton, Postmaster General William T. Barry, and Major Lewis. The dispute had reached its crisis. When the announcement was made that the Secretary of State had offered to resign, the Secretary of War said he would resign too, inasmuch as his wife had been largely responsible for the disturbance. Jackson was now in a position to dismiss all the others. They came in, he said, as a unit, and they ought to go out as a unit. Accordingly Secretary of the Treasury Ingham and Secretary of the Navy Branch presented their resignations. Major Eaton was infuriated, especially at Mr. Ingham; he planned to administer a sound thrashing in revenge; but Mr. Ingham managed to escape out of Washington in a stage coach one morning before daylight.

President Jackson determined to allow Postmaster General Barry, a friend of the Eatons, to retain his place in the Cabinet; but all the others had to go. The problem that now confronted the old warrior was to select an entirely new Cabinet, with the exception of the Postmaster General. Edward Livingston, who had been serving as Ambassador to France, was named Secretary of State. Levi Woodbury, of New Hampshire, was chosen to head the Navy Department. They assumed their duties in May, 1831.

For Attorney General the President was searching for an able lawyer, upon whom he could call in the emergency for legal advice. Taney's qualifications had been placed before the old warrior. The Marylander had been suggested for the Attorney Generalship by Dr. William Jones, a Washington physician, but a native of Maryland, and a close friend of Old Hickory. Dr. Jones told the President that Taney, at that time the Attorney General of Maryland, had been a Federalist for some years but was now a strong friend of his Administration.

Francis Scott Key heard that the name of his brother-in-law had been mentioned to the President. But Key did not urge the appointment. Indeed, on the contrary, he hoped that Jackson would retain Mr. Berrien in the Cabinet. One day in June, 1831, the poet lawyer from Georgetown happened to meet Mr. Berrien on a journey into Washington. The Attorney General said that he was willing to resign, if General Jackson wanted him.

"But," he said, "if I resign, who do you think will take my place?"

Key replied: "Buchanan, I suppose, more likely than anyone else. Taney has been mentioned. But I don't believe Jackson will offer him the appointment."

When Key arrived home — after conferring with Mr. Berrien, Secretary of State Livingston and Secretary of the Navy Woodbury — a message was waiting for him to come to the White House at once. He did not wait until morning; with characteristic alertness he hastened back to Washington.

It was quite late in the evening when the Georgetown lawyer was ushered into the White House. A solitary lamp burned in the vestibule. Candles dimly lighted the rooms inside. He found the old warrior tired and worn. The man who was now the Nation's Chief Executive was unlike the dashing hero of early days. His health was broken, his spirits depressed, by grief over his beloved Rachel, by the exertions of the campaign, by the worries of the Presidency. His shoulders were slightly stooped, his chest was flat. Key could detect that the burdens of office had been bearing down heavily upon the old man's gradually weakening body. But his firm mouth, and his strong jaw and cheek-bones, and his flashing blue eyes showed the inflexible warrior that was in him.

Presently General Jackson told Key the purpose of the summons — he wanted to ask Key his opinion about appointing Taney Attorney General. As a matter of fact, Taney was not seeking the position, and Key did not recommend his brother-in-law's appointment. He thought the President would be wise to retain Mr. Berrien. The rupture in the Cabinet had been a source of satisfaction to the Adams-Clay people. The newspapers were asking the cause of the resignations. The anti-Administration editors were hinting that the "American Pompadour" had caused the dissolution of the Cabinet. Duff Green, in the *Telegraph*, laid the blame for the political upheaval upon the petticoat controversy, charging that the President had forced the members of the Cabinet to accept Peggy Eaton or else hand in their resignations. Francis Scott Key therefore suggested to the President that, since Mrs. Berrien had been opposed to Mrs. Eaton, the retention of Mr. Berrien as Attorney General might make it appear to the world that the quarrel over Peggy had not been the cause of the resignations after all. This, in Key's opinion, would produce "a good effect upon the affairs of the party."

But Key's line of reasoning did not appeal to the stern old warrior. Mrs. Berrien had been unfair to Peggy; he had decided to get rid of all the Cabinet members, except Postmaster General Barry; and he refused to modify his plans.

In view of this decision of the President, Key promised him to write to Taney at once. Here are the highlights of his letter:

G. T. 14 June, 31.

My Dear Taney

I had some talk with Berrien in our journey, & found that he expected he was to resign, but thought he was willing (if the Press was so) to remain. He inquired what was thought and said upon the subject. I told him . . . that it would gratify some of the General's friends if he could be retained, and I told him that that was your opinion, & that you thought it desirable to the party that he should continue in the Cabinet. . . . .

Upon getting home I found a note from the Pres requesting me to call out & see him, & I went, of course, though it was almost 9 o'clock. He said he wanted to tell me confidentially that he wished to offer you the place of Atty-Gen & he wanted to know if it would be acceptable to you. I told him that some of your friends had told you that the appointment would be probably offered to you & that I had conversed with you recently upon the subject, that I believed you would prefer his continuing Berrien, thinking such a thing would be conducive to the success of the Administration. . . . .

He said at once that was entirely out of the question, that he would have been glad to retain B. [Berrien] that he thought highly of him, but that it was a necessary part of the arrangement he had been compelled to make, was understood as such, & that he could not go back from it. He was very decisive. . . .

He said it would give pleasure to his heart to understand that you would, that he would feel gratified to have you in his counsels, that your doctrines upon the leading Constitutional questions he knew to be sound, & your standing in the Supreme Court he well knew from Baldwin & others. He requested I would write and let you know your answer as soon as possible. . . .

I do not think you ought to have any hesitation in

> accepting. I believe it is one of those instances in which the Gen[l] has acted from his own impulses, & that you will find yourself both as to him and his Cabinet, acting with men who know and value you & with whom you will have the influence you ought to have & which you can do something efficient with. . . .

Taney replied that he would accept; and on June 16th Key made another trip to the White House. At the hour of his arrival the President was conferring with Postmaster General Barry, the only one to escape the axe as a result of Peggy Eaton's quarrel. Jackson and Barry were delighted to hear that Taney was willing to accept the Attorney Generalship. The old warrior reassured Key that the duties of the office would not interfere with Taney's practice in Baltimore—he would not even be obliged to move from Baltimore to Washington, if he did not care to do so.

Key then told the President that the only thing that bothered Taney in considering the place in the Cabinet was the fact that his appearance had been entered in a number of cases in the Court of Appeals of Maryland at Annapolis, and he did not want to neglect them.

"That," retorted the grim old hero, "will make no difficulty in any event. I don't want Taney to let the office interfere with his business. And I don't suppose it will interfere in any material degree. But, as it is, Berrien wants to stay a little while longer to get the business of his office cleaned up. When he is ready to go, he will say so, and we will let Taney know."

Mr. Berrien, however, preferred to quit at once. And in a few days Roger Brooke Taney took the oath of office as Attorney General of the United States. From the very beginning the gaunt man from Maryland was one of the most trusted advisers of the President. The confidence which the President had in him was revealed in a letter written by Postmaster General Barry at the President's direction, inquiring whether Mr. Taney was also willing to take charge of the War Department until the arival of the new Secretary of War. Jackson had chosen Lewis Cass of Ohio as Secretary of War, and Louis McLane of Delaware as Secretary of the Treasury; but they were not ready to qualify until some time in August. The new Attorney General agreed to act as Secretary of War *ad interim*, thereby gaining the distinction of holding two Cabinet portfolios at the same time.

Thus was finally settled one of the most picturesque imbroglios in American History — the only petticoat quarrel ever to disrupt the Cabinet.

The National Republicans charged that General Jackson, under the influence of Mrs. Eaton, was trying to dominate society as well as politics. The Jackson Democrats denied these accusations. At a Fourth of July banquet in Georgetown, at which Francis Scott Key presided, a resolution was adopted denying the charge that Jackson was endeavoring to "control the private intercourse of society." When the National Republicans read this resolution, they accused the author of the National Anthem of being a hypocrite — because he had been the legal adviser of Rev. Campbell, the instigator of the charges against Peggy Eaton, as well as a close friend of General Jackson.

CHAPTER XVIII

Jackson and Liberty

PRIOR TO THE Jackson Administration Francis Scott Key looked upon politics as sordid and repulsive. But after Jackson entered the White House, a great political controversy arose which not only bound him with a strong bond of affection to the old warrior, but also captured his interest in politics. It was the famous upheaval over Nullification.

The tariff act of 1828 had been obnoxious to the South; and in 1830 Senator Robert Y. Hayne enunciated the doctrine of Nullification — that a State had the right to ignore any act of Congress which did not please the State. "The South," declared the Senator, "is acting on a principle she has always held sacred — resistance to unauthorized taxation."

Daniel Webster, in his immortal reply to the South Carolinian, presented the Constitutional view of the Nationalists — that the people had declared the Constitution to be the supreme law of the land; that the right to decide on the validity of acts of Congress rested in the Judiciary; and that the assumption by the several States of this authority would destroy the foundations of the Republic. Key, an ardent patriot and a Nationalist at heart, was delighted with Senator Webster's logic and majestic eloquence. The closing tribute to the Stars and Stripes — the flag which Webster called "the glorious ensign of the republic" — brought a particular thrill to the Poet of the Flag:

> When my eyes shall be turned to behold, for the last time, the sun in heaven, may I not see him shining on the broken and dishonored fragments of a once-glorious Union; on States dissevered, discordant, belligerent; on a land rent with civil feuds, or drenched, it may be, in fraternal blood! Let their last feeble and lingering glance rather behold the glorious ensign of the republic, now known and honored throughout the earth, still full high advanced, its arms and trophies streaming in their original luster, not a stripe erased or polluted, nor a single star obscured, bearing for its motto no such miserable interrogatory as "What is all this worth?" nor those other words of delusion and folly, "Liberty, first, and Union afterwards"; but everywhere, spread all over the land, and in every wind under the whole heavens, that other sentiment, dear to every American heart — "Liberty and Union, now and forever, one and inseparable!"

Among the statesmen of the day there was a wide difference of opinion regarding the seriousness of the dangers that threatened the Republic. There were some men, like Senator Benton, who were unable to detect any sign of approaching calamity. These men hooted at the very idea that America was in peril. There were others like Justice Story, who were so greatly alarmed that they cried out that nothing but a miracle could save the Union from destruction. Francis Scott Key did not underestimate the seriousness of the situation. He admitted, as the troubled weeks passed, that he was worried by the prospect of fratricidal war. But in April, 1830 — a few months after Webster's reply to Hayne — an utterance of President Jackson gave immeasurable encouragement to the soul of the poet lawyer. Up to this time the old patriot had not expressed himself publicly on the question of Nullification. Since he had come from the South, many of the Southern politicians thought that he would sympathize with the Nullifiers. But at the Jefferson Day banquet in Washington, when he was called upon for a toast, he stood up, like a Banquo looking at an ugly spectre; and hurled defiance at the Nullifiers with the thrilling toast: "Our Federal Union: It must be preserved!" It was a prophetic utterance: four bloody years of war — to be witnessed by Taney, but not by Jackson and Key — were necessary for its fulfillment.

President Jackson's defiance of the Nullifiers enraged the South — especially the hotheads in South Carolina — and the insistence of the Southern leaders in favor of Nullification grew each day fiercer and more determined. Key detested the theory of Nullification. Like Jackson and Taney, he saw the danger in the doctrine that a State could resist a law merely because the law was distasteful. But, relying on Providence in time of peril to give America men of patriotism and courage like General Washington and General Jackson, the pious lawyer felt confident that the Constitution would endure. Even though Civil War should come, he predicted that not a single star would ever be removed from the Star-Spangled Banner. Gazing into the future, he gave utterance to his prediction that while clashes would occur between the States, the storms would be calmed, and the Union would be preserved. "But," he asked, speaking of the troubles between the North and the South, "do they portend a dissolution of our Union?" "No!" he replied. "The tree of Liberty may be shaken by these blasts, but its roots are in all our hearts, and it will stand."

This prophecy was contained in an oration which Key delivered in the rotunda of the Capitol on July 4, 1831. For weeks a committee of prominent men had been planning the Fourth of July celebration for Washington, including a patriotic ceremony at noon, at which the author of *The Star-Spangled Banner* was to be the speaker. This was to be followed by a banquet in the afternoon and fireworks at night.

Before noon of that day a large crowd had assembled at the Capitol. Atop the stately building the American flag floated in the breeze. The meridian salute gave notice for the opening of the exercises. The cylindrical walls of the rotunda beneath the great dome echoed the martial tones of the United States Marine Band.

Mayor John P. Van Ness of Washington, a former Congressman from New York, who was chairman of the committee of arrangements, called the meeting to order. He first called on Edward Van Ness to read the Declaration of Independence. He then introduced the lawyer from Georgetown as the orator of the day.

Francis Scott Key, slender of build, vibrant with energy, now approaching fifty-two, stepped forward like one half his years. It had been nearly seventeen years since he had written the National Anthem. With each passing year he had become more widely known not only as the author of a popular patriotic song but also as a man of dynamic personality.

In his opening remarks, Key said that the crowd before him had assembled for the purpose of discharging a holy duty. "We have opened the records of time," he declared, "and read that bright page that proclaimed to the world the solemn purpose of the Fathers of our Country, and the sacred pledge they gave for its fulfillment. The pledge has been redeemed — the purpose is accomplished — and we are here, in the rich possession of what valor has won, and wisdom has preserved for us."[1]

For some minutes the speaker described the scene in the Continental Congress in 1776, when the Declaration of Independence was unrolled and the members of the Congress pledged their lives, their fortunes, and their sacred honor. This, he said, was a scene of grandeur, and the names of the Signers have gone forth to an admiring world and will be handed down to distant generations. "They sleep," he said, "in honored graves, a rescued land their monument, and their names engraven on the hearts of their countrymen." All of them had passed away except one — the venerable Charles Carroll of Carollton, now approaching ninety-four, whose days had been prolonged so "that he might see the rich fruits of a patriot's labors and that the world might see, in the grateful homage of a thankful people, the reward that awaits such labors."

The theme of Key's speech was "The Blessing of Liberty." He referred to the United States as a "broad and beautiful land" rich in the gifts of Heaven. He mentioned the in-

1.—*Oration Delivered by Francis S. Key, Esq., in the Rotunda of the Capitol, July* 4, 1831. Rare Book Room, Library of Congress. Subsequent references to Key's address are from the same source.

heritance of this favored portion of the earth as one of the blessings of Providence. "But human happiness," he declared, "requires more than any land, however enriched by Nature and adorned by art, can give."

Another blessing which called for thanksgiving was the rescue of America from the grip of Great Britain. "But," Key declared, "had this been all, had nothing further been effected for the security and happiness of a delivered people, it might have proved a short-lived joy. Too often have such struggles terminated, even when successful, only in a change of masters. Too often some new misrule has started up in the weakness and disorder of a period of revolution, more intolerable than that which was overthrown."

No dictatorship had appeared in this country. At the outbreak of the Revolution, the patriot leaders looked ahead to the close of the war. At the very moment when they were planning resistance to the British Crown, they declared not only "what they meant to put down" but also "what they meant to set up." Consequently they succeeded. "Had their measures been dictated by less wisdom or courage, they would have made it a much less work, a far inferior project. They might have determined upon resistance, blindly leaving it to circumstances to guide them in its course and in its results." They might have given allegiance to some other Power, in consideration of protection. Or they might have established a new dynasty, calling the head of some favored family to the throne. For either of these schemes "very respectable authorities" could be found. But the Founding Fathers had been raised up by God for the special purpose of establishing this Republic:

> That a people could govern themselves — a people neither born nor bred to such a business — would never have been the opinion of men who took their views from the learning of that day, which had been made the pensioned advocate of power. In those days, if a writer was inclined to defend popular governments, there were not many parts of the world where it could be done with safety; while the doctrines that denounced such governments had hosts of retainers, everywhere maintained and richly rewarded. . . . Under such circumstances, and in such times, no ordinary men could have put forth the Declaration of American Independence. And the men who made this fearless appeal to God and the world, in behalf of the long violated and almost forgotten rights of mankind, were no ordinary men. They were fitted by Providence to the exigency to which they were called. There were men of learning among them, but they were also men of wisdom. There were many others summoned from their farms and workshops, to whom politics was, in a great measure, a new study. But they brought to it strong minds and devoted hearts, and, bowing to no human authority, determined to work out its questions for themselves. They were not ignorant of man and the affairs of the world, and they knew perfectly the men they represented and the things around them. With such qualifications it is not wonderful that they mastered their subject, and became legislators and statesmen, such as the world has rarely witnessed. From such men, no evil of sophistry could hide the truth; and no fear of man could deter them from maintaining it. Hence we see in the declaration of their purpose that bold and eloquent avowal of the great principles of Truth and Freedom to which we have been listening. Hence they put at issue, in the holy strife upon which they were entering, the establish-

ment of a government which should rest upon no other foundation than the will of the people.

The orator explained how the wisdom of the members of the Continental Congress was manifested in American victory. "It was the avowal of these principles and this purpose," he maintained, "that sanctified their Cause, justified their appeal to Heaven, and gave it its success." In the Common Cause the Nation was welded together. The people saw that "their dearest rights were to be sustained or lost forever." Thus did the Colonies become a Nation of Patriots. "The friends of Civil Liberty were awakened. They saw that upon our fields was to be decided the fate of Nations, the destiny of Man. The benevolent of every land gave us their sympathy and prayers, some gave us — a gift never to be forgotten — themselves." And so he agreed with the poet that such a Cause is seldom unsuccessful:

> Power usurp'd
> Is weakness when oppos'd: conscious of wrong,
> 'Tis pusillanimous and prone to flight.
> But men that once conceive the glowing thought
> Of Freedom, in that hope itself possess
> All that the contest calls for — spirit, strength,
> The scorn of danger and united hearts:
> The surest presage of the good they seek.

"It is, therefore," exclaimed Francis Scott Key, "that I invite you this day to remember not only the defeat of Usurpation but the establishment of Freedom — that we are not only relieved from a yoke of bondage, but exalted above kings — and that to the men whose deeds we this day commemorate, we are indebted for the wisdom which devised and secured to the land they had delivered the blessing of a free Constitution. This was the crown of their labours — this is the crown of our rejoicing."

At this point the orator allued to the difficulties that confronted the framers of the Constitution in 1787. "They were no common difficulties that presented themselves," he declared, "when the principles they had proclaimed were to be brought into a system, adapted to the situation and circumstances of the community for which it was intended." According to Francis Scott Key, these problems were happily solved. "The people," he explained, "were to form a General Government of limited and defined powers, intended to secure the common interest — the States to be independent republics, in all other respects having exclusive power in whatsoever concerned their separate interests." But, the orator continued, it was not to be expected that the boundaries of power could be defined with such a degree of exactness that all doubt and controversy would forever be prevented. "Human language," he asserted, "cannot make nice distinctions with perfect accuracy, and if we resort to the spirit of an instrument for its construction, we enter a still broader field of disputation."

Thereupon Key urged that the Federal Government be kept free from encroachments by the States, and that the States be protected from Federal usurpation:

> From the nature of institutions thus organized, it follows of necessity that they must in some measure be exposed to two opposite dangers. The one is, that

as the tendency of power is ever encroaching, the General Government may become a vast consolidated dominion, with immense resources and unlimited patronage, dangerous to the power of the States and the rights of the people. The other is, that the States will gradually weaken the powers of the General Government and dissolve the Union.

It is not easy to see how these dangers could have been removed, or more effectually guarded against. It must be left (as it is) to the good sense of the people to exercise their vigilance towards both. Experience will determine (if it has not already done so) which is the most to be apprehended and how the tendencies of each are to be checked. On whichever side encroachments may appear, let a double guard be set to arrest its progress, and let us patiently wait the correcting voice of the people, expressed as the Constitution prescribes. We must become a very different people from those who devised this Constitution, if, with the remedy in our hands and the dangers foreseen, they are permitted to come upon us.

The speaker now referred to the trials of the young Republic. Fifty-five years had passed since the Continental Congress proclaimed American independence. The Constitution had been found to be our bulwark of freedom, and nothing less than "degenerates" were those citizens who failed to uphold it:

May we not take hope and courage from the past? More than half a century has gone over us. Many trials have been endured. Times of peace, of war, of general and local excitements have passed away — and we are safe. Our scheme of Government was looked upon by the world as an experiment. The friends of Arbitrary Power predicted its failure, the friends of Freedom regarded it with apprehension. It has out-

> lived these hopes and fears—and most unworthy of our inheritance, degenerate sons of our Fathers shall we be, if we suffer it to perish in our hands.

Here the lawyer from Georgetown extolled America as a prosperous country. With pride in his native land and his American citizenship, Key declared that the United States enjoyed the respect of every Nation in the world.

> Is there anything in the aspect of the present to throw a gloom upon our joy? Are any of the blessings of Providence withheld from us? Any of the improvements of Art or Science denied to us? Is not the face of our country rich in the beauties of Nature, the labors of industry, the profusion of plenty? Where can the patriot look without saying with glistening eye and heart of rapture, "This is my own, my native land"? And are not the kingdoms of the earth looking to us with respect, as the Nation that will "neither do nor suffer wrong"? And are not the oppressed of the world thronging to our happy shores, to behold and partake our joy? Are not our people improving like their country? Growing not only in physical but intellectual strength? Where is benevolent enterprise more active and untiring? Where are the charities of life more cherished, and where does Religion, the great promoter of happiness, achieve more successfully her peaceful triumph?

Step by step the poet lawyer prepared his audience for a eulogy of Andrew Jackson.

> If thus improved and improving in other things, are we deteriorating in patriotism? Is our country less loved, as it becomes more worthy of our love? This is the preserving virtue of republics. This was most conspicuously the virtue of Americans: shining not

> only among the chiefs and leaders of the Nation, but pervading all classes of the people and animating the humblest follower in the ranks. Splendid instances of this in our history will recur to your memories. The men of those days were in nothing more remarkable than in their disinterested devotion to the public good. The workings of selfish ambition, so natural to the corrupt heart of man, were subdued to the all-absorbing love of country. Sacrifices of personal interests and feelings to the Common Cause seemed not only submitted to, but to be sought for; and the zeal and energy of those days were seen, not in seeking the honors and emoluments of office, but in the faithful discharge of its duties.

Key was now ready to compare Jackson with George Washington. "Are these virtues still extant?" he inquired. "Is there no generous enthusiasm to follow these bright examples? Can we point to no instance of high official station seeking the man who would not seek it? Can we find no man drawing the eyes of an admiring and grateful country upon him only by the splendor of his services?" He was ready, of course, to answer these questions. "Yes, my countrymen," he exclaimed, "we have such a man. It may yet be said of our land, as of Rome, 'she hath not lost the breed of noble men, and we have a people, wise and patriotic, who delight to honor him.' "

It was at this juncture that Key alluded to the clamor in the South for Nullification. With President Jackson's oath of allegiance to the Constitution – "Our Federal Union: It must be preserved!" – ringing in his ears, strengthening his faith in the solidarity of the Nation, Key exclaimed:

> Are the dangers, to which I have alluded as threatening the perpetuity of our institutions, more formidable at present than in past periods of our history? There are (as there often have been) agitation and loud complaints of oppression in some of our States. But do they portend a dissolution of our Union? Is there any portion of our country that will not bear much wrong, and bear it long, before so desperate a remedy is resorted to? Let them appeal to the great body of their countrymen; and let them patiently abide the result of that appeal. To determine upon the justice of their complaints may require time.... But it can not be believed that the Nation, when it sees undoubted evidence of the unjust and unequal operation of a system, will desire or permit any portion of the country to bear burthens for another. Patriotism, like charity, (of which virtue it is a branch) will teach the complainers to "suffer long and be kind." And the same virtue will teach their opponents to bear with their complaints, examine them emphatically, and not "seek their own" (particularly through doubtful questions) to the injury of their brethren. This is the Constitutional remedy for wrongs. It is a safe one: and, sooner, or later, it is a sure one. The people... may occasionally err, but they always mean to do right, and give them time and information, and they will seldom do otherwise. These agitations will be thus calmed. The tree of Liberty may be shaken by these blasts, but its roots are in all our hearts, and it will stand.

So much for the danger of weakening the General Government. Now the opposite danger: that the General Government might become "a vast consolidated dominion, with immense resources and unlimited patronage, dangerous to the power of the States and the rights of the people." An illustration of this peril was to be seen in the demand for internal improvements. In 1830 Congress passed an act to build a highway in Kentucky. President Jackson vetoed it, thus challenging the principle of internal improvements advocated by John Quincy Adams, Henry Clay and John C. Calhoun. The veto indicated to Mr. Calhoun that he was losing his influence in the Democratic party; and indeed the President, by his attitude on the Kentucky road, did rob Calhoun of his favorite policies and "weakened him so much that his enemies dared to proceed to destroy him utterly." Francis Scott Key commended the President for vetoing the Kentucky road bill. He saw the grave danger that lay in placing unlimited powers in the hands of the President. In praising General Jackson for curbing internal improvements at the expense of the Federal Government he declared:

> Let us remember that it has been said "The Union must be preserved"—and that he who said it hath already done much to maintain it.

Having paid a glowing tribute to the old warrior in the White House, Key now moved toward his conclusion. Urgently he appealed for patriotism:

> I have said that patriotism is the preserving virtue of republics. Let this virtue wither, and selfish ambition assume its place as the motive for action, and the Republic is lost. Here, my countrymen, is the sole ground of danger. We are in a state of unexampled national prosperity, and to nations as to individuals great are the hazards and responsibilities of such a state. Times of difficulty and danger give men their virtues, and prove and exalt them. We become listless and luxurious in times of ease and security. Men

who inherit an estate generally prize it and enjoy it less than the ancestor who earned it; and we who inherit Freedom may learn to value it less than the men who won it. Let us not indulge the unworthy thought that to us is left the privilege of enjoyment, without the obligations of duty. We are responsible for the most sacred of trusts — to our country — to the world — to our God. Let us not imagine that nothing is left for us to do. This is never the condition of an individual or a nation. Patriotism may still find its appropriate labours among us. There are yet things to be done. . . . Abundant as are the blessings around us, there are evils to be seen — not to be hid in despair or mourned over in heartless despondency, but to be looked at, and met, and overcome, with the spirit of men who think nothing that concerns its honour and happiness above the power of such a country to accomplish. Many and great will be the toils and triumphs of patriotism before our whole land shall present to the eye of Heaven what Heaven has given us the means of making it — a picture of human happiness without a blot. The spirit of this virtue still abides among us. Let us exercise and cherish it. . . . The present time then is a time for joy; another year has passed over us and adds its proof to that of those before it of the stability of the blessings of Freedom.

The speaker now came to the climax of his oration. If Freedom flourishes in this country, will the rest of the world look on in apathy? His answer was an eloquent appeal to the American people to keep burning the fire that had been kindled by their Fathers in 1776:

No, my countrymen, we hold a rich deposit in trust for ourselves and for all our brethren of mankind. It is the fire of Liberty. If it becomes extinguished, our darkened land will cast a mournful shadow over the

> nations — if it lives, its blaze will enlighten and gladden the whole earth. Already hath its pure flame ascended, and kindled more than one noble strife. The kingdoms of the earth are moved. The friends of man are awakened, and the arm of the patriot is strong and his heart steadfast, as he thinks of our glory . . . . We hold too this deposit from God, who warmed the hearts of our Fathers with a sense of their rights and their duties, and heard their appeal — and we hold it for Him, to sustain it for His great purpose in bestowing it — the good of man.

And so, convinced that the world is growing better, Francis Scott Key had faith in the prophecy that men would beat their swords into plowshares and their spears into pruning hooks. He prophesied that the world would establish a "Holy family of Nations" — bound together by love; not by law or by armaments — to make Isaiah's dream come true:

> However darkly we may speculate upon the future destiny of nations, we have a light shining on distant days which cannot mislead us — the holy light of prophecy. This tells us of the coming of a brighter day than has ever shone upon a fallen world — a day when man will find no foe in man — when "nations will learn war no more" — but live together in love as members of one great family upon earth under the care of the common Father of us all. There are signs in the times in which we live, which indicate the dawning of that day of brightness.

In an eloquent conclusion Key pictured the glorious privilege that is his who engages in the cause of international peace:

> Is it not a glorious privilege to be permitted to labour in such a cause and for such a consummation? To see that in promoting the freedom and the happiness of the world, by sustaining our own, we work with the bounteous Giver of Good in effecting His purposes of love to man; and that we work for Him—for the glory of His name and the welfare of His creation. He it is who rules the nations and reigns in the hearts of men. May we look to Him that we may understand and feel and fulfill the high duties He has placed before us. And as the world advances to this sure period of its destined blessedness, and as people after people put forth their strength and join the Holy Family of Nations that love us as brethren and "learn war no more," shall not this, our land, and this, our day, be "freshly remembered"? And that which is now celebrated as the birthday of Freedom to a Nation be honoured as the birthday of Freedom to the World?

In the crowd that had gathered in the rotunda there were few, if any, of the followers of Henry Clay. Indeed, Mr. Clay's friends considered the Fourth of July celebration as a shrewd political trick—a scheme to promote the candidacy of President Jackson for reëlection. As a matter of fact, the National Republicans had arranged for a Fourth of July celebration of their own, entirely apart from that arranged by Mayor Van Ness and his committee. Duff Green, no longer a friend of Jackson, revealed that the Democrats had placed the arrangements for the Fourth of July celebration in the hands of a "Jackson committee"; that the ceremonies were partisan, not patriotic; and that the friends of Mr. Clay had "no option but to celebrate it by themselves." Accordingly, at the time Key was delivering his oration in the Capitol, Philip Richard

Fendall, an enemy of President Jackson, was delivering an oration in the City Hall to the friends of Henry Clay.

In the late afternoon the Jacksonians held a dinner in Carusi's assembly hall. It was an elegant affair. Among those at the banquet table were members of the Cabinet, foreign diplomats, and others prominent in Washington society. The Marine Band added to the gaiety of the occasion.

The banquet was followed by a great array of toasts, each accompanied by a salute from the artillery. First came thirteen toasts specially arranged by the committee. A musical selection accompanied each toast. Key's anthem was the tenth on the list. The following were the toasts and songs that accompanied them: (1) The Day: the principles it has consecrated are extending throughout the world; *Hail Columbia;* (2) Our Country; *Yankee Doodle;* (3) the Union of the States and the preservation of our Liberties: they are inseparable; *The Meeting of the Waters;* (4) The President of the United States; *Jackson's March;* (5) The Memory of Washington and Jefferson; *Roslin Castle;* (6) Lafayette; *Marseillaise Hymn;* (7) Charles Carroll and our Revolutionary Fathers; *Auld Lang Syne;* (8) The People; *Jefferson's March;* (9) Our Foreign Relations; *Hail to the Chief;* (10) The Army and Navy; *The Star-Spangled Banner;* (11) A Free Press; *Franklin's March;* (12) General Information; *Washington's March;* (13) The Fair: Gallantry is born to defend them; *Come Haste to the Wedding.*

After the thirteen toasts had been drunk, Mayor Van Ness called on M. Serrurier, Minister from France. He responded with a toast to "The Two Anniversaries of July: equally dear to the friends of self-government and of a strong and wise liberty in the United States and in France."

The Chargé d'Affaires of the Portuguese Embassy, when called upon by the Mayor, showed his familiarity with Key's anthem when he said in a toast to the President of the United States: "And may, as long as the world shall last, the Star-Spangled Banner continue to shine as the prosperous emblem of the happiest confederation!"

Then followed an array of toasts from the Secretary of War, the Secretary of the Navy, the Postmaster General, and the Acting Secretary of the Treasury; from Amos Kendall and W. B. Lewis, members of the Kitchen Cabinet; and from a score of others. A letter was read from Attorney General Taney, expressing his regret that he was prevented from attending the banquet by important engagements in Annapolis.

During the long program virtually all the officials in the Administration were honored. To the poet lawyer a toast was offered by Dr. Robert Mayo: "To Francis S. Key, Orator of the Day, and Author of *The Star-Spangled Banner*: his eloquence and poetry alike inspired by the loftiest spirit of Patriotism."

Two days later—July 6, 1831—the Jackson leaders of the District of Columbia who lived west of Rock Creek met in the Lancaster school house in Georgetown. Dr. Charles A. Beatty presided. Resolutions were presented by Francis Scott Key, praising Andrew Jackson's record as President and pledging hearty coöperation in the campaign for his reëlection. Referring to Jackson's candidacy as "the great cause of the people," Key recommended that a committee of fifty voters be appointed by Dr. Beatty to give support to the campaign. In addition to Key, Col. Thomas Corcoran, James Dunlop and General John Mason spoke in support of the resolutions. After the resolutions were adopted, Key was named on the committee of fifty. It was still ten months before the Democratic Convention. But the pious lawyer, who heretofore had cried out so frequently against party spirit, was now one of the first politicians to take the stump for General Jackson.

In the Spring of 1832 the President was nominated at Baltimore. Mr. Clay was chosen as the candidate of the National Republicans. As the parties were launching their campaigns, a tariff act was passed by Congress imposing additional duties on imported goods. Again the people of South Carolina were infuriated. The spectre of Secession raised its head.

As the Fourth of July approached again, the poet lawyer was called upon to write a hymn to be sung by the children of the Sunday Schools of Georgetown on Independence Day. In this hymn—a fine example of patriotic ardor and the spirit of thanksgiving—Key wrote that America was then enjoying "peace and rest," and implored the "God of our Sires" to continue to vouchsafe His never-failing aid to "this favor'd land." This is the hymn which was sung at the celebration by the children of Georgetown:

Hymn for July 4, 1832

I

Before the Lord we bow,
The God who reigns above,
And rules the world below,
Boundless in pow'r and love.
Our thanks we bring,
In joy and praise
Our hearts we raise
To heav'n's high King.

II

The nation thou hast blest
May well thy love declare,
Enjoying peace and rest,
Protected by thy care.
For this fair land,
For this bright day,
Our thanks we pay,
Gifts of thine hand!

III

Our fathers sought thee, Lord!
And on thy help relied:
Thou heard'st and gav'st the word,
And all their need supplied.
Led by thy hand
To victory,
They hail'd a free
And rescued land.

IV

God of our Sires! that hand
Be now, as then, display'd
To give this favor'd land
Thy never-failing aid.

Still may it be
Thy fix'd abode!
Be thou, our God!
Thy people, we!

V

May ev'ry mountain height,
Each vale and forest green,
Shine in thy word's pure light,
And it's rich fruits be seen!
May ev'ry tongue
Be tun'd to praise,
And joined to raise
A grateful song!

VI

Earth! hear thy Maker's voice,
The great Redeemer own!
Believe, obey, rejoice,
Bright is the promis'd crown.
Cast down thy pride,
Thy sin deplore,
And bow before
The Crucified.

VII

And when, in pow'r He comes,
O! may our native land,
From all it's rending tombs
Send forth a glorious band,
A countless throng
Ever to sign
To heav'n's high King,
Salvation's song!

The campaign between President Jackson and Mr. Clay ended with an overwhelming victory for the old warrior in the White House. Key was elated by the tremendous majorities. But in midst of the rejoicing there came distressing news from the South. On November 24, 1832, the South Carolina Convention, called to consider the Nullification Ordinance, declared that the tariff acts were "null, void, and no law, nor binding upon this State, its officers or citizens." The Ordinance not only directed the Legislature to take measures to prevent the enforcement of the tariff acts within the State, but set forth that, if the Federal Government attempted to enforce the law, the people of South Carolina would hold themselves "absolved from all further obligation to maintain or preserve their political connection with the people of the other States."

President Jackson, claiming that his reëlection expressed the people's approval of his attitude on Nullification, decided to issue a Proclamation setting forth his views on the subject. The Congress convened on December 3rd; but the President's Message made no allusion to the imminence of Civil War. Nevertheless, on the very day that his Message was read in Congress, the brave old patriot was preparing his appeal to the American people. It was almost midnight. Before his fireplace in the White House he sat puffing his pipe and meditating. The Message had been prepared by his Secretary of State: but he would add the final touches. "Going over to the table on which always stood the picture of his Rachel, and the Bible to which she had been devoted," says one of Jackson's biographers, "he wrote a conclusion to the Proclamation in the nature of a touching appeal to the patriotic memories of the South Carolinians." On December 10, 1832, the old warrior issued the historic Proclamation in answer to the defiance of South Carolina. The President denied the right of a State to nullify an act of Congress; announced his resolve to crush Nullification as treason; and warned that the authority of the National Government would be maintained at any cost. The grim old patriot appealed to the American people to sustain him, and his Proclamation thrilled the Nation like a bugle call.

Francis Scott Key watched with increasing anxiety the dramatic procession of events. He wanted to do his part to uphold the Constitution. He was delighted with the Proclamation. He pledged his support to the President in maintaining the Union. Even Daniel Webster and John Quincy Adams modified their opinions about General Jackson, constrained as they were to give their support to him in his crusade for the preservation of the Republic.

There was no one more aware than Key that President Jackson despised any man who gave the slightest comfort to the Nullifiers. When, for instance, Thomas Charlton wrote to Key from Savannah in November, 1832, to ask for help in seeking an appointment from the President, the Georgetown cousin replied: "It has occurred to me however that this is a matter that will certainly be settled by your Representatives in Congress. . . . I hope you are not a Nullifier. For if you are, I think that will nullify all your hopes."

The people looked on with intense interest when Mr. Calhoun took his seat in the Senate. The old warrior in the White House was ready to seize him and imprison him for treason. But the day of Secession had not yet arrived. The pious lawyer at Georgetown, a zealous advocate of peace, breathed a sigh of relief when he heard that Senator Clay had proposed a compromise measure which won the support of Senator Calhoun. Then, early in 1833, came the news from Charleston that the Nullifiers had decided to suspend the Ordinance of Nullification pending the discussions in Congress. And eventually the tariff bill sponsored by Senator Clay was passed by Congress and was signed by President Jackson.

CHAPTER XIX

Defender of Sam Houston

ON MARCH 31, 1832 – but a few days after President Jackson's renomination by the Democratic National Convention – the members in the House of Representatives were engaged in a debate concerning a fraud which was alleged to have been committed by a collector of the customs. One of the Congressmen who participated in the debate was William Stanberry of Ohio, who made a bitter attack upon the Jackson Administration. Charging that the Government was saturated with corruption, he cited a case in Ohio where the superintendent of the Cumberland Road had defrauded both the contractors and the Government, and nevertheless was not removed from office. He declared there were many other officials, known to be dishonest, who were allowed to remain in office, even after evidence of their dishonesty had been sent to the President. Congressman Stanberry then hurled an insinuation against former Secretary of War Eaton and Sam Houston, intimate friend of the President. "Was the late Secretary of War removed," he asked, "in consequence of his attempt fraudulently to give to Governor Houston the contract for Indian rations?"

Two days later this question was printed in Duff Green's newspaper. Sam Houston, then in Washington, rushed to the Capitol in a rage. He was anxious to get immediate revenge.

Houston was just thirty-nine. Born near Lexington, Virginia, he was taken into East Tennessee, then a part of North Carolina, after his father's death. One day, when young Sam had disappeared, it was learned that he had crossed the Tennessee River and was living with the Cherokee Indians. His brothers, who went into the Indian country to search for him, found him lying under a tree at the wigwam of Chief Oo-loo-te-ka. They found that he had been adopted by the Indian Chief and had been named Co-lon-neh — meaning "the Raven." The brothers urged the runaway boy to come home, but he replied that the freedom of the red men suited him better than the tyranny that he found at home. So he stayed with the Indians more than a year. Finally he returned to civilization; and after conducting a private school for a short time, became a student at an academy. At twenty he closed his books to enlist in the army then being raised for the war with Great Britain. He took part in the campaign against the Creeks, and received an ugly wound from a barbed arrow. General Jackson urged him not to return to the field, but he insisted on leading the attack on the Indians at Tallapoosa in 1814. In that battle he fell in the moment of victory with two bullet wounds in his body, wounds from which he never entirely recovered. For months his life hung by a thread. He was taken to his mother's home to die; but the Tennessee air proved beneficial; and in 1815 he rejoined his regiment and continued his army life until 1818. When he returned to Tennessee he took up the study of law. At thirty

Houston was elected to Congress, and two years later was reëlected. In 1827, through Jackson's influence, he became Governor of Tennessee; in January, 1829, the Governor was married; in April of the same year his bride left him; he then resigned the governorship, and returned to the wild life of the Indians. Crossing the Mississippi, the former Governor took up his habitation with the Cherokees, his old friends, who had emigrated to what is now Arkansas. He was adopted by Chief Oo-loo-te-ka as a member of the Cherokee Nation; he lived the life of the painted savage; and often drowned his memories in alcohol. Then came the news of the death of his mother. He returned home, and at the bedside of his mother there came a reformation of his soul. He determined then to live no longer as an exile with the Indians.

In 1831 Sam Houston set out with a delegation of Cherokees on a trip to Washington to call on President Jackson. They stopped at Nashville, where the former Governor showed the Indians through the Hermitage. While making an inspection of the grounds, Houston cut a hickory sapling and made it into a walking stick. It was this hickory cane that Houston was ready to use upon Congressman Stanberry. At the Capitol the Tennessee giant met James K. Polk, then a member of Congress from Tennessee, who persuaded him to leave the building without doing any violence.

Houston now decided to send a message to Stanberry to ask the Congressman whether he admitted making the statement as it was quoted in the press. The Raven's message was delivered by Congressman Cave Johnson of Tennessee. Mr. Stanberry asked one of his colleagues to hand this reply to

Mr. Johnson: "I cannot recognize the right of Mr. Houston to make this request."

As the days passed Congressman Stanberry became more and more alarmed. One of the Ohio Senators urged him to carry two pistols and a dirk. But he saw nothing of Houston until the night of Friday, April 13th. That evening about eight o'clock Houston was strolling on Pennsylvania Avenue with Congressman Blair of Tennessee and Senator Buckner of Missouri. Congressman Stanberry, who had just crossed the avenue, stepped upon the sidewalk. It was long past sundown. The avenue was lighted by dim street-lamps.

"Are you Mr. Stanberry?" demanded Sam Houston.

"Yes, sir," replied the Congressman from Ohio.

"Then," shouted Houston, "you are a damned rascal!"

As he shouted, the Tennesseean slammed down his hickory stick upon Stanberry's head. Stanberry threw up his hands and staggered back. Houston leaped upon him and threw him down. Stanberry cried to his assailant to stop; but the enraged man continued with his blows. Fortunately for Stanberry, Houston's right arm had been weakened slightly by a wound received at the battle of To-ho-pe-ka; and Stanberry managed to turn on his side and draw out a pistol from the right pocket of his pantaloons. He cocked the pistol and aimed at Houston's chest. He pulled the trigger. As the gunlock snapped, the flint struck particles of fire — but the charge did not explode. Houston grabbed the pistol, and struck the Congressman several more times with his hickory cane. Senator Buckner, who was watching the fight, told Houston it was about time to stop. Congressman Stanberry, lying prostrate on the sidewalk, asked Houston why he was trying to assassinate him. Houston said he was not trying to assassinate him: he was punishing him for trying to ruin his reputation. By this time a large crowd had gathered. When some one in the crowd advised Houston not to punish the Congressman too severely, Houston replied that he was attending to his own business: he had chastised "the damned scoundrel," and he was ready to answer for anything he had done.

Congressman Stanberry, badly bruised, was taken to his bed. The next day he notified the House of Representatives of the attack. In his message, which he sent to Speaker Andrew Stevenson, he said: "I was waylaid in the street, near to my boarding-house, last night, about eight o'clock, and attacked, knocked down by a bludgeon, and severely bruised and wounded, by Samuel Houston, late of Tennessee, for words spoken in my place in the House of Representatives; by reason of which, I am confined to my bed, and unable to discharge my duties in the House, and attend to the interests of my constituents. I communicate this information to you and request that you will lay it before the House."

A motion was made that Houston be arrested and brought before the bar of the House. Four Representatives from Tennessee and a scattering of Members from other States opposed the arrest; but the motion was adopted by a vote of 145 to 25.

When the former Governor of Tennessee was brought before the House as a prisoner on April 16, 1832, the galleries were crowded. Towering more than six feet, he was a commanding figure. He wore a buckskin coat with a fur collar, and he carried his hickory stick. Down the aisle of the historic chamber he walked in the custody of the sergeant-at-arms. When he reached the Speaker's desk, the Speaker pronounced the charge against him, and asked him if he wished counsel and witnesses. Houston, himself a member of the Bar, said that he did not want counsel to represent him, but did want to produce witnesses.

Two days later the House was ready to proceed with the trial of Sam Houston, military hero, lawyer, former Member of Congress, former Governor of Tennessee, and protégé of President Jackson. In the meantime, Houston had changed his mind about his plan of defense: he had conferred with Francis Scott Key and had decided to let the Georgetown lawyer defend him. Accordingly, on April 18th, Congressman Johnson of Tennessee presented a motion that Houston be allowed the privilege of counsel before the bar of the House. The motion was adopted; and when Houston was brought in, he was accompanied by the poet lawyer. The Colossus in Buckskin, accompanied by his attorney, slight and slender of build, walked to the Speaker's desk.

"Samuel Houston," said Speaker Stevenson, "are you now ready to proceed to your trial?"

"I am ready!" was Houston's firm reply.

At this point Key made a motion that no Member of the House, who had formed or expressed an opinion on the guilt or innocence of the accused, should sit in judgment in the case.

The motion electrified the House. Houston and Key were asked to leave the chamber while the motion was being discussed. One of Stanberry's colleagues from Ohio branded Key's suggestion as equivalent to "disgracing one of his brothers on that floor." Congressman Thomas H. Crawford of Pennsylvania replied that in a criminal case the Congressmen sat as both judges and jurors, and he swore that he would never consent to the trial of any man, while some of the Members who were to sit in judgment were not able to do justice to the accused. It was evident that the House was divided between the friends of President Jackson and his enemies. Congressman Tristam Burges of Rhode Island was indignant because he felt that Key had questioned the fairness of Members of the House: he charged that Key must have known that no one had a right to expel a Member of Congress from his seat; and he expressed regret that Key had made such an unfortunate motion. Key, while waiting in the lobby with the prisoner, and hearing the echoes from the virulent debate, realized that he had made a mistake. He sent word to the Speaker that he wished to withdraw the motion. This permission was granted, and soon afterwards the Tennessee giant and his lawyer again marched down the aisle.

Speaker Stevenson now asked Houston this question: "Do you admit or deny that you assaulted and beat the said Stanberry, as he has represented in the letter which has been read, and a copy of which has been delivered to you by order of the House?" The prisoner replied that his lawyer would answer the question.

Francis Scott Key then arose and addressed the chair. He read a statement that the accused denied that he had assaulted and beat Stanberry as represented in the letter; that the accused admitted he was indignant when he read the remark made by Stanberry on the floor of the House; that the accused was armed only with "an ordinary walking stick," while Stanberry was armed with pistols; that he met Stanberry after the House had adjourned and a half mile from the Capitol; that he denied any intention of committing a contempt of the House, or a breach of the privileges of its members; denied that the act involved any such contempt or breach; and averred that he was fully prepared to justify his conduct by proof and argument.

The Speaker then asked the Raven: "Do you admit or deny that the said assault and beating were done for and on account of words spoken by the said Stanberry in the House of Representatives in debate?"

Houston replied that his lawyer had already answered that question.

Congressman Stanberry was absent; so the trial was suspended until the next day. Meanwhile the House refused to allow bail.

On Thursday, April 19, 1832, the House of Representatives began the taking of testimony in the trial of Houston. Mr. Stanberry, the first witness, narrated the details of the assault and battery. Questions were propounded by the members of the special committee chosen to conduct the proscecution. Francis Scott Key subjected the Ohio Congressman to a rigid cross-examination. After the clerk had read aloud Stanberry's speech, in which fraud was insinuated, Key hurled this question at the Congressman: "These remarks, thus published, impute fraud to the accused. Had you then, or have you now, any and what evidence of the correctness of such imputation?" Congressman Stanberry explained that he had intended his accusation against former Secretary of War Eaton, and that he had mentioned Governor Houston's name merely to identify the transaction. Key thought that the witness was evading the issue, and kept up a withering fire of questions. Some of the Members felt that the defense counsel was too harsh and too persistent; they jumped to their feet to protect their fellow Member. A snarl ensued; and at five o'clock the House adjourned for the day.

On the following day the wrangle continued. But Key finally won his point: and Congressman Stanberry was ordered to answer whether he had any evidence of fraud on the part of Sam Houston. The Congressman admitted reluctantly that he believed Houston did participate in the attempted fraud. He added that bids for the contract for the Indian rations were asked for in 1830, that Houston was in Washington at that time, and that he was known to be "a man of broken fortunes and blasted reputation."

On the next day, April 21st, Key was still engaged in the cross-examination. Congressman Stanberry testified that his severest injuries were on the head as a result of the blows from the hickory cane, but that a bone in his left hand was fractured and both arms were bruised.

The trial of Sam Houston had now attracted nation-wide attention. In spite of a strong feeling of sympathy for the assaulted Congressman, Francis Scott Key was waging one of the hardest battles of his career with remarkable courage.

Most of the people, except blind partisans, believed that whether there was fraud or not, the giant from Tennessee had no right to assault one of the Nation's lawmakers as he did. One of the Baltimore newspapers in commenting on the case said: "But, let the truth of these charges be what they may, it is impossible to admit the right of individuals thus to punish representatives of the people, for words spoken in debate. If so, Col. Benton's famous prophecy has met its fulfilment—'that members of Congress would be compelled to legislate with pistols in their belts.'"

When the trial entered the second week, Francis Scott Key called Senator Alexander Buckner of Missouri as a witness for the accused. Mr. Key held up the famous hickory cane, and inquired:

"Is the stick, now shown to you, the one used by the accused on that occasion?"

"I think it is," replied the Senator from Missouri.

Senator Buckner made light of the assault. And Congressman Stanberry thought the Missourian was trying to cast ridicule upon him. In a fit of anger Stanberry branded the Senator's testimony as "destitute of truth and infamous." Later, however, he withdrew this statement and apologized.

On Thursday, April 26th, with the taking of testimony concluded, Attorney Key was ready to begin his argument in defense of Sam Houston. The scene was a colorful one. Behind the Speaker's desk, beneath a sweeping arch, was a figure of Liberty. On either side of the desk were flag-draped panels, one containing a portrait of George Washington, the other a portrait of Lafayette. Every seat on the floor was occupied, and in the aisles were chairs for privileged guests. The gallery was filled to capacity with diplomats and others prominent in Washington society.

When the author of the National Anthem arose, he first called attention to the importance of the case. "The duty I am now to discharge," he said, "of submitting the defense of Samuel Houston to this honorable House, would be a far lighter one to the House and to myself, if I could consider this the case of Samuel Houston alone... But, Sir, this cause cannot fail to have consequences, for good or for evil, extending to distant days, when the accused and all around him may be forgotten. It is thought to affect the high privileges of this great House; and it is certain that it affects the still higher privileges of a still greater House — the people of this great Republic."

While Sam Houston was under arrest, his lawyer was endeavoring to make it appear that the prisoner was occupying "a post of honor" on the floor of the House. "He is proud," Key exclaimed, "as an American citizen, to stand here, representing the great body of the people, whose rights, he trusts, will be vindicated in his person. And I am proud, as an American lawyer, to stand by such a man in such a case."

Before delving into the law and facts of the case, Key offered an apology for the motion which he had made at the outset of the trial. In the course of a trial, he said, things sometimes occur — it may be through the mistakes of its advocates or the mistakes of others — that excite prejudice and ill feeling. For example, he himself had been criticized for damaging Houston's case by seeking to challenge a member of the House alleged to have formed and expressed an opinion unfavorable to the accused. He therefore made a plea to the Congressmen that they would not allow any mistake that he had made to prejudice them against his client. "It was my own act," he confessed, "and from my own suggestion. I thought it my client's right, and consequently my duty. I hope I also may be excused if, in my ignorance of this dark subject, parliamentary law, I thought the rules of proceeding in the tribunals to which I had been accustomed, intended to secure to every man a fair and impartial trial, might be applicable here."

There was one other observation he wanted to make before proceeding to a discussion of the law and the facts — this was the attitude of the press. In a case like this, he said, when a question of constitutional rights was to be considered, the very least that ought to be expected of the press — "the privileged guardian of the people's rights" — was that it would remain impartial. Instead of that, the press was attempting to inflame the people as well as the members of the House against the accused in order to prevent a calm and unprejudiced consideration of the case. Some of the newspapers, he charged, even contained malicious misrepresentations. Regarding Houston's strength he declared:

> The accused has been represented as a man of violence and blood, conscious of superior strength, lying in wait as an assassin; in personal vigor as a Hercules. These exaggerated descriptions of his character have been wholly unconfirmed by the proof; and whatever the appearance of his person might indicate, he is

> shown to be a weak and disabled man, not likely to be tempted to violence by the assurance of success. He had once, indeed, an arm fit to execute the strong impulses of a brave heart — but that arm he had given to his country. On the field of one of her most perilous battles it had been raised in her defense . . . and on that field it had fallen, crushed and mangled, to his side. Hercules, too, could not be painted without his club — and language could hardly be found to convey an adequate idea of the terrific weapon with which this assassin was armed. I thought it proper that, instead of the picture, the club itself should be exhibited. The House have seen it; and I could not help remembering, on seeing an honourable gentleman measuring it, and comparing it with his finger, the venerable judge who is said to have presented his thumb to show the dimensions of the stick with which, in those strange old times, the law allowed a man to chastise his wife.

Key now launched into his main argument — that the House of Representatives did not have the power to try the case. As a matter of fact, a ruffian had brutally assaulted a Congressman for words which he had spoken in debate on the floor of the House, and the House has the right to protect its members. Nevertheless, the ruffian's lawyer continued to ramble on for two hours, trying to make the Congressmen believe that they had no jurisdiction in the matter.

It was quite true, as Key asserted, that the members of Congress were subjected too much to the influence of politics and passion to enable them to act as calm and fair-minded judges. With amazing courage he condemned the Congressmen for being unable to decide with impartiality:

> It can never be proper that a party prosecuting offences against itself shall be the judges to try and

> punish.... The prisoner is allowed counsel, but the privilege of arguing with his judges, and refuting their arguments, will generally be of little use to him. It would be hard enough to have such fearful odds against him in numbers and talents, as opposing advocates; but after such an encounter, to have to look to the same persons for judgment would present almost a hopeless prospect. The counsel, in such an encounter, might possibly also meet some things still more fearful than superior numbers and talents. There may hereafter be, upon a bench of two hundred and fifty judges (of which this House will consist), such a thing as a captious, impatient judge. He may think some of the questions or arguments of the counsel... 'trifling,' and he may be, as such judges generally are, armed with the most withering powers of rebuke and invective; and he may be provoked to make the counsel feel, for such an offence, all the thunder and lightning of judicial ire. It is true that the inferiority of the counsel, his humble and unprivileged condition, as a permitted guest in this great Hall, would generally protect him from being thus assailed and disabled; but these circumstances... might possibly be sometimes forgotten.

As twilight approached Key was asked to suspend his argument; and the House adjourned for the day. That night he was taken ill. The long and grueling battle in defense of Sam Houston had been taxing his strength. On the morning of April 27th he was unable to go to the Capitol. He thought he would be strong enough to resume his argument on the following day; but he had overestimated his strength; he was so weakened that he was unable to return to the Capitol until the 3rd of May.

On resuming the argument of the case, Key continued

to lash the members of the House for sitting in judgment in a criminal case. He contrasted the members of Congress with the Justices of the Supreme Court — to the disparagement of the members of Congress. Said he:

> Let the Supreme Court of the United States and the House of Representatives be compared, in respect to their duties and powers under the Constitution.... Where more safely (if safely anywhere) could this high and indefinite power of privilege be trusted, than in that supreme tribunal? What scheme or object of policy can the judges of that Court have the means, even if they should have the wish, to accomplish?... Public opinion expects (and I trust not vainly) that the men exalted to that high station, when they put on the robes of justice, will lay aside the uniforms of political warfare. To them are committed the scales of justice to be held, with high and steady hand, above the reach of every breath of the storms of party strife that may rage beneath them. To them is given the sword of justice, to guard the Constitution, the tree of life to the people, from every violation. How differently is this House constituted! And for what different purposes! Here must necessarily meet the leaders of all conflicting principles and parties. This must be the arena on which all the popular contests incident to our free institutions are to be fought out. Every temptation to the abuse of power that can be imagined will be found here.

But this was not all. Francis Scott Key now proceeded to sound a warning against legislative tyranny. He declared that the usurpation of power had always come gradually and under the pretext of promoting the welfare of the people. "From the days of Caesar to the present time," he asserted, "all power has been considered by those, who nevertheless have assumed it, as a most troublesome and dangerous thing, to be taken with great reluctance. The crown must be thrice offered, and thrice refused, and only accepted at last for the sake of the people, to be blessed under its rule."

At this point the poet lawyer took the opportunity to give a word of praise for the Administration of President Jackson. He called attention to the "present times of security," but at the same time issued a warning against Chief Executives who might be found to be corrupt and tyrannical in the future years. His warning was contained in the form of a question: "And if bad men shall ever gain the ascendancy in our councils, if a corrupt Executive shall ever command a corrupt majority here, (and the statesman must look beyond the present times of security, and guard against such dangers) may not such a power be wielded to any purpose of oppression?"

Key now subscribed to the truth of the adage that eternal vigilance is the price of liberty. "A free Constitution can be nowhere safely written," he exclaimed, "but in the hearts of a virtuous and vigilant people, who shall watch and restrain the first step of power or privilege that passes the limits assigned to it." The trial of Houston he denounced as a usurpation of power by the House of Representatives. "Surely the men who framed this Constitution," he declared, "would have thrown their unfinished work with indignation from their hands, if they could have foreseen that a day like this was so soon to come, when here, in this hall, it should be gravely debated whether power, undefined and unlimited but by the discretion of the holders, should be adjudged under the Constitution to be lodged here, or there, or anywhere, in any human hands."

Passing finally to his conclusion, Key asserted that, even assuming that the House of Representatives did have the power to try the case against Houston, it was the duty of the House to refuse to punish an unfortunate man in a "hard case." While the prisoner was accused of being "a man of ruined fortunes and blasted reputation" who had attempted to defraud the Government, as a matter of fact he had heard the call of his country in the hour of danger; he had taken his humble stand "in the lowest rank of her defenders"; he had risen to distinction "among the honored and the brave"; and he had caught "the approving eye of one [General Jackson] who is ever prompt to see and proud to exalt merit, however humble."

It was true, Key admitted, that Sam Houston was "a man of ruined fortunes," for out of the horrors of war he brought "no other spoils than the scars of honest wounds, and the sword which his valor had won." But it was not true that Houston was a man of "blasted reputation." In his final appeal to the House to guard the name of Sam Houston from the breath of censure, Key exclaimed to the Speaker: "Sir, the man who inherits an honorable name, or who gains it with ease or by accident, prizes it as a rich possession; but the man who has won it as the accused has, and won it only as he has, will cherish it as his only earthly treasure."

When Key concluded his speech, Houston remarked that he wanted to address the House too. His request was granted, but his speech was deferred until the following Monday. In the meantime President Jackson sent word that he wanted to see him. Houston, still clothed in buckskin, hurried to the White House. General Jackson asked the Colossus in Buckskin whether he had any other clothes. He replied that he had not; whereupon his old commander gave him some money, with the request that he dress like a gentleman and thereby strengthen his defense. So Houston went to a tailor, and ordered a coat of fine material that reached to his knees, trousers of the latest style, and a vest of white satin.

At noon on Monday, May 7, 1832, Houston was led again to the bar of the House. He bowed in front of the dais. The Speaker nodded to him to proceed. This was the first time in his life, he began, that he had ever been accused of violating the law. He recalled his four years of service in Congress as a Representative from Tennessee. He admitted that adversity had overtaken him. But he exclaimed: "Though the ploughshare of ruin has been driving over me and laid waste my brightest hopes, yet I am proud to think that, under all circumstances, I have endeavored to sustain the laws of my country and to support her institutions." He contended that the liberties of more than twelve million people were at stake because of the great principle involved in his case. He scoffed at the idea that President Jackson was plotting to usurp the powers of Congress. "They have conjured up," he declared of Jackson's enemies, "the spectre of a Chief Magistrate who may have his bullies and his myrmidons, and may employ them to carry measures in the House by practices the most nefarious." No single individual, he contended, would ever be able to overthrow the liberties of the American people: if any danger of tyranny ever appeared, it would be the tyranny of Congress. No tyrant ever grasped the reins of power, he declared, until after they were put into his hands by a corrupt legislative body. "And when Caesar trampled on the liberties of his country," he pointed out, "it was because a corrupt and factious Senate had placed the sceptre in his hands and tendered him the crown." At one point the gallery applauded and a bouquet of flowers fell at his feet. Solemnly he picked up the flowers and bowed. Then he launched upon a denunciation of the men for giving him an unfair trial. Not only had one of his witnesses been insulted on the stand, but his lawyer had been treated with disrespect. "A gentleman," he said, giving a description of Francis Scott Key, "whose bland and amiable manners should at least have shielded him from everything like rudeness or indignity. A gentleman whose intelligence raises him to a distinguished eminence in society, and the fruits of whose genius will be a proud legacy to posterity. He was entitled, as it seems to me, especially when engaged in behalf of an accused man, to respectful consideration and gentlemanly treatment." Houston now compared himself to St. Paul as he stood before Ananias, recalling that the high priest commanded those that stood by him to smite the Apostle on the mouth. "God," Houston quoted St. Paul's rebuke, "shall smite thee, thou whited wall: for sittest thou to judge me after the law, and commandest me to be smitten contrary to the law?"

Francis Scott Key sat in the front row, marveling at

the brave frontiersman. For two hours the Raven spoke. Just how much help he received from his lawyer in preparing the speech is not known; but his peroration contained a tribute to the Star-Spangled Banner, expressed Key's lofty ideals of patriotism, and endorsed one of his favorite theories about human life — that luxury is a vice that endangers the Republic.

The question now before the House was whether Samuel Houston was guilty of a violation of the privileges of the House. For several days the oratorical combat raged. Congressman Polk, who had voted against the arrest of his fellow Tennesseean, branded the entire proceeding as a usurpation of power, and asserted that the conduct of the trial showed that the members of the House were highly unfit to sit in judgment. "What excitement and warmth of feeling have we witnessed on this trial! How unlike grave judges have we occasionally appeared!"

The days slowly passed. The speeches seemed interminable. Finally, when darkness came on May 11th, the lights were brought in, and John Dickson, Congressman from New York, raised his voice against the prisoner. The gentleman from New York sounded a warning against the Administration dominated by the old man in the White House. He prophesied that the corruption of General Jackson and his followers would lead to violence. He feared the collapse of industry, the disheartening of genius, the mourning of patriotism, and the silencing of the tongue of eloquence. In a tremulous voice he warned: "Consternation, terror, and tyranny, desolation and ruin will overspread the land: your rulers will be Domitians, Tiberiuses, and Neroes, *and the people — slaves!*"

By this time the patience of the members of the House was completely exhausted. It was after nine o'clock. Cries for the question resounded through the chamber. The motion to declare Houston guilty was finally put by the Speaker. The roll was called, and Houston was found guilty by a vote of 106 to 89.

Houston's punishment was very mild. He was sentenced to be called before the Speaker and reprimanded — then he would be discharged from further custody. Some of the Congressmen thirsted for something more than a "schoolboy's punishment," but the motion to give only a reprimand was passed by a vote of 96 to 84.

And so, at noon on Monday, May 14, 1832, Sam Houston presented himself and again the aisles and the gallery were crowded. Speaker Stevenson, as he proceeded to give the reprimand to the prisoner, paid a glowing tribute to the eloquence and the ability of Francis Scott Key as the attorney for the defense. "You have been heard in person in your defense," said the Speaker to the Raven. "You have been ably and eloquently defended by eminent counsel, and every facility afforded you to place your cause fully and fairly before the House."

CHAPTER XX

Mediator in Alabama

KEY'S ADMIRATION FOR President Jackson now led to an appointment to an important Government office. The poet lawyer was offered the position of United States District Attorney for the District of Columbia — a legal position which promised to help him rather than interfere with his profession. The appointment was confirmed by the Senate on January 29, 1833.

During his first year as United States Attorney, Key received a call from the President to go on a special mission to Alabama. Its object was to mediate between Federal and State officials in their contest for jurisdiction over the lands that had been ceded by the Creek Indians. For some years the Indians of the South — the Cherokees, the Chickasaws, the Choctaws, the Creeks, and other tribes — were being pushed westward to make way for the white man. In 1832 the Upper Creeks of Alabama — this faction of the Creek Confederacy lived along the Coosa and Tallapoosa Rivers — reluctantly made an agreement at Cusseta to cede to the United States Government all their domain in exchange for special reservations west of the Mississippi. The Creeks did not want to leave the ancient hunting grounds of their fathers, hallowed by the memories of a grim past, and made sacred by familiar haunts. They were not savage nomads;

they occupied modest homes, tilled the soil, raised horses and cattle, and traded among themselves and with their white neighbors. So the Treaty of Cusseta made provision for surveys of special reservations, on which the Indians would be allowed to remain if they desired. According to the terms of the Treaty, no whites were to settle in these reservations for a period of five years; and no whites were to settle in any of the ceded territory at all until after the surveys were completed and the allotments were made to the Indians. As soon as it became known that the Creeks had ceded their land to the Government, about twenty-five thousand people rushed in to grab the choice locations. The task of removing these intruders was imposed by law upon the United States Marshal for the Southern District of Alabama. The Marshal made preparations to carry out the orders of the President; but he soon realized the difficulties that confronted him. In the Summer of 1832 he ordered some intruders to leave a little settlement along the banks of the Chattahoochee; but they refused to go; they disputed the right of the Marshal to remove them. The Marshal reported the trouble to the nearest army post, Fort Mitchell. This post was located in Russell County, Alabama, about ten miles south of Columbus, Georgia. A detachment of soldiers under the command of a Lieutenant of the United States Army hurried to the scene. Before long the village was a mass of flames. A State warrant was issued for the arrest of the Lieutenant; but when the Deputy Sheriff attempted to serve it, he was pierced by a Federal bayonet. Governor John Gayle of Alabama, in his Message to the Legislature in

December, called attention to the controversy in emphatic terms. "If it shall be considered as the true constitutional doctrine," he said, "that a State can remain a member of the Union, and at the same time place her citizens beyond the reach of its laws, ours will not be the shadow of a government, and for all practical purposes it will be dissolved.... As sure as it shall succeed, its triumph will be stained with fraternal blood, and the proudest of its trophies will be the destruction of constitutional liberty."

In the Summer of 1833, the embers of hatred broke out anew. Several Indian chiefs called upon the United States Marshal and laid complaints against a squatter named Hardeman Owens. The Indians swore that Owens had not only taken their fields from them, but had also killed their horses and hogs. The Marshal went to the scene, about twenty miles from Fort Mitchell, and ordered Owens to leave. Owens refused. So the Marshal went to Fort Mitchell, and returned shortly with a detachment of United States soldiers. Owens was placed under arrest; and then he made a promise to the soldiers that, if they would release him, he would leave the ceded territory. So they let him go. After the Marshal had gone about fifteen miles, however, he was overtaken by a group of Indians, who had lost the stoic calm and traditional bravery of their race. They said that Owens had threatened to burn their homes and kill any person who dared to come upon his property. The Marshal turned his horse, and hurried back to the scene. Just as he was riding up to the gate, a frightened Indian warned that Owens had set a powder mine in the house. The powder exploded; but, thanks to the Indian, no one was injured. The soldiers again set out to arrest the daring squatter. He was overtaken; but he resisted arrest. Just as he was about to fire his pistol at one of the soldiers he was shot dead.

District Attorney Key, as well as President Jackson and Attorney General Taney, heard the rumblings of discontent that echoed from Alabama. In course of time news reached the White House that some of the United States soldiers had been indicted for the murder of Hardeman Owens. Major James L. McIntosh, the commanding officer at Fort Mitchell, refused to surrender any of his men to the civil authorities and warned the Sheriff to stay away. When the Sheriff reported Major McIntosh's defiance to the County Court, the Judge asked Governor Gayle to call out the State Militia. Strong indignation had been aroused throughout the State by the action of the Federal authorities, for the State of Alabama claimed juridsiction over the territory which had been ceded by the Indians. Mass meetings were held, at which resolutions were adopted declaring that the forcible removal of the settlers by Federal troops was subversive of the sovereignty of the State. Fortunately Governor Gayle was cool-headed. At the same time that he called for Militia in the newly formed counties, he urged the people to "guard against all undue excitement." But he plainly wrote, in a letter to Lewis Cass, Secretary of War, on October 2, 1833, that the Federal Government had admitted the jurisdiction of the State in the ceded territory, and the State had the right to enforce its jurisdiction. On October 7th the Governor issued a Proclamation, urging the settlers to obey all processes from the Federal and the State Courts and to abstain from any acts of unlawful violence toward the Indians. The settlers respected the Governor's admonition, and a clash was momentarily averted.

President Jackson gave orders to protect the rights of the Federal Government in Alabama. The Secretary of War accordingly replied to Governor Gayle that while the State of Alabama had obtained jurisdiction over the ceded district, the United States Government owned the land, and that the United States Army would be ordered to remove all intruders from the Government's property by order of the President.

A few days later, as the controversy over the Indian lands was on the verge of actual hostilities, President Jackson and Secretary Cass concluded that it would be wise for the United States Government to send a conciliator to Alabama to confer with officials of the State. District Attorney Key was the man they selected for the mission. At the request of the President, Secretary Cass notified Key of his duties. In his letter, dated October 31, 1833, Mr. Cass requested the District Attorney to proceed at once to Alabama, to confer with the Governor and other officials of the State, with the United States Marshal and the District Attorney for the Southern District of Alabama, and with the Army officers, in the hope of effecting a reconciliation.

Key accepted the call of his Government with characteristic enthusiasm. He was now past fifty-four; but he set out on the trip to the South with the same energy and zeal which he displayed nearly twenty years before when he obtained the permission of President Madison to use the cartel ship to seek the release of Dr. Beanes from the British fleet.

Within a few days Key was in Tuscaloosa, the Capital of Alabama. With such amazing speed did he proceed with his mission that within six days he had not only secured the Gorernor's promise of coöperation, but he had also made progress by conferring with the leading members of the Legislature.

Governor Gayle was now in a very embarrassing position. He had not only supported General Jackson for the Presidency, but he had also commended Jackson's resistance to Nullification. But now the Governor was in a quandary. As Key explained to his brother-in-law, now Secretary of the Treasury, in a letter written at Tuscaloosa on November 6th: "If he [Governor Gayle] offends the Nullifiers he is not sure of appeasing all the Union Men, and if he says he is satisfied with the United States he will be sure to offend the Nullifiers."

So tense was the situation in the Alabama Capital that a new fusion party was threatened by Governor Gayle's friends and the Nullifiers to resist the Federal authorities. Francis Scott Key, however, was not frightened by these rumors: he believed that Governor Gayle would not be willing to consent to it. "Again," said Key in his letter to Taney, "there are some Union men so displeased with the Governor that they do not altogether like making up the quarrel on such terms as would be acceptable to him and his friends. It is difficult to say yet with certainty how it may end." It was evident that the Governor was in a dilemma; but Key was gratified to find that the Governor was "quite disposed to a pacific course."

In the Legislature a committee had been named in each House to consider that part of Governor Gayle's message which related to the controversy over the Indian lands. The Governor, who was now preparing to submit a more detailed statement to the Legislature, gratified Francis Scott Key by promising he would report that he was satisfied with the proposals of the United States Government. Key then showed the Governor a message which he had received on the subject from Colonel Abert. Colonel Abert's statement was so reassuring that the Governor made a visit to Key's room to suggest that the statement be published. Key, however, suspecting that the Colonel's communication was not intended for publication, did not approve of the Governor's suggestion. "He has since appeared satisfied," Key reported to his brother-in-law, "and says he shall make his communication immediately, and will aid in promoting proper measures to prevent any further difficulties."

Considering the attitude of the Governor, Key felt confident that the Legislature would ultimately give its coöperation to prevent armed conflict between the National and the State authorities. The United States District Attorney for Alabama was now expected from Mobile. "As soon as I can have my conference with the District Attorney," he wrote Taney, "I shall look homewards, and I hope to be with you by New Year's Day." One of Key's fears was that the squatters might take unfair advantage of the Indians. "It is much to be apprehended," he reported, "that the speculators will harass the Indians with the State laws; and I am sure that the only effectual way of saving them will be to buy their land and send them off."

Having aided materially in relieving the tension in the State Capital, Key now set out for Fort Mitchell, about two hundred miles east of Tuscaloosa. Arriving there on November 11th, he soon was in conference with Major McIntosh, the commanding officer. The lawyer from Georgetown found that the Major, an old veteran of Mr. Madison's War, was embittered by the fact that his soldiers had been indicted for murder. He swore that he would stand firm in his determination to resist the arrest of his men.

One of the soldiers who was stationed there at that time said many years afterwards that Francis Scott Key, in pleading with Major McIntosh referred to the constitutional principles involved in the dispute and pointed out that the Major's action would set a precedent for posterity.

Whereupon the Major exclaimed: "Let posterity take care of itself! The people down here want to hang my men for doing their duty! I must take care of my men!"

But the emissary from the White House was not disheartened. He continued to plead, as only he could do who had turned the hearts of Cockburn, Cochrane and Ross to win the release of Dr. Beanes. He "laboured hard" to convince Major McIntosh that it was not right for the soldiers who had been indicted to resist or evade legal process.

Key's arguments were effective. For Major McIntosh finally admitted that it would be the wisest course to allow the Sheriff to arrest the indicted men.

"But," warned the Major, "if any of the men are thrown in jail, not an officer or soldier will ever move again to turn off an intruder; but they will refuse in a body and take their chance of a Court Martial!"

The poet lawyer engaged in long conversations with the soldiers. He wanted to find out what they thought of the action of the Grand Jury. He found that most of the boys were willing to stand trial, but he was not so certain how they would feel if they found they were unable to get bail.

On the morning of November 14th Key left the Fort for a day's trip to the county seat of Russell County to make some further investigations. He first rode to the Clerk's office "nine miles off in a wilderness." Here he was unable to find any information regarding the criminal proceedings. As he wrote to Taney, partly in humor, partly in irony, he supposed the records were "kept in a candle box or basket." Undaunted, he then set out for the Court House, which was located about nine miles further. When he finally located the Court House, he found it to be "a sort of shantee of rough plank." In this crude temple of justice the conciliator met a lawyer from Columbus named Seaborn Jones, who had come to Alabama to offer advice to the Grand Jury, the Sheriff and the Court.

Key felt rather disgusted with the situation in Russell County. While the Treaty of Cusseta did not make it mandatory for the United States Government to drive off intruders from the Indian lands, his opinion was that the Government had the right to withdraw its indulgence to intruders whenever it pleased. Even now, before the surveys for the reservations for the Indians had been completed, the State officials were hindering the Government in the performance of its duty.

Giving good-bye to the soldiers at Fort Mitchell, Key returned to Tuscaloosa to see what had developed in the meantime at the State Capitol. He learned that Governor Gayle was striving to avoid armed conflict between the Federal and the State troops. While the Governor had the authority to call out the Militia to enforce processes of the State Courts, he had refrained from doing so. He had taken no drastic action; but had merely sent a report of the Owens case to Secretary of War Cass for the consideration of the President.

Alabama was seething with excitement. The Jackson Democrats insisted on the importance of upholding the Federal Government. One of the Mobile newspapers reported: "We have just learned from an authentic source that orders have been issued from Headquarters for the immediate marching of ten companies of United States artillery, completely equipped for the field, to Fort Mitchell in this State. This detachment, added to the troops already stationed at that post, will constitute an effective force of fourteen companies." The Nullifiers scoffed at the very name of Andrew Jackson, and urged Governor Gayle to prepare for battle.

As the shouts of defiance rang through the halls of the State Capitol, and the bugle signalled the mobilization of troops, the pious emissary from the White House decided that he would relax and pray. He would offer his prayers in silence for the intercession of "the Power that has made and preserved us a Nation." But at the same time he would do his part in promoting conciliation by serving as an "Ambassador of Good Will." A pleasing conversationalist, he delighted the "literary and fashionable circles of the little city with the brilliancy and wit of his conversation."

One of the homes in which Key spent many pleasant hours was the Governor's Mansion. The Governor's wife, a woman of poetic talent and culture, became intensely interested in the talented visitor from the National Capital. "Mr. Francis Scott Key, the District Attorney for the District of Columbia," Mrs. Gayle wrote in her Diary, "is here at present for the purpose of assisting to settle the Creek controversy. He is very pleasant — intelligent, you at once perceive, and somewhat peculiar in his manners. He is a little, nay, a good deal absent in company, not always attending when others converse, and often abruptly breaking in with a question, though evidently unconscious of what he has done. His countenance is not remarkable when at rest, but as soon as he lifts his eyes, usually fixed upon some object near the floor, the man of sense, of fancy, and the *poet* is at once seen. But the crowning trait of his character, I have just discovered — he is a Christian."

Key was very fond of children, and he soon became a warm friend of the children of Governor and Mrs. Gayle. He was especially fond of little Sarah, aged nine. She had an album, like most little misses of her day, and now she had an opportunity to ask the author of *The Star-Spangled Banner* to write something in her album. Key was delighted to make a contribution to his little friend's book: in it he pretended to prophesy the young lady's future happiness. The opening lines show the poet's tenderness:

Lines Written in Sarah Gayle's Album

Thine hand, fair little maiden — let me see
How run the mystic lines of destiny?
A poet once (so ladies kindly said
Of the enthusiast their charms had made),
I may, though cold and dead the poet's fire,
Touch with a kindred hand the prophet's lyre.
The face too I must look upon, for there
I once could read more plainly of the fair.
With hands and face, those tell-tales of the heart,
If I have not forgotten all my art,
Some secrets of thy fate I may impart. . . .

In the midst of important diplomatic duties, Key turned to religious discussions whenever he had the opportunity. In the Governor's Mansion he opened his prayer book and hymnal and read to the children. Mrs. Gayle related in her Diary: "He has been to see me frequently and sat an hour or two last night chatting to me and the children. He made Sarah read for him and then he read for her some of the fine hymns and psalms in the *Book of Common Prayer* — one of his own, beginning 'Lord With Glowing Heart I'd Praise Thee' is in it. He seems to be fervently pious and I dearly love to hear him talk on the subject. He speaks with much simplicity upon it, and it is his own remark that religion is a system of simplicity, nothing metaphysical in it or what is not suited to all."

Another little miss who wished some original verses from the pen of Francis Scott Key was Margaret Kornegay, a niece of United States Senator William R. King of Alabama. Little Margaret asked Mrs. Gayle if she would ask Mr. Key for her. The Governor's wife, a woman of some poetic talent, wrote an anonymous request in rhyme:

To Mr. F. S. Key

Thanks, gentle Fairy! now my album take,
And place it on his table, ere he wake;
Then whisper that a maiden, all unknown,
Claims from the poet's hand a trifling boon:
Trifling, perchance, to him, but oh! not so
To her whose heart has thrilled, long, long ago,
As his inspiring lays came to her ear,
Lending the stranger's name an interest dear.
A timid girl may yet be bold to admire
The Poet's fervor and the Patriot's fire. . . .

Mrs. Gayle's poem, written on December 10th, and little Miss Kornegay's album were placed in Mr. Key's room while he was out. When he returned to the room and saw the poem, he penned a clever reply. As the "timid girl" did not divulge her name, he wrote his stanzas to Miss ——. The poem shows how he revelled in the natural beauties of Alabama, the leisurely charm of the South, and the generous hospitality of the Southern people. Incidentally the poem discredits the story which arose some years after his death that he could neither sing nor distinguish one tune from another, and that when he was serenaded by the Tuscaloosa band with a rendition of *The Star-Spangled Banner* he did not recognize the tune. For in the poem he says:

And — to a Poet, oh, how dear! —
My own song sweetly chanted here.

The anonymous poem to Mr. Key had referred to him as a "stranger." Denying that he was a "stranger," he explained very felicitously the ties that bound him to the little

Southern girl who had called him Poet, Patriot, and Christian. These are some of the lines which he inscribed in little Margaret's book in Tuscaloosa on December 13, 1833:[1]

To Miss — —

And is it so? a thousand miles apart,
Has lay of mine e'er touched a gifted heart?
Brightened the eye of beauty? won her smile?
Rich recompense for all the poet's toil!

We are not strangers: in our hearts we own
Chords that must ever beat in unison.
The same touch wakens them; in all we see,
Or hear, or feel, we own a sympathy.
We look where Nature's charms in beauty rise,
And the same transport glistens in our eyes.
The joys of others cheer us, and we keep
A ready tear, to weep with those that weep.

Yes, though Columbia's land be wide —
Though Chesapeake's broad waters glide
Far distant from the forest shores
Where Alabama's current roars;
Yet over all this land so fair
Still waves the flag of stripe and star;
Still on the Warrior's banks is seen,
And shines in Coosa's valleys green;
By Alabama's maiden sung,
With patriot heart, and tuneful tongue.
Yes! I have looked around me here,
And felt I was no foreigner:
Each friendly hand's frank offered clasp
Tells me it is a brother's grasp;
My own I deem these rushing floods —
My own, these wild and waving woods;
And — to a Poet, oh, how dear! —

1.—The full text of this poem, as well as many others quoted in this work, are included in Key's *Poems.*

My own songs sweetly chanted here.
The joy with which these scenes I view
Tells me this is my country too!
These sunny plains I freely roam —
I am no outcast from a home;
No wanderer on a foreign strand:
"This is my own, my native land."

By this time the crisis in Alabama had passed. President Jackson, while eager to give the Indian the protection of the American flag, had no desire to interfere with the processes of the State Courts: on the contrary his Secretary of War ordered Major McIntosh to facilitate any investigations which the State authorities deemed necessary. The old warrior in the White House furthermore assured Senator King that the United States Government would not give any trouble to the settlers in the Indian territory, except those who molested the Indians.

Accordingly, on December 16, 1833, Francis Scott Key, as General Jackson's duly authorized representative, addressed an official communication to Governor Gayle, stipulating the terms he was authorized to offer on behalf of the controversy. Key gave assurance that the Federal officials would not drive away any of the settlers from the lands outside the Indian reservations; that the surveys of the reservations were expected to be completed within one month; and that even the squatters settling on Indian reservations would be allowed to remain, if they paid the Indians for the land they took.

Governor Gayle replied that the terms were satisfactory to him. After all, the real purpose of the Government's order for the removal of the settlers was to assert the authority of the Government to protect the Indians in the domain ceded by the Treaty of Cusseta; and as long as the Indians were satisfied the main objective was accomplished.

So the controversy between the Federal Government and the State was now virtually at an end. And there is no doubt that Francis Scott Key played an important rôle in helping to bring order out of chaos. Largely as a result of his negotiations — not to speak of the value of his placid manner during the crisis — an agreement was reached which was satisfactory to all parties concerned — the President, the Secretary of War, the United States Marshal, the District Attorney, the military officers at Fort Mitchell, the Governor, the members of the Legislature, the Judges and other State officials, the settlers, and the Indians. Moreover, the controversy was brought to an end without bloodshed, without coercion, and even without resort to the Courts.

It is true that Key's proposal was not officially accepted by the Legislature. Some of the firebrands in Alabama were still shouting about "usurpations of power, subversive of government and destructive of civil liberty." Nevertheless the compromise was received by the people of Alabama with such hearty approval that the resolutions of indignation in the House were never reported out by the committee. Governor Gayle, in a message to the Legislature, expressed his delight in the happy outcome of the negotiations. He was gratified not only because a calamity had been averted in the new counties, but also because the principal object sought by the

State had been attained — to uphold the sovereignty of the State and the security of the people.

Key was now ready to leave for home. On December 18, 1833, after being engaged on his mission for six weeks, he said farewell to his friends in Tuscaloosa, and hurried off to reach his home in Georgetown in time for the Christmas holidays. When he arrived at his home, now decorated with Christmas greens, he carried with him a big supply of Christmas gifts for Anne and the children — as well as a great array of stories about his adventure — stories about his horse-back rides through the wilderness; the life of the Negroes on the Alabama plantations; the strange customs and rituals of the Creek Indians; the soldiers at Fort Mitchell; the scenes in the Legislature at Tuscaloosa; and the visits to the Governor's Mansion. It was the longest trip he had ever made; and his return home in time for the holidays, with the satisfaction of knowing that he had rendered an important service to his country, made this Yuletide one of the happiest in his life.

The conciliator left home for a while to make a hurried trip to Washington to report to the old chieftain in the White House. Needless to say, General Jackson was gratified to learn that the diplomatic mission had been crowned with success.

While complete amity was restored between the Federal Government and the State of Alabama, there occurred one incident which caused lifelong animosity between President Jackson and Governor Gayle. The *Globe,* one of Jackson's newspapers in Washington, published a statement charging that the trouble in Alabama had been occasioned by sordid motives of the State officials. Governor Gayle was aroused by the insinuation; and, although he had been a supporter of General Jackson, he swore that he would never again support him after the outrageous "charges of corrupt speculation and furnishing a combination with Nullifiers"—charges which he believed were printed "with the approbation, if not at the instance, of the President." Senator King tried to appease Governor Gayle by explaining that the *Globe* did not speak officially for Andrew Jackson or any of the leaders of his Administration. "The editor of that paper," Senator King explained, "is perfectly reckless in his course, and although it is considered in the country as the official paper, God help the Administration if it had to be held responsible for all of Blair's indiscretions." But John Gayle was deeply offended, and he was determined to quit the party of Andrew Jackson. Editor Blair offered an apology; and Key wrote to Governor Gayle on June 11, 1834, to call attention to the retraction with the hope that it would satitsfy him and bring him back into the Democratic fold. "You have seen no doubt," Key explained, "that the *Globe* has at last done you justice and acknowledged its fault. Blair is rather awkward in such matters, but I hope he has done it in a way satisfactory to you. It is unfortunte that he is too easily led into such attacks, and in your case, I have no doubt that some enemy of yours at home prompted him in his course towards you." But it was of no avail. Mr. Gayle had made up his mind. He deserted his old political companions, and joined the Whig party; he was elected to Congress; and later was appointed United States District Judge by President Zachary Taylor.

However, the main quarrel between the Federal Government and the State of Alabama had been adjusted. The turmoil in Tuscaloosa and on the Indian frontier subsided; and in March, 1834, Secretary of War Cass notified Governor Gayle that the troops which had been ordered into Alabama had been withdrawn. Only the regular garrison at Fort Mitchell remained in the Creek country.

As for Major McIntosh's soldiers, no trial for murder was ever held. The indicted Lieutenant and his detachment were allowed to give bail; but they were never required to appear in court for trial. The unfortunate soldier, who verily deserved praises for shooting Hardeman Owens to save one of his comrades, deserted the army. For a time District Attorney Key thought that he might be called back to Alabama to represent the Government at the trial. But when it became evident that the trial would never be held, he wrote to Governor Gayle: "As the officers and soldiers will not be forthcoming to take their trial, I shall not have the pleasure of defending them, and you will have to forfeit their bond."

From now on the Indian problem in Alabama was left in the hands of Governor Gayle. In a letter to the Governor on June 11, 1834, Key reported: "I called on the Secretary of War soon after receiving your letter, and he expressed the fullest confidence in you and his willingness to leave the whole matter [of Indian troubles] to yourself." And thus the curtain fell on one of the colorful scenes in Alabama's history—

a scene which has been described as "one of the most interesting and important episodes in the history of the State."

In the years that followed, often were the times when Francis Scott Key in his reveries brought back to recollection his thrilling adventures in the deep South. And during these remaining years there were no fonder memories than those that clustered about the Governor's Mansion in far-away Tuscaloosa. "I have often thought of Tuscaloosa and your family circle," he once wrote to Mrs. Gayle, "and could I transport myself as easily as my thoughts, I should still be a frequent visitor."

Often too he thought of the fate of the rapidly vanishing Indians. Gradually the red men were being forced back from their native haunts. They were loath to leave; but Fate decreed that they had to make their agonizing trek across the prairies. Francis Scott Key's adventures in Alabama were an interlude in the tragic drama of the exile of the Creek tribes as described by Althea Bass:

> Then the farewells were said, the cattle sold,
> And the deserted cabins and the fields
> Of corn and melons choked with weedy growth,
> Left far behind, too, were the burial mounds
> Where lay the bones of their great ancestors
> Abandoned to the white man's greedy plow,
> And then began the long march to the West,
> The trackless way that every Indian learned
> To call the Trail of Tears.

O say can you see ~~through~~ by the dawn's early light,
What so proudly we hail'd at the twilight's last gleaming,
Whose broad stripes & bright stars through the perilous fight
O'er the ramparts we watch'd, were so gallantly streaming?
And the rocket's red glare, the bomb bursting in air,
Gave proof through the night that our flag was still there;
O say does that star-spangled banner yet wave
O'er the land of the free & the home of the brave?

On the shore dimly seen through the mists of the deep,
Where the foe's haughty host in dread silence reposes,
What is that which the breeze, o'er the towering steep,
As it fitfully blows, half conceals, half discloses?
Now it catches the gleam of the morning's first beam,
In full glory reflected now shines in the stream,
'Tis the star-spangled banner — O long may it wave
O'er the land of the free & the home of the brave!

And where is that band who so vauntingly swore,
That the havoc of war & the battle's confusion
A home & a Country should leave us no more?
— ~~[illegible]~~ Their blood has wash'd out their foul footstep's pollution.
No refuge could save the hireling & slave
From the terror of flight or the gloom of the grave,
And the star-spangled banner in triumph doth wave
O'er the land of the free & the home of the brave.

O thus be it ever when freemen shall stand
Between their lov'd home & the war's desolation!
Blest with vict'ry & peace may the heav'n rescued land
Praise the power that hath made & preserv'd us a nation!
Then conquer we must, when our cause it is just,
And this be our motto — "In God is our trust,"
And the star-spangled banner in triumph shall wave
O'er the land of the free & the home of the brave. —

FACSIMILE OF THE MANUSCRIPT
OF "THE STAR-SPANGLED BANNER"

CHAPTER XXI

The Moneyed Monster

FROM THE TIME that General Jackson entered the White House, Francis Scott Key was familiar with the old warrior's hostility to the Bank of the United States. This, the second bank to be sponsored by the National Government (the first having been destroyed by the Jeffersonians in Congress in 1811) was incorporated in 1816 for a period of twenty years to meet the financial difficulties entailed by the war and to restore the soundness of paper currency. It had an authorized capital of thirty-five million dollars, partly subscribed by the Government; on its board of directors there were twenty-five men, twenty of whom were chosen by the stockholders and five appointed by the President of the United States. The Bank had given the Nation a sound currency; it had been capably managed; and it enjoyed the confidence of the financial world. But there had been breathed into Jackson's ear the suspicion that its influence had been injected into politics; and Jackson, who was totally ignorant of finance, inserted a threatening warning to the Bank in his first annual message to Congress in December, 1829. After affirming that the charter of the bank would expire in 1836, the President contended: "Both the constitutionality and the expediency of the law creating this bank are well questioned by a large portion of our fellow-citizens, and it must be admitted by all that it has failed in the great end of establishing a uniform and sound currency."

Nicholas Biddle, a native of Philadelphia, was the President of the Bank. He had been appointed by President Monroe as a director of the Bank in 1819, and had been elevated to the Presidency of the Bank in 1823, when only thirty-seven. He was a man of quick action and intense energy; he had a magnetic personality; and his self-confidence and iron will made him the dominating figure on the board of directors. Somewhat alarmed over President Jackson's attitude regarding the Bank, Mr. Biddle urged his friends to try to influence the President to change his views. But the old warrior, in his second annual message to Congress in December, 1830, insisted: "Nothing has occurred to lessen in any degree the dangers which many of our citizens apprehend from that institution as at present organized."

In spite of the ominous warnings, however, Mr. Biddle felt confident that, in the event Congress should enact a new charter, Jackson would not be so bold as to veto it. So when Congress convened in December, 1831, a bill to recharter the Bank was introduced. Then it was that the shrill voice of Francis Scott Key's Virginia friend, John Randolph, was heard. Randolph's fear was that General Jackson might weaken in his antagonism to the "Chestnut Street Monster." But the President retorted that under no condition would he ever give his sanction to the Bank of the United States. With a suspicion of banks in general, Jackson had a particular suspicion of the Bank of the United States, inasmuch as a third of its stock had passed into foreign hands.

The bill to recharter the Bank was passed by Congress on July 3, 1832, and on the following day it was sent to the President. Jackson had determined to veto it. Taney was asked to prepare a message explaining the veto, and he wrote it with "an eye to the coming campaign." Within six days the act of Congress was returned with a vehement message. Naturally the friends of the Bank were alarmed. They regarded the message as the appeal of a demagogue to the passions of the masses. "It has all the fury of a chained panther biting the bars of his cage," Mr. Biddle avowed. "It is really a manifesto of anarchy."

It was only natural that Francis Scott Key, an appointee of President Jackson, should be an enemy of the Bank of the United States. Key knew that his own brother-in-law, to whom he was devoted, was advising the old warrior to assail the Bank. Accordingly, as Jackson's campaign for reëlection advanced, the poet lawyer became more and more deeply convinced that the Bank was a monster of special privilege that was corrupting American political life. Key had heard some ugly charges too that the Kitchen Cabinet — this included such astute politicians as Amos Kendall, Major W. B. Lewis, and F. P. Blair — was scheming to arouse the jealousy of the masses against the bankers. But the members of the Kitchen Cabinet were scheming to keep Jackson in power; and Key had perfect faith in Jackson.

Henry Clay, Jackson's opponent for the Presidency, insisted that the Bank of the United States was one of the main issues of the campaign. Mr. Clay called Andrew Jackson narrow-minded and stubborn; he regarded men like Taney and Key who were endorsing Jackson's crusade against the Bank, as dangerous demagogues. The conservative people throughout the country were deeply disturbed at the trend of events. So alarmed was Chief Justice Marshall that he "all but despaired of the future of the Republic."

But the masses knew as much about finance and banking as did Andrew Jackson – and that was very little – but they knew that Andrew Jackson was the hero of New Orleans and the champion of the common people; and he was the man who now dared to attack the moneyed monster. Among the charges against the Bank were these: that the directors received their appointments through political influence; that Mr. Biddle had given special favors to certain Members of Congress, such as loaning money on insufficient security; that he had subsidized the press by loaning money to newspapers and making them his tools; and that the Bank had used money at the polls against Andrew Jackson. The officials of the Bank denied that they had ever employed corrupt methods in lobbying with the Congressmen; but they could not deny that, after Jackson opened his fight against the Bank, Mr. Biddle followed "the morally wrong and practically unwise policy of loaning money without proper security to editors and Members of Congress."

And so, as the tide of Democracy swept again over the land, Andrew Jackson was triumphantly reëlected. There were many people who were hoping that the Bank issue could be evaded. Not so Andrew Jackson. The monster had showed its teeth: it was now his turn to pursue the monster. He regarded his reëlection as a verdict endorsing his veto of the Bank bill. Nothing, therefore, would suffice less than the complete annihilation of the monster. Since, however, the majority in Congress favored a new charter for the Bank, it was evident that if a blow were to be struck, it had to be struck by the Executive. Accordingly, Jackson determined upon his plan to remove the Government deposits from the Bank in order to hinder it in its fight for a new charter at the next session of Congress. But the only man who could withdraw the Government deposits was the Secretary of the Treasury. Without delay the plan was presented to the members of the Cabinet. Taney and Barry were against the Bank; Livingston and Cass were for it; Woodbury was evasive. Secretary of the Treasury McLane waited two months before he was ready to give his reply, but finally he opposed the President's scheme.

Determined at all costs to remove the deposits, the President decided to reorganize the Cabinet in the hope of accomplishing his plan before the Congress reassembled in December. He arranged to send Mr. Livingston to Paris, and to transfer Mr. McLane to the State Department. He then appointed William J. Duane of Philadelphia Secretary of the Treasury, because Duane was known to be unfriendly to the Bank. Duane accepted the Treasury portfolio; but the old warrior later discovered to his dismay that Duane was unwilling to order the removal of the Government deposits without the sanction of Congress.

In the Summer of 1833 Jackson went on a trip to New England. While in Boston he was stricken with a hemorrhage of the lungs—his hemorrhages were becoming increasingly frequent—and it put an end to his trip. The old man turned back, physically feeble, but with an iron determination to resume in Washington his battle with the "Hydra of corruption." The monster was now threatening to fight with savage intensity. Already Mr. Biddle had ordered his twenty-six branch banks to call in loans and reduce the circulation of bank notes. He also caused an avalanche of petitions to be sent to the White House in favor of the continuation of the Bank.

Early in September President Jackson requested Secretary Duane to give the order for removal. But the Secretary refused. The President then asked Taney to prepare a brief on the subject. This paper, read to the Cabinet on September 18, 1833, stated: "Whatever may be the opinion of others, the President considers his reëlection as a decision of the people against the bank." It recommended the immediate removal of the deposits. For five days the President plead with Duane. But Duane shook his head. He said he not only refused to order the removal of the deposits, but he also refused to resign. The old warrior hesitated no longer. On September 23rd Duane was ousted from the Cabinet. Taney, in the meantime, was giving assurance that while he had no desire to change his place in the Cabinet, he would not shrink from duty if called upon by the President. And on the day when Duane went out, Taney came in as head of the Treasury Department.

Francis Scott Key, in his early years a dreamer and a lover of peace, had been toughened under Old Hickory's magnetic influence into a militant political warrior with galvanized convictions. He remained the poet with the poet's dreams; but, according to the testimony of one who knew him, "in his political opinions, as in everything else, he was decided; in political action, ardent, zealous, fearless." He was now convinced that Nicholas Biddle, even if he had done nothing worse, had subsidized a number of newspaper editors and had held the sword over the heads of some of the members of Congress. He not only approved Taney's order for the removal of the deposits, but also offered his own services to the President.

Early in November, 1833 when he was in the midst of his diplomatic duties in Alabama, Key was eager to hear how Jackson and Taney were faring in their battle with the Bank.

"I feel anxious," Key wrote at Tuscaloosa in a letter to his brother-in-law, "to hear how you and the Senate will agree. I think I see that Biddle is to resign. I trust you will be able to keep your Banks up."

Upon his return to Washington, Key heard that Mr. Biddle's friends in the Senate had prepared themselves to defy the gray-haired veteran in the White House. On the day after Christmas, Senator Clay introduced two resolutions aimed at the Administration — one charging that Jackson had assumed power in violation of the Constitution; the other declaring that the reasons which Taney gave for the removal of the deposits were "unsatisfactory and insufficient." In denouncing the President as a tyrant, Senator Clay was greeted with wild applause from the galleries. Both of the resolutions were adopted by the Senate.

In June, 1832, near the close of the session, President

Jackson sent to the Senate the nomination of Taney as Secretary of Treasury. The nomination was rejected — the first time in American History that the Senate had ever rejected the nomination of a Cabinet officer. The action of the Senate, however, did not surprise Taney or Key. They were aware that the Senate was controlled by Clay, Webster, and Calhoun — Jackson's arch enemies. Taney resigned immediately as Secretary of the Treasury. But as he stepped down to private life he was assured by the old patriot in the White House that he was one of the martyrs in "the great struggle to redeem our Republic from the corrupt domination of a great moneyed power."

During the following Winter a newspaper editor in New York proposed that all the anti-Jackson forces should form a coalition under the name of Whigs. The Whigs in England had fought against the tyranny of the King. America needed a similar party to fight against the tyranny of King Andrew! The suggestion was adopted. And thus a new political party came into being in America.

Maryland, the home of Mr. Taney, promised to be one of the spectacular battle grounds of the campaign of 1834. As early as May, the Whigs met in Frederick and denounced President Jackson for his "high-handed and arbitrary abuses of power." Dr. John Tyler presided, and addresses were delivered by William Schley, Richard Potts, Francis Brengle, and James M. Coale. Several weeks later the Whig newspaper at Frederick charged that Taney, by indoctrinating Jackson with "puerile nonsense" about a metallic currency, had "duped and deceived a childish and superannuated man."

Taney was given a royal welcome by the Jacksonians when he returned to Baltimore on July 21st to resume the practice of law. On the following day he decided to accept an invitation to speak at a dinner in Frederick. "I am, as you know," he replied to the committee, "no great *diner out,* and my habits have not altered since you knew me. And the only places at which I could consent to accept such invitations are my two homes, Frederick and Baltimore." The committee selected August 6th as the date for the affair; and Taney replied that he would come by way of Washington. "I shall come up," he said, "in my own carriage and be at Clarksburg the first night, or at Rockville so as to reach Frederick at any hour that may be appointed, or if equally suitable to your arrangements I may come in the stage. I prefer staying at Bartgis's and prefer very much a dinner or barbecue as our friends can generally attend."

An invitation to the dinner was mailed to Senator Thomas H. Benton of Missouri, Jackson's champion in the Senate, whose advocacy of the "currency of the Constitution" brought him the sobriquet of "old Bullion." Invitations were also sent to Vice President Van Buren and the members of the Cabinet. But regrets were sent by officials of the Administration. There was one of Jackson's appointees, however, who accepted. It was the Frederick County son who was now the United States District Attorney for the District of Columbia. He made arrangements to accompany his brother-in-law on the trip to Frederick.

Soon the great day arrived — August 6, 1834 — the day of jubilee for the Jackson Democrats of Frederick County. A burning sun was rising in the sky as Taney and Key lumbered up the road to Frederick. It was about an hour before noon when they reached the Monocacy bridge. Here they were greeted by the reception committee, headed by Congressman Francis Thomas, with about fifty men on horseback. A barouche was waiting for the distinguished visitors. Into it climbed Taney and Key, Congressman Thomas and George W. Ent, another member of the reception committee.

Shortly before noon the cavalcade clattered into Frederick. The arrival was announced by the blast of a bugle and the firing of a cannon on Barracks Hill. The cavalcade had grown larger on its way into Frederick: there were about one hundred men on horseback as escorts for the barouche as it passed by the Revolutionary Barracks down Market Street, the main street of the town. Taney and Key were given an ovation by the crowds that lined the sidewalks. Certainly it was the most enthusiastic greeting ever accorded to any visitors since the time of the reception to Lafayette ten years before.

When the parade came to an end at Matthias E. Bartgis's Tavern, Congressman Thomas delivered an address of welcome. Mr. Thomas, who had been the chairman of the House committee appointed to investigate the affairs of the Bank of the United States, expressed gratitude to Taney for the services he had rendered as a Member of the Cabinet.

Mr. Taney, a very frail man now past fifty-seven, had managed to exist by means of simple habits and serenity of disposition. He was possessed of an ardent temperament; but he held his temper under control and seldom displayed any emotion. "When Mr. Taney rose to speak," said one of his Baltimore neighbors, "you saw a tall, square-shouldered man, flat breasted in a degree to be remarked upon, with a stoop that made his shoulders even more prominent, a face without one good feature, a mouth unusually large, in which were discolored and irregular teeth, the gums of which were visible when he smiled, dressed always in black, his clothes sitting ill upon him, his hands spare with projecting veins—in a word, a gaunt, ungainly man. His voice, too, was hollow, as the voice of one who was consumptive. And yet, when he began to speak, you never thought of his personal appearance, so clear, so simple, so admirably arranged, were his low voiced words. He used no gestures. He used even emphasis but sparely. There was an air of so much sincerity in all he said that it was next to impossible to believe he could be wrong." In his extemporaneous remarks in front of the tavern, Taney said that he cherished many recollections of his life in Frederick, and that the kindness of the people of Frederick would remain in his memory until the latest hour of his life. He gave assurance that "the gray-haired patriot" in the White House would defend his fellow countrymen from the impending peril of "the worst of all possible governments—a money aristocracy." He said that, during a long period of time, he had advised the President to take the step which he "finally made his mind to adopt." Under such circumstances, he continued, he could not with honor have shrunk from the responsibility of executing the measure when he himself was called upon by the President to perform it. Taney then told of the vilification that had been directed against him for his act, but he realized that abuse is something that can not be avoided in politics. "No man who has at any period of the world stood forth to maintain the liberties of the people against a moneyed aristocracy grasping at power," he asserted, "has ever met with a different fate. Its unrelenting, unquenchable hate has never failed to pursue him to the last hour of his life, and when in his grave."

When he had fininshed, Taney was accorded a burst of applause, and the local band struck up a familiar air. It was now about noon, but Taney and Key still had an hour or two to relax until the time for the dinner, which was to be served in the Court House yard. The Whig editor ironically predicted that the gold currency advocates would have the iron railing around the Court House yard burnished with gold, and the viands and wines served in gold vessels, in honor of the "great Apostle of Finance" who had been thrown out of office. It was after two o'clock when a blast of the bugle announced that the feast was ready. A procession was formed and the marchers escorted Mr. Taney and Mr. Key to the Court House.

The Court House yard was gaily decorated with flags and bunting. Beneath the trees, which gave shelter from the scorching sun, seventeen tables were spread with the bounties of the season. More than four hundred Democrats took seats around the festive boards. Hundreds of onlookers stood outside the iron fence. Back of the chairman's seat was a portrait of George Washington. To the left was a portrait of

Thomas Jefferson. On the right was a full-length likeness of President Jackson.

After the regular toasts had been drunk, Taney was called upon for a speech. He commenced by observing that never since the days of the Revolution had such mighty efforts been made to alarm the people and spread "ruin and dismay over this great and happy Nation." But he placed the blame for the panic upon the Bank: there was a run upon the State banks for specie; those who had money hoarded it; debtors were unable to borrow; real estate was sacrificed at forced sales; and farm products were sold to speculators at reduced prices. But, said Taney, the local banks had stood firm; farm products had risen in value; specie was flowing into the country and the currency was about to be improved by a plentiful circulation of gold. The crisis had passed; but the battle was not over. The issue before the country was more than the mere question of recharting the Bank. The source of controversy, he said, lay deeper. The Bank was the citadel of the moneyed power. For the first time in the history of the country the financiers had united and had fought openly with the use of money to take possession of the Government. The issue was boldly presented. "On the one side stands the Bank, representing and concentrating the moneyed power—haughty, arrogant, overbearing, and selfish, demanding submission to its will; threatening vengeance to those who oppose it, and pouring its poisoned arrows on those whom it hates. On the other side are the friends of equal rights; firm and unbroken in spirit, battling for the liberties of the people, with a courage and firmness, worthy of their cause, and of their often tried and venerable chieftain, who stands at their head." And so Taney opposed any compromise with the Bank whatsoever. He opposed any charter of a central Bank, even though limited in capital and limited in powers. "Yield but an inch," he said, "and you will be driven to the wall, and instead of the rich inheritance of liberty which you received from your fathers, you will bequeath to your descendants slavery and chains — the worst of slavery, that of submission to the will of a cold, heartless, soulless, vindictive moneyed corporation." In conclusion he said: "However others may choose, I cannot doubt your determination. I have lived too long among you, and know too well the stuff you are made of, to doubt the decision to be made here." And then he proposed his toast to: "Frederick County — Rich in the production of its soil — but richer far in the patriotism and manly independence of its citizens."

At the close of Taney's address, a toast was offered to his brother-in-law. This was expressed to "Francis S. Key — A friend of the administration and an incorruptible patriot; worthy of being honored, wherever genius is admired or liberty cherished, as the author of *The Star-Spangled Banner*."

Upwards of thirty years had passed since Key had lived in Frederick as a young member of the Bar. He had just celebrated his fifty-fifth birthday a few days before. His face was now wrinkled. But his mind was far more alert than it was thirty years before. In his speech he agreed with Taney that the Bank of the United States was a monster of greed and corruption; but as Taney had covered the subject so thoroughly he devoted most of his time to the anthem which had been mentioned in the toast. He went back twenty years to that thrilling night in 1814 when he paced the deck of his little cartel ship and listened to the cannonade of the British guns; and he recalled his elation when he caught the glimpse of the Stars and Stripes that waved over Fort McHenry at daybreak. With some feeling of pride he said:

> You have been pleased to declare your approbation of my song. Praise to a poet could not be otherwise than acceptable; but it is peculiarly gratifying to me, to know that, in obeying the impulse of my own feelings, I have awakened yours. The song, I know, came from the heart, and if it has made its way to the hearts of men, whose devotion to their country and the great cause of Fredom I know so well, I could not pretend to be insensible to such a compliment.
>
> You have recalled to my recollection the circumstances under which I was impelled to this effort. I saw the flag of my country waving over a city — the strength and pride of my native State — a city devoted to plunder and desolution by its assailants. I witnessed the preparation for its assaults, and I saw the array of its enemies as they advanced to the attack. I heard the sound of battle; the noise of the conflict fell upon my listening ear, and told me that "the brave and the free" had met the invaders. Then did I remember that Maryland had called her sons to the defense of that flag and that they were the sons of sires who had left their crimson footprints on the snows of the North and poured out the blood of patriots like water on the sands of the South. Then did I remember that there were gathered around that banner, among its defenders, men who had heard and answered the call of their country — from these mountain sides, from this beautiful valley, and from this fair city of my native County; and though I walked upon a deck surrounded by a

> hostile fleet, detained as a prisoner, yet was my step firm, and my heart strong, as these recollections came upon me. Through the clouds of war, the stars of that banner still shone in my view, and I saw the discomfited host of its assailants driven back in ignominy to their ships. Then, in that hour of deliverance and joyful triumph, my heart spoke; and "Does not such a country, and such defenders of their country, deserve a song?" was its question. With it came an inspiration not to be resisted; and even though it had been a hanging matter to make a song, I must have written it. Let the praise, then, if any be due, be given, not to me, who only did what I could not help doing; not to the writer, but to the inspirers of the song!

After an eloquent recital of the bravery of "the rude militia" mustered "with unexampled wisdom and success" by General Jackson for the defense of New Orleans, Francis Scott Key continued:

> But I will return to the song: this company has thought it worthy the honor of a toast. Perhaps you are not unreasonable in placing so high an estimate upon a song. It has been said by one, thought wise in the knowledge of human nature, that "if he could be allowed to make a nation's songs, he cared not who made its laws."
>
> I will undertake to say that if a Nation's songs are of any importance to it, there is but one way of providing a supply of them. I have adverted to the occasions, of which I have spoken, for the purpose of showing that way. If National poets, who shall keep alive the sacred fire of patriotism in the hearts of the people, are desirable to a country, the country must deserve them; must put forth her patriots and heroes, whose deeds alone can furnish the necessary inspiration. When a country is thus worthy of the lyre, she will command its highest efforts. But if, ever forgetful

> of her past and present glory, she shall cease to be "the land of the free and the home of the brave," and become the purchased possession of a company of stock-jobbers and speculators; if her people are to become the vassals of a great moneyed corporation, and to bow down to her pensioned and privileged nobility; if the patriots, who shall dare to arraign her corruptions and denounce her usurpation, are to be sacrificed upon her gilded altar; such a country may furnish venal orators and presses, but the soul of National Poetry will be gone. That Muse will "never bow the knee in Mammon's fane." No, the patriots of such a land must hide their shame in her deepest forests, and her bards must hang their harps upon the willows. Such a people, thus corrupted and degraded —
>
> "Living, shall forfeit fair renown,
> And, doubly dying, shall go down
> To the vile dust, from whence they sprung,
> Unwept, unhonoured, and unsung."
>
> I again thank you for the honor you have done me; but I can only take my share of it. I was but the instrument in executing what you have been pleased to praise; it was dictated and inspired by the gallantry and patriotism of the sons of Maryland. The honor is due, not to me who made the song, but to the heroism of those who made me make it.
>
> I will therefore propose as a toast — The real authors of the song, "The Defenders of *The Star-Spangled Banner*: What they would not strike to a foe, they will never sell to traitors."

Thus ended the fête of the Frederick Country Democrats in celebration of the removal of the deposits from the United States Bank. It was a festival in which Taney was the chief guest of honor, with Key as a subordinate figure; but when the guns were opened by the Whig editor a week later,

Key received his full share of abuse. Like Taney he was rebuked for deserting the ranks of Federalism. So was Congressman Thomas. The occupants of the barouche, which came into Frederick on the day of the celebration, were classified as follows:

> Democrats: George W. Ent — 1.
> Federalists: Roger B. Taney, Francis S. Key, Francis Thomas — 3.
> Majority of Federalists — 2, to say nothing of the horses and driver.

The District Attorney from Georgetown was also condemmed by the Whig editor for participating in the celebration. The editor said that Taney had been invited to Frederick to stimulate interest in the Democratic campaign; and notwithsanding the fact that Jackson had deprecated the interference of Federal officials with State elections, Key — "one of Jackson's officers," who stood "very near the person of the President and in especial favor with the Kitchen Cabinet" — was openly engaged in electioneering for the Democratic party. Key had already heard the Whigs in the Capital denounce the confidential advisers of the President as "kitchen rats" fattening off "the Treasury larder"; but at no time did he lose his implicit confidence in the President.

One week later the same editor launched another venomous attack upon Key for his "exhibition of the interference of an officer of the Federal Government with our local politicals." He stated that it was nauseating to see "public officers travelling through our country preaching the glories of the golden currency, and exhibiting, as we learn Mr. Taney and Mr. Key have done, Eagles and Half Eagles with a view of deluding the ignorant and unwary."

It was not long before the ugly charge of bribery was publicly hurled at the pious poet lawyer. According to his usual custom he was spending his vacation of several months at Terra Rubra. In his own district — Taneytown — the sentiment was strong in favor of the Whigs; accordingly whenever the chance presented itself he discussed the issues of the campaign with neighboring farmers in an effort to show that the hard times were caused by the bankers and not by the Administration. As a result of his interest in the campaign, there appeared in the Whig organ a venomous letter accusing Key of gross deception. This communication — perhaps the vilest ever published against the name of the author of the National Anthem — ran as follows:

> *To the Hon. Francis S. Key,*
>
> SIR. — The citizens of the northern and eastern parts of Frederick county will readily understand my motive for addressing you. If I have not been misinformed, you have devoted the best part of the summer to their service, and I learn that, upon the eve of your departure, you left some enduring memorials of your visit amongst them, in the shape of golden coin.
>
> You, sir, are an officer of the Federal Government. The income which you derive from your office is said to exceed FIVE THOUSAND DOLLARS a year. Is is possible that this can be honestly earned, or that the public duties for which it is received can be faithfully discharged, if you can afford to idle away the summer in enlightening the people of Frederick County upon the subjects of coin and currency?
>
> You, Sir, are, I am told, *an appointee of Gen. Jackson.* Do you recollect that in his inaugural address, he de-

clared that he would give his utmost attention to the "*correction of those abuses which have brought the patronage of the Federal Government into conflict with the Freedom of elections?*" Is the master you serve a hypocrite, or do you enjoy so common a share of his favour as to dare with impunity to act directly contrary to his principles? Let us hear your reply. They who fostered your youth — they who warmed you into being, demand an answer.

You are, I am told, a strict and professedly scrupulous member of the church. Is it consistent with the doctrines of that church, that you should devote yourself to the low and degrading task of systematically deceiving the people? Do you believe, sir, that a man who conscientiously carries his religion beyond professions, can approach a fellow being whom he knows to be ignorant, with the deliberate design of duping him by exhibiting to him a piece of gold coin and telling him that that is the Jackson money which is to be plenty throughout the land? Sir, *my* religion teaches me that there is nothing so abhorrent in the sight of God as wilful deception, and I believe in my soul that every man having a mind ordinarily well informed, unless, (as in charity I will suppose you to be) totally blinded by partizan zeal, who exhibits a half eagle to the ignorant and deluded men who are commonly the objects of such attentions, with a view of influencing their suffrages, is, knowingly, guilty of deception.

Have you, sir, been content to confine yourself to the performance of the duties enjoined upon you by your office or had you been satisfied to direct your electioneering missiles from the District of Columbia, I should not have deemed you worthy of my attention. But, sir, I cannot permit my county to be polluted with the interference of Federal officers, in its local elections, without drawing the attention of my fellow citizens to the agent in the work. I charge you, sir — an officer in the pay of the General Government — a confidential friend of the President — a member of what is termed the Kitchen Cabinet—with having visited Frederick County, ostensibly for the purpose of attending to your domestic business—but really with the design of DISTRIBUTING GOLD. Are you falsely accused? If so, make it appear, and you will find no one readier to do you justice than myself. If not, then, sir, I say you have been engaged in a work unsuitable to your dignity as a man, your duty as an officer and your professions as a Christian.

TERRA RUBRA.

Such is the sordid drama of party politics—a drama of ambition and hate, loyalty and treachery, jubilee and remorse. Here was the grim opportunity for the Whigs to spread the cry of "Bribery"! A Democrat in Baltimore was collecting gold coins to be distributed by the politicians in Frederick County! Congressman Thomas was one of the daring "propagators of the Golden humbug." Mr. Key was another. And who was foolish enough to say that the distribution of the gold was not for the purpose of influencing the election? "Does any one believe," asked the Whig editor, "that Mr. Key is so much in love with the people of this county as to devote his days and nights to their service without some hope of reward?"

President Jackson and his friends remained adamant in their histility to the Bank of the United States. The Congress refused to pass the bill to recharter the Bank; and in 1836 the "monster" collapsed.

CHAPTER XXII

Jackson's Providential Escape

ON JANUARY 30, 1835, a funeral service was held in the House chamber in the National Capital for Congressman Warren R. Davis of South Carolina. Many high officials of the Government, including President Jackson, attended. After the ceremony had started, a young man sauntered through the rotunda into the House lobby, and glancing into the House chamber recognized the President. Before the service was over, the young man came out of the building and stood unnoticed behind one of the columns on the east portico of the Capitol.

The throng presently came pouring out of the rotunda. President Jackson was accompanied by Levi Woodbury, Secretary of the Treasury, and Mahlon Dickerson, Secretary of the Navy. The lurking man near the door waited until Jackson emerged leaning on the right arm of Mr. Woodbury; and then, when Jackson was within six or eight feet, he drew a pistol from an inside coat pocket, aimed it at Jackson's heart, and pulled the trigger. The percussion cap exploded with a loud noise, but did not ignite the powder in the tube. The man dropped the pistol and pulled out another. The crowd was thrown into a panic. Quick as a flash the old hero from the White House raised his cane and started for his assailant. At the same moment Lieutenant Gedney, of the United States Navy, made a lunge for the man; but just as the Lieutenant seized him, he jerked aside and aimed a second pistol at the President. This time the muzzle almost touched the President's breast. The pistol snapped with a loud report; but again the percussion cap exploded without igniting the charge.

Above the din of the crowd was heard the shrill voice of General Jackson. "Let me alone! Let me alone!" shouted the brave old veteran, brandishing his hickory cane and rushing furiously toward the assailant. "Let me get him! They can't kill me! I can take care of myself!"

The culprit, bewildered by the failure of both of his weapons, tried to escape, but the Naval officer soon had him down. Jackson was ready to inflict summary punishment upon the assassin; and it was only with great difficulty that he was restrained from violence. "I know where this came from!" he cried, suspecting that it was a plot hatched by his political enemies. He was assured, however, that he was surrounded by his friends; that the assassin had been placed under arrest; and that it was advisable to let the law take its course. Somewhat pacified, Old Hickory was finally persuaded to proceed to his carriage.

General Hunter, the United States Marshal for the District, assisted by Sergeant-at-Arms Randolph of the House, dragged the culprit to a carriage and drove him to the City Hall for a preliminary hearing. District Attorney Francis Scott Key was immediately notified. On arriving in the court room of the United States Circuit Court, Key caught his first glimpse of the prisoner. He was small in stature, had black hair, and appeared to be about thirty-five. He was neatly dressed.

When Chief Judge Cranch was ready for the hearing, District Attorney Key presented a number of witnesses—including the Secretary of the Treasury, the Secretary of the Navy, Congressman Burd of Pennsylvania, who picked up the pistols from the steps, Lieutenant Gedney, and Sergeant-at-Arms Randolph. The pistols were made of brass, the barrels being about six inches long. After a ball was taken out of one of them with a screw, the pistol was found to contain a heavy charge of powder.

The traverser, named Richard Lawrence, remained composed during all the excitement. After Key had offered the Government's testimony, Judge Cranch asked Lawrence if he wished to cross-examine the witnesses or make any statement. He replied he did not.

Judge Cranch then announced that he would hold the traverser for trial, and set the bail at $1,000. At this point Key urged the Court to require a higher bail on account of the seriousness of the crime. Judge Cranch replied that he was impressed with the District Attorney's remarks, but because of the constitutional prohibition against excessive bail, he could not require a penalty of more than $1,500 for such an offense. Many of the President's friends complained that Judge Cranch was too lenient. One of the newspapers remarked: "So if any of our patriots should think fit to furnish this sum to stand the forfeiture, we may have this desperate man with new weapons of destruction at the next levee." Lawrence, however, went to jail.

News of the attempted assassination of the President spread rapidly. Soon the whole country was asking: Who is Richard Lawrence? President Jackson was convinced that Lawrence had been hired to kill him — that there were rascals in the Whig party who would stoop to any dastardly crime to advance their interests. A number of threatening letters had been received at the White House. One of them sent this warning to the old warrior: "Damn your old soul, remove them deposites back again, and recharter the bank, or you will certainly be shot in less than two weeks, and that by myself!"

Francis Scott Key knew of the suspicions which General Jackson and some of his friends harbored; but he did not know of any evidence of a conspiracy. Of one thing Key felt sure: the dramatic occurrence on the steps of the Capitol was unmistakable proof that Andrew Jackson was living under divine protection. To the pious District Attorney the fact that both of the pistols failed to discharge, when aimed directly at the President, was a miracle — a clear indication that the Deity was on the side of the Democratic Administration. And there were many other worshippers of General Jackson who held the same opinion. "Providence," said the editor of one of the Jackson papers, "has ever guarded the life of the man who has been destined to preserve and raise his country's glory, and maintain the cause of the people. In the multitude of instances in which he has hazarded his person for his country, it was never in more imminent danger than on yesterday." But the Whigs merely scoffed at this idea; some of them believed Lawrence had not shaken the barrel enough before ramming in the powder and the ball, and consequently the powder failed to penetrate through the small tube leading to the cap; while others gave the explanation that the dampness of the atmosphere had spoiled the priming.

While Key was convinced that the life of the President had been saved by providential intervention, nevertheless he decided to test the pistols – a prudent thing to do in preparing for the trial. So he made experiments with the pistols with the aid of Marshal Hunter. The experiments served to strengthen Key's belief in "providential interference."

Key also directed an investigation into Lawrence's past. An investigator, calling at Lawrence's boarding house, learned that Lawrence had been of unsound mind for more than a year. The investigator then called on the prisoner's sister, Mrs. Redfern, who said that her brother was born in England and came to America when he was a boy; that he had made his living as a painter; but that after he was rejected by a young lady he became listless and talked of going back to England. She said he went to Philadelphia and New York with the idea of sailing for England; but returned to Washington claiming that the ship owners were in conspiracy against him and refused to give him passage, but that he would soon have a vessel of his own. She added that he became irritable; and once when he struck her, her husband had him arrested. The investigator then called on Samuel Drury, who occupied a room next to Lawrence's paint shop. Drury told of Lawrence's claim to the throne of England – the boys in the neighborhood had already begun to taunt him by calling him King Richard III — and the notion that if he could get rid of the President he could use the influence of the American Government to enforce his claim to the Crown. Drury also disclosed that Lawrence had inquired, on the evening before the funeral of Congressman Davis, whether the President was planning to attend the service; and the next morning, after talking and laughing to himself in his shop, he slammed the lid on a box and shouted in a loud voice, "I'll be damned if I don't do it!"

Key also made arrangements for a psychiatric examination of the prisoner. Two well-known Washington physicians, Dr. N. P. Causin and Dr. Thomas Sewall, were selected to make the examination. They went to the jail and asked Lawrence a number of questions. He answered them willingly. He said that he left England when he was about twelve, that he was temperate, and that he did not gamble. He said that he called at the White House and asked the President for some money — he needed the money for his trip to England — but the President refused him. He said that he changed both of his pistols from flintlocks to percussion locks; that he tried them a number of times, and had never known them to fail to discharge; that he loaded them, using a pencil for a ramrod, for the purpose of killing President Jackson. He said that he was in the rotunda of the Capitol when Jackson arrived, but did not shoot at that time because he did not want to interfere with the funeral. Asked if he had felt any fear in trying to assassinate the President, he said not in the least until after the second pistol missed fire and he saw General Jackson coming after him with upraised cane. The physicians then proceeded to the subject of the prisoner's hallucinations, inquiring why he wanted to kill the President. Then it was that Lawrence commenced his tirade, insisting that his only remedy was to get President Jackson out of the way. When he was asked what benefit he expected to derive from the assassination, he replied that the laboring man would be enabled to get work, and money would be more plentiful.

"Why would money be more plentiful?" Lawrence was asked.

"Because," he replied, "we could get it more easily from the Bank of the United States."

For two hours, Dr. Causin and Dr. Sewall interrogated him. But during the entire time the dapper young prisoner remained "tranquil and unconcerned." He clung stubbornly to his contention that his family had been deprived of the British throne, and that if he could kill the President of the United States he could then proceed to assert his rights in London. On completing their examination, the physicians reported that Lawrence was "laboring under extensive mental hallucination."

Notwithstanding the manifest mental derangement of Lawrence, the Jackson newspapers continued to print ugly rumors concerning a conspiracy to assassinate President Jackson. Senator Calhoun, condemned by the *Globe* for making predictions of National disaster, thereby inflaming cranks like Lawrence against the Chief Executive, denounced this newspaper as a "base and prostitute" organ of the Administration. But the *Globe* continued to publish the charges of conspiracy. "Every hour," the editor said, "brings new proof to show that Lawrence had been operated on to seek the President's life, precisely as we had supposed from the moment we learned that he had been an attendant on the debates in Congress."

District Attorney Key learned that it was Senator George Poindexter of Mississippi, who was suspected by the President of being chief conspirator. Years before Poindexter and Jackson had been intimate friends, Poindexter having served on Jackson's staff during the war; but a quarrel over patronage had turned them into bitter enemies. The Mississippian joined the Whig party; voted in the Senate for the "moneyed monster"; and did everything else he could to offend Jackson. Soon after the attempted assassination on the steps of the Capitol, affidavits were received at the White House alleging that Richard Lawrence had been seen in the office of Senator Poindexter just a few days before the attempt. Poindexter was enraged by the insinuations. He appealed to the Senate for an investigation of the infamous charges. Thus was forced to an issue "a perfectly foolish notion of Jackson's." Henry Clay, amazed to hear that the President was a party to a scheme to implicate a Senator in "so foul a transaction," nevertheless consented to the appointment of a committee to investigate the accusations. Within a few days Senator Poindexter was exonerated from all suspicion. Thus ended what some historians have considered to be "the most unfortunate incident in the career of Andrew Jackson."

Meanwhile Richard Lawrence idled away his time in jail for two months and a half. One of his symptoms was insensibility to cold. On some of the coldest days of the Winter he let his fire go out and sat in his dismal cell in his shirt sleeves.

The trial of Lawrence was held in the United States Circuit Court in April, 1835. The prisoner presented a striking appearance as he was led into the court room. He wore a gray sport coat, brown pantaloons, black vest, and black cravat. With tranquil self-assurance he sat beside his lawyers, William L. and James F. Brent. On the bench sat Chief Judge Cranch and Associate Judges Morsell and Thruston.

After the witnesses were called, District Attorney Key addressed the Court. He had not proceeded very far, however, before Lawrence jumped from his chair and asked how they could hold him as a prisoner when he was entitled to be the King of England. Judge Cranch ordered him to take his seat and to let his counsel manage his case for him. At this point Attorney William L. Brent inquired whether it would be possible to dispense with the prisoner's presence in the court room because of his mental conditions.

This caused Lawrence to leap up again.

"I want to know, since I have the sword, why —"

Again he was stopped by the Court. Mr. Brent repeated that he thought it would be impossible to proceed with the trial if the traverser remained in the court room. But the Court explained that an accused person always has the right to be present when tried for a crime, and that it was preferable to have the trial proceed in the usual manner.

So the clerk began to call the panel. As he was reading the names, Lawrence jumped up again, looking like a maniac.

"I want to know if it is right to call a jury," he shouted. "I certainly am King of Great Britain —"

"You must sit down and be quiet, Mr. Lawrence," demanded Judge Cranch, "until you are called on to speak!"

Lawrence grumbled for some time before his attorneys succeeded in pulling him to his seat. The clerk then returned to the call of the panel; and after many challenges the twelve chosen jurymen took their places in the jury box.

Francis Scott Key then arose and announced that he was ready to open the case for the Government. His opening statement was lucid and logical. He said:

> The prisoner before the jury, Richard Lawrence, is charged with an offence which is — at least in this part of the world — of very rare occurrence. This renders it all the more necessary that I shall give a statement as to the nature of the evidence which I shall produce in the case; and further because many rumors wide of the truth have gone abroad, as usually happens in such cases.
>
> The prisoner is charged with an assault, with intent to kill and murder; and the object of that assault was the Chief Magistrate of the Nation. There are two counts in the indictment — one charging the assault with intent to kill; and the other stating more particularly the manner, the instruments, etc.
>
> This is an offence which by our laws is a mere misdemeanor, and punishable by fine and imprisonment. The station or office of the object of this crime is to be left entirely out of the question; and it is to be considered in the same light as though committed on the most humble individual in the country. The framers of our Constitution did not think it was necessary to surround the Chief Magistrate with any additional protection than those laws which are deemed sufficient

> for the citizen holding the most obscure station in life. The love of order and of justice has theretofore been found — and I hope will continue to be found — sufficient for this purpose. The members of the jury are not to look on the extraordinary and providential delivery of the President from the danger of the prisoner's act; but, free from any anxiety, to judge the case according to the evidence which will be offered...
>
> In the present case, the prisoner has committed an assault, certainly with a murderous intent. If under a state of total insanity, the jury will then have to consider what the public safety requires; if only under the influence of partial insanity, you are then to examine into the character of the delusion under which the prisoner has been laboring; to ascertain the connection between the act committed and that delusion; and to see whether it was delusion, and delusion alone, which induced the act.

Key then referred to the English case of Hadfield, in which the charge was the attempted assassination of King George III. He read from the argument of Lord Erskine, Hadfield's lawyer, to prove that it was not enough to show merely a mental delusion in order to save a criminal from punishment, but that it was also necessary to establish a connection between the delusion and the act committed. Key remarked that he was "perfectly willing" to allow Lawrence's attorneys to have the benefit of the arguments which were used by "the eminent Erskine" with success in the Hadfield case.

Explaining his theory of the accountability of a lunatic for the commission of a crime, Key stated to the Court:

> If then the jury shall be of the opinion that the prisoner was, at the time of committing the assault, under a delusion, and shall believe that that delusion originated the act, he is certainly not guilty.... But if it appears that the prisoner is a man of violent temper and capricious humors, that the act did not spring from delusion, but from other causes, then the jury can not acquit him from the consequences of his crime.
>
> I will lay before you not only the evidence as to the manner of the act, his appearance and behaviour before the jury, but also the instruments, which you will see were as well calculated to accomplish the purpose designed, and as well prepared for it, as they could have been by any man of intelligence. By the withdrawal of the charge of one of these pistols before the judge on the occasion of the first examination of the prisoner, it was found that it consisted of a ball well fitted to the piece and powder of a very fine quality. The other pistol was examined on the succeeding day, and was fired off without any alteration of its charge. The powder was distinctly seen in the tube; and it was fired off repeatedly after this. This, then, is sufficient to show that there was no defect in the pistols or their loading; and also the deadly intent of the prisoner, which was so happily frustrated by providential interference.
>
> I know that all these acts could be done even by a man of unsound mind; but still there are circumstances to be considered in this case, in which the guilt or innocence of the prisoner must depend on the issue whether he is properly to be considered as having been an accountable human agent at the time he committed the crime.

Thus did Francis Scott Key, while surrounded by bitter party spirit, demonstrate that as an officer of the Court he was striving to aid in the administration of justice, and that he was not seeking as a prosecutor the plaudits of his party leaders.

One of the newspaper men who attended the trial said that Key "did not lose his calmness, allowing only a sense of justice and a desire for the truth to influence him in the matter."

Key's star witnesses were Secretary Woodbury of the Treasury, Secretary Dickerson of the Navy, Lieutenant Gedney, and Marshal Hunter. After they had testified, Key did a very unusual thing: he called on one of the presiding judges, Chief Judge Cranch, to testify. The purpose of this testimony was to show Lawrence's demeanor on the day of the assault.

When all of the Government's testimony had been offered, Mr. Brent asked the Court once more to allow the prisoner to leave the court room. He said that it would be very painful to everybody if the prisoner remained in the room during the introduction of the defense testimony.

At this point Lawrence jumped to his feet again and shouted in a loud voice, insisting that General Jackson owed him some money and also that money was due him from the United States Bank.

"All of you in this room," he shouted, "are my subjects, and —"

A Deputy Marshal grabbed the prisoner and tried to push him into his seat.

The prisoner turned to the officer with an air of haughty indignation, and said: "Mind your own business, or I will treat you with severity!"

Then, turning to the judges, Lawrence said with a tone of confidence: "Gentlemen, it is for me to pass upon you — and not for you to pass upon me!"

When the accused was finally silenced, Mr. Brent again pleaded to the Court to give his client permission to leave the room in order to prevent a "painful exhibition." He added that he hoped the District Attorney would give his sanction to this request. Key replied that he had no objection — it was immaterial to him whether the prisoner stayed in the room or not — but he added:

"I myself have no power to grant the prisoner permission to leave the court room.

After some deliberation the judges ruled that Lawrence had the privilege of withdrawing from the room if he wished to do so.

Once more Lawrence jumped up like a wild man yelling that he denied the authority of the Court to try him.

"I am my own man!" he cried. "I want my revenue!"

The Brents had difficulty in quieting their client but they finally pacified him by telling him that he would get his rights.

"Yes," said Lawrence angrily, "but when?"

"Today," replied his senior lawyer assuringly.

The accused was pleased to hear that he would get his rights so promptly, and sat down with a feeling of relief.

Mr. Brent, enabled at last to proceed with the defense, then paid an unusual tribute to Francis Scott Key, declaring that the United States Attorney had presented such an "able exposition of the law" that the defense considered it unnecessary to bother the Court or the jury with any additional statement regarding the law of the case. Mr. Brent stated that nothing remained to be proved except the "morbid delusion" of the accused. He accordingly proceeded to call the witnesses for the defense.

When the first defense witness, named Redfern, a brother-in-law of the accused, was on the stand, Mr. Brent asked him if Lawrence owned two estates in England. The witness answered that he did not know of any such estates. Mr. Brent then called on the prisoner to give the names of the estates.

With a serious expression Lawrence answered: "Tregear and Kinnany!"

Among the defense witnesses were a number of prominent doctors who qualified as experts. One of them, Dr. Worthington, explained the two kinds of mania: with one the patient is dejected, with the other the patient is haughty. He placed Lawrence in the second class — known as astromania. Dr. Worthington testified that insensibility to cold is one of the symptoms of mania. On cross-examination by Key, the doctor admitted that Lawrence was quite sane in his conversation until the subject of money was mentioned.

Dr. Causin testified that he visited Lawrence at the jail about twenty times, and had always found him calm and agreeable. He made a distinction between partial insanity and morbid delusion or false imagination.

Dr. Hall diagnosed Lawrence's trouble as morbid delusion. Attorney Brent asked the doctor if he considered Lawrence a lunatic. He replied that he did.

Dr. Sewall gave his opinion that the accused was

unable to distinguish between right and wrong—that he was laboring under mania—not merely monomania.

Key asked Dr. Sewall on cross-examination if he had ever read Shakespeare's *Hamlet*. The doctor replied that he had not only read it but had seen it on the stage.

"Then," said the poet lawyer, "do you believe that an actor could portray the monomania of Hamlet so well as to make a person believe it a reality?"

Dr. Sewall replied that this was difficult to say.

One of the witnesses, a cousin of the prisoner, testified that Lawrence's father had died with a deranged mind. More than twenty witnesses in all testified for the defense. Mr. Brent announced that he did not desire to make any argument of the case.

The jury retired to their room—they took with them a copy of the verdict in the case of Hadfield—and within five minutes they returned with their verdict: "We find him not guilty, he having been under the influence of insanity at the time he committed the act."

The Court remanded Lawrence to jail until arrangements could be made to send him to an institution to prevent him from doing further mischief. Soon afterwards he was taken to the Asylum for the Insane, near Washington. Here the unfortunate man, with staring eyes and grave countenance, languished for nearly forty years until the time of his death.

ROGER BROOKE TANEY

From the miniature in the Taney Home

CHAPTER XXIII

Taney Succeeds Marshall

FRANCIS SCOTT KEY reached the forefront of the legal profession during the last years of John Marshall. The incorruptible integrity of the pious lawyer aided him in his rise to success. On one occasion there came a murmur of doubt as to his reliability from one of his clients in New York, for whom he was making a collection, and Key replied frankly that his reputation would bear any investigation that one wished to make. "I do not want you to trust me (strange and uncommon as your objections are)," he wrote, "and would rather you would come yourself. But I must be gone by the beginning of the next week, and you must therefore be here by the time I mention. If you cannot come then, Mr. Ward will tell you who I am. Mr. Ogden also or almost any Gentleman of the Bar in New York can tell you whether you may safely trust me to do what I have been doing all my life, collecting people's money for them and sending it to them." But any doubt concerning his trustworthiness was removed when Key was met in person. One illustration of utmost confidence in him was afforded by William R. Hallett, who was a member of the Alabama Legislature at the time Key was a visitor in Tuscaloosa. In 1835 Mr. Hallett asked Key to handle some matters for him during his absence abroad; and in 1838 he sent Key a check for one thousand dollars to retain his services in behalf of a friend to make sure that Key would not take any matters against him. Another illustration of complete confidence was a request which Key received from Alabama to select an attorney to represent the opposite side of a case in which he appeared. The writer said: "As you are engaged against the claim of Follin, I would be greatly obliged to you to request Mr. Swann, or such other gentleman of the profession as you may select, to represent the interests of Follin's widow and children."

So striking was Key's personality that he was likened by some of his admirers to Wilberforce "in the charms of his taste, conversation and manners, and in his habits of thought and action." He had been blessed with a fine intellect, inheriting, so his friends believed, some of that "creative power which is called genius." His amazing store of energy and his retentive memory also helped to make him one of the leaders of the American Bar. Rev. Brooke said of him: "Every faculty of his mind was active, every sinew of his body seemed instinct with energy. When upwards of sixty years of age, his step was so light, quick and elastic, that his more rapid walking was like flying. His memory, too, was remarkable, rarely needing the aid of written notes or memoranda for any purpose." While he spent much of his time in Church work and the Colonization movement, he managed to acquire a rather broad knowledge of the law. His quickness of perception and his resourcefulness aided in making him an excellent lawyer. Then too he was a talented orator. "His voice," according to Rev. Brooke's description, "was sonorous and mellow; his articulation remarkably distinct; and his gesture graceful, earnest and free from the semblance of art. His countenance was extraordinary. It was brilliant, and seemed to shed sparkling beams upon his words as they fell from his lips. In his impassioned moments, it was like lightning, charging his sentences with electrical power! His self possession, too, was admirable. He was rarely baulked or thrown from his track; and sometimes, under the excitement of an interruption, his mind sped with the smoothness and velocity of a locomotive!" Reverdy Johnson recalled after many years that Key's reasoning before the Courts was "logical and powerful" and his speeches to juries "beautifully eloquent."

In 1834 Key was a colleague of Daniel Webster and Walter Jones in an important suit against the Chesapeake and Ohio Canal Company. They were representing a man named Binney, a riparian owner along the Potomac at Little Falls, who was claiming the right to divert the stream for manufacturing purposes. Among the spectators in the Supreme Court room was a young man from Boston, who had just begun the practice of law. The youth, Charles Sumner, was thrilled by what he saw and heard. The contrast between Senator Webster and District Attorney Key was very marked. Webster was portly and impressive, in dark blue broadcloth coat and trousers, high white collar and fancy cravat, colored waistcoat, and black silk stockings. Key was thin and slightly stooped; his face was seamed with wrinkles; his features were aquiline; his keen blue eyes were deep-set. Key wore his hair like Milton, whom some people thought he resembled. Young Sumner jotted down his impressions of the scene:

> Mr. F. S. Key is now speaking in the Supreme Court, where I write these lines.... Key has not prepared himself, and now speaks from his preparation on the trial below, relying upon a quickness and facility of language rather than upon research. Walter Jones... is in the same plight.... And *our* Webster fills up the remiss triumvirate. He, like Jones, is doing the labor in Court which should have been done out of Court. In fact, politics have entirely swamped his whole time and talents. All here declare that he has neglected his cases this Term in a remarkable manner. It is now whispered in the room that he has not looked at the present case, though the amount at stake is estimated at half a million dollars.

Another appeal which Francis Scott Key argued before Marshall in 1834 was a dispute over the estate of Thaddeus Kosciusko. The Polish patriot had made two wills, the second of which was signed in Paris in 1806. While residing in Switzerland in 1817, Count Kosciusko was killed by a fall from his horse; and in the following year the Czar, seeking to win the affection of his Polish subjects by a gracious gesture, ordered the body of their great leader brought home and buried in the Cathedral of Cracow. Francis Scott Key contended that the will which Kosciusko signed in Paris revoked the earlier one. But the case was a very complicated one, and the Supreme Court refrained from deciding whether the will made in Paris was valid under French law as well as under the law of the United States. Justice Joseph Story observed that, in the event the case came again before the Supreme Court, the attorneys should produce additional information because of the "complicated circumstances" and the "important bearings of foreign law" in the litigation.

At the 1835 term of the Supreme Court, Key appeared as counsel in as many as twelve appeals. Chief Justice Marshall was now seventy-nine. Key, although a political enemy of Marshall, had admired him for many years for his unaffected manner and his brilliant intellect. Often, when the Court was not in session, the Georgetown lawyer enjoyed the fun and the laughter of the kindly jurist. The placid manner of Marshall was never disturbed; but when the time came for the Court to convene, a transformation came over him. "Clad in the robes of his great office, with the Associate Justices on either side of him, no king on a throne," says his biographer, "ever appeared more majestic than did John Marshall. The kindly look was still in his eye, the mildness still in his tones, the benignity in his features. But a gravity of bearing, a firmness of manner, a concentration and intentness of mind, seemed literally to take possession of the man." When approaching eighty Marshall's mind was still clear and vigorous, and his disposition was as gentle as ever; but he was disheartened by his declining physical strength. Nevertheless he remained at his post and attended to his duties with scrupulous care to the very end.

Some of the appeals in which Key participated before Marshall in 1835 were cases of considerable magnitude. In one which arose in Carolina, the amount involved was about $30,000. Key represented the Bank of Georgia, which was seeking to set aside the judgment; but the Supreme Court held that the judgment was valid.

In another case at this term Key appeared as a colleague of Daniel Webster in behalf of the contractors who had built eight locks on the Chesapeake and Ohio Canal. The contractors had won a verdict against the Canal Company for nearly $20,000. The judgment was affirmed by the Supreme Court.

As the Summer approached, John Marshall's health grew steadily worse. He was tormented by an incurable disease of the liver. In his eightieth year, his prospects for recovery were very slight. With marvelous fortitude he journeyed to Philadelphia to obtain medical treatment. But he grew gradually weaker, and on July 6, 1835, the venerable Chief Justice passed away in Philadelphia.

Within a few days after John Marshall's burial in Richmond, the name of Roger Brooke Taney was mentioned in the newspapers as his possible successor. But during the Summer and Fall of 1835, President Jackson refused to make any announcement of the appointment.

During the closing days of 1835, Taney and Key were absorbed in the controversies resulting from the collapse of the Bank of Maryland at Baltimore. Certain officials of the Bank were charged with having lost about a third of a million dollars. The Bank's depositors, after waiting for an accounting for about a year and a half, grew impatient and indignant. So bitter was the feeling against the bankers that a mob surged about the city looking for revenge; the rioters broke into the homes of some of the men who were supposed to be responsible for the failure of the Bank. One of the heaviest losers was Reverdy Johnson, a personal friend of Taney. Taney took the view that all those who had sustained losses from the mob were entitled to reimbursement from the City of Baltimore;

and he promised that if a bill were introduced in the Legislature to order the City to pay the victims, he would go to Annapolis to speak in favor of it.

President Jackson sent Taney's nomination for Chief Justice to the Senate on December 28, 1835; but it was not until March, 1836, that the Jacksonians were ready to vote for the confirmation. Vice President Van Buren, who presided over the Senate, was now ready for action. But Mr. Taney asked for delay. He said that he had promised to speak at Annapolis in support of the bill to reimburse the sufferers in the Baltimore riots; that he had received threatening letters warning him that his house would be demolished if he did so; and that he would be criticized if he allowed the donning of the judicial robe to interfere with his promise. He denounced one of the Baltimore papers for using political prejudice to inflame the Jackson Democrats against the sufferers, for one of them, Reverdy Johnson, was a prominent Whig. Such propaganda, Taney believed, was "most mischievous" — it exercised "a sort of Terrorism" over everything connected with the defunct Bank — and he owed it to his own reputation to make the argument in favor of the bill before the Legislature. So he advised the President that any efforts to expedite action upon the nomination were "very mistaken ones."

In the meantime, by means of correspondence with Key, Taney had been keeping in close touch with the old warrior in the White House. When, for instance, it was rumored in Baltimore that Andrew Jackson was opposed to the indemnity bill — the rumors had probably been started to influence members of the Legislature to vote against it — Taney requested his brother-in-law to call at the White House and inquire if there was any truth in the report. Key was glad to comply with the request. Arriving at the White House on the morning of March 14th, he was immediately ushered in before the gray-haired veteran.

"No! Positively no!" roared General Jackson. "Those whose homes were destroyed ought to be paid in full!"

Without delay Key dashed off a message to Taney to tell him of the President's denial:

Key To Taney

Washington, March 14th, 1836

My Dear Taney:

I got your letter this morning, and am surprised you have not received mine of Saturday.

I saw the President this morning. He expressed himself, as I wrote you he did before, in strong and decided terms, that the persons whose property had been destroyed ought to be fully indemnified by the community where the outrage had occurred, and denied positively that he had ever expressed any other opinion. He allows me to say this to you, and to say that you may make any use of it you please.

Your nomination was to have been called up to-day. It will most probably be done to-morrow.

Yours truly,

F. S. KEY

Before receiving this letter, Taney wrote to Vice President Van Buren that the hearing on the indemnity bill at Annapolis had been postponed, and now he felt that he had done everything that he needed to do in behalf of Senator

Johnson and other sufferers from the mob to show that he had not been shaken by intimidation from the "discharge of a clear duty." Having presented the memoranda, which he had intended to use, to John V. L. McMahon, he did not wish his nomination for Chief Justice to be postponed in the Senate any longer. He feared that if he asked for further postponement, his chance of confirmation might be jeopardized. With such suddenness and positiveness did Taney change his mind that he rebuked his brother-in-law for seeking further delay on confirmation in the Senate. In caustic language he wrote to Van Buren: "My sincere and excellent, but most injudicious friend, Mr. Key, has put to hazard by his conduct all the prospects of my future life and that too for a matter in which I have no interest and in which I have already made greater sacrifices of feeling and interest than the parties had any right to ask for."

As a matter of fact, poor Key had been amazingly prompt and diligent in carrying out Taney's wishes. On the very day that Taney was blaming Key for tardiness and indiscretion, the Vice President placed Taney's nomination before the Senate. Webster, Clay, and Calhoun tried to block the appointment; but the nomination was confirmed by a vote of 29 to 15.

Congratulations now poured in upon the new Chief Justice. For a whole week he was overwhelmed with "the calls of friends and the calls of business." Then he sat down at his desk to answer the pile of congratulations. The first acknowledgment which he wrote was to his friend, William M. Beall of Frederick, who had supported him in all of his political battles. To him he extended deep appreciation for his "manly and public and active support" throughout the "most trying and doubtful seasons." And then with utmost frankness he said:

> For my political battles are over, and I must devote myself to the calm but high duties of the station with which I am honored.... The office I have received I prefer to any in the Government and is the only one I ever felt any ambition to obtain. I would not have accepted a nomination for the Vice Presidency.... My large family and slender pecuniary means put that office out of the question. Besides it has nothing in itself to make it an object of ambition unless it be regarded as a step towards the highest office in the Government.... The one I have received is the one I most desired as an object of honest ambition, and I trust I shall so discharge its duties as to give my friends no cause to regret the support they have given me.

During the Summer of 1836 President Jackson went on a Northern trip, and the exertions of the journey greatly weakened him. He returned to the White House in a critical condition. Another hemorrhage of the lungs kept him in bed for some time. But, ill almost unto death, the grim old warrior maintained the same invincible spirit and the same iron will and determination which he had displayed at New Orleans as the commander of the American troops.

Another campaign was now being waged for the Presidency. The Whig candidates were William Henry Harrison of Ohio, Senator Hugh L. White of Tennessee, and Senator Webster of Massachusetts. They lashed at Jackson and his candidate with most violent denunciation; but the little Magician remained as suave as ever. He refused to stoop to bitter personal quarrels. Because of the split in the Whig party, Van Buren was elected as Jackson's successor.

Little now remained for President Jackson to do except to make a number of appointments. Francis Scott Key's term as United States District Attorney was about to expire. Accordingly, on December 12, 1836, Jackson nominated him for a second term. And on January 9, 1837, Key's reappointment was confirmed by the Senate.

The dawn of Inauguration Day in 1837 found the old warrior so ill that he could hardly get out of bed. But his spirit remained indomitable. Feeble and bent, his hair snowy white, and the lines deepened in his face, he made preparations to attend the final ceremony. Entering his phaeton, made by pieces of wood from *Old Ironsides* and presented to him by the Democrats of New York, he rode to the Capitol with President-elect Van Buren.

At the Capitol General Jackson listened to the man whom he had selected for his successor; while Taney, the man whom he had chosen as Chief Justice, administered the Presidential oath. It was on this eventful day that Old Hickory, advanced in age and broken in frame, issued "his counsels of age and experience" to the American people. And thus came to a close the colorful "reign" of Andrew Jackson. He had not accomplished his desire of shooting Henry Clay or of hanging Calhoun, but he managed to win his share of political victories. He was ready to return now to "the calm of his beloved Hermitage, among his old friends and faithful slaves, and near the tomb of his idolized Rachel." The twilight was closing in upon him. He knew that it was time to go.

At the time that Andrew Jackson was closing his career as Chief Executive, Roger Brooke Taney was just beginning his career as Chief Justice. It was in 1837 that Taney occupied the Supreme Court Bench for the first time. And from that time on, Francis Scott Key argued a long list of cases before his brother-in-law. One of the first of these cases was an echo of the long-fought controversy between Edward Livingston and Benjamin Story. After the proceedings had been sent back to Louisiana, Mr. Story's counsel petitioned Chief Justice Taney in 1837 for a mandamus to compel the District Judge to sign a bill of exceptions to bring the entire record back to Washington. Key, representing Mrs. Louise Livingston, objected to the issuance of the writ. Taney, deciding in his brother-in-law's favor, remarked, "A bill of exceptions is altogether unknown in chancery practice."

Key's first slavery case before Chief Justice Taney was argued in 1838. Like the Dred Scott case, which rocked the Nation many years later, it arose in Missouri. And like the Dred Scott case, it was a suit for assault and battery instituted to test the validity of a person's servitude. The slave, named Marguerite, while "a woman of color," was not a full-blooded Negress, but a descendant of a Natchez Indian woman. Key assisted Senator Thomas H. Benton in representing the slaveholder in the case. Benjamin F. Butler, Attorney General of the United States, represented the Indian girl. Associate Justice Story, selected by the Chief Justice to hand down the opinion, dismissed the case for lack of jurisdiction.

The most noteworthy case which the poet lawyer argued before Chief Justice Taney at the 1837 term, and indeed one of the most historic cases in which he ever participated, was Kendall *vs.* United States. The plaintiffs in this case had entered into contracts with Postmaster General Barry to transport the United States mails; and when Amos Kendall succeeded Barry as Postmaster General in 1835 he revoked some of the credits that Barry had given in settlement of the claims. The contractors appealed to Congress for relief, and in 1836 Congress passed an act authorizing the Solicitor of the Treasury to make an adjustment of the claims. Kendall had allowed the claimants about $122,000; but the Solicitor of the Treasury held that they were entitled to about $162,000. When they applied to Kendall again, he refused to comply with the award, contending that the Solicitor had exceeded his authority by misconstruing the act. Again the claimants applied to Congress for relief, but the members of Congress took the position that no further legislation was needed on the subject. The contractors then petitioned the Circuit Court of the District of Columbia to compel Postmaster General Kendall to settle the claims; and the Circuit Court issued a mandamus ordering him to make the settlement.

Attorney General Butler and District Attorney Key, representing the Postmaster General, brought a writ of error to the Supreme Court.

When the appeal came before the Supreme Court in 1838, Key was prepared to make an exhaustive argument concerning the powers of the three coördinate branches of the Government under the Constitution — probably the most thorough interpretation of the Constitution he ever made during his entire career at the Bar. Arising to address Chief Justice Taney and the eight Associates, he said that the mandamus directed to Mr. Kendall was an attempt of the Judiciary to exercise power unwarranted by the Constitution — an invasion of the prerogatives of the Executive Department. Boldly he declared that the Judiciary was just as apt to usurp power as the President or the Congress. It might not necessarily be wilful usurpation: it might merely be error of judgment; for, he reminded the solemn jurists, "nothing human is infallible," and a Court might make a mistake in determining the extent of its own powers just as easily as it might make a mistake on any other question. Then he exclaimed: "I am gratified that the contest is brought here — here, where all encroachments upon the Constitution will be brought to the same impartial test; where this high tribunal will watch with double vigilance, and revoke with all its dignity, judicial encroachments."

Furthermore, Key rapped the Circuit Court for holding that the President was powerless to see that the duties of the Postmaster General were properly performed. The Constitution, he said, had cast upon the President the duty of seeing that the laws are faithfully executed. Moreover, the American people had always held the President responsible for the acts of his subordinates. In addition, he insisted, the management of the Post Office Department was clearly an executive, and not a judicial, function; and the Postmaster General could act more promptly and with greater uniformity than the Courts scattered throughout the nation. For, he reminded the jurists, "Judicial robes are not the garments for quick action."

Richard S. Coxe and Reverdy Johnson were the counsel for the postal contractors. Mr. Coxe was venomous in his reply. He charged that Kendall had hung out the flag of defiance to the Senate, to the Solicitor of the Treasury, and to the United States Circuit Court. And he declared that Key's contention – that a citizen whose property is illegally withheld by a public official has no remedy except to appeal to the President – was "a monstrous heresy, slavish in the extreme."

The closing argument was made by Attorney General Butler, who expressed regret that the attorneys for the claimants had indulged in "reiterated and unsparing censures" in the Supreme Court room – one spot which had been regarded as "holy ground" and where questions of constitutional law could be discussed "with calmness of mind and liberality of temper." The Attorney General observed that the responsibility of the President for acts of members of the Cabinet had been understood by every President from George Washington to Van Buren. He quoted Alexander Hamilton: "He who is to execute the laws, must first judge for himself of their meaning." When, therefore, the lawyers for the claimants denied the power of the President in this respect, they spoke, he said, "with very little historic accuracy."

When the case was finally presented to Chief Justice Taney and his Associates for their deliberation, the majority of the Court rejected Key's view that the Court had no power to order a Cabinet officer to perform his duty. Justice Thompson, in delivering the opinion of the Court, said: "This is a doctrine that cannot receive the sanction of this Court. It would be vesting in the President a dispensing power which has no countenance for its support in any part of the Constitutition, and is asserting a principle which, if carried out in its results to all cases falling within it, would be clothing the President with a power entirely to control the legislation of Congress, and paralyze the administration of justice." Justices Story, McLean, Baldwin, Wayne, and McKinley concurred. The effect of the decision was to hold that the mandamus directed to Posmaster General Kendall did not control him in the performance of a duty of an executive character, but of "a mere ministerial act, which neither he nor the President had any authority to deny or control."

Chief Justice Taney and Associate Justices Barbour and Catron dissented. As soon as it became known that Taney took the view that the Judiciary did not have the right to issue the writ of mandamus against the Postmaster General – one of the members of Jackson's Kitchen Cabinet – the Whig newspapers launched a scurrilous attack on the Chief Justice; while the majority opinion was praised as "a beacon to mark demagogues in office, for all future time, the point at which their presumption and tyrannous disposition will be rebuked and effectively stayed." Chief Justice Taney was now receiving his first baptism of fire since he donned the judicial robe – accused of partisan prejudice as Chief Justice in behalf of Amos Kendall.

In a letter to Chief Justice Taney, Richard Peters, the Court Reporter, referred to the bitter attacks in the press. Taney replied blandly: "The daily press, from the nature of things, can never be 'the field of fame' for Judges: and I am so sensible that it is the last place that we should voluntarily select for our discussions, that on more occasions than one, where I have seen my opinions at Circuit incorrectly stated, I have declined publishing the opinion really delivered, because I did not think it proper for a Judge of the Supreme Court to go into the newspapers to discuss legal questions."

Francis Scott Key lived less than seven years after Taney's elevation to the Bench. And so he was destined to hear but a small part of the vilification to be heaped upon the Chief Justice during his years as Chief Justice. But if Key could return to life today, he would discover that his brother-in-law, for whose elevation to the Bench he worked so arduously, is now extolled by the Bench and Bar as the peer of John Marshall. And had he been living in 1931, he could have heard his brother-in-law eulogized by another Chief Justice, Charles Evans Hughes, as a bust of Taney was unveiled in Frederick: "With the passing of the years, and the softening of old asperities, the arduous service nobly rendered by Roger Brooke Taney has received its fitting recognition. He bore his wounds with the fortitude of an invincible spirit. He was a great Chief Justice."

CHAPTER XXIV

Domestic and Social Life

KEY'S DISAPPROVAL of the theater and all other "vain amusements" was widely known. His constant thought was his duty to his family, to his church, and to mankind. Disliking display, he gave very little attention to the styles in clothes; he was "careless in his dress," according to one of his daughters-in-law, but "no matter what he put on he looked well in it." One story which corroborates the tradition of Key's indifference to fashion has been handed down in the Key family: it relates that once, after he had been bantered for combing his curly hair in too stylish a manner, he not only changed the style of his hair-dress but, fearing he was becoming vain, removed the mirror from his bedroom.

During the Jackson Administration there was a riot of drinking, gambling, dancing, and scandal. During this era, Key, because of his Puritanical notions, was looked upon by most of the gayer Washingtonians as "staid and sober-minded." One writer, in describing the Jackson period as the "age of gallantry as well as gossip," says, "If the admirer of John Forsyth's daughter proposed in a Valentine Day verse throbbing with adolescent passion, the more staid and sober-minded Francis Scott Key wrote, in a fine hand, religious hymns for the pleasure of her mother."

In spite of his seriousness and piety, however, Key was

genial and cheerful in his moments of relaxation. He was by nature a friendly man, full of humor, and life and enthusiasm. While dignified he was modest and courteous. He was considerate and kind to every man, black and white, rich and poor. In his own home he was a delightful host. A bit of doggerel verse that Key dashed off one busy day to serve as a message to Polly indicates his spontaneous hospitality:

Mrs. Key will hereby see
That Judges two or three,
And one or two more,
So as to make exactly four,
Will dine with her to-day;
And as they cannot stay,
Four o'clock the hour must be
For dinner, and six for tea
And toast and coffee.
So saith her humble servant,

F. S. KEY

After a lapse of fifty years Key's daughter-in-law recalled an occasion when the children in their merriment gathered all the tin pans they could find around the house, marched off to his law office and banged away until they forced him to close his books. He emerged from his office good-naturedly, joined the frolickers, and became "one of the merriest of the crowd."

With all his devotion to duty, and all his afflictions, Key found it possible to derive much happiness in life. His sense of humor was sparkling and cheerful. One of his poems, addressed to his friend, Judge James S. Morsell, petitioned the Court for a writ of habeas corpus for an old mare that was "cold, hungry, and weary." His petition read as follows:

Petition For A Habeas Corpus

To the Honorable James Sewall Morsell, one
Of the Judges of the County of Washington:

May it please your Honor to hear the petition
Of a poor old mare in a miserable condition,
Who has come this cold night to beg that your Honor
Will consider her case and take pity upon her,
Her master has turned her out in the street,
And the stones are too hard to lie down on, or eat;
Entertainment for horses she sees everywhere,
But, alas! there is none, as it seems, for a mare.
She has wandered about, cold, hungry, and weary,
And can't even get in the Penitentiary,
For the watchmen all swear it is more than they dare,
Or Mr. Edes either, to put the mare there,
So she went to a lawyer to know what to do,
And was told she must come and lay her case before you,
That you an injunction or *ha. cor.* would grant;
And if that means *hay* and *corn,* it is just what I want.

Your petitioner, therefore, prays your Honor will not fail,
To send her to a stable and her master to jail;
And such other relief to grant as your Honor thinks meet,
Such as chopped straw or oats, for an old mare to eat.
With a trough full of these and a rack full of hay,
Your petitioner will ever, as in duty bound, pray.

One story, which has been handed down for one hundred years in the Potts family testifies to Key's sunny disposition. According to this story, Key called one day at the home of Richard Potts, Jr., overlooking Court Park.

"Why, Frank!" Mrs. Potts exclaimed in surprise. "Where are your shoes?"

To which Key replied: "The last time I was here you complained because my shoes were muddy. So this time I left them at the door!"

Opposed though he was to all the "vain amusements" of the day, the pious lawyer had no objection to whiskey, tobacco or snuff. One of his old receipts shows that he bought at a nearby store a pint of whiskey for twelve and a half cents together with a box of shoe polish and other household necessities. His fondness for tobacco is demonstrated by a poem which he wrote to one of his cousins to express his appreciation for the repairs she made to his pouch for tobacco and snuff:

To My Cousin Mary

For Mending My Tobacco Pouch

My conscience has given me several twitches
For not having thanked my fair coz. for her stitches;
The pouch that contains the best part of my riches
She has made safe and sound by her excellent stitches;
And whenever I take it from waistcoat or breeches,
I enjoy my quid and admire the stitches.
She has sent me a note all in rhyme also, which is
Still more to be praised than these praiseworthy stitches.
I sometimes have seen "few and far between" stitches,
The stitchers of which should be thrown in the ditches,
For no one need care where such vile things he pitches,
And nothing's more vile than such stitchers and stitches,
Such stitchers were taught in a time scarce of switches,
Or they ne'er would have stitched such detestable stitches;

For this saying, I'm told, a sort of distich is
Among the most eminent teachers of stitches:
That experience proves "few and far between" switches
Will always produce "few and far between" stitches.
But my sweet cousin's skill so much me bewitches,
I must give her a sonnet in praise of her stitches:

Thy stitches are not "few and far between,"
As other stitches very often are,
And many things besides, as I have seen,
In this sad world, where good things are so rare,
But they are even, neat, and close enough
My treasured sweet to hold in purest plight;
To keep tobacco safe, and even snuff,
And thus at once eyes, nose, and mouth delight.

They're like thy smiles, fair cousin, frequent, bright,
They're like the rows of pearls those smiles display;
They're like the fingers that did make them, white
And delicate, but not so long as they.

At dinners and all festive occasions, the merrymakers usually called on Key's Muse to add to the gaiety of the occasion. Although his lighter verses were written on the spur of the moment, and not intended for publication, they nevertheless display the cleverness of the poet's mind. "He spoke quickly and with energy," said one who knew him, "and no one ever conversed with him without recognizing his ability." On one occasion, on January 12, 1833, he attended a wedding and a Twelfth Night party in Annapolis. The bride was Miss Josephine Harwood, and the groom Edward Tilton, an officer in the Navy. The wedding night was enlivened by the crowning of the Twelfth Night Queen in the bride's home. The Twelfth Night, patterned after the European festival of Epiphany, was the occasion for reunion and merrymaking incident to the close of the Christmas festivities. Miss Katherine Murray was chosen as the Queen. Francis Scott Key, who was one of the guests at the wedding, contributed a poem for the "coronation." This is the first verse:

Here is a crown, but where is the Queen
With brow of beauty, and grace of mien,
    And worthy such gift to demand?
Whose power all hearts shall ever confess,
Whose smile shall bless and frown depress
    And every look command?

On another occasion Key entertained the guests at a party with a riddle in rhyme. This too showed the originality of the poet:

A Riddle

I made myself, and though no form have I,
Am fairer than the fairest you can spy;
The sun I outshine in his mid-day light,
And yet am darker than the darkest night;
Hotter am I than fire, than ice more cold,
Richer than purest gems or finest gold;
Yet I am never either bought or sold.
The man that wants me never yet was seen;
The poor alone possess me; yet the mean
And grudging rich oft give me to the poor,
Who yet are not made richer than before.
The blindest see me, and the deafest hear,
Cowards defy me, and the bravest fear:
If you're a fool, you know me; if you grow
In knowledge, me you soon will cease to know.
Get me—and low and poor thy state will be;
Forget me—and no equal shalt thou see.

Now catch me if you can — I'm sometimes caught,
Though never thought worth catching, never sought,
Am I still hid? Then let whoever tries
To see me, give it up, and shut his eyes.

Whether any of the guests succeeded in solving the riddle has not been recorded in history; but the answer is contained in the one word – Nothing!

When in his fifties, after residing in Georgetown about thirty years, Key moved his family into Washington. Polly had given birth to eleven children. One had drowned in the Potomac. Five – Elizabeth, Maria, Frank, John, and Anna – had married and left home. Another, Daniel, was absent from home most of the time, having become an officer in the Navy. Consequently there were only four left at home – Philip Barton, who was planning to study law, Ellen, Alice, and Charles.

Two of the children were soon to come to sudden ends. One of these was Daniel, who had just returned home from the Mediterranean. On the cruise young Key had quarreled with another midshipman named Sherburne, and he challenged Sherburne to a duel. On June 23, 1836, the two Naval officers marched upon the "field of honor" on a farm in Prince George's County, several miles from Washington. The first shots failed to take effect, but on the second exchange Daniel reeled and fell. The bullet penetrated his left side, and the wound bled profusely. In about thirty minutes the twenty-year-old midshipman was dead. On account of the prominence of the young man's father, the tragedy caused a "very deep sensation" – it was even rumored in the press that Sherburne was discharged from the Navy — and the sympathy for the Key family was "strong and universal."

Strengthened in faith through the passing years, Francis Scott Key bore up under his new affliction with amazing fortitude. He recalled the assurance which St. Paul gave in one of his Epistles: "And we know that all things work together for good to them that love God." It was just a few weeks before when he quoted these words of cheer in a letter to his son John. Tall, sturdy and handsome, John was now twenty-seven. He had been admitted to the Bar; and in one of his father's criminal cases, in which the accused was charged with the burning of the United States Treasury Building, he helped to prosecute the incendiary and send him to the penitentiary. John had been in Chicago, trying to get a position, and when he failed to get it he became distressed. The Poet lawyer assured his son that God's plans are always for the best. His letter to his son gives a glimpse into his buoyant soul:

Key To His Son John

Washington

24th May, 1936

My Dear John

I returned from the Woodyard yesterday and found your letter. Your mother went there with the children on Saturday, and will perhaps go on and see Frank and pay a short visit to Annapolis. Our house here is painting and she will stay away while it is about, which I suppose will be all this week.

Do not distress yourself about losing your trip to Chicago. It was most probably no loss. I am sure it is best so. I wish you could believe that it is always so — that if we do our duty and trust to Providence, the promise that "all things shall work together for our good" shall be fulfilled to us. I hope we may go out together and look about us and see where you can best fix — very probably there are other situations much better than Chicago. Our Court is still sitting; but we get on very slowly. I hope by the middle or latter end of June we may get off. But it will be too slow going on horseback.

You need not write to Mr. Kendall about your letter. He has, you know, nothing to do with it. Dr. Jones is the Postmaster — but you need not write to him either. He could tell nothing about it. I fear Tommy is in fault. I wrote your letter and one to Mr. Beall in Fred[k] late, and it was a dark night, and Tommy is very scary about going out in the night, ever since some man (as he says) tried one night to catch him. Now as you did not get your letter, nor Beall his, I fear Tommy did not put them in.

I do not expect to join the Strawberry party — but if your mother goes, you and Virginia must meet her there.

With love to Virginia

Yr affec father

F. S. KEY

Upwards of a year later John was stricken with an excruciating pain. His illness was desperate but brief. In a few days, on May 21, 1837, he was released from his agony by death. Thus were Frank and Polly bereaved of another promising son, and in their "fresh and heavy affliction" they had the "sincere sympathy of every heart."

Witnessing the uncertainty of life, Francis Scott Key, his face lined with sorrow, decided now to devote his attention to the preparation of his will. He had written a will many years before, when he was in his thirties; but he recognized the importance of executing another in order to give protection to John's widow (John had married Virginia Ringgold, the attractive daughter of General Samuel Ringgold of Washington County, Maryland) and her two little boys, as well as to Polly. He willed Terra Rubra to Polly for life, but he wanted Virginia to make her home there as long as she remained a widow. He believed that Terra Rubra would be the "most comfortable and desirable residence" for Polly; but, if she preferred to live somewhere else, he authorized the sale of the property. But whatever the arrangements might be he hoped that Polly would provide everything she could spare for the "comfortable" maintenance of Virginia. He bequeathed his law library to Philip Barton, with the hope that his use of it would enable him to assist Ellen, Alice, and Charles, and Virginia's children. From his general library he directed that each of his children should be allowed to select six books, while each grandchild should have one. He gave his watch to Francis Scott Key, Jr. His seal he gave to Charles. His Negro slaves were to belong to Polly as long as she lived, if she wanted them; but he hoped that she would manumit them while she lived. All other personal property was ordered to be sold, the interest from the proceeds of sale to be divided between Polly as long as she lived and Virginia as long as she remained a widow. Finally he selected as his executor his son-in-law, Charles Howard of Baltimore. When the will was drafted, December

9, 1837, he called in three witnesses, and signed his name in their presence.

Frank and Polly were dearly fond of Terra Rubra. Here they could relax and enjoy the annual reunions with their children and grandchildren. One of Key's granddaughters once wrote her recollections of him at "dear old Pipe Creek": "We would all asemble in August, and start in two stages drawn by four horses each, and the four-horse wagon from Pipe Creek came down for us too, and grandfather rode beside us on horseback." The author of the National Anthem would romp with his grandchildren and re-live his boyhood days in dreams. "No one," it has been written, "who saw Key only in the retirement of domestic life, participating in the sports of his children, his dreamy eyes melting with tenderness, his sensitive mouth wreathed in smiles, could believe that this same gentle, courteous gentleman was capable of becoming the fiery Rupert of the forum, the Bayard of debate."

The land of Terra Rubra was fertile and valuable. While Key sold off about one hunderd acres in 1817 and over one hundred acres in 1820, he still owned a very large plantation. In 1824 there was a debt of five thousand dollars on the property, but the estate was worth several times this amount. Late in the Autumn, Key would linger about his birthplace, loathe to go back to the city. In one of his letters to Clotworthy Birnie, of Taneytown, written just before leaving for Washington in November, he expressed the hope that he would be able to return to Pipe Creek "early in the Spring." In the same letter he asked Mr. Birnie to send "as many of the Grape Vine roots" as he could spare. The Keys and the Birnies were intimate friends; they often exchanged farm products, live stock, and advice. In one letter Polly referred to several barrels of apples and a quantity of cider which she had presented to Mr. Birnie and his wife and daughters. In another letter she inquired whether it was advisable to sell their cattle promptly or to wait for a higher price. Polly was a good manager, and she attended faithfully to her domestic duties. An idea of some of the chores around the house in Washington is afforded by an old statement rendered to the Keys by a carpenter: among the items are those for "repairing the chicken coop," "making a stand for the ash-hopper," "grinding a hatchet for the son," and "making two doors to let the dogs out."

For many years Key kept in touch with the management of the farm, with the prices of the grain market, and with the means of transportation. Back in the Monroe Administration, he advised the operator of the mill at Ceresville, three miles north of Frederick, that Georgetown was "as good a market for flour as Baltimore," and reported that the stone work on the canal locks on the Potomac had been completed, that the gates had been hung, and that navigation would soon be improved. In later years Key took an active interest in the Chesapeake and Ohio Canal Company: in 1836, when the State of Maryland offered to subscribe three million dollars to enable the Company to complete the Canal to Cumberland and the financiers in Washington were reluctant to accept the offer because of a jealous distrust of the Baltimore interests, Key took a prominent part in the discussion of the question at the meeting of stockholders. But Key kept his farm more for pleasure than for profit. He was too "impulsive and generous in spending money" to accumulate wealth; moreover, he was an indulgent master, one who was "fairly idolized" by his tenants and his slaves; and so it was commonly said around the neighborhood that "Farmer Key spent all the money Lawyer Key made."

Nevertheless, Farmer Key was compensated amply by the happiness which his farm afforded him. He was very fond of his horses and dogs, and nothing gave him more exhilarating diversion than a horseback ride. Slender all his life, he thanked God that there was "not an ounce of superfluous flesh upon him." Never losing the exuberance of youth, he enjoyed horseback riding even after he had passed sixty. Nor did he mind storm and rain; often he expressed his enjoyment in being out in "weather that would deter ordinary mortals from stirring about." Once, thrilled by a fine ride, he penned these stanzas to his saddle horse:

To My Steed

'Tis sweet to breathe freely the balmy air,
  And walk where we will, at morn, eve, or noon,
When the step keeps time with the bounding heart,
  And the strings of life are all in tune.

'Tis sweet to be rocked on the ocean's swell
  When the fresh breeze fills the sail,
And the light bark leaps o'er the dancing waves,
  And laughs at the rising gale.

But give me the steady and fearless seat
  On the back of the gallant steed
That knows no check to his flying feet
  But the hand that rules his speed!

In the Blue Ridge Mountains there were resorts where the air and the medicinal springs attracted visitors for many miles round about. White Sulphur Springs, where Key spent a part of his vacation in the Summer of 1838, nestled in a charming spot in the mountains. It had rows of cozy cottages, a large dining hall and a ball room. In the Summer it was a colorful scene – cavaliers in riding habit . . . saddle horses and hunting dogs . . . a gay barouche drawn by prancing horses . . . sulkies and buggies . . . hacks for the older people . . . Negro servants hurrying to and fro . . . crowds of noisy children . . . quoits flying in the air. But as aristocratic and as healthful as the resort was, Key soon grew tired of it. He enjoyed the music and the gaiety of the dance; but when he awoke in the morning he found, as many others did in those days, that he had been bitten badly by fleas. Consequently, before taking his departure, he gave some advice to those who were planning to visit the resort:

Written At White Sulphur Springs

A word of advice about matters and things
May be useful to people who come to the Springs,
First, there's a bell in the morning that rings
To awaken the people who come to the Springs,
And the folks fix their ribbons and tie up their strings,
And look very beautiful here at the Springs.

There's an insect or two, called a flea, that here stings
The skins of the people who stay at the Springs;
There's a broom and a half here, for nobody brings
Such implements here, to sweep out the Springs;
There's a maid and a half, too, for one of them swings
Rather much to one side; for she's lame at the Springs.

There's a bawling all day — but the ball at night clings
The most to my fancy of all at the Springs,
To conclude, though some things here might do e'en
for kings,
If you wish to fare well, say farewell to the Springs.

From time to time Francis Scott Key received news from the old warrior at the Hermitage. The former President had passed through a racking illness, with swelling in the head and painful sores and even occasional delirium. But in 1839, when a suit was brought by Dr. Robert Mayo against Editor Frank Blair, of the *Globe*, with Key as the newspaper man's attorney, General Jackson had recovered sufficiently to write to Blair in his old-time spirit: "What a set of villains we were surrounded with in Washington . . . Even Mayo, that the Secretary of War and myself kept literally from starving, under assurance of friendship, purloined my confidential letter, handed it to Adams to do me an injury. This will recoil upon these confederate scamps' heads, I hope. Say to my friend Key to spare them not, as the receiver of stolen goods is as bad as the thief."

In the Fall of 1839 Chief Justice Taney received an invitation to visit the Hermitage; but the Chief Justice, who was none too strong himself, was reluctant to make the long journey to Tennessee at that time. All hope of making the trip to Jackson's home vanished in the Spring of 1840, when Mrs. Taney had the misfortune to break one of her legs. As a result of the accident Key's sister was confined to her bedroom all through the Summer; it was not until August that the splints were removed from her leg; and it was many more weeks before she was able to walk down stairs.

Key and Taney, now living near each other in Washington, spent many pleasant hours together. Before the close of 1839 the Whigs nominated General Harrison for President; and Key and Taney regretted the apathy that existed in the Democratic party especially in view of the popularity of the hero of Tippecanoe. But the day of active participation in politics was past for both Key and Taney.

In a letter written in the Spring of 1840, to Andrew Stevenson, Minister to England, the Speaker of the House at the time of Sam Houston's trial, Key said mournfully: "Often this winter have the Chief Justice and myself, condoling with each other about our prospects in the political way, talked over our old conflicts, and the way they were met, and on these occasions you were never forgotten. And often I think I see what our leaders ought to be doing, and they are doing nothing, or worse than nothing, and remember your course in perilous times, I say to myself

> 'O for one hour of Wallace wight
> Or well skill'd Bruce, to rule the fight.'

In the months that followed the country witnessed a stirring contest between General Harrison and President Van Buren. The Democrats were aroused from their lethargy, and Francis Scott Key became more hopeful of victory. In another letter to Mr. Stevenson in July, 1840, he reported: "Congress has just adjourned, after a shocking session—such as to make many friends of the free Government feel some degree of fear that our experiment, after all, may fail. If it does fail, the place of breaking down is the House of

Representatives. How can you account for this? Our people are evidently improving in every way. And yet their representatives are growing worse and worse. It puzzles me to account for this. We have the prospect of a great struggle before us, but I think we shall succeed – that is, if we stand on our present ground and make no more blunders."

But in all parts of the Nation the Whigs conducted their campaign with wild enthusiasm. They adopted the Log Cabin as the symbol of their campaign. They mounted log cabins on wheels and drew them through the streets while singing their song about "Tippecanoe and Tyler too." As a parody on Woodworth's ballad, *The Old Oaken Bucket*, the Whigs sang for their refrain:

> The iron-armed soldier, the true-hearted soldier,
> The gallant old soldier of Tippecanoe.

To make General Harrison more popular with the masses, the Whigs proclaimed that he drank hard cider while the aristocratic Martin Van Buren drank wine from silver vessels. So the Whigs sang:

> Let Van from his coolers of silver drink wine,
> And lounge on his cushioned settee,
> Our man on his buck-eye bench can recline,
> Content with hard cider is he.

These pretensions about Log Cabin and Hard Cider were too overpowering for the red-headed man in the White House, notwithstanding all his good luck and his magical powers. The Little Magician was unable to stem the popular tide in favor of General Harrison. A few weeks after the election –

December 16, 1840 – President Van Buren reappointed Key as United States District Attorney. The nomination was confirmed by the Senate on December 29th to take effect on January 29, 1841.

On the 4th of March another immense crowd jammed the Nation's Capital to witness the inauguration of General Harrison. Replicas of log cabins moved down Pennsylvania Avenue in the inaugural parade; coonskins hung from the floats to symbolize the frontier. General Harrison rode to the Capitol on horseback; and he was sworn into office by Chief Justice Taney.

The President's tenure of office was brief. His physical resistance had been lowered by the turmoil of the campaign and the annoyance of office-seekers, and he fell a victim of pneumonia. On April 4th – exactly one month after the inauguration – the idol of the Whigs was dead. It was the first time a President had died in office. All through the land the people, irrespective of politics, mourned for the gallant old hero. In one of the newspapers in New York there appeared a poem that expressed the sorrow of the people:

> Death sitteth in the Capital! His sable wing
> Flung back its shadow o'er a country's hope
> And lo! a nation bendeth down in tears.

During General Harrison's brief Administration, Francis Scott Key was making arrangements for a trip to Iowa, which became a territory in 1838. As early as March 9th he wrote to General George W. Jones, of Dubuque, Iowa, that he hoped to have the pleasure of seeing him. Journeying across the

Allegheny Mountains in April, he finally reached the Ohio River, and then took a boat and descended to the Mississippi. From the deck he caught a glimpse of the late President Harrison's country estate at North Bend. Key went as far west as Fort Madison. It was a long journey, but the glimpse of the Western States was an enjoyable revelation.

On June 1, 1841, after an absence of about six weeks, he arrived back in Baltimore. "He is much pleased," said one of his sons, "with Iowa and the West." From Baltimore he hastened over to Washington, and once again he was in the arms of Polly.

About two months after President Harrison's death, a group of Georgetown Whigs requested President Tyler to remove Robert White as Collector of the Customs for the port of Georgetown. Not only had White supported President Van Buren, but he had arranged for a Democratic meeting in Georgetown at which Harrison was accused of being the candidate of the Abolitionists—an "Abolitionist of fraud and concealment" conspiring with "dangerous fanatics" in a "mad warfare" upon the peace, prosperity, and lives of the American people. The Whigs clamored for White's removal, claiming that he had denounced Harrison and his friends with "vile calumny and slander." White was ousted; and shortly afterwards he filed a suit for slander in the United States Circuit Court against these who had made the accusations against him. Key was White's counsel. The Court held that the letter of complaint sent by the Whigs to President Tyler was a privileged communication and was therefore inadmissable as evidence. Had Key lived a short time longer than he did, he would have seen his defeat turned into victory — for the United States Supreme Court, in reversing the Circuit Court, held that a public man puts his character in issue only "so far as it may respect his fitness and qualifications for the office," and that the publication of calumny against a public official or candidate for public office is an "offense dangerous to the people" and deserving punishment since the people may be deceived thereby and may be caused to reject their best citizens "to their great injury, and it may be, to the loss of their liberties."

CHAPTER XXV

The Cry for Abolition

FOR MORE than a quarter of a century Francis Scott Key was an ardent advocate of Colonization. He never lost hope that this project would eventually rid the United States of slavery. In a speech which he delivered on October 21, 1829, in the Middle Dutch Church in New York, he reported with optimism that the expense of transporting Negroes from this country to Africa had fallen from about $100 to $25 each, and he declared that slavery was decreasing in Maryland, the State of his birth.

The State of Maryland had long been in favor of the scheme of Colonization. In 1831 the Legislature, after having appropriated $1,000 a year for several years to the American Colonization Society, authorized the formation of a State Colonization Society and gave to the Society an appropriation of $20,000 to establish a colony of its own in Africa. A constitution for the colony was drafted by John H. B. Latrobe, secretary of the Society; and Dr. James Hall, who had just returned from Africa, agreed to return as the leader of the Maryland group.

Near the close of 1833 Key was delighted to hear that a ship had sailed from Baltimore, flying a flag designed by the Maryland Colonization Society—a flag of alternate red and white stripes with a Greek Cross in a field of blue. On board the vessel were nineteen emancipated Negroes under the leadership of Dr. Hall. In February, 1834, the ship cast anchor in the harbor of Cape Palmas. And thus was established a new "nation"—Maryland in Liberia, consisting of nineteen Negroes from Maryland and thirty-four others picked up along the way.

But the advocates of Colonization were like a few men trying to extinguish a conflagration with several buckets of water. In 1830 there were in Maryland more than 100,000 slaves; in the District of Columbia, small as it was, there were more than 6,000. In Virginia the number of slaves showed an increase of about 45,000 in ten years. North Carolina had an increase of 40,000, and South Carolina more than 50,000 in the decade from 1820 to 1830. The total slave population in the United States was more than 2,000,000, and it was steadily growing. It is no wonder that Colonization was a subject of ridicule. There were thousands of critics who assailed the scheme of transporting the colored people of the United States to Africa as "absolutely absurd" and "absolutely pernicious." William Lloyd Garrison, publisher of *The Liberator*, claimed that the number of slaves smuggled into the South every year was seven times the number of Negroes sent to Africa by the Colonizationists in a period of fifteen years.

Sponsored by Mr. Garrison, the American Anti-Slavery Society was organized in Philadelphia in 1833. This group declared that it was the duty of the people and the Government of the United States to eradicate slavery "by moral and political action."

Francis Scott Key had already publicly expressed his opposition of the Abolitionists. In an address before the Pennsylvania Colonization Society in 1829, he expressed his belief that unconditional abolition would be dangerous, and that sudden emancipation was frequently "anything but a blessing" either to the slave or to the State. Henry Clay held the same opinion: he believed that, while emancipation would be unwise unless the Negroes were removed from this country, the shipment of Negroes back to Africa would be "the greatest blessing on earth, which Heaven, in its mercy, could now bestow on this Nation."

And, indeed, it was undeniable that the great difficulty about Garrison's plan was the problem of what to do with the Negroes after their emancipation. After being dependent all their lives, they often sank after their manumission into indolence, and their settlements became breeding-places of vice. Therefore, many of the leaders in the South – and indeed quite a few in the North – looked upon the Abolitionists as agitators who were imperilling the Nation. On a number of occasions meetings of the Abolitionists were broken up, and leaders of the movement were violently handled by mobs. In 1835 the people of Charleston, South Carolina, seized the mail and burned the abolition literature; and Postmaster General Kendall refused to take any steps to prosecute.

But the agitation went on. In 1835 Wendell Phillips, witnessing the mobbing of Garrison, resolved to enter the crusade for the abolition of slavery. From that hour the young Boston orator's voice resounded throughout the land.

The first martyr in the cause was Rev. Elijah P. Lovejoy, who was shot at midnight, November 7, 1837, while defending a new abolition press.

Each year the question brought graver concern to public officials. The Abolitionists insisted, for example, that it was the duty of Congress to abolish slavery in the District of Columbia in order to "efface so foul a blot from the national escutcheon"; but President Van Buren averred that he was opposed to any attempt to abolish slavery in the District against the wishes of the slaveholding States. At that time the value of the slaves in the United States amounted to approximately one billion dollars.

When therefore Francis Scott Key deplored the agitation of the Abolitionists and warned that the violent methods of the fanatics would endanger the safety of the people, he was in accord with the overwhelming sentiment of the South, if not the great majority of the level-headed people of the North. His ideas coincided with those of Abraham Lincoln — for in 1837 Lincoln, then a member of the Illinois Legislature, signed a statement that, while slavery was "founded on injustice and bad policy," the promulgation of abolition doctrines tended "rather to increase than abate its evils." Furthermore, Lincoln was an advocate of Colonization.

As a matter of fact, men of sound judgment, like Francis Scott Key, Abraham Lincoln, and Henry Clay were sound in their view that the passionate appeals of the Abolitionists were retarding, rather than promoting, the crusade for human freedom. For the Abolitionists had gone to extremes — especially against the churches, many of which had refrained from denouncing slavery — and men like Key and Lincoln and Clay and hundreds of thousands of others, while opposed to slavery, were not willing to attack the Church or the State.

While the politicians of the South were printing their briefs in support of the institution of slavery, the clergy were speaking on such texts as "Cursed be Canaan; a servant of servants shall he be unto his brethren"; and "Servants, be obedient to them that are your masters." At a public meeting in South Carolina, Rev. J. H. Thornwell declared that slavery as it existed in the South was not an evil, but was "consistent with the principles of revealed religion," and that the actions of the misguided fanatics was "un-Christian and inhuman, leading, necessarily, to anarchy and bloodshed." At a church meeting in Mississippi in 1835 it was resolved that any person who circulated incendiary abolition literature was "justly worthy, in the sight of man and God, of immediate Death." In 1836 the General Conference of the Methodist Church, meeting in Cincinnati, adopted a resolution disclaiming any desire to interfere with the institution of slavery, and denouncing the actions of the Abolitionists as "treasonable and wicked." Rev. Robert M. Anderson, a Presbyterian, declared at one of the sessions of his church: "If there be any stray goat of a minister among you tainted with the bloodhound principles of Abolitionism, let him be ferreted out, silenced, excommunicated and left to the public to dispose of him in other respects." And one of the clergymen connected with the American Colonization Society gave that trenchant advice: "The best way to meet the Abolitionists is with cold steel and Dupont's best."

In 1836 District Attorney Key prosecuted Dr. Reuben Crandall, an Abolitionist agitator, on an indictment for "publishing libels with intent to excite sedition and insurrection among the slaves and colored people" of the District of Columbia. In his speech in the Circuit Court of the District, Key declared that the Negroes of the South were happy, and he condemned the Abolitionists for bringing their "fiend-like doctrines" to the cabins of the slaves.

In 1838, at a church conference in the North, a committee was chosen to correspond with prominent churchmen in the South to ascertain the attitude of the Church in the Southern states with respect to slavery. One of the questionnaires was mailed by Rev. Benjamin Tappan to Francis Scott Key. The letter reached Washington when the District Attorney was vacationing in the Blue Ridge Mountains of Virginia; but in October, after his return to Washington, he wrote a comprehensive reply. Before answering the questions, Key stated his own attitude on slavery:

> I was born in Maryland, and have always lived in a slave State — am pretty well acquainted with the Middle States, and have been as far as Alabama to the South. No northern man began the world with more enthusiasm against slavery than I did. For forty years and upward I have had the greatest desire to see Maryland become a free State, and the strongest conviction that she could become so. That desire and the convictions have not abated in the least — I feel sure that it will be so. I have always been endeavoring to aid in promoting that object, and do so still. I consider it now in the course of accomplishment; and, could I give you all the facts in my possession and the results of my observation and experience for many years, I

> believe you would come to this conclusion — that there is now a field open to the labors of all who wish to promote emancipation, to which they should direct and confine their efforts, and that such efforts, *pursued in the right way,* would accomplish more in comparatively a few years, than has ever been yet effected; and with these great advantages — that the discussion arising from this delicate and exciting subject would be everywhere quieted, and the condition of the slaves in the other States greatly meliorated. Had I time, I would like to go to the North and maintain these propositions.

Key then proceeded to reply to the questions. The first question was: "Does the opinion generally prevail among the ministers and members of Southern churches, that slaveholding, as practiced in this country, is sanctioned by the Word of God? If this is not their opinion, how do they justify themselves in holding slaves?" Key asserted that the general belief in the South was that the Scriptures contained "neither an express sanction nor an express prohibition on the subject." The Golden Rule, he declared, ought to "govern all possible cases of human conduct." In other words, Key believed that slaveholding was either right or wrong, according to the way it was practised. If practised according to the Golden Rule, it was sanctioned by the Word of God. If practised otherwise — if slaves were bought and sold for the mere purpose of profit, or made to work without any regard for their welfare — it was not sanctioned by the Word of God.

Rev. Tappan's second question was: "Do professors of religion forfeit their Christian character by buying and selling slaves, as they may find it convenient? Or do they subject themselves to censure and discipline by any immorality or ill treatment of which they might be guilty toward their slaves?" Key soon disposed of this query by asserting that he had never heard of any professors of religion who bought or sold slaves for profit. "Such conduct, or any immorality or ill treatment towards their slaves," said the poet lawyer, "would forfeit their Christian character and privileges, if their minister did his duty."

Third: "Since the discussion of slavery in the Legislature of Virginia a few years since, has there been in that State any change of opinion more favorable to the continuance of the present system? If so, to what causes is that to be attributed?" To this Key replied that a distinct change of opinion had taken place in the Middle States—particularly in the State of Maryland. Some, who had favored Colonization, he said, had avowed themselves not only against Colonization, but also against any agitation against slavery. "I attribute this," Key declared, "to the publications and efforts of the Abolitionists."

Fourth: "Is it the general belief of human and Christian Colonizationists in the South that slaves ought not to be emancipated, unless they are also sent out of the country? If this is their opinion, on what is it founded? Were they set free, would not their labor still be needed, and might it not be secured on terms more advantageous to both parties than under present arrangements?" Key replied that the Colonizationists were universally opposed to the emancipation of slaves, unless arrangements were made for their exportation. He added that the Negroes constituted "a distinct and inferior race of people, which all experience proves to be the greatest evil that afflicts a community."

"Is there any good reason to believe," was the fifth question, "that anything of importance, generally speaking, will be done to prepare the slaves for freedom, before they are made free?" To this the poet lawyer replied: "As the Colonization scheme advances, I think much will be done. Many masters will prepare their young slaves for such a change. . . . And if a desire to return to their fathers' land should become general (as I trust it will) both among the slaves and free blacks, nothing could be better calculated to improve and exalt the whole colored race. It would encourage them to good conduct, industry, temperance, and all those efforts that men make to better their condition."

The next question was: "Is there not an undercurrent of opinion and feeling in the South among the more enlightened and philanthropic, and is it not widening and strengthening, against the continuance of the present system, and an increasing conviction that it may safely and advantageously be abolished?" Key denied any such trend of opinion. He declared that although he came in contact with "men of all sorts," he had never heard any opinion favorable to emancipation, unless connected with the condition of Colonization.

The final question was: "What, in your opinion, has been the effect, upon the whole, at the South, of the efforts of Abolitionists?" Key stated that the efforts of the Abolitionists had been most unfortunate. "There is," he declared, "a great unfavorable change of opinion and feeling in the whites towards the blacks, which, I think, cannot be otherwise accounted for; and the whole colored race have been injured by these efforts. The free and the slaves have both been subjected to more restraint."

Before closing his letter, Key commented on the change that had taken place in the attitude of the Methodist Church regarding slavery. "Methodists formerly denounced slavery in general terms," he explained, "as it is now denounced at the North. . . . They were not allowed by their discipline to continue in the church, if they purchased and held slaves. . . . The rule of discipline is now changed. . . . If it is considered that he has bought from a mercenary motive, for gain alone, without any inducements of kindness or favor towards the slave, he is censured and suspended from his church privileges, and made to do what is thought right, or excommunicated. . . . If he has bought from kindness to the slave, to prevent the separation of a family, or in any way with the bettering of his condition, he is allowed to hold him, and is considered as having acted consistently with Christian charity."

Meanwhile the Abolitionists and the Colonizationists continued their crusades. The Abolitionists contended that the Negroes who were emancipated and shipped to Africa were sent to their doom — that they would fall as victims either of the African fever or the barbarity of the native tribes. The Abolitionists also charged that the Colonizationists had ulterior ends in view — that the whole project was a sinister scheme of the Clay machine. But Francis Scott Key, like many other advocates of Colonization remained as ardent as ever in favor of the project. At one of the meetings in 1838, at which Congressman James Garland of Virginia pleaded for a united South in behalf of Colonization, District Attorney Key concurred in the plea, referred to the wholesome influence of the Society, and urged greater exertions in behalf of the cause.

In 1840 Key read in the *Westminster Review* that the British Government was contemplating establishing a colony in Africa. He was immensely pleased. "This is a good project," he wrote to Minister Stevenson at London. "It will break up the Slave trade—and nothing else will. It will civilize Africa, and open an immense trade to the world. It will aid our Colonization operations; and gradually and safely, and to the advantage of all concerned, open a way to rid us of Slavery."

Of all the addresses which Key delivered on the subject of slavery his last was the most noteworthy. It was delivered on May 9, 1842, before the American Colonization Society in support of his resolution urging the United States Government (1) to promote commerce with Africa, (2) to suppress the slave traffic, and (3) to protect the American colonies on the coast of Africa.

First, in behalf of American commerce, Key painted a glowing picture of Africa, which he said was unsurpassed by any other quarter of the globe for "the fertility of its soil, the excellence of its climate, and the richness and variety of its products." Here he burst into a flash of eloquence:

> Light has pierced into the thick darkness that has long enveloped that outcast Continent, and the treasures and blessings of a benignant Providence are seen to smile in all her plains and wave in all her forests.
>
> It is true this fair creation of God has been marred

by the wickedness of Man. A trade, abominable and detestable beyond all epithets that can be given to it, at the very name of which the blood curdles, and no man hears it, who

— "having human feelings, does not blush
And hang his head, to think himself a man,"

has long since desolated Africa, and disgraced the world.

This trade has been stamped with the double curse of offended Heaven — curse to the givers and rceivers of the guilty traffic — to Africa, in the wretchedness, rapine and murder of her children; to her rapacious tempters in innumerable, just and fearful retributions.

The wrath of God has been manifested at this crying iniquity on the blood-stained borders of all her coasts, where the angry elements are let loose against this inhuman trade. What is the stormy cloud that darkens these infested shores, but the frown of the Almighty? What the fierce tornado, but the blasting of the breath of displeasure?

It is true that, under this curse, Africa has long groaned and bled, and many a fair field, and happy village, and crowded town, has been made a wilderness.

It is true she is still an awful sufferer. Even now, while we are speaking of her wrongs, some distant and peaceful hamlet, hitherto beyond the reach of the spoiler, hidden, and hoped to be secured by intervening forests, has been hunted out and surrounded, and its sleep awakened by the shout of the ruffians.

Already, Key asserted, colonies had been established where the natives no longer heard "the signal gun of their cruel spoilers." In the place of the slave traffic, a lawful commerce had been substituted under which the African was rising to his "true rank and conditions as a man." He referred to the dye woods and other products of the African forests to justify Government aid to promote American commerce.

Key then advanced to the second part of the resolution — America's duty to suppress the slave trade. The Congress, he maintained, had the power to suppress it as an enemy of lawful commerce. He cited the effort of Great Britain to suppress the slave traffic, referring particularly to the Treaty of Madrid, under which the British Government agreed to pay to Spain £400,000 for the abolition of the traffic. "Here," he declared, "we have the gratification of seeing that the great and proud land of our ancestors has zealously and powerfully seconded the declarations and acts of our Government for the suppression of this crime. . . . Mr. Wilberforce, the best and greatest of her statesmen, in1818 in a speech in the House of Commons upon the Spanish Treaty, speaking of the sum paid to Spain for acceding to the abolition of the trade, said he could not but think that the grant to Spain would be more than repaid to Great Britain in commercial advantage by the opening of a great Continent to British industry." Thus had two great Nations pledged themselves to unite in "the noble and holy resolution of effacing this foul blot from the face of the earth." To Key it was "a design of Providence." And now, he declared, the American Colonization Society had the opportunity to render a valuable service to the Nation by impressing upon Congress the fact that the slave traffic had been increasing, rather than diminishing, in extent and in brutality. "This pestilential crime," he declared, "now sweeps from Africa every year upwards of half a million of her people!"

In a blaze of righteous indignation he denounced the beast-like men who traded in human souls:

> It is now a fearful and horrid process, carried on under the constant dread of pursuit, in sharp fast sailing vessels, with the malice and fury of fiends. The wretched victims are wedged together in the foul and close recesses of these prisons, with scarcely space enough to each for the heart to swell in the agony of its despair. The very slave traders of former days would be shocked to look into the hold of a modern slave ship. If, in the days of Clarkson and Wilberforce, when the pictures of the interior of the vessels then in use roused the indignation of their countrymen, a slave trader of that day could have been shown the representations now given of vessels recently captured by British cruisers, and he could have been told that the cruelty of his trade would ever reach such a measure of enormity, he would have indignantly repelled such an intimation, and said—"Am I a dog that I should do such things?"

But, Key deplored, all the efforts to capture the slave vessels had effected no diminution of the awful traffic. It was manifest that more drastic methods were needed. "The question now," he said, "is, what shall these means be?" Would it be possible to stop the building of slave ships? No! Key was wise enough to know that reform could be obtained by education far better than by legislation. Relief could be gained, he exclaimed, by means of Commerce, Civilization, and Colonization! Let England and America coöperate, he urged, to give Commerce, Civilization, and Colonization to Africa! "Let the officers of our respective Naval forces, detached to execute this service," he advised, "be instructed to act in concert—

to visit the most extensive slave marts, convene the Kings and Chiefs before them, and let them know that these two Nations have united their forces to abolish the trade. Let treaties of amity and commerce be thus formed along the coast, and all the facilities and inducements of commerce be opened between the natives and the people of both Governments, and with all the world. Thus, and thus only, can the solemn pledge of England and America be redeemed, the rescue of Africa accomplished, and the cause of humanity and the prosperity and honor of the world sustained as they ought to be."

Finally, Key turned to the third part of the resolution — the protection of the African Colonies. He contended that the faith of the United States Government was pledged to their protection. During the Monroe Administration, an act was passed by Congress prohibiting the slave traffic and providing that all slaves seized in the traffic should be taken back to Africa in United States vessels; and Key argued that Congress certainly never contemplated that the slaves, which were taken back to Africa, were to be left to perish or to be seized again by the traders. Indeed, he pointed out, agents had been appointed by the President to receive the Negroes on the coast of Africa: and it was natural to expect that the agents as well as the Negreos were to be given the protection of the American flag. "The humane policy of those measures," declared the orator, "has never been changed. Agents are still appointed. Cargoes of captured Africans have been received there, and they are now a portion of a civilized and prosperous community. . . . How can this work of our hands be abandoned?"

Key became eloquent again, as he paid his final tribute

to the cause of Colonization. "I have never doubted its success. From its origin, when first proposed by the venerated Finley, to the present time, in its darkest day, I have never doubted. It originated in Christian hope and benevolence, and it has the favor of Heaven; and that favor has been manifested in all its course. Christians and patriots came around it. . . . And this Convention has the gratification of seeing that under the impulse of the feelings which has called it into existence, there are still American statesmen ready and able to maintain it."

Before passing on to his conclusion, Key returned once more to the horrors of the slave trade. The call for help, he exclaimed, should be heard by all mankind. "Who can be unconcerned and know that things like these are done upon the earth we inhabit? . . . All—all are guilty in His sight—not only those who *perpetrate* but those who *permit* the outrage... Let all join in a work of mercy that shall appease the wrath of Heaven and win the smiles of angels. . . . This work will be done—the voice of inspiration has proclaimed it, and fulfilling prophecies around us show that the dawning of this day of brightness is at hand. . . . Africa will take to her bleeding bosom her long lost children; and they shall wipe away her tears of agony—break off all her chains—enlighten all her darkness, and the days of her abasement shall be ended."

The poet lawyer's peroration was a stirring appeal to his fellow countrymen. It contained an eloquent reference to the American flag—his final opportunity to speak of "The Star-Spangled Banner" which he loved so well:

> The call is to our country. I trust that she will nobly answer it. I think I value, as I ought, her deeds of patriotism and valor, the triumphs achieved by her flag. But when that standard flings forth its folds over the destitute and abandoned; when it calls together the outcasts of a dark and distant land, guides them to a happy heritage, and there waves over them, their pride and their protection; then are its stars a constellation of glory; then does it achieve a higher triumph than its proudest battle fields have won. This is the boon that I ask for my country — not the renown that arms or arts can give, but a name and example that shall enlighten and animate the world, by being active and eminent in a work of mercy — that she shall show her gratitude to Heaven for the blessings she has received, by the blessings she bestows — and secure the protection of Heaven by fulfilling its high behests in sending forth its light to those who are in darkness. I covet for my native land the honor of repairing the wrongs, and re-peopling the desolations of injured Africa, and restoring her to a place among the Nations of the earth, thus making a great Continent, redeemed and enlightened by her labors, a living monument to her praise.

The oration made a profound impression upon the Convention. It was ordered to be printed in pamphlet form so that it could be distributed to the members of Congress. A copy was also sent to the White House for presentation to President Tyler "with Mr. Key's compliments."

Meanwhile the black man in the South continued to play on his banjo and to enjoy his watermelon and his possum. He had not made himself a slave; he had not brought himself here; nor was he now asking for permission to leave the country. He enjoyed life day by day as best he could, seemingly unconcerned with the raging tempest of which he was the cause.

FOUR MONUMENTS TO FRANCIS SCOTT KEY

Above: Monument at Eutaw Place and Lanvale Street, Baltimore; Monument in Golden Gate Park, San Francisco

Below: Monument at Fort McHenry; Monument over Key's grave in Mt. Olivet Cemetery, Frederick, Maryland

CHAPTER XXVI

Faith in Immortality

ON MOVING into Washington, Frank and Polly became members of Trinity Church. According to the old pew rent receipts, the Keys occupied Pew 35, which cost forty dollars a year. At the age of sixty, Key was just as active in church work as he had been at any time during his life in Georgetown. Trinity parish, like the Georgetown parishes, sent him as a delegate to the Diocesan Conventions. At one of these sessions, held in 1838, after the death of Bishop William Murray Stone, Rev. Dr. John Johns and Rev. Dr. William E. Wyatt were nominated for Bishop. Since neither obtained the necessary two-thirds majority on account of the rivalry between the High and the Low Churchmen, a committee was chosen to confer in a "spirit of Christian conciliation" to recommend a candidate in the hope of preserving the "harmony of the Church." Key was selected as one of the conferees. It was only after many hours of conciliation that Rev. Dr. William R. Whittingham, of the faculty of the General Theological Seminary, New York, was elected as the Bishop of Maryland.

From now on the poet lawyer spent a great part of his time in meditating about the future life. His faith remained implicit; his philosophy became more serene. The things that he saw and read constantly reminded him of the promise of the future life. When he read some lines written by Fawcett on revising the scenes of his early life, he penned the following stanzas:

On Reading Fawcett's Lines

So sings the world's fond slave! so flies the dream
  Of life's gay morn; so sinks the meteor ray
Of fancy into darkness; and no beam
  Of purer light shines on the wanderer's way.

So sings not he who soars on other wings
  Than fancy lends him; whom a cheering faith
Warms and sustains, and whose freed spirit springs
  To joys that bloom beyond the reach of death.

And thou would'st live again! again dream o'er
  The wild and feverish visions of thy youth
Again to wake in sorrow, and deplore
  Thy wanderings from the peaceful paths of truth!

Yet yield not to despair! be born again,
  And thou shalt live a life of joy and peace,
Shall die a death of triumph, and thy strain
  Be changed to notes of rapture ne'er to cease.

Life on this earth, according to Key's credo, is a temporary existence where the soul "has no home," and after this life is over, the soul is welcomed at the gates of Heaven with the songs of the angels. This belief he expresed in a poem:

The Home of the Soul

O! where can the soul find relief from its foes,
A shelter of safety, a home of repose?
Can earth's brightest summit, or deepest hid vale,
Give a refuge no sorrow nor sin can assail?
            No, no, there's no home!
There's no home on earth; the soul has no home.

Shall it leave the low earth, and soar to the sky,
And seek an abode in the mansions on high?
In the bright realms of bliss shall a dwelling be given,
Yes, yes, there's a home!
There's a home in high heaven; the soul has a home!

O! holy and sweet its rest shall be there,
Free forever from sin, from sorrow and care;
And the loud hallelujahs of angels shall rise
To welcome the soul to its home in the skies.
Home, home, home of the soul!
The bosom of God is the home of the soul.

Key's concept of the Universe, like that of the Israelites, was that the earth is enveloped by atmosphere in which the clouds gather; above the atmosphere is the firmament — the location of the sun and the moon and the stars; and above the firmament is Heaven — the abode of God and the angels. The only difference between Key's concept and the ancient one was that he believed the celestial bodies to be in motion. But he believed that Heaven far exceeded anything on earth in grandeur. He tried to visualize the "high seats of bliss" offered to those who attain everlasting life; and he recalled what St. Paul had written to the Corinthians: "Eye hath not seen, nor ear heard, neither have entered into the heart of man, the things which God hath prepared for them that love him." With St. Paul's assurance in mind, the pious lawyer wrote a poem on Heaven, declaring his belief in the glories "yet to be revealed," and concluding with this stanza:

To tell of those high seats of bliss,
The seraph's song imperfect proves,
Their builder is the mighty God —
The mansions are for those He loves.

One evening Key thought of his departed mother, as he sat with his aged cousin, Eleanor Potts, at her home in Frederick. Her home was the three-story brick mansion in which General Lafayette was entertained in 1824, overlooking Court Park. Cousin Nelly, now totally blind, was a beautiful character. As Key and his saintly cousin sat together in the twilight, she played on her guitar an old song—a song which she had heard Key's mother sing to him when he was a little boy. He listened intently. Fifty years had passed since he had heard it at his mother's knee. But he recognized it instantly. For several hours he sat with his old cousin, chatting about the past and the hope of eternal life. Before leaving on the following day for Pipe Creek Key promised to write a poem especially for Cousin Nelly. This he did on October 22, 1840. When he returned to Frederick shortly afterwards, he called again at her home and read to her the lines which he dedicated to her:[1]

To Mrs. Eleanor Potts

I sat beside an aged saint,
It was a pleasure there to be,
Her kind and gentle words to hear,
Her calm contented face to see.

She sat in darkness — day's fair light
Had often come and gone:
Gilding the scenes she long had lov'd
No more for her they shone.

And fond familiar voices paid
Affection's homage there,
And as their words of love and truth
Fell on her charmed ear,

1.—The manuscript of the poem is owned by Miss Eleanor M. Johnson, Frederick, Md., great-granddaughter of Mrs. Potts.

She could but think, how great the bliss
  If she again could ever trace
The looks of love she knew were there
  Upon each well-remember'd face.

But she had long since felt and said
  Of all this — "It is well."
And the bow'd spirit rose, sustain'd
  Its peace and hope to tell.

She sat in darkness — but the gloom
  Was only on the body's eye,
And cover'd with the cloud of night
  Only the objects that were nigh.

But the mind's eye that cloud could pierce
  And things far off descry,
Beyond the bounds of this dull earth
  And its encircling sky.

She sat in darkness — but a light
  Was hers of heavenly ray,
Shining upon a home on high,
  And lighting all her way.

The "light of other days" was hers,
  Of happy days now past and gone.
It call'd up friends long lov'd and mourn'd,
  And sweetly round her shone.

'Twas then, as by her side I sat,
  She softy touch'd the light guitar,
And tones that had my childhood charm'd,
  Fell sweetly, sadly on my ear.

I had not heard them since — The sounds
  Thrill'd through my quivering frame,
And scenes and friends and joys, long past,
  Quick, at their bidding came.

Those sounds call'd up a mother's form,
  Her voice, her love and care,

When at her feet, a happy child,
  I drank with greedy ear.

The songs she lov'd, of power to charm
  And to exalt the heart,
That thoughts and feelings like her own
  They might to me impart.

And if the magic power of song
  Its influence o'er me ever threw,
And haply some small meed of fame
  To lay of mine be ever due,

These early teachings at her knee—
  To these the high-priz'd boon I owe,
With all the blessings I have known,
  And all I ever hope to know.

I could but thank her for the strain
  That call'd up these forgotten lays,
And kindly bade me share with her,
  The "light of other days."

And I pray'd that the light of the days to come
  Might brighter and brighter prove,
And the gloom of this darken'd world be lost
  In the light of the world above.

Now that he was reducing his legal practice and spending a great part of his time at Pipe Creek, Key availed himself of the opportunity to meditate on the subject of immortality. He had always believed in immortality; now he was trying to prove it. First of all, he thought of God's justice. He could not believe that God could be so unjust as to give the same fate—annihilation—to both the godly and ungodly. His reference to the "aged saint" was virtually a description of himself:

> He had passed the world's trials; he has been acquainted with the "sweet uses of adversity," and learned wisdom, and seen God's hand in many blessings, and learned love. He is at peace. The evening of his day has come, his work is almost done; the discipline of this life is passed, the world's cares are laid aside, and his treasure and his thoughts are in Heaven. "He knows in whom he has believed," and is waiting for his summons. And what is that summons for which all things in a long life of probation have been preparing him? For which joys and sorrows, hopes and fears, helps and hindrances, trials and temptations, have been teaching, and enlightening, and purifying, and strengthening him? Is it to perish in a grave? Impossible. God cannot have made such a work for such an end.

Then too Key experienced the "feeling" of immortality: as Addison put it—

> Else whence this pleasing hope, this fond desire,
> This longing after immortality?

Not only did he experience the inner promptings of the soul, but he saw the outward and visible signs of immortality in the Universe. "Man has been taught by everything within him and around him," Key observed, "and made to feel and know that he is immortal."

As a third reason, Key recalled the promise of the Word of God. He saw the advancement of man — even though he did not believe in Evolution — through God's discipline. "God himself," he said, "has taught him by His Spirit, led him by His hand, armed him for the conflict with sin and temptation, and given him the victory; will he now deny him the Crown, and give him to the grave?" This he could not believe. Man had been elevated above the animals of the world. He had been endowed with "holy and heavenly affections." He had been made " a fit associate for the angels." Death, therefore, was the beginning, not the end, of life.

So the aging poet compared the death of man to the metamorphosis of the worm into the butterfly. He imagined that he could hear the insect singing to him about the long sleep which it was planning to take in the cocoon, only to burst forth later into a life of freedom and beauty. On January 31, 1841, he wrote the song of the lowly worm spinning its cocoon, beginning:

The Worm's Death Song

O! let me alone — I've a work to be done
   That can brook not a moment's delay;
While yet I breathe I must spin and weave,
   And may rest not night nor day.

Food and sleep I will never know
   Till my blessed work be done:
Then my rest shall be sweet, in the winding-sheet
   That around me I have spun.

Somehow there was a feeling in Key's soul that the end of his mortal life would come to him rather soon. But he was fully prepared for the final summons. In 1841, he had received about $56,000 of Mexican Claim Certificates; so he drafted a codicil to bequeath these securities. After setting aside his usual tithe for charitable purposes, he bequeathed $1,000 of them to the Maryland Colonization Society, $1,000 to the Domestic and $1,000 to the Foreign

Missions of the Episcopal Church, and $1,000 to the American Bible Society. He gave $10,000 to Virginia and her boys, $5,000 to Alice, $5,000 to Ellen, $5,000 to Charles, $600 to the widow of his Cousin John Grosh, and all the remainder to Polly. He signed the codicil in Washington on January 5, 1842.

Key's fondness for his family is revealed in an affectionate letter, written to his nine-year-old granddaughter, Ellen Turner:

Key To Ellen Turner

Washington, 4th March, '42.

My Dear Ellen:

I am afraid you have got tired of waiting for my letter, and I must promise you the next time you write to answer you sooner. I was glad to see you could write so clever a letter, and I hope you will give your little fingers a good chance to be useful as they are growing by practicing them every day in sewing and writing. Some young ladies are proud of their hands and take great pains to keep them white and nice; but, unless they learn to sew and write neatly, they are good for nothing. I hope you will remember this, and keep your pens and needles going briskly.

But fingers are not able, as you know, to write letters of themselves. You must have thoughts, and then put your thoughts into words, and then spell the words right, and then set the fingers agoing. You see, therefore, that you must learn to think and to express your thoughts. Reading and considering and trying to understand and remember what you read will help you in this, and I hope, therefore you will be fond of reading.

This summer I want your father and mother to

bring you all to Pipe Creek, and then I shall hear you read and talk and shall be much pleased to find you (as I hope I shall) much improved in every respect and as good as clever. You shall see these two smart little cousins, who will be new acquaintances and very fond of you. The older of them, Clarence, reads now almost like a man; the other is too little to read, but is learning his letters.

I want to see Frank very much. When I get you all at Pipe Creek, I think I shall start a school — a reading and writing school and a riding school — and I hope we shall all be very happy.

Tell your father and mother that we are now looking out for them. Our winter is fine, and the flowers in bloom. I suppose your mother's garden is beautiful. Your grandma and aunts and Barton and Charles all sent their love to you, and give mine to father and mother and all the children.

Your affectionate grandfather,

F. S. KEY.

In April, 1842, Key heard that his old college chum, Daniel Murray, was critically ill. He made a trip to his old friend's home near Elk Ridge. When he arrived he found that Murray was dying. "He had arranged all his affairs," Key narrated soon afterwards, "talked in the most cheerful, consoling manner to his family and friends, and sent messages of affectionate regard to those who were absent. He received me with great animation, and a smile that showed he was filled with all joy and peace."

The dying man gazed at the pious lawyer. "Now," said Murray hoarsely, disclosing his peace of mind in all his suffering, "I owe it all to you; though I never told you, and you never knew it."

Key looked at him in amazement. The dying man motioned to him to come nearer to the bed.

"Now," Murray whispered, "I will tell you what I've never told you or any one in the world. When we first met, and you were a little boy, your good mother had taught you a hymn, which you used to repeat aloud every night in getting into bed. That hymn made a deep impression on me, and it has never been lost. You did not know it; but I learned it by heart from hearing you repeat it. From that time to this day, I have never gone to my rest at night without repeating to myself that hymn and praying. It has had a wonderful effect on me all my life. When I was at sea, I never forgot it under any circumstances. Once, when I was in command of a small brig we had captured from the French in the Mediterranean, I remembered the hymn, and the first order I gave was for all hands on board the ship to have a meeting for reading and prayer. It had a fine effect on the men."

The dying man dropped back on his pillow, repeating slowly the words of the hymn. Key, in the lapse of fifty years, had forgotten it completely. He jotted down the words with a pencil as Murray recited them. As the servants came in, Murray gave to each an affectionate farewell together with words of advice and encouragement.

Gradually the man's life ebbed away. But on his face was an expression of radiant peace until the last. "A few minutes before he expired," Key recalled, "he was told his departure was near, and asked if he still felt the hopes and happiness he had expressed. He expressed his assent by a smile and the pressure of his hand; and soon these, and all other indications of life, gently and almost imperceptibly disappeared."

The dying words of Daniel Murray made a profound impression upon Francis Scott Key. How strange it all was! "A pious mother teaches her child a hymn. It makes no impression upon his heart, and is soon effaced from his memory. But its work is done, and its fruits appear in the heart and life of another." While abashed at his own shallowness, Key found consolation in the thought that his mother's prayers had been answered. "Her wayward child had forgotten her instructions, but they had made for him a friend, whose influence and counsel and example restrained and strengthened him in the dangerous paths of youth, whose life had taught him how to live, and whose death hath now taught him how to die."

At harvest time Key returned to Pipe Creek for a brief visit to inspect his crops and to order some repairs around the farm. The fields enchanted him as never before. In the harvest, as in the sky, he saw the hand of God. As he arrived on the farm, he was greeted with affection by his faithful slaves. He liked to talk with them. He said that their conversation was refreshing after listening so long to lawyers and members of Congress. What a relaxation it was to sit on the broad piazza and look out over the peaceful fields! In writing to Polly he showed how dearly he loved his birthplace, in preference to the "dust and smoke and noise and nonsense" of the city:

Key To His Wife

My dear P........,

I have had a nice journey. There was nobody I knew in the car, so that I had it all to myself, & I took out more than half of it in sleep. After dinner at Cousin H's, I got a horse, quiet enough to let me continue my naps occasionally, & reached here just in time to avoid a fine shower. It is raining again to-day, but I buttoned on my old water-proof, & rode about the farm, & to two or three of the neighbors, & have just returned, quite dry & comfortable.

As this rain, if it continues, may detain me beyond Monday, & the Mail goes to-day, I determined to write. If I do not come on Monday, you may look for me, (if you should think it a thing worth looking for,) every day — & tell any body that wants me, they may do the same.

I find it a most agreeable change, to get away from following up Members of Congress & secretaries & clerks, worrying them & they worrying me; to have no body to talk to but Uncle Clem, & Aunt Prissy, & to walk or sit in the Piazza, & look around upon the fields of green & gold, instead of dusty avenues — From Fred^{k} Town, here, the country is enchanting. There has not been for 20 yrs, such a harvest. In every field, the grain is either cut down & piled up in shocks that "stand so thick that the valley seems to laugh & sing," or is waving in its beauty, or falling before the merry reapers. Such are the fields of gold — Then the corn, & the grass cover all the others with their various shades of green. Old *Timothy* has grown so rank & fat, & his head so heavy, that he is lying down in all the meadows. Clem says, we shall make three times the quantity of hay we did last summer. I do not think I have seen such wheat since I was a boy. — The garden is rather wild, but every thing there seems flourishing — I must send up a Gardener — We have fine prospects of fruit — Henny says there is a smart quantity of ice in the ice-house. She is quite well again: & they all seem anxious to have you all here again. But I must have a few things done first. Harvest must be over — & the old spring house pulled quite down, — It is now nearly so, & built up again. — I found all well & happy & every thing thriving in the abundance of this beautiful season, except your poor Suk. She was in disgrace, & tied head & foot together. Clem had condemned her to this punishment for her misdoings — or to speak more properly — un-doings — You know how she used to open the gates last Summer. It seems, in the course of her studies in the Winter, she has so improved in her knowledge of mechanics, that she now opens anything. Bolts and bars, she now understands as well as latches, & draws them downwards or upwards or sideways, as their construction requires, & goes into the stables or feed rooms as she pleases. She certainly, by overhearing you, or in some other way, has found out who she belongs to, & supposes of course she has a right to every thing — & she takes with her, on these occasions a large party — So that Clem found it necessary to bring down these high notions of hers. As I could not bear to see her head brought so low, — on a level with her *understanding*, I have commuted her punishment, to that of solitary confinement, & had her untied, & turned into the cow stable, & have ordered her to be well supplied with grass, corn &c. I hope, that she will be improved by ruminating in solitude, upon her past ways. You must speak to her when you come up, for without reformation, it will never do to take her to Washington — You might find her some morning, on the sofa, in your parlor —

The sun is just peeping out, & everything glistening. How shall I break through the temptations around me here, to go back to the dust & smoke & noise, & nonsense of the City?

"How can I renounce, the boundless store
Of charms which Nature to her votary yields?"

I will tell you how I shall manage it.—I will think of one, (you know who it is,) that

——————— "were she as far
As that vast shore, wash'd by the furthest sea
I would adventure, for such merchandise"—

With love to the children—

Ever yrs

F. S. KEY

On his return to Washington a few days later, Key found it difficult to keep his mind from the "fields of green and gold." Again he thought of the transitoriness of life, as he compared the life of man to the harvest, recalling the Song of David, "The days of man are but as grass; for he flourisheth as a flower of the field. For as soon as the wind goeth over it, it is gone, and the place thereof shall know it no more."

After attending to some business affairs in Washington, Key returned to Pipe Creek for the remainder of the Summer. The happy days sped by. The trees took on their Autumn colors. But still he remained. In the tranquillity of Pipe Creek he heard strange murmurs in his soul. He was well and hearty, and only sixty-three; but he seemed to have a vague presentiment that his earthly life was drawing to a close. As this strange feeling surged through his soul, he found comfort in Robert Burns's *John Anderson, My Jo.* On October 13, 1842, in the stillness of the mansion which echoed the voices of his father and mother, he copied these words of the Scottish bard:

John Anderson, my jo, John,
  We clamb the hill thegither;
And mony a cantie day, John,
  We've had wi' ane anither:
Now we maun totter down, John,
  And hand in hand we'll go,
And sleep thegither at the foot,
  John Anderson, my jo.

Then he added another stanza, simulating the Scottish brogue:

John Anderson, my jo, John,
  From that sleep again we'll wake,
When anither day's fair light
  On our opened eyes shall break,
And we'll rise in youth and beauty
  To that bright land to go,
When life and love shall last for aye,
  John Anderson, my jo.

As Winter set in, the poet lawyer said good-bye to the scenes of his childhood, and returned to Washington. Polly remained for a while on the farm, and saw the beauty of the landscape when the earth was covered with a blanket of snow.

In a letter to Polly, which he wrote in Washington on December 3, 1842, Key said:

> Tell the girls & boys I suppose they were delighted to see the snow — Ellen may perhaps be frightened by the fear it will keep her longer there and keep every body away — but if I can manage to get away from the Court I shall not mind the snow. — I must be in Court on Monday next: but I think in a day or two after that, I can get away for 3 or 4 days, perhaps for a week. —
>
> Do make them write to me — all who choose to let

> me see how they like the Country now — & that they have brightness enough, in & among themselves, to chear (sic) the gloom of a deep snow in the Country. . .
>
> I hope the Wash house and Pump&ca are all done — or at least made safe & comfortable — & that you have water enough. — & that Clem gives you fire enough.

On Saturday, January 7, 1843, Key left for Baltimore to attend to some legal affairs. He had not been feeling entirely well since New Year's Day, and had been taking some medicine; but he seemed as cheerful as ever.

On his trip from Washington to Baltimore he made a draft of a poem called *The Nobleman's Son,* based on the Lord's miracle at Capernaum. This poem — the last that Key ever wrote — contained these prophetic lines:

> But the dwellings of earth, whether high or low,
> Or mighty and massive their walls,
> Cannot keep in joy, or keep out woe —
> They must open when misery calls.
>
> And sorrow, and sickness, and death will come
> When sent, and with step as sure
> They pass through the gates of the gilded dome
> As the cottager's open door.
>
> "Ask what thou wilt," commands He still;
> Fear not, thou shalt be heard;
> Only believe — He can, He will
> Speak the life-giving word.
>
> It may not be that life that spends
> In care and pain its breath,
> That runs its weary course, and ends
> At last, and soon, in death.

But a gift beyond thy poor request
  May to thy prayers be given:
A life to be spent in the mansions of rest,
  And the endless bliss of Heaven.

Arriving in Baltimore on Saturday evening, Key went to the home of his daughter "Lizzie" – Mrs. Charles Howard. On the next morning he wanted to go to church, but he was troubled with a sore throat. As it was raining, his daughter persuaded him to stay in bed. Dr. Buckler was called. The doctor did not think his patient was very sick, but he advised him to stay in bed for a day or two, and to drink plenty of warm barley water. But on Monday the patient's condition was much worse. Pleurisy had set in. He complained of fever and a severe pain in his side. Not even yet, however, did his relatives think he was seriously ill. On Tuesday his fever was lower, and it was thought that he would soon recover. Polly arrived at his bedside, and about daybreak Wednesday she was alarmed by a decided change for the worse. The pleurisy had developed into pneumonia. Several times Key was cupped and bled.

All day long the sick man's mind wandered in a delirium. He was not totally unconscious, for whenever he was asked whether he wanted a drink of water he would reply "yes" or "no."

Once he said huskily: "I cannot agree to that proposition. Tell them not to bother me."

From time to time Key repeated passages from the Bible or from his favorite hymns. Once he muttered something about crowns and thorns.

Once during the day one of the women said to him: "Shall I read to you?"

"Yes, my dear," he answered.

"What shall I read?" she inquired.

"The 91st Psalm," he whispered.

She read the first two verses; and the patient tried to listen, but in a few moments he rambled off to something else.

Word was sent to all the children that their father was critically ill; but he sank so rapidly that only one child—Maria—arrived to see him alive. He did not recognize her.

About seven o'clock in the evening Key fell into a deep sleep from which he never awoke. So peacefully did he slumber that those around his bedside were unable to tell the exact moment when the summons came: it was about eight o'clock on Wednesday evening, January 11, 1843, when the soul took its flight.

The members of the family were not the only ones who felt the loss. Thousands of Key's fellow countrymen were saddened with grief. On Thursday the United States Supreme Court adjourned in respect to his memory. On Friday the *Baltimore American* declared: "Francis S. Key, the author of *The Star-Spangled Banner*, is no more. So long as patriotism dwells amongst us, so long will this Song be the theme of our Nation."

The huge battle flag, which waved over Fort McHenry in 1814 and inspired the writing of the National Anthem, was offered to the family for use at the funeral. And everywhere on Saturday the American flag was lowered at half mast when the body of the poet lawyer was buried in the graveyard of St. Paul's Church.

Many years later it was recalled that Key had expressed a wish to be buried "'neath the shadows of the everlasting hills" in Frederick County. And so in 1866 his body was removed from Baltimore to a family lot in Mt. Olivet Cemetery in Frederick.

Only a small headstone marked his grave. But year after year Key's fame grew. In 1887 a monument, created in Rome by William W. Story, was erected in Key's honor in Golden Gate Park in San Francisco, through the generosity of Mr. James Lick. Then in 1898 the body was re-interred in Mt. Olivet Cemetery under a handsome monument designed by Alexander Doyle of New York. In 1911 there was dedicated in Baltimore another Key monument, the Marburg Memorial by the French sculptor, Antonin Mercié. And finally on June 14, 1922, there was unveiled at Fort McHenry a gigantic Orpheus, by Charles H. Niehaus, which was made possible by an appropriation of the Congress of the United States.

But the monuments of bronze and stone are not the greatest tributes of the American people to Francis Scott Key. His finest memorial is his song of victory which has inspired his fellow countrymen from generation to generation in American patriotism. His anthem is his greatest service to his country. Through it Francis Scott Key has become immortal.

The author of this book attended the dedication exercises at Fort McHenry on Flag Day in 1922, and heard President Warren G. Harding pay his beautiful tribute to the Poet of the Flag.

"That the song became instantly popular," said President Harding on that occasion, "and when set to music it was immediately adopted as the anthem of militant Americanism, testifies that already, more than a century ago, the conviction of a great nationalism and a great destiny had taken hold upon the American people. To give ringing voice to such a conviction, to such an aspiration, was one of the greatest services which any man could do for the young Republic. That was the service of Francis Scott Key. It was not the production of soul-stirring lines, thrilling with martial appeal; it was the contribution of this great hymn toward creating that sense of national pride and that realization of responsibility for a great adventure in behalf of humanity, which became at last the inspiration of union preserved and of nationalism established."

"The intervening century," President Harding declared in conclusion, "has brought our country power and high place. It has cast upon us heavy problems of a world in the turmoil of a new time. We need all the inspiration and faith which fired his glowing soul of patriotism. No generation of men has ever come into the world to find its path smoothed, or to find its problems solved for it in advance. Solution is the fit price we pay for our great inheritance of liberty and opportunity.

"The outstanding and reassuring thought of today is the supreme exaltation of Key in the hour of great trial to reveal the soul of a patriot in the night of surpassing anxiety and devotion to country.

"No concern for self narrowed his thought. No glorification of the individual marred his vision. No pursuit of fame set his soul ablaze. No personal advantage hindered his pen. His country and his concern for its safety were combined in his all-consuming thought; the Nation was the great uplifting, and exalting love. In this impassioned, anxious, self-sacrificing, exalting, and exulting love of country, transcending all else, Key reached the sublime heights, and wrote the poetic revelation of an American soul aflame.

"If our generation is called to shoulder unprecedented burdens, it may rejoice in unexampled strength. Everlastingly right in the great fundamentals, we may face the future with every confidence, providing men give first of heart and soul to the Republic and its righteous institutions, and give first thought and unfailing devotion to the Nation's perpetuity.

"An American citizenship of the high and simple faith of Francis Scott Key, aflame for defense, and no less devoted in meeting the problems of peace, will add to the lustre of the banner he so proudly acclaimed. Every glittering star is fixed, every worth-while procession is the more impressive for its bearing, every passion for country is refined by its unfolding. On ships of mercy or vessels of war, in the armed camp or at the memorials of peace, in rejoicing procession or flying from the staff over the simple temples of the schooling youth of America — everywhere it pleases the eye, and reassures the heart and stirs the soul, until we sing in all confidence with the poet-patriot —

"The Star-Spangled Banner in triumph shall wave
O'er the land of the free and the home of the brave."

Bibliography

ADAMS, WILLIAM FREDERICK, *compiler.* Commodore Joshua Barney, United States Navy. Springfield, Mass. 1912.

ADDISON, *Rev.* WALTER DULANY. *See* Murray, Elizabeth H.

African Repository.

American Colonization Society. Annual Reports, 1-72. 1818-89.

ANDREWS, MATTHEW PAGE. History of Maryland: Providence and State. New York. 1929.

ANNE ARUNDEL COUNTY, MARYLAND. Marriage Record. 1777—1813. Folio 79.

APPLETON, NATHAN. The Star-Spangled Banner. Address delivered in Boston, June 14, 1877.

ARMISTED, *Lt. Col.* GEORGE. Report to James Monroe, Secretary of War, September 24, 1814. [Volume 1 of *The Patriotic Marylander* for 1914.]

BABCOCK, LOUIS L. The War of 1812 on the Niagara Frontier. Buffalo. 1927.

BARNARD, HENRY. The South Atlantic States in 1833, as seen by a New Englander. [Volume 13 of *Maryland Historical Magazine* for 1918.]

BARNEY, JOSHUA. *See* Adams, William Frederick; Paine, Ralph D.

BARTOW, ANNA KEY, Recollections of Francis Scott Key. [Volume 12 of *Modern Culture* for 1900.]

BASSETT, JOHN SPENCER. The Life of Andrew Jackson. 2 vols. New York. 1911.

BEANES, *Dr.* WILLIAM. *See* Magruder, Caleb Clarke, Jr.

BEVERIDGE, ALBERT J. The Life of John Marshall. 4 vols. Boston. 1916–19.

BLAKE, W. O. The History of Slavery and the Slave Trade, Ancient and Modern. The African Slave Trade and the Political History of Slavery in the United States. Columbus. 1859.

BLEDSOE, ALBERT TAYLOR. An Essay on Liberty and Slavery. Philadelphia. 1856.

BOND, *Judge* CARROLL T. The Court of Appeals of Maryland: A History. Baltimore. 1928.

BOWERS, CLAUDE G. The Party Battles of the Jackson Period. Boston. 1922.

BOYLE, ESMERALDA. Biographical Sketches of Distinguished Marylanders. Baltimore. 1877.

BRADFORD, GAMALIEL. Damaged Souls. Boston. 1923.

BROOKE, *Rev.* JOHN T. A Sketch of the Character of the Late Francis Scott Key, Esq. Address delivered in Christ Church, Cincinnati, January 29, 1843.

BROWN, WILLIAM HORACE. The Story of a Bank. An Account of the Fortunes and Misfortunes of the Second Bank of the United States, with a preliminary Sketch of the First Bank. Boston. 1912.

BRUCE, WILLIAM CABELL. John Randolph of Roanoke. 2 vols. New York. 1922.

BRYAN, WILHELMUS BOGART. A History of the National Capital. 2 vols. New York. 1914–16.

BUCHHOLZ, HEINRICH EWALD. Governors of Maryland. Baltimore. 1906–08.

CARPENTER, JOHN C. "The Star-Spangled Banner." [*Century Magazine* for July, 1894.]

CATTERALL, RALPH C. H. The Second Bank of the United States. Chicago. 1903.

CLAGGETT, *Bishop* THOMAS JOHN. *See* Utley, George B.

COCKBURN, *Rear Admiral* GEORGE. Admiral Cockburn's Plan. Letter of Admiral Cochrane. [Volume 6 of *Maryland Historical Magazine* for 1911.]

COLSTON, FREDERICK M. The Battle of North Point. [Volume 2 of *Maryland Historical Magazine* for 1907.]

Columbia Historical Society, Records of.

DECATUR, STEPHEN. *See* Waldo, S. Putnam.

DIDIER, EUGENE L. Key as a Lawyer. [*The Green Bag*. Boston. May, 1904.]

DISTRICT OF COLUMBIA: Land Records. Orphans' Court Records.

EARLE, SWEPSON. The Chesapeake Bay Country. Baltimore. 1923.

EATON, PEGGY. *See* Pollack, Queena.

ECKER, *Mrs.* GRACE DUNLOP. A Portrait of Old George Town. Richmond. 1933.

ESCHBACH, *Rev.* E. R. Historic Sketch of the Evengelical Reformed Church of Frederick, Maryland. Frederick. 1894.

ESSARY, J. FREDERICK. Maryland in National Politics. Baltimore. 1932.

EYSTER, NELLIE BLESSING. "The Star-Spangled Banner": An Hour with an Octogenarian. [Volume 43 of *Harper's New Monthly Magazine* for 1871.]

FARIS, JOHN T. Historic Shrines of America. New York. 1918.

FOOTE, HENRY STUART. Casket of Reminiscences. Washington. 1874.

FOX, EARLY LEE. The American Colonization Society. 1817–1840. [Series 37 of Johns Hopkins University Studies.]

FREDERICK COUNTY, MARYLAND. Land Records. 1813, 1817, 1820, 1824.

GARLAND, HUGH ALFRED. The Life of John Randolph of Roanoke. 2 vols. New York. 1850.

GODDARD, HENRY P. Luther Martin: The "Federal Bull-Dog." [No. 24 of *Maryland Historical Society Fund-Publication.*] Baltimore. 1887.

GREELEY, HORACE. The American Conflict. 2 vols. Hartford. 1864–67.

HARDING, WARREN GAMALIEL. Address of the President of the United States delivered at the Dedication of the Francis Scott Key Memorial at Fort McHenry, June 14, 1922.

HENSEL, W. U. Long May it Wave. [*The Philadelphia Press* for August 1, 1881.]

HICKS, FREDERICK C. The Flag of the United States. Washington. 1926.

HIGGINS, EDWIN. The National Anthem, "The Star-Spangled Banner." Baltimore. 1898.

HILLIS, NEWELL DWIGHT. The Battle of Principles. A Study of the Heroism and Eloquence of the Anti-Slavery Conflict. New York. 1912.

HOUSTON, SAM. *See* James, Marquis.

HOWARD, McHENRY. Date of Francis Scott Key's Birth. [Volume 2 of *Maryland Historical Magazine* for 1907.]

HUMPHREYS, HECTOR. *See* St. John's College.

IDE, EMILY KATHERINE. The Star-Spangled Banner, and a Sketch of the Life of the Author, Francis Scott Key. Boston. 1914.

Inquiry Respecting the Capture of Washington by the British. Rare Book Collection, Library of Congress.

JACKSON, ANDREW. *See* Bassett, John Spencer; Bowers, Claude G.; Johnson, Gerald W.

JACKSON, RICHARD P. The Chronicles of Georgetown, D. C. Washington. 1878.

JAMES, MARQUIS. The Raven: A Biography of Sam Houston. Indianapolis. 1929.

JOHNS, *Right Rev.* J. A Memoir of the Life of the Right Rev. William Meade, D.D., Bishop of the Protestant Episcopal Church in the Diocese of Virginia. Baltimore. 1867.

JOHNSON, GERALD W. Andrew Jackson: An Epic in Homespun. New York. 1927.

——— Randolph of Roanoke: A Political Fantastic. New York. 1929.

JOHNSTON, CHRISTOPHER. Key Family. [Volume 5 of *Maryland Historical Magazine* for 1910.]

——— Lloyd Family. [Volume 7 of *Maryland Historical Magazine* for 1912.]

KENNEDY, JOHN PENDLETON. Memoirs of the Life of William Wirt. 2 vols. Philadelphia. 1849.

KEY, FRANCIS SCOTT. An Oration delivered by Francis S. Key, Esq., before the Washington Society of Alexandria, February 22, 1814.

——— Oration delivered by Francis S. Key, Esq., in the Rotunda of the Capitol, July 4, 1831.

——— Speech delivered by Francis Scott Key in the House of Representatives as counsel for Sam Houston. Gales and Seaton's Register of Debates in Congress, Volume 82, pp. 2597-2620.

——— The Power of Literature and its Connexion with Religion. Oration delivered at Bristol College, July 23, 1834. Pamphlet in Boston Public Library.

——— Speech delivered by Francis Scott Key on the trial of Reuben Crandall, M.D., before the Circuit Court of the District of Columbia. Washington. 1836.

——— Poems of the Late Francis S. Key, Esq., with an Introductory Letter by Chief Justice Taney. New York. 1857.

——— Daniel Murray, Late Lieutenant in the American Navy. [Volume 20 of *Maryland Historical Magazine* for 1925.]

KEY-SMITH, FRANCIS SCOTT. A Sketch of Francis Scott Key, with a glimpse of his Ancestors. [Volume 12 of *Columbia Historical Magazine* for 1909.]

——— Francis Scott Key, Author of "The Star-Spangled Banner," What Else he Was and Who. Washington. 1911.

——— The Story of the Star-Spangled Banner. [*Current History* for May, 1930.]

KING, RUFUS. Life and Correspondence, comprising his Letters, Private and Official, his Public Documents and his Speeches. Edited by Charles Ray King. 6 vols. New York. 1894–1900.

LANE, *Mrs.* JULIAN C. Key and Allied Families. Macon, Ga. 1931.

LATROBE, JOHN H. B. *See* Semmes, John E.

LOWELL, JOHN. Mr. Madison's War. By "A New England Farmer." Boston. 1812.

McCANN, WALTER EDGAR. Francis Scott Key. [Frank Leslie's Popular *Monthly* for May, 1888.]

McCORVEY, THOMAS CHALMERS. The Mission of Francis Scott Key to Alabama in 1833. [Reprint from Volume 4 of *Transactions, Alabama Historical Society*] Montgomery, Ala. 1904.

MACKENZIE, GEORGE N. Colonial Families of the United States of America. Boston. 1907.

MAGRUDER, CALEB CLARKE, JR. Dr. William Beanes, the Incidental Cause of the Authorship of the Star-Spangled Banner. [Volume 22 of *Records of the Columbia Historical Society* for 1919.]

MANUSCRIPTS:

Jacob Engelbrecht's Diary, Frederick, Md.
Francis Scott Key's Diary.
Key MSS. Carroll County, Md.
Key MSS. Frederick, Md.

Key MSS. Library of Congress.
Key MSS. Maryland Diocesan Library.
Key MSS. Maryland Historical Society.
St. John's College. Records.
Anne Key Taney. Poetry Album. Taney Home.
Taney MSS. Maryland Historical Society. [Volume 5 of *Maryland Historical Magazine* for 1910.
Taney MSS. Roger Brooke Taney Home, Frederick, Md.

MARINE, WILLIAM M. The British Invasion of Maryland, 1812–1825. Baltimore. 1913.
MARTIN, LUTHER. *See* Goddard, Henry P.
MARYLAND:
Archives of Maryland.
Court of Appeals Reports.
Laws of Maryland.
Maryland Historical Magazine.
MEADE, *Bishop* WILLIAM. Old Churches, Ministers, and Families of Virginia. 2 vols. Richmond. 1910. *See* Johns, J.
MURRAY, ELIZABETH H. One Hundred Years Ago, or the Life and Times of the Rev. Walter Dulany Addison, 1769–1848. Philadelphia. 1895.
MURRAY, DANIEL. *See* Key, Francis Scott.

NEWSPAPERS:
Annapolis, Md.
Maryland Gazette, 1790; November 20, 1800.
Baltimore, Md.
American, January 13, 1843.
Sun, January, 1843; September 23, 1928.
Frederick, Md.
Bartgis's Federal Gazette, September 5, 1798.
Herald, March 10, 1804.
News, August 9, 1898.
Political Examiner and Public Advertiser, August 30, 1820; July 6, 1831; May 21, July 2, 30, August 6, 13, 20, September 24, October 1, 8, 1834.
Georgetown, D. C.
Metropolitan, July 8, 1836.
Mobile, Ala.
Commercial Register, December, 1833.
Philadelphia, Pa.
Press, August 1, 1881.
Washington, D. C.
Federalist, December 21, 1805.
Globe, January 31, 1835.
National Intelligencer, June 4, 1811; March 18, 1812; July 4, 1831; April 2, July 11, November 2, 1832.

Niles's Weekly Register. Baltimore. 1811-1849.

PAINE, RALPH D. Joshua Barney: A Forgotten Hero of Blue Water. New York. 1924.

PICKETT, LaSALLE CORBELL. Poet of the Flag. Volume 90 of *Lippincott's Monthly Magazine* for July, 1912.

POLLACK, QUEENA. Peggy Eaton: Democracy's Mistress. New York. 1931.

PREBLE, *Rear Admiral* GEORGE HENRY. "The Star-Spangled Banner." [Volume 31 of *New England Historical and Genealogical Register* for 1877.]

——— Three Historic Flags and Three September Victories. [Volume 28 of *New England Historical and Genealogical Register* for 1874.]

PROTESTANT EPISCOPAL CHURCH. Historical Notes of All Saints Parish, Frederick, Md., 1742–1908. Frederick. 1908.

——— Journals of the Conventions of the Protestant Episcopal Church of the Diocese of Maryland.

——— Journals of the Proceedings of the Bishops, Clergy, and Laity of the Protestant Episcopal Church in the United States of America, in General Convention. 1817–41.

QUINCY, EDMUND. Life of Josiah Quincy. Boston. 1874.

RANDOLPH, JOHN. Letters to a Young Relative. 1806–22. Philadelphia. 1834. *See* Bradford, Gamaliel; Bruce, William Cabell; Garland, Hugh Alfred; Johnson, Gerald W.

REDWAY, VIRGINIA LARKIN. The Carrs, American Music Publishers. [*The Musical Quarterly* for January, 1932.]

RICHARDSON, HESTER DORSEY. Side-lights on Maryland History. 2 vols. Baltimore. 1903.

RICHARDSON, JAMES DANIEL, *compiler*. A Compilation of the Messages and Papers of the Presidents, 1789–1897. 10 vols. Washington. 1900.

ROOSEVELT, THEODORE. The Naval War of 1812. New York. 1882.

SAMS, CONWAY W., *and* RILEY, ELIHU S. The Bench and Bar of Maryland: A History, 1634 to 1901. 2 vols. Chicago. 1901.

SCHARF, JOHN THOMAS. History of Maryland. 3 vols. Baltimore. 1879.

——— History of Western Maryland. 2 vols. Philadelphia. 1882.

SEMMES, JOHN E. John H. B. Latrobe and His Times, 1803–1891. Baltimore. 1917.

SHAW, JOHN. Poems, by the late Doctor John Shaw. Philadelphia and Baltimore. 1810.

SHEPHERD, HENRY E. The Representative Authors of Maryland. New York. 1911.

SHIPPEN, REBECCA LLOYD. The Original Manuscript of "The Star-Spangled Banner." [Volume 25 of *Pennsylvania Magazine of History and Biography* for 1901.]

SMITH, *Major General* SAMUEL. Official Report to the Secretary of War, September 19, 1814.

SONNECK, OSCAR GEORGE THEODORE. "The Star-Spangled Banner." Washington. 1914.

STEINER, BERNARD CHRISTIAN. Life of Roger Brooke Taney. Baltimore. 1922.

ST. JOHN'S COLLEGE. An Address of the Visitors and Governors of St. John's College to the Senate of Maryland. 1784.

——— Memoirs Read at the Meeting of the Alumni, February 22, 1853, by Rev. Dr. Hector Humphreys, Fifth President of St. John's College.

——— Minutes of the Board of Visitors and Governors, 1786–1826.

SWISHER, CARL BRENT. Roger B. Taney. New York. 1935.

TANEY, ROGER BROOKE. Mr. Taney's Speech, at the Public Festival Given to him by the Jackson Republicans of Frederick County, Maryland, August 6, 1834. Rare Book Collection, Library of Congress. Letter to Henry V. D. Johns. Introductory Letter in Poems of the Late Francis S. Key, Esq. Washington. 1856. *See* Steiner, Bernard Christian; Swisher, Carl Brent; Tyler, Samuel.

TYLER, SAMUEL. Memoir of Roger Brooke Taney, LL. D. Baltimore. 1872.

UHLER, JOHN EARLE. The Delphian Club [Volume 20 of *Maryland Historical Magazine* for 1925.]

UNITED STATES CONGRESS. Debates and Proceedings in the Congress of the United States. Twenty-first Congress, First Session.

——— Memorial of the American Colonization Society. Twenty-first Congress, First Session. Document No. 277. 1830.

——— Report of Select Committee on Memorial of American Colonization Society. Twenty-first Congress, First Session. Report No. 348. 1830.

——— Hearing before the Committee on the Judiciary. Sixty-eighth Congress, First Session. Legislation to make "The Star-Spangled Banner" the National Anthem. 1924.

——— Hearings before the Committee on the Judiciary, Seventy-first Congress, Second Session. Legislation to make "The Star-Spangled Banner" the National Anthem. 1930.

——— United States Senate. Executive Journal. 1833. 1836. 1840.

UNITED STATES NAVY DEPARTMENT. Records during administration of President James Monroe.

UNITED STATES WAR DEPARTMENT. Records of Francis Scott Key's military service.

UNITED STATES SUPREME COURT. Reports of Cases adjudged.

4 Cranch. 1807–08.

5 to 9 Cranch. 1809–15.

1 to 4 Wheaton. 1816–19.

5 to 8 Wheaton. 1820–23.

9 to 12 Wheaton. 1824–27.

1 to 4 Peters. 1828–30.

5 to 8 Peters. 1831–34.
9 to 12 Peters. 1835–38.
13 to 16 Peters. 1839–42.

UTLEY, GEORGE B. The Life and Times of Thomas John Claggett. Chicago. 1913.

VAN SANTVOORD, GEORGE. Sketches of the Lives and Judicial Services of the Chief-Justices of the Supreme Court of the United States. New York. 1854.

WALDO, S. PUTNAM. The Life and Character of Stephen Decatur. Middletown, Conn. 1822.

WASHINGTON, GEORGE. Farewell Address to the Peoples of the United States. September 17, 1796.

WARREN, CHARLES. The Supreme Court in United States History. 3 vols. Boston. 1922.

WATTERSON, HENRY. Address at the Unveiling of Francis Scott Key Monument at Frederick, Maryland, August 9, 1898. New York. 1906.

WEBSTER, JOHN A. Narrative regarding the attack on Fort McHenry. 1853. [*Baltimore Sun* for September 23, 1928.]

WEYBRIGHT, VICTOR. Spangled Banner: The Story of Francis Scott Key. New York. 1935.

WHITLOCK, BRAND. LaFayette. 2 vols. New York. 1929.

WILLIAMS, T. J. C. History of Frederick County, Maryland. Hagerstown, Md. 1910.

WIRT, WILLIAM. *See* Kennedy, John Pendleton.

WROTH, LAWRENCE C. Francis Scott Key as a Churchman. [Volume 4 of *Maryland Historical Magazine* for 1909.]

Index